Cycling
Full Circle

Happy cycling... :)

6/6/12

Cycling Full Circle

a lone woman's 2-year pilgrimage round the world

Astrid Domingo Molyneux

Quicksilver Publications

First published by Quicksilver Publications in the United Kingdom
in 2012

978-0-9571875-2-8   Cycling Full Circle – Hard cover
978-0-9571875-3-5   Cycling Full Circle – Soft cover
978-0-9571875-4-2   Cycling Full Circle – eBook (Kindle)
978-0-9571875-5-9   Cycling Full Circle – (eBook – other)

www.cyclingfullcircle.com

Typeset in Times 11pt.
All photographs by Astrid Domingo Molyneux.
Printed by Berforts Group Limited, Stevenage, Hertfordshire.

Dedication

To my gorgeous children,
Jessica and Daniel

And in loving memory of my
darling Mum, 1923–1974

Come to me
all you who are weary and heavy burdened
and I will give you rest

Charities

I took advantage of my trip to try and raise awareness of the work of a couple of charities in whose work I have had a long-standing interest. During the two years, I had the enormous privilege of visiting hospitals and a leprosy colony in India and Nepal run by The Leprosy Mission, as well as a couple of schools for deaf children in Cyprus and India and a chain of deaf-staffed cafés in Nepal.

The Leprosy Mission – www.leprosymission.org

Every year between 200,000 and 300,000 people are diagnosed with leprosy and an estimated 2–3 million people around the world are disabled because of it.

The Leprosy Mission works to enhance the quality of lives of leprosy victims and their families: through total eradication of the disease, help and support for those affected, removal of stigma and its devastating effects, not only on individuals, but also their families.

Deaf Studies Trust – www.deafstudiestrust.org

The Deaf Studies Trust (DST) is a national charity set up for the benefit of the Deaf community in the UK. It aims to apply research-based knowledge to practical issues for Deaf children and adults.

The charity's main target is to improve communication and understanding. This will enhance the quality of Deaf people's lives, as well as make a contribution to society as a whole.

Contents

List of Maps

About the Author

Astrid Domingo Molyneux was born in England in 1956 in County Durham, the middle child of a Norwegian mother and English father, sister to two brothers. The family moved to the Midlands when she was age four and a half.

On leaving school, Astrid moved to the Southwest where she qualified as a physiotherapist, thereafter working in Wales, the Middle East and Bristol.

Eventually she became a full-time mother for eleven years to her two children, Jessica and Daniel. She acquired British Sign Language skills, leading to a job in administration at the Centre for Deaf Studies at Bristol University.

Eleven years later she was granted leave of absence to cycle round the world.

Introduction

Gosh, aren't you brave!

This is invariably the first comment made by anyone about my trip. But if I had thought that myself, I would never have gone in the first place. It was just that once the idea had planted itself, it refused to go away. On the contrary, it blossomed and flourished, in the end becoming its own reality, by which time I had no qualms about undertaking the trip.

But how did it start in the first place? After all, I am not a macho male in his mid-twenties; rather, a middle-aged mum in mid-menopause. All I can say is, beware charity shops, they can seriously damage your comfort zone! That was where, in September 2005, I casually picked up a benignly-entitled paperback, *A Bike Ride* by Anne Mustoe, a middle-aged headmistress who had cycled solo round the world some twenty years previously. By the end of reading her book I was thinking, 'I'd like to do that,' followed by, 'Well, if she can do it, why can't I?'

And so I did.

As much as anything, this was a journey of faith and I could not go unless it was with God's blessing, or even better, with the notion that it was his idea in the first place. Why? I had been brought up traditionally in the Church of England, turned away as a teenager, then started searching and made a personal commitment in my twenties. I have been on the journey ever since, one full of perplexing and frustrating questions, but underpinned by an unshakeable belief in the love of God. I wanted to deepen that relationship.

The ease with which my plans advanced smoothly and effortlessly convinced me that this trip was right for me. Even so, the following summer, 2006, I went on a 10-day cycling taster trip to Scotland to see if cycle touring was even my thing. After all, I had never done more than go off for a day's cycle ride at the most. It turned out to be about the best holiday I had ever had, a clear confirmation of the validity of my trip.

In December that same year, at a joint birthday party with my daughter and son – landmark 50, 21, 18 years respectively – I blithely announced to all present, 'At some point in the future, I am going to cycle round the world.'

'Yeah, right,' encouraged the sceptical voices, 'like we all do!' Undaunted, my plans continued unabated.

The discovery of the wonders of a virtually maintenance-free bicycle, to offset my almost total ignorance of anything mechanical, was a joyful revelation. The casual inquiry at work as to whether they would care to give me a 2-year sabbatical, followed by their disarmingly quick response, 'Yes, when do you want to go?' saw me plucking from the air a random date for the following year, 2008. All this, followed by a favourable financial arrangement with my father, left me with almost no excuses. The final jigsaw piece was some timely, but crucial, surgery six months before my departure date.

However, it was not all plain sailing. The hardest thing was acknowledging the understandable concerns of family and friends for my safety and well being – alone out there in the big bad world – whilst steadfastly ignoring them. My utter conviction about the 'rightness' of the trip was my staunch ally.

Apart from the physical, mental, intellectual and spiritual challenges of such a venture, I also wanted to see for myself the goodness of ordinary people. So much in the news is taken up in reporting, with sensational delight, the wars, conflicts, misery and suffering in the world that I wished to witness for myself the redress of balance that must surely exist alongside these negative forces. I went on the premise that most people do not seek world power and domination over others, or become fierce religious fanatics forcing others to share their viewpoint. Surely, just as at home, people throughout the world desire a peaceful life, wishing to live harmoniously with their neighbour, enjoying essential needs of shelter, sustenance and society and basic rights of freedom and fear from persecution. I was pretty confident I would find this on my trip; it would merely be a confirmation of what other cycling travellers had already reported. Even so, I wanted to experience it for myself.

I was not disappointed. The world is a beautiful place and the people therein. That's not to say there is no dissatisfaction, frustration, helplessness, ugliness, sadness, sorrow. It is that, despite these, the instinctive desire of most people to demonstrate kindness to one another flows as living water and their underlying goodness shines as a light in the world.

Astrid Domingo Molyneux (May 2012)

Part 1

Almondsbury
to
Jerusalem

*Now the Lord said to Abram, 'Go from your country
and your kindred and your father's house.'
So Abram went, as the Lord had told him.*
Genesis 12

England

6 – 9 May 2008

Bath, Bournemouth, Poole

Can it really be just two and a half years since I picked up that benignly subversive book? A mere eighteen months since my confident announcement, 'At some point in the future, I shall be cycling round the world'? Has it actually come now to the point of embarking on an excursion that is luring me away from the familiar into the unknown, separating me from those I love dearly? It appears so.

My elder brother, Rick, arrives the night before, my younger brother, Cogs, the morning of my departure. Cogs and I discuss security of my front panniers: how to stop them being easily lifted by a passing opportunist, at the same time not being a tedious hassle for me when removing and replacing them. He comes up with a simple idea: to screw a small u-bend shackle onto one of the restraining clips of each pannier, thereby preventing the clip from lifting and releasing, at the same time being fairly quick for me to operate. When not in use, each shackle dangles from a piece of cord neatly spliced and attached to the carrying strap of its pannier.

As the time of departure arrives, a significant little crowd of family, friends and neighbours gathers outside the house. Standing in my driveway, under the cherry tree pendulous with pastel pink blossom, I take in as much as I can of the scene, suddenly acutely aware that I shall not be seeing my beloved children, my home sweet home, these familiar, friendly faces again for two whole years.

After much bonhomie, a short speech and a cycle once around the block, finally, after two and a half years of preparation, it is time. On 6 May 2008, at 10.15 am, I cycle away from my home in Almondsbury, to encouraging cheers, clicking cameras and well-wishes, the dichotomy

3

of sadness and excitement – and, admittedly, some trepidation, bubbling (or is it churning?) within me.

The weather is almost balmy: warm and sunny, with a light breeze. Accompanying me for this first day are my son and two brothers; my daughter does not do cycling. At the end of the road we turn left, left again, onto and along the busy A38, looking over to the right for a final look at the unforgettably familiar sight of the old and the new Severn bridges. On then under the M5 motorway, past Filton airport, at the crest of the next hill pausing briefly for photos – my tall, gangly, teenage son insisting on removing his helmet and re-working his hair before posing for the camera.

Our departure was timed to coincide with the customary morning coffee break at the Centre for Deaf Studies at Bristol University, when deaf and hearing staff daily prise themselves away from their office desks to meet in the coffee room during this period, face-to-face encounters being essential in the visual environment of sign language communication.

I came to be working at the Centre as a result of attending British Sign Language classes. Formerly a physiotherapist, I changed career to become a full-time mum for eleven years to my two children, Jessica and Daniel. During this time I started learning British Sign Language, the result of watching a friend and her deaf parents-in-law signing to each other and, like many people, I was entranced by the beauty of the language. After attending classes for a couple of years, a temporary job in administration came up at the Centre. It was only for six months, but as my father likes to say, 'There's nowt s' permanent as temp'ry.' Gradually I became a permanent fixture, eleven years at the time of my trip departure. This is my place of work from which I have been granted a 2-year and 3-month sabbatical to cycle round the world: two years for the cycling, three months to re-acclimatise on my return.

Eight miles to the Centre for Deaf Studies brings us punctually to the coffee and cake break and another touching send-off, with balloons, poppers and more photographs, as well as one colleague reiterating that she plans to join me in North America to cycle a section. A friend presents me with one of those old-fashioned 'ding-ding' bicycle bells, which we fit onto the handlebars, alongside a little plastic hand from the deaf staff, a touching reminder of my signing colleagues. After speeches, smiles, sobbing farewells (well, slight exaggeration), my entourage and I

4

set off once more. Of the balloons, one bursts just down the road, the other between Bristol and Bath. We descend Park Street, cross the city centre and join the Bristol–Bath cycle track, the first Sustrans cycle route in the country and thirteen miles of easy gradient along a disused railway path.

Considering it is a weekday, there is a surprising number of pedestrians and cyclists along the path, the pace, at times, slowing to a leisurely loiter, and we take longer than expected to reach Bath. For the final leg to a friends' house, we have a steep, oh so very steep hill, up which I puffingly feel my hundred and twenty pounds of bicycle and baggage. But that is forgotten when we are greeted with champagne and hugs by friends, Jane and Peter, and my daughter and boyfriend, who duly arrived by car.

It is now three thirty and the thought of continuing another twenty miles or so does not hold that much appeal, even though there are a mere twenty-eight on the clock. I need little persuasion, therefore, to graciously acquiesce to the offer of an exclusive campsite in the back garden. I pitch my tent, the front door perfectly placed to appreciate a picturesque panorama of Bath set in the bowl of surrounding hills.

And now another round of goodbyes ensues. But, away from the partying of the previous partings, these are rather more subdued and reluctant, prolonged embraces with my two brothers, heart-aching hugs with my children. Jessica will be in her mid twenties on next meeting, Daniel will have celebrated his key-to-the-door twenty-first. They leave and I watch until they disappear into the distance, waving forlornly.

Despite careful planning for this trip, inadequacies are already showing up. During the night I strive haplessly for some degree of comfort from my pillowed bundle of clothes. After a fitful sleep, I awake in the morning to the hush of a suspended mist in the valley, bright sunshine above; partake of perfect scrambled eggs, porridge oozing with darkly-melting muscovado sugar, richly-brewed coffee. And more final farewells.

Eight thirty next morning sees me sailing down the steep hill, through the centre of Bath, to join the Kennet & Avon canal towpath, striking for Bournemouth and another friend's house. It is a bit of a tall order, about seventy-five miles, to reach my desired destination today and I am quite prepared to stop short for the night. I meander along the canal – could the whole trip be so easy and congenial? There is a stillness in the air, as you only experience beside water. Quietly smiling with pleasure at the passing languid scenery, I note the varied names of numerous narrowboats: Just So, Lady of Mann, Utopia, Chaos, Crinkly Starfish.

The day turns out to be much longer than it should have been, not helped by the fact that I manage to become lost as soon as I veer away from the canal! Is this a foretaste of things to come? Desire somehow overcomes deliberation, as, instead of sensibly stopping short, I persevere with dogged determination for a marathon thirteen and a half hours and eighty-four miles, eventually to arrive in Bournemouth, in the dark, at friend Colin's house. I am feeling very unwell: in a shaky stupor, light-headedly hungry and immensely tired – but extremely glad to be with a familiar face.

Colin and his Norwegian wife, Inger, are friends from Saudi days, twenty years previously. During my three years in the Middle East, I learned a smattering of Arabic, written and spoken, and something of the culture, useful now for this excursion.

I stay for two nights, after which it is a pleasant cycle ride along the seafront towards the neighbouring harbour town of Poole. A text message from my children makes the surprising announcement that they are currently driving down with their partners and a friend, for the (definitely) last time, to wave me off on the late-night ferry to Cherbourg. I pedal on in excited anticipation.

To be honest, I have had some doubts during the last couple of days that I am capable of doing the trip. In the two and a half years since the notion implanted itself so confidently, I have blithely prepared for this moment. Now though, uncertainty is skulking in the shadows, offering all kinds of tempting negatives: I am not the greatest of map-readers; my experience of cycle touring is alarmingly limited; I can barely mend a puncture. Yes, I have a load of bicycle spares with me, but how on earth do I tighten, loosen, replace a spoke or a brake pad?! And what about camping? It is definitely not my first port of call for a comfortable night's accommodation, getting up and dressed in the middle of the night to traipse over a soggy field to the dubious communal loo block. And let's not forget potential encounters with nasty beasties and creepy-crawlies, such as slithery snakes and spindly spiders, dangerous dogs and marauding men.

How on earth am I going to cope – all on my own?

Then I find a letter from my children, secreted into my map case.

What they each write is wonderful: loving, selfless and full of encouragement. My daughter's letter is affirming.

'I just wanted to make sure you knew how proud I am of you. This is an amazing thing you are doing and I have admiration pouring from my very soul . . . You can't come back until you're ready, and when you do we will still be here. Have a fantastic time. You are going into the unknown, the dark. But follow the light and you will return.'

My son's letter is reassuring.

'Don't worry about us . . . Just enjoy yourself, have no regrets, but be safe . . . Wherever you are, however many times you have read this letter, take a picture. Of anything. Something that will remind you of us.'

I know this venture of mine is not easy for my children, even though my son's initial reaction was, 'Yeah, go for it, Mum!' My daughter's, on the other hand, was to be angry with me, pronouncing, 'You're going to be killed!' Of course, I can understand their fears and worries. After all, the media is effective propaganda for such feelings and beliefs. But, even without that, I am their mother, and would it not be slightly odd if they did not display doubts and concerns? If it was either of them going off, I would be reacting in the same way. Therefore, to have these letters from them is, and will be throughout my two years, a huge support and encouragement. They are amazing children and I feel truly blessed. I entrust them both to God's care, realising that missing them is going to be the hardest part of the trip.

And now, finally, finally, I really am leaving the shores of England, to an emotional parting with my children and to feeling, overwhelmingly, very much on my own. Wow! This is really it! Eyes brimming, I push my bicycle onto the ferry, away from my children. A while later, the vessel slips its moorings and sails silently out on the night tide, heading for the far side of the Channel.

*   *   *

France

10 May – 1 June 2008

Cherbourg, Grandecamp, Port de Bessin, Pirou, Genêts, Beauvoir, Rennes, Guéméné-Penfao, Nantes, Nesmy, Ile de Ré, Chatelaillon, St Augustin, Mesches sur Gironde, Blaye, Gradignan, Labouhèyre, St Paul des Dax, St Palais, St Jean Pied de Port

The shortest sea crossings are in the northern hemisphere. Having decided that I would much prefer to cross watery bits by sea rather than air, this largely dictates my general route round the world.

Other factors also come into account: there would seem to be too many rainforests and too few roads to traverse South America. Top to bottom of the Americas would double my trip time. As for Africa, well, I never fancied that by bicycle; much too arduous terrain and definitely to be kept away from after listening to one guy's account of his journey of masochistic self-discovery. In fact, I was nearly put off my whole trip in the early planning days after hearing him talk about his nigh suicidal, four-and-a-half year, circumglobal jaunt. His name is Alastair Humphreys. Great guy, undoubtedly; intrepid, most certainly; and full of useful advice to my question,'What should I do to guard against bears in Alaska?' 'What bears?' came the blythely dismissive reply (as it happens, he was to be disappoint-ingly accurate). And I was right about the suicidal description; whoever heard of anyone of right mind cycling across Siberia in the depths of winter?

As for sea crossings by ship rather than flying, that was an easy decision. Hanging around forever at airports; severe baggage restrictions; interminable, tedious, demeaning security checks; dismantling your bicycle, packing it up, unpacking it (oh look, dear, your back light seems to be hanging a bit loose), attempts to reassemble it; are really not my idea of the spiritually or emotionally enhancing experience I wanted. Crossings by ship, boat and ferry, on the other hand, would be blissful experiences, leaving me wanting to do them all over again.

The ferry crossing is uneventfully calm and I duly arrive in Cherbourg, nervously wheeling my bicycle out from the dark bowels of the boat into a bright, sunny morning. I make my way into the centre, intent on buying a French SIM card for my mobile phone as soon as possible, my children and family having sternly stressed the importance of regular contact for their peace of mind. I have a choice of two networks, Orange or Buoyges. For some reason I choose the unknown latter. Big mistake. Even the procedure for buying it involves finding a photocopying service to make a copy of my passport to accompany the application form. Finally, I come away with the SIM card. It is yet to be installed and set up on my phone.

From Cherbourg I cycle eastwards along the coast for about sixty miles, stopping for the night at a small rough and ready campsite in a village called Grandecamp. Seated in front of the door of my tent, I attempt to activate the SIM card, but, unable to make it speak English, it becomes dispiritingly complicated to set up. I resort to asking a nearby middle-aged couple for help. My French is hesitant and it is a struggle, but they happily sort it out and, with great relief, I am at last able to send a reporting-in text to my children.

Whilst cooking my evening meal on my campstove, I try to feel excited about my first day in France, but only manage to feel overwhelmed by extreme homesickness and loneliness, utterly daunted by the hugeness of my mission.

After a reasonable night's sleep, I decide not to rush the day, choosing first to wander down to the beach and drink in the beautiful view, savouring the calm moment.

I have never visited the Normandy beaches and now take the opportunity to do so. As I cycle along, I notice that portions of roads have been named after soldiers, of different ranks and from different countries, presumably killed along that particular stretch.

At Colleville-sur-mer, I follow a signpost to an American war cemetery, overlooking Omaha Beach. Music plays quietly in the neatly-manicured grounds; people move solemnly and silently from one section to the next. A heavy feeling of pathos hangs pervasively over the fields of numerous, nameless white crosses, poignant reminders of the sacrifice, 'For their tomorrow, we gave our today.'

It is barely after noon when I stop early for the day at a campsite in Port de Besillon. I wash my cycling clothes and hang them to dry on the line I have attached between two trees, made from the three bungee cords that secure my tent bag on top of the rear panniers.

After an amble by the sea along the deserted, pebbly beach, I prepare a culinary delight of *escalope de dinde* (sounds more exotic than turkey cutlet), boiled potatoes and tomatoes, accompanied by a glass or two of red wine. Afterwards, I laze in the sun listening to songs on my ipod (a gift from my children), beginning to feel more buoyant about my trip.

The approach to the town of Bayeux is dominated by three church spires, tranquilly heralding their divine purpose. I head for the museum and the 'tapestry' (technically, an embroidery), surprisingly disproportioned at 230 feet long by only 12 inches high. It shows a fascinatingly detailed description of the events leading up to and including the Battle of Hastings in 1066, possibly the only historical date remembered by every English person from their school days.

My course now zigzags back in a westerly direction, arriving on the opposite coast of the Cherbourg peninsula at a seaside campsite at Piron. Reception is closed (it is a Sunday), remaining so the following morning, affording no opportunity to pay. Unbelievably, the toilet block is also closed. What to do? There I am, jigging away in desperation, mentally ready for an urgent pee, distressingly thwarted from doing so. But, in the middle of the courtyard, I spot a drain. Feeling slightly self-conscious and overexposed, I do, however, manage to exchange qualms of propriety for unrestrained, blissful relief.

The pleasure of early morning stillness is now enhanced by the evocative smell of yeasty homebaking emanating from a boulangerie. I purchase breakfast of croissant and *pain aux raisin*, stopping at a wayside picnic table to eat it. Pre-trip, such fare would have been a rare, calorific indulgence, but is now tantalisingly acceptable. I turn off the main road onto peaceful, rural lanes, passing fields of frilly and smooth lettuces being picked, packed and sent off on tractor trailers. Away from the noisy, unfriendly major roads, it is soulfully satisfying to savour the moment of where I am, rather than hankering after where I am headed.

I arrive in Granville-sur-mer (home of Christian Dior) at noon, seeking out a cyber café to check emails and sit out the heat of the sun.

By the time I come out, it is raining – hard. But I have a riding cape, a leaving present from my younger brother. He cycles almost daily to work in London and swears by the cape; preferable to rain jackets, and their simulation of a Turkish bath, and rain trousers, which disconcertingly restrict the ability to swing your leg up and over the cross bar. A cape is well-ventilated and keeps upper legs dry, with the additional advantage of having various other uses, such as picnic mat, or, occasionally, discreet loo screen.

I continue to Genêt, where, in the misty distance, I glimpse my first view of Le Mont St Michel. I meet my first cycle tourer, Johanne, a German student, who has been on the road for two months of an intended 8-month trip around Europe.

Le Mont St Michel is at the end of a causeway on an island, on which a church was built in the eighth century. Legend has it that Archangel Michael instructed Aubert, bishop of Avranches, to build a church on this rock, but that he duly ignored him; until, that is, on the third visit, Michael burned a hole into the bishop's skull with his finger, which finally seemed to get the point across, and the church was duly built. This was later replaced by an imposing abbey, impressive enough at the time to be referred to as 'an image of the Heavenly Jerusalem on earth.'

I tried thirty years ago to visit the Mount when on a hitchhiking holiday around Brittany with a student friend, but did not quite make it. Here now, a second opportunity. I am dismayed, therefore, to find that I have no battery charge for my camera. Even though I have two batteries. Why? My intention of being green and power-fully self-sufficient is showing signs of being frustrated. I am supposed to be cycling with a large, flexible solar panel on the top of my rear bags, charging my camera, mobile and ipod. But no. The panels themselves seem to be working fine; the only trouble is, the connectors are not. No connectors, no charge, no power, no pictures. *Quel dommage* and what a pity.

I am a little wary about leaving my bicycle unattended whilst sightseeing, but reckon I can hardly go all the way round the world without stopping occasionally for a closer look at some of the wonders on offer. In Bayeux, I parked and locked my bicycle to railings inside the grounds near the entrance, asking the staff to keep an eye on it. Here, I lean it up against the wall of the bridge on the lead-up to the entrance. I surmise that, as well as being in full view of everyone, it is too heavy and conspicuous for a passing opportunist to abscond with it.

I ascend the steeply-stepped hillside leading up to the ancient abbey. Inside the cool, dark building is a holy, hushed atmosphere. It is easy to sense the presence of people down the centuries worshipping in this lofty building, glimpsing the promise of heaven on earth.

I return to my bicycle, still there, and make my way to a campsite in nearby Beauvoir. The helpful site manager offers to charge my camera batteries overnight. I cook a meal prepared from the meagre ingredients offered in the camp shop: pasta swirls and rehydrated vegetable soup, topped with a splodge of camembert; unappetisingly un-haute cuisine, but filling.

In the evening, the heavens open and I experience the dubious pleasure of sitting in my tent, listening to the drumming rain and watching the water visibly rising towards the lip of my tent, picturing myself haplessly floating away. The rain comes down even more intensely, as though a fire hose has been turned on maximum power pointing straight down. The continuous rumbling thunder and a sky full of flashing lightning make quite a daunting scenario. Tent, bicycle and I, though, are up to the challenge, singing to each other to keep our minds suitably distracted.

After a reasonable night, considering the circumstances, I am up and off promptly in the morning. The sky is overcast, air cool, no wind; in fact, pretty good cycling conditions. Quiet country lanes again, the last twenty miles spent pleasurably in the company of the Canal d'Ille et Rance all the way to Rennes. The tenth day of my trip and time for a rest day.

My (loose) plan is to cycle five days and rest two, so that I do not go too long without a break, as well as a chance to catch up on house-keeping duties: washing clothes, deleting photos from the camera, repacking my panniers more efficiently.

Whilst in Rennes, I manage to find a small, local repair shop, where the owner is willing to solder my broken battery charger connector. This is in direct contrast to the big stores who don't even bother looking at the broken item, straightaway advocating that I purchase a new one – even though there is none available.

The municipal campground is good. Surprisingly, unlike private ones, these seem to be the ones that provide loo paper. I am starting to realise that most towns and cities in France have municipal campsites, a fact that helps to allay one of my biggest anxieties, 'Where am I going to sleep at night?' Wild camping in France is forbidden, thus forcing me to find an approved site, regardless of how many additional miles of cycling this might entail towards the end of the day.

I am now feeling more confident and at ease, even to the extent of enjoying myself a great deal – surely, a significant aim of my trip. Whenever I miss my children I read their touching letters, invariably, as instructed, taking a photo. The letters and envelope are decorated with sunflowers, hence one particularly pertinent picture incorporates a field of sunflowers as the background.

Packing up my tent in the morning, after another torrential rainstorm throughout the night, I try to wipe it dry, to no avail. It always manages to remain wet and so I end up carrying a couple of pounds of undesirable extra weight. Other cyclists say they are able to dry theirs completely, packed and ready to depart within an hour. It beats me how they do it. Maybe they blow them dry.

A magnificent hailstorm attacks me in the afternoon, triumphantly soaking me in the thirty seconds before I snatch my cape from the pannier. Arriving at tonight's campsite, I receive a warm welcome from Claire, the friendly manageress, and offered a helping hand from a chap with a hammer, who interrupts his game of boules to drive my tent pegs into the impenetrable ground.

I stay two nights, even though I have just had two in Rennes. My left knee has been troubling me for a few days so it seems a good idea to take it easy. Rest day being a Sunday, I pop along to the church in the village centre for the morning service. It does not really matter that I do not understand the content, the traditional order of service is universal enough to be able to follow events. Really, it is just a matter of following what everyone else does: sit down, stand up, exchange the peace, say, 'Amen', and queue up to receive communion. During a special quiet moment afterwards, an inner peace affirms, 'I am with you.'

The following day, I manage to take the wrong road out of town and become lost, so do not know exactly where I am when I hit the 500-mile mark. It is a small but smugly satisfying milestone. Just 19,500 miles to go then . . .

My next port of call is Nantes, capital of the Loire region, a pretty town with a thirteenth century castle surrounded by a moat. The campsite I choose is recommended as four stars by both Rough Guide and Claire at the previous campsite. Well, I should like to see the others because quite frankly, four stars do not immediately spring to mind. The place is soulless, reception staff are not particularly friendly, there are no provisions in the shop and there seem to be some dodgy characters camping here.

I leave my bicycle at the campsite, taking a tram to the town centre in search of a suitable store to buy a replacement connector for my solar panel. Unfortunately, the repair has not been totally successful and now the other end seems to be loose. Not only this, but my Freeloader solar charger is also not behaving itself; my ipod charging only intermittently. The time-wasting and frustration now associated with these unreliable appliances have become an unnecessary and unwelcome stress. I kick myself for having bought them last minute, leaving insufficient time to test the gadgets properly. The store has no replacement connectors, but one of the staff, Patrick, generously gives me a mains lead for my camera battery charger – at no cost. I thank him, take a photo of him for my records and leave the store with a smile on my face. Unfortunately, this marks the death knell for my solar charging as I finally admit defeat for this particular device.

Whilst in town, I also buy three large-scale maps for the rest of my time in France in order to make the most of the small country roads.

Back at the campsite, a new tent has appeared near mine, complete with bicycle and trailer. The following morning the owner appears, we chat and he offers me freshly brewed coffee. Jean is following the Santiago de Compostella route, a popular pilgrimage route in northern Spain and on my itinerary as a side trip. This is the fourth time Jean has travelled the pilgrimage; each trip along a different designated route, of which there are four in France.

A characteristic of many French people is that they speak very quickly, Jean being no exception. Most of what he says goes over my head, although after a few repetitions and requests to speak at a slower pace (which he manages for half a sentence), as well as the occasional English word thrown in, there is a level of understanding between us. We are both leaving the city in the same direction and Jean offers to guide me to the outskirts. I accept his offer readily, prompted by the desire not to become lost in the melée of traffic and unfamiliar streets.

On the way, we pause at both the cathedral, taking turns to peek inside whilst the other looks after the bicycles, and the thirteenth-century moated castle. Jean confidently navigates us to the other side of the city, where we bid each other farewell, accompanied by an exchange of email addresses and an invitation for him and his wife to visit me in England in a couple of years' time. As he reckons to travel twenty-five to thirty miles a day and I, forty to fifty, we shall not necessarily meet up again.

I now find myself on a busy road (according to the map, the road should not be this busy), congratulating myself that at least I have not made the same mistake as the previous year on a pre-trip tour of Brittany, when I ended up on the hard shoulder of an E road (which happens to be a motorway). Ooops. I even tried convincing the two policemen who pulled up behind me in their squad car, when I paused to consult my map, that it could not possibly be a motorway. They were impressively patient, gently insisting that I needed to leave at the next exit just up the road.

And now? Well, it slowly dawns on me that I have indeed done the same thing. The horrible shock of it fires up my adrenalin levels to send me scuttling along the hard shoulder to the nearest exit, desperate to get off as soon as I can – before those two kind policemen come by.

The rest of the day is marvellous. My map reading shows signs of improving; the initially flat, then gently undulating terrain makes for easy cycling; the weather is superb, enabling me to remove my layers and expose my arms to the sun for the first time in a week.

This pleasurable day culminates at the restaurant campsite in Nesmy, when I am bought glasses of Loire rosé by a couple of the locals. Maybe it is a subconscious wish to see more of the immediate area, but the next day finds me going around in a circle for nine and a half miles before returning almost to my starting point an hour later. I have no idea how this happened, but the pattern is set for the day, as I continue to take wrong turnings. I think it must just be my little Raven having a mind of her own.

Most cycle tourers seem to give a name to their bicycles: Achilles, Emma, Evans, Alchemy. I had not thought too consciously about this, but, over time, the natural reference to mine became Raven.

Unimaginatively coined after the model of my bicycle (a Thorn Raven Tour), it turns out to be a very apt name: not only do I often feel as free as a bird flying along on my bicycle, but also, it is a raven that is first to leave the ark in search of land, of new beginnings, of a renewed life; and it is a raven sent by God to sustain Elijah by bringing food for him every day. All this symbolism fits perfectly with the main themes of my trip: exploration, renewal, reliance, replenishment; the name Raven could not have been more appropriate.

A day cyclist, Nadine, joins me for a short distance. It seems every person I now meet travels the Santiago Camino. As with many pilgrims, Nadine does not have time to complete it in one go and so is accomplishing it in sections, annually progressing her route, a couple of weeks at a time, finally to arrive in Santiago, maybe years down the line.

She directs me to a canal path that should take me much of the way to La Rochelle. Although still on the Atlantic coast, I notice that the houses now have terracotta-tiled roofs, so that, cycling over the summit of a hill, the view of a village nestling in the green hills evokes a Mediterranean landscape.

I arrive in La Rochelle, having already covered sixty-eight miles, generally more than enough for one day, fifty being the daily working distance. After all, I am not in the game of wanting to try and break any records. What short-lived joy is there in that?

The first campsite is closed. At the second, there is no one at reception, nor is there any response to swinging the rope of the large bell outside the front door of the main building. Phoning the number displayed on the door brings no one. I wait. Nothing. Wait some more. No one comes. I leave reluctantly, following the cycle route over the 2-mile long bridge to the Ile de Ré. On the way past La Rochelle airport, I see a Ryanair plane, watch it take off and think, 'Oh, don't they fly into Bristol?' Feeling weirdly close to home, I muse how easy it would be to pop back for a brief visit.

I cycle all round the island looking for a desirable campsite. In the end, admitting defeat, I trudge into the one back near the bridge, disappointed that it is not quite what I had had in mind. It is not pretty, has no character, merely utilitarian. My cyclometer shows eighty miles. I am tired and hungry and could murder a beer, but there appears to be nowhere selling any. Miserably putting up the tent, I become increasingly annoyed at the poor quality of the mostly bent tent pegs, especially considering the price I paid for the tent itself. The last straw comes when I cannot push them into the ground.

So what do I do? I resort to my instant survival mechanism: I quietly cry. And feel so much better. After the wonderfully restorative powers of a hot shower and sumptuous campfire meal of fish 'bouillabaise' and apple turnover, I am almost cheery.

I admit to myself that grotty is an attitude and that mine in the last couple of hours has been just that. The good thing is that only I am in control of my attitude and so it is only I who can do something about it. Talking to myself out loud helps.

In the morning, I have an unexpected but welcome surprise: my tent is quite dry. I am bizarrely delighted at this great start to the day. Simple pleasures for simple minds. In happy spirits, I pack up and cycle back over the bridge and into La Rochelle, a sea port with a marina situated in the centre of town. I locate an internet café, persuade the manager to put my bicycle safely inside, write a journal entry on my website and check and respond to emails. Then down to the moored boats, to sit basking in the sun, eating my lunch and admiring my rather peculiar tan marks, specifically on my feet from wearing sandals.

The first campsite at the end of the day is at Aytre, but at a €20 (£16) minimum, two-person charge, I am not going to succumb to a lone camper penalty (the first time this has happened) and so continue up the road to Chatelaillon and a friendlier site at €5. I meet a long-term camper, Claudius, who has been obliged to move to this area for work, living here during the summer, returning every so often to his home in Toulouse to visit his family. He invites me to cook my food under the shelter of his rain awning, where we share our respective meals. In the morning, Claudius sends me off with a flat-palms, knuckle-rapping farewell.

At the entrance to the walled city of Brouage is a sign indicating its history as a sixteenth-century seaport capital of the salt trade, frequented by Flemish and Dutch ships loading up with salt. Cycling through the grey, cobbled streets of the centre, I notice something leaning against the wall of a church: a Thorn bicycle – like mine. Then I notice the Brooks saddle -like mine. Could the owner be a Brit? Indeed he could and is and sitting outside the café opposite.

He buys me tea and biscuits and we chat about our various trips. Ken is cycling for three weeks, supposedly with three friends, but they seem to be lagging behind. They took the ferry from Plymouth to Santander in northern Spain and are now cycling around the coast and up to Brittany for the return ferry from Roscoff to Portsmouth.

Soon after continuing our separate ways, the friends come along. After hearing about my trip and then inspecting my bicycle, they impart much useful advice about bicycle care and maintenance, clearly shocked at the rusty appearance of my chain, neither cleaned nor oiled thus far

along the road. They proceed to spray every moving part they can find —
I did not realise there were so many – at the end of which they present
me with the remainder of the can of the general cure-all, WD40, with the
unequivocal command, 'Use it.'

I think I have just been admonished by Derek, Ursula and Alan for
my lack of care towards my loyal Raven, so no gold star for me then. I
vow from now on to be assiduous in treating her with more respect and
attention.

Over the bridge to Marennes, I come face to face with a long uphill,
but, being such a well-designed gradient and with Raven freshly oiled,
we fly up effortlessly in top gear, to be met by a stiff headwind at the
summit.

The campsite at St Augustin is not really open for the season –
although which 'season', I am not sure, as we are already in the third
week of May – and the hot water has to be turned on especially for me.
The farm on which this campsite stands produces and sells its own rosé
wine, but the smallest bottle is one and a half litres. I can always pour
the undrunk amount into one of my three water bottles. A couple of eggs
for a breakfast fry-up complete my farm purchases. A little later, Tony, a
gently-spoken Filippino who was buying wine at the same time, comes
by from his nearby campsite to present me with a litre of orange juice. I
am touched by his thoughtful generosity. As with the wine, the
remainder finds a home in a second water bottle, but I am rapidly
running out of vessels in which to carry the base essential.

The forecast for the weekend is a continuation of the gloomy rain. It
becomes heavy during the night and, in the morning, I find myself
peering warily out of my front door, watching helplessly as the water
gleefully rises up towards the lip of the entrance. I sit there, watching,
praying, 'Please don't let it flow over into the tent – and, particularly,
please don't let that big slow-worm right there by the entrance, doing a
great snake impression, come in either.' To take my mind off things, and
to use the time constructively, I manicure my nails.

The rain finally stops mid morning, the waters begin to recede and I
paddle my way out, by now desperate to go to the loo. The funny thing
is that, in the whole of the campsite, the only pooled water is
surrounding my tent. It is not as though there was a lack of choice of
pitches, mine being the only tent, but I managed to plonk it in a little
hollow, rather than on raised ground. Not my most astute decision.

In theory, this should be a weekend rest stop, but there is no way I am going to spend another wet night camping. I inquire in the next town about chambres d'hôtes, but they are too expensive. I come across a mobile home park in Mesches-sur-Gironde and go in. The manager, Valerie, turns out to be American. What joy to have a flowing conversation with an English-speaking person – plus two nights in a comfortable caravan. As I do not have the requisite two hundred and fifty euro deposit for the mobile home, I am obliged to surrender my driving licence. It is not immediately obvious to me how I would tow away the mobile home with my bicycle, having left my towbar at home, but 'rules is rules.'

Being in the dry, warm, cosy mobile home is about as perfect as it gets in my current frame of mind; just what I need to restore my spirits. I wash and dry my clothes, clean Raven, hang out my tent to dry, cook food on a real cooker, use a real kettle to boil water for my tea, take a shower in the warmth and privacy of my own place – sleep in a real bed. In other words, I luxuriate. I have been so mean with my budget, for fear of overspending, that I needed such a wake up call to realise that it is okay, occasionally, to treat myself.

During the day, I barefoot the beach, echo call the caves, steadfastly loll in the cloudy sun and read the first of the three books I brought with me, which, up until now, have been sitting in the bottom of my panniers. On leaving, I promise to send Valerie a postcard from India, as it is on her wishlist of countries to see before she dies.

Being in Bordeaux wine country, I pass vineyards galore. The terrain is flat, the cycling effortless. In the town of Blaye, complete with ancient castle, walls and moat looking out to sea, I pitch my tent in one of the hedged plots in the municipal campsite, situated regally within the castle grounds.

The next morning, whilst waiting for the ferry across the river Gironde, I happen upon the French guy, Jean, the speedy talker with the trailer bicycle. On the ferry, we chat to an elderly chap who has just purchased a hundred and seventy-five pounds of fresh asparagus to bottle entirely for his own consumption, it being his 'Big Passion.'

On the other side of the river, Jean and I keep company for a few miles before parting again. He suggests I become a pilgrim, if for no other reason than to give me the opportunity of staying in the dry each night in cheap pilgrim accommodation. Last night, for instance, whilst I was coping with camping in the wet, he had stayed in the dry in a local B&B, at a reduced rate because of being a pilgrim. It seems like an eminently sensible suggestion.

Included in my itinerary is cycling to the three great Christian pilgrim destinations: Santiago, Rome, Jerusalem. If I had done my homework properly beforehand, I could have signed up as a Santiago pilgrim in England and following the prescribed route, staying at refuges. Better late than never, though, and, encouraged by Jean's experience, I make my way to the cathedral in Bordeaux to acquire my pilgrim passport. But they are not available here and I must go to Gradignan, which happens to be south of Bordeaux and on my route. One of the cathedral volunteers gives me an address and a telephone number for the refuge, even calling ahead to confirm a place for me.

The skies gradually darken as I head south, arriving in Gradignan just as the rain buckets down. By this time, it is dark and the downpour merciless. I feel like a drowned rat. Shortly after phoning the refuge for directions, a car pulls up in front of me.

'Hello. Are you Astrid?'

'Yes.'

'Welcome,' he responds with a wry smile, 'the refuge is just five hundred metres up the road on the right.'

He has just finished work, is on his way home and was looking out for me. I could have hugged him. In a few minutes, I am knocking on the door of a big old house, the scallop shell above the lintel confirming this is the right place. The door quickly opens and I am ushered inside to the warmest of welcomes.

'Bring your bicycle inside, spread out your wet tent on the chairs over there. Don't worry about it dripping all over the floor; not a problem. Have a glass of wine.'

Happily divesting myself of my sodden clothes, I am delighted and relieved to be in the warm and dry and in company. Although I get on with myself quite well, I do not hanker to be on my own all the time; it can be rather lonely. I am usually the only single person on the campsite, not much interaction occurring with other campers. Here, however, in this pilgrim refuge, are others in the same boat, so the feeling of isolation does not arise.

A memorable moment this evening is when I complete the required paperwork and am duly presented with my *carte de crédenciels de pélérin*, my pilgrim passport, and a large scallop shell, the symbol of the Camino, which I attach to the front of my handlebar basket. I am now a bonafide pilgrim; and one happy, dry, bunny.

Pilgrim refuges provide at least basic needs: shelter, a sleeping place, personal washing facilities and toilet and, generally, some means of preparing food. Some will be in private homes, some attached to churches or monasteries and convents, some in the form of commercial hostels. Here, in this comfortable, renovated old building I have my own room and share a communal washroom.

The other pilgrims are all walkers. One has a *charette*, a trailer, which attaches to a harness around his chest and waist. It means there is no heavy weight to be carried on his back and he says it is not cumbersome or uncomfortable. I am entranced by it, as I was with Jean's bicycle trailer, but do not think either would be something I would adopt; sometimes I have difficulty enough negotiating the bicycle on its own without an articulated attachment increasing the challenge.

In the morning before setting off, I wander around the grounds, tranquil and peaceful, halting at the statue in front of the building, the Pilgrim at Rest. He is sitting on a bench leaning on his upright staff, one ankle resting on the opposite knee, broad-brimmed hat on the bench by his side. He appears to be in deep meditation of his journey, looking up to heaven, as though having a mental conversation with God.

'Well, Lord, how do you think we are doing so far? We certainly see life on the road, don't we? Tell me again why we are doing this? Ah, to see what life has in store for me. Would you like to be a little more specific? Just wait and see? Hmm . . . the life is full of surprises tack. Well, thanks for that; it's always good to talk.'

Happily armed with a list of refuges along the route for the next couple of days, I arrive in a small town and stop for a short refreshment break, whereupon along comes a familiar yellow shirt and cycle trailer. I cannot understand it. If Jean reckons to cover twenty miles a day less than me, how is it that we keep on bumping into each other?

He suggests we cycle along together, as he has a particularly creative route for the day – and so it turns out. Most of it is along forest dirt tracks, new to me, as I have been sticking religiously to firm, comfortable, tarmac. I am not sure if I am grateful to becycling with him or not. It is pleasurable being away from the roads, even though, for the most part, they are not particularly busy, but some of the surfaces on

Jean's route leave something to be desired, especially the soft, sandy, slippery surfaces when my back wheel is intent on heading off in the opposite direction to the front wheel.

We stop for lunch at a crossroads in the middle of a forest. There is an easy bonhomie between us, with Jean chattering away in French, blissfully unconcerned as to whether or not I am responding to anything he says; probably just as well, considering for the most part I have no idea what he is talking about. In the early afternoon he goes off to find a friend's house with whom he is staying the night, whilst I continue another twenty miles to my next refuge in Labouhèyre.

In the village, I follow the simple instructions, 'Look for the red roof,' to arrive on the doorstep of the home of Jacques and Jacqueline. They decided to open their home to pilgrims after having walked the Camino themselves, their house being situated on the route. Breakfast is included in the fixed price, which is a bit more than most refuges at € 15.

I park my bicycle in the safety of the garden shed. There is already another bicycle inside, belonging to a Dutch pilgrim. He, too, is cycling from his home all the way to Santiago, although currently has developed a problem with his bicycle that he hopes to get sorted the following day. He proceeds to show me his pilgrim passport, in which are numerous stamps, of which he is rather proud. Each time a pilgrim stays in a refuge or visits particular church buildings, he can usually obtain a stamp. In fact, in order to qualify for a pilgrim certificate in Santiago, a sufficient number need to be acquired.

On departure, Jacques and Jacqueline touchingly present me with a small metal scallop shell on a keyring, to accompany me on my pilgrimage round the world.

Today I visit the Convent of the Sisters of St Vincent de Paul near Dax. St Vincent worked with the poor and marginalised of seventeenth-century French society, setting up hospitals for the sick, the needy and the aged, homes for abandoned children and for galley slaves (he himself had been captured by pirates and sold as a slave). His life and works were remarkable and continue today throughout the world. His deep, personal faith in God and his compassion for people are displayed clearly in his kind and gentle face.

I consider staying overnight, but decide I want to travel a bit further today and so continue to the town of St Paul des Dax; so much bustlier than the calm of the convent. The basic refuge comprises a room with three bunk beds, a microwave, a table and a couple of chairs squeezed in; showers situated across the courtyard. Raven opts for the storeroom next door. Two other pilgrims have already arrived: a young French-Canadian girl and a middle-aged French guy, the two having met a few days ago and now walking together. Later in the early evening comes another chap, whom I had seen walking earlier in the day. He is a master baker, completing the Camino in stages during his holidays. The attraction of the pilgrimage for him is the reflective solitude it offers, as well as the opportunity to appreciate and savour the beauty of God's world, afforded by this slow pace.

In the morning, the three of them are up and off at the crack of dawn. A dark, early start for walkers is usual, sometimes as extreme as four or five o'clock; whereas, for cyclists, it is much more civilised, between eight and nine.

During the morning, Jean and I cross paths and join forces; we must stop meeting like this. We encounter a couple of donkeys, on their first pilgrimage to Santiago, enjoying a well-earned break, whilst munching on a snack of juicy grass in the dappled shade. They are enjoying the easygoing friendliness of the pilgrim road, especially having already met two other pairs of donkeys with whom to exchange, '*Bon camino.*'

And that is what I am finding: this easy camaraderie with total strangers, either pilgrims or passersby who, on noticing the scallop shell on my basket, invariably call out the familiar pilgrim greeting. I love it.

As yesterday, Jean heads for the home of another friend, I to St Palais, aiming for the big church in the centre, my starting point for locating the refuge. A pilgrim rests on a bench outside the church. He would seem to be more in keeping with the traditional ethos of this genre of traveller, for he has none of the oversized, overstuffed, hi-tech backpacks of the contemporary species, containing a month's supply of underwear and a rotating five-day wardrobe. Instead, he carries barely more than that which he is wearing, appearing totally relaxed and unflurried. He gives me detailed directions to the refuge and I ask if he intends to spend the night there also. But he prefers to keep on walking, during the night and day, resting where and when he feels the need. To me this seems to be the epitome of romantic, uncluttered freedom; I should like the nerve to do the same.

On arrival at the Franciscan monastery, there is a gregarious greeting from the genial host, Flavio. He is an Italian, who shares his time between work in his home country and volunteering here in the monastery for four months each year. He loves the whole concept of the Camino and wants to help others benefit from it. Whenever he goes on pilgrimages himself he travels light, generally opting to sleep rough, often in church porchways, much like the chap on the bench.

He shows me to my own delightful little bedroom, complete with sweet-smelling sheets and towel. Along the corridor is a bathroom and the prospect of a luxuriating soak before bedtime. He invites me to give him any clothes to be washed, directs me to the kitchen, where breakfast is served each morning, then leaves me to make myself at home. Later, I use the internet in the office for a couple of hours, to check my emails and, because the trip to Santiago is a sideways detour, investigate the best means of public transport back to France. It does not even occur to me to consider cycling the return journey. Although some cyclists do, even some of the walkers, all the way back home to France, Italy, Switzerland, Belgium or – wherever. They must be mad.

At breakfast I meet cyclists, Liliane and Huguette, travelling from their homes in northern France. They are in their seventies, avid cyclists and have travelled the Camino many times before, as well as undertaken numerous other cycling trips. These spritely, elderly women are inspirational, great advocates for a continuing active life in advancing years.

My side trip to Santiago means that I shall be returning through St Palais to rejoin my main route. Therefore, why not take advantage of this to temporarily shed myself of one or two items to make my burden considerably lighter (especially I think of the upcoming ascent of the Pyrenees)? I leave behind my tent and camping stuff, cycle spares, books, maps, and, hmm, big decision, my party outfit – will I, won't I? Yep, leave it behind. My party outfit comprises aubergine silk skirt, cream and lace silk camisole and blouse, accessorised with lilac pashmina, amethyst-coloured necklace and earrings, small black handbag and strappy, heeled sandals. Sadly to date, there has not been much call to wear them on the campsites and can I really envisage the likelihood of a dressy dinner date on the pilgrim road to Santiago? Rash maybe, but the decision is made. And now see – rather feel – the difference in weight. Scaling the Pyrenees is going to be a piece of cake. Yum.

Liliane, Huguette and I phone ahead and book tonight's beds in St Jean Pied de Port. The two women set off before me; I am waiting until the current downpour ceases, or at least eases.

For the past week I have been spoilt with the terrain, which has been overridingly flat. Today, though, it begins to undulate, hardly unexpected with the prospect of mountains looming and, in fact, quite desirable in order to lessen the shock of a sudden onslaught of gruelling gradients. I am treated to my first glimpse of the Pyrenees and my heart flutters at the imminent challenge. I stop by the side of the road to eat my lunch of bread and cheese, gazing at this distant view. On the point of setting off again, I am not totally surprised to spot a familiar person trundling up the hill. Jean and I continue the final few miles into St Jean Pied de Port. I clock up 1,000 miles.

It is an early arrival for once, just 1.30 pm. Spotting Liliane and Huguette outside a café, I join them, Jean continuing to the *Centre d'Acceuil des Pélérins* to find accommodation. The women finish their lunch and we make our way to the refuge.

Considering St Jean Pied de Port is the mecca for the main confluence of pilgrims on the *Camino de St Jacques*, it is a surprisingly small town, taking a while to find on any map. As well as the main starting point for thousands of pilgrims each year, it is the converging point for three of the four French routes. The town nestles at the foothills of the Pyrenees, the great range of mountains stretching all the way from the Atlantic to the Mediterranean coast, naturally separating France and Spain as it goes. The old town is surrounded by the remains of a defensive wall, walkable in parts. With the enormous popularity of travelling this pilgrimage, it is inevitable that business acumen will align itself with religious fervour, as seen in the numerous trinket shops throughout the place. Amongst nicknacks on sale is an assortment of miniature models of archetypal pilgrims in long woollen cloaks, wide-brimmed hats, staff in hand. And they do exist, having seen a flesh and blood version for myself.

I attend a service in an ancient church in the old part of town. It is in Basque and, in common with half of the congregation I understand nothing, quite happy to appreciate the church building, the ambience of the service and the knowledge that I am taking part in an act of worship. Afterwards I stroll along the city walls and down to the river on the edge of town, weaving through the throngs of pilgrims and tourists in the small side streets, where I stop to buy a sweet, sticky regional speciality as sugar injections for the following day.

On the morning of the assault, the weather is cool and overcast. The road wends along a quiet, forested road, flattish for the first few miles beside the river before starting to climb. At some point I must have passed over into Spain, but with no border control in evidence, it is a mystery when this happened. Progress is slow, down in my lowest granny gear, but hey, at least I'm not walking. I pass a couple of Belgian cyclists, Otto and Gerrard, who have paused to 'admire the view' (which generally translates as, 'Oh boy, I need a rest!'). The weather is a cool, rainy mist, but I soon warm up enough with the effort to unlayer to bare arms, a right decision as long as I keep moving.

As I ascend, the road becomes busier. Cyclists take it in turns to overtake each other and walkers appear, seemingly from nowhere, most of their route being well away from the road.

Up I slog, slowly the summit looms. . . push those pedals. . . one. . . two. . . three. . . ah, made it.

Quite painless, really.

*　　*　　*

Spain

2 – 16 June 2008

*Pamplona, Estella, Navarette, Belorado, Estepar,
Carrion do los Condo, Léon, Murias do Rechivaldo,
Villafranca, Samos, Melide, SANTIAGO*

The Camino de Santiago de Compostella, or The Way of St James,
has been a popular pilgrimage route since the ninth century. The remains
of the apostle, St James, whose mother was a sister or cousin of Mary,
the mother of Jesus, were brought by boat from Jerusalem to northern
Spain and buried at the site where Santiago de Compostella now stands.
It is said that the boat carrying the body was approaching the coast of the
Iberian Peninsula, when a storm blew up and swept the body overboard.
After some time, it was washed ashore, undamaged, covered with
scallop shells. The scallop shell is the symbol for the Camino.

Over 100,000 pilgrims each year travel to Santiago. They are not
nowadays always Christians, although it is probably fair to say that the
majority are looking for some sort of spiritual or personal experience,
possibly achieved even through the physical act of walking (or cycling)
the pilgrimage route. On arrival in Santiago and on production of the
appropriately-stamped credentials, the pilgrim receives a *compostella*, a
certificate, calligraphed with the person's Latin name. A service in the
Cathedral every day at noon is *de rigeur* for the majority of pilgrims,
whether or not they are of a Christian persuasion. It is part of the
pilgrimage experience, a fitting end to their efforts.

Cyclists and walkers eagerly gather at this first summit, excited and
relieved that this primary major hurdle has been accomplished, and
expressing surprised satisfaction that it was not as arduous as they had

imagined. People mill around, pose for memento photos beside the summit sign, Ibañeta 1,057 metres, and hail those stranger friends they passed on the ascent, congratulations all round on each other's efforts. Otto and Gerrard appear, then Liliane and Huguette, and we all join together as members of the Mutual Admiration Society.

A short time later, I notice a vaguely familiar face; ah yes, the Dutch guy with the multi-stamped pilgrim passport. We greet each other. He still has some problem or other with his bicycle but, a short way down in the small village of Roncesvalle, a group of half-a-dozen gregarious Italian cyclists, with their own support vehicle, delightedly provide a comrade-in-arms with the vital tool he needs to carry out the repair.

He and I then end up travelling together for the rest of the day. To be honest, I have quite envied the way other pilgrims have buddied up with co-travellers and find myself enjoying the company, especially shared moments of pleasure in the surrounding landscape. Having up until now thought it would be difficult to cycle with someone else, I am surprised that we seem fairly compatible: I feel neither pressure to keep up with him, nor frustration at not travelling at a faster pace. It is quite different from travelling on my own.

We breeze down glorious downhills, interspersed with a couple of smallish ascents, then a long one, up and over a second pass. We take it in turns to overtake each other, I on the descents, he on the uphills, waiting respectfully for each other at strategic points. On one occasion we watch eagles majestically gliding and circling the hillside, counting twenty of them. (Later, the sighting lost some of its impact when I am told they were European vultures!)

An attempt by my cycling companion to teach me the Dutch word for 'poppy' fails when I mishear it as *glomp rose* (I never do learn the real word), which slips into becoming his nickname, Glomp Rose or GR.

Ending the day in Pamplona, we head for the designated refuge, a vast, commercial, 100-bed, open-plan dormitory affair on two levels. It feels jarringly strange after the intimate, homely places to date. This difference is accentuated in the morning, when we are ordered out by 9 am – sharp. A shock for one poor guy who is thrown out onto the street still tying his boots.

GR guides us out of the city – and we become slightly lost. This is paradoxically reassuring, suggesting that my own map-reading skills are not as questionable as previously self-accused. Once the right route is

28

located, we have a delightful day cycling on picturesque, virtually traffic-free, country roads through medieval villages, the likes of Puenta de la Reina. Crossing over the ancient 6-arched, mellowed stone bridge into this historic village, we pay a visit to the church to be impressed by its grandly ornate, gilded interior, more in keeping with a cathedral than a parochial church.

We are travelling the Dutch St Jakob Way, which mostly follows the regular scenic cycling route but with a few picturesque diversions thrown in for good measure. I have no detailed route description myself, naïvely under the impression that the way would be so well signposted there would be no need for one. Not necessarily the case. Therefore, a companion in possession of a detailed guide, as well as someone with whom to while away otherwise solitary evenings, are two good reasons to count my blessings.

In the town of Estella, our accommodation is much more in keeping with my expectation of a welcoming, homely refuge. Payment is a donativo – it is up to each person how much they give. This place is currently run by Eudit from Hungary, who spends two months a year as a volunteer, generally working for two weeks in any one refuge, before moving on to another.

Early morning, 6 am, and the Spanish pilgrims are up and about, clearly of the opinion that everybody else should be awake at the same time. GR and I maintain corpse-like slumbers until they leave, before emerging for a peaceful, unhurried breakfast of baguette and real coffee, courtesy of Eudit, before setting off at a civilised eight o'clock. Part of our day brings us in line with the walkers for a taste of the real camino, a stony dirt track, bumpity-bumping us along on our heavy-laden road tourers, as we weave intently in and out of the walkers. Hearty '*buen caminos*' constantly abound, at least at the beginning of the day, becoming more desultory later on as tiredness sets in.

The town of Navarette offers another richly gilded church interior, more elaborate, if that were possible, than the day before. We wander around the village, the curiosity of an open door getting the better of us as we pause to watch a potter in his workshop throw a lump of clay onto the wheel, adeptly transform it into a utilitarian vessel, promptly placing it in a neat row with the others awaiting their turn to be fired and glazed.

After a tediously noisy night (it only takes one loud snorer to disturb everyone else's sleep, when all you want to do is go and pour a jug of cold water over the perpetrator), we contend with an overcast day spouting occasional rain and cold enough to be still wearing socks, windproof jacket and head buff. It may be late May, but at over 3,500 feet, the air is pretty chilly.

The passing wayside is an oil-painting of vivid poppy reds and cornflower blues, soft clouds of rape yellows and daisy whites, stiffly-stemmed grasses rising from their midst. This vibrant display borders a mellow yellow meadow of bearded barley stretching away into the middle distance. It is a fabulously florid time of year to travel the Camino.

Although I am hugely enjoying travelling with a companion, I wonder sometimes whether I should be striking off on my own, as that is how I had envisaged travelling to Santiago, using it as a time of contemplation and meditation. Prior to the start of my trip, I had prayed that I would be discerning about the people I would meet, and so something in me now wonders if meeting this particular pilgrim has a specific purpose. Or is it merely coincidence that we have encountered each other whilst on pilgrimage? We shall see.

The villages we travel through have a dilapidated charm, although maybe the locals do not see it in quite the same way, the disrepair of many buildings and lack of maintenance of roads suggesting an unwilling poverty. For the second time we join the walkers on the actual *chemin*, a short, but arduous stretch of rutted, potholed surfaces. Personally, I am happy to stick to the roads.

In the cathedral city of Burgos we take a brief respite beside the Bronze Pilgrim on the park bench outside the cathedral, before continuing a further fourteen miles to Estepar and a motel, there being no refuge nearby. As we arrive, a Dutch cycling couple, Hans and Yolande, lean out of the window of their room in greeting. They are combining their journey to Santiago with raising money for an Altzheimer's charity; something that strikes a chord with me as my father is caring for his wife who suffers from the ghastly condition. The four of us join up for dinner in the motel restaurant, an opportunity for GR to take a break from always speaking English with me.

We opt for a rest day here, to spend in Burgos and visit the cathedral. It takes a bit of ingenuity to reach the city: after waiting for various non-existent buses, GR finally flags down a poor, unsuspecting woman, who generously offers (although not really having much option) to drive us to the city outskirts. We then walk to the centre and the cathedral, a pale-grey building of ornate spires and castellated turrets. Amongst other things inside is the the tomb of El Cid, the legendary military leader of the eleventh century.

On our return to Estepar, we eat lunch, spend a couple of hours cleaning and oiling our bicycles, then loll in the sweltering sun, swigging cold beers. I also try to identify a persistent noise on my bicycle, which appeared yesterday. Cycling up and down the road, head dipped precariously below the crossbar, ears alert, I try unsuccessfully to pinpoint the source of the noise. With a bit of luck, it will just go away.

The next day, we meet a couple of Dutch stalwarts cycling the return journey, and a pair of outward bound Italians, one with an inflatable cushion on his saddle and a big tube of baby cream to hand (or should that be to bottom?). In contrast to everyone else, they both declaim how difficult the ascent to Roncesvalles had been, taking them seven hours to reach the summit (about twice as long as anyone else), early on resorting to pushing their bicycles up. But they are persisting and not giving up, so bravo to them.

Tonight's stop is Carrion de los Condes, arriving mid afternoon at a monastery refuge. We witness a scene that is surprisingly common: a coach arrives, its occupants disgorge, queue at the monastery to obtain their pilgrim stamps, wander around the town for as much as twenty minutes, before rushing back onto the coach, onward to their next pilgrim-stamp stop. It begs the question, why?

A regular feature on the Camino route is that pilgrim menus are on offer in all the towns and villages. This comprises a set meal: an entrée of two to four options (soup, salad, pasta), main course (meat, fish) served with chips, followed by caramel pudding or yoghurt and fruit for dessert; plus half a carafe of house wine, water and bread. Not gourmet, but very satisfying, and a welcome service to the impoverished pilgrim.

We arrive in Léon, its centre dominated by the imperious thirteenth-century gothic cathedral with lavish, richly-toned, stained glass windows. We meet Cony, an affable German professional cyclist, sponsored by Ortlieb (makers of excellent waterproof panniers) to participate in long-distance cycling events. He is set on completing the Camino in double-quick time, having only a small time-frame in between his sponsored events. As I am finding, those travelling the Camino do so for all sorts of quirky reasons.

The monastic refuge separates into female/male dormitories; unusual, as most of them are mixed. Fortunately for me, mine is a quiet 20-bed affair with just two other occupants. Unfortunately for GR and Cony, their quarters are packed to the gunwhales with snoring bedfellows.

The following day finds us crossing paths again with Hans and Yolande, Otto and Gerrard. It is all very chummy. A brief but gruelling spate along the *chemin* does nothing to make me envious of the mud-splattered mountain-bikers rough riding the whole way along the off-road route.

In Murias, the only other occupant in this night's refuge is Konia, a young Japanese woman who joins us in the evening at a nearby restaurant, where we sit outside in the warm evening sun. She speaks no Spanish or English, in fact, no languages other than Japanese, and yet she has undertaken to walk the Camino on her own. If your desire is to be with your own thoughts for any length of time, this must surely be the way to go about it. I have a sneaking admiration for her.

Personally biased, of course, but the universalism of English has much going for it and so I wonder how I shall fare in similar situations to Konia further on in my trip. I suspect that China and Japan are likely to be my most challenging countries through which to navigate, if only from the obvious perspective of roadsigns written in an alternative alphabet. By the same token, though, Greece and the Middle East could be of an equal challenge.

In the meantime, we smile, point, gesture and mime, accompanied by suitable facial contortions, in attempts at conversation, interspersed with companionable silences. Being just three in a refuge does not guarantee uninterrupted sleep; throughout the night Konia snores – loudly.

The next day starts with a long twelve-mile climb from 1,500 to 5,000 feet. It is cyclable all the way to the top of the pass, albeit in granny gears, which I manage, GR does not, resorting to walking – not that there is any rivalry between us, of course.

The landscape is beautiful, swathes of broom decorating the rolling hills, at first yellow, changing to white as we climb higher. At the top, we are rewarded with an intoxicating panorama of interweaving hills and valleys which gradually blurs into a hazy blue horizon.

What goes up must come down and the free-flowing descent swiftly brings us back to our day's starting height. Picturesquely situated on the hillside overlooking the medieval town of Villafranca de Bierzo, tonight's albergue initially appears quaint, but we soon realise it is run on totally commercial lines. The sardine-packed bunk beds hardly afford enough room to sidle between them; the showers are freezing cold and the breakfast in the morning is a total rip-off, not even enough bread for the later eaters (or is it that the first-comers are merely greedy pigs?).

Today we cannot help but be aware that not all pilgrims are of a contemplative nature, when the peace and quiet is broken by two German women we have encountered previously, a constant yakety-yak on their lips that, impressively, requires no pause for breath.

The monastic refuge in Samos stretches along the banks of a gently flowing tree-lined river, the soft afternoon sun bathing the grazing cows in honey yellow. The walls inside the dormitory are gaily decorated with hand-painted murals of lively medieval angels and pilgrims, horses and goats – on the banks of a gently flowing tree-lined river.

The following day we arrive in Mélide, on the eve of reaching our destination. The pilgrim refuge quite rightly gives priority to walkers, so instead of waiting three hours for bed confirmation or continuing to the next refuge we opt for a moderately-priced hotel.

In the morning, I awake to a fever of anticipation, for today we reach our destination, Santiago. The sun blazes down as we pick our way along quiet, country lanes through quiet country villages, no traffic, no other cyclists, our senses pervaded by the intoxicating perfume of eucalyptus forests. Each turn of the road anticipates our first view of our destination, until finally, there before us is Santiago.

We make our way towards the centre, exultant congratulatory greetings emanating from all directions as we pass countless pilgrims, their rhythmic plodding having taken on a buoyant air as they too are drawn into the thrill of finally reaching their long-awaited destination.

Arriving in the centre, the crowded narrow lanes oblige us to dismount, to walk with our bicycles as we enter the open space of the main plaza. The rising façade of the iconic Cathedral of Santiago de Compostela stands before us.

It is a reverential moment. What can you do, but stand and stare and send up a prayer of thanks for countless blessings: safe arrival, pilgrim fellowship, supportive friends, loving family, beautiful creation, a delightful cycling companion and a Divine travelling companion too.

We queue up for our pilgrim certificates and the following day attend the noonday pilgrim service in the cathedral. We also meet up with Hans and Yolande for a celebratory meal; I text my father, 'Happy 85th Birthday.'

GR buys me a pair of silver scallop shell earrings as a keepsake, before accompanying me to the coach station for my return journey to France, to continue my easterly direction. He is cycling to the west coast to Cap Finisterre, Land's End, a traditional additional journey's end for the Santiago pilgrim. We decide to keep in touch.

In order to comply with cycle-on-a-coach rules, it is necessary to remove pedals and re-attach them facing inwards, loosen the handlebars to straighten them in line with the bicycle, remove the front wheel and fix it to the frame with plastic ties, lower the saddle, then finish off this procedure by swathing the entire bicycle in a whole roll of clingfilm. I have never done any of these things before so I am thankful for my pilgrim friend to show me how.

The coach arrives, we load my bicycle and baggage in the hold, give each other a hug; I climb aboard and we wave each other goodbye as the coach pulls out into the dark and wet night. It is an emotional parting. I hate goodbyes at the best of times, feeling this one more than I should like.

Apart from that, it is a soulfully satisfying end to the beginning of my trip, topped with a touch of smug pleasure at my achievement so far.

* * *

France

17 June – 8 July 2008

*St Palais, Lescar, Marciae, Beaupuy, Toulouse, Castel Naudary,
Trèbes, Capestang, Vias, Loupian, La Grande Motte,
St Gilles, Salon, Cassis, La Seyne-sur-Mer, Boulouris-sur-Mer,
St Laurent du Var*

The crowded coach travels through the night to Bilbao, arriving in
the cold, unfriendly hours just before dawn. There is a 2-hour wait on
the draughty station for the connecting coach, which arrives late, the
rude, impatient driver only able to vent an aggressive, '*Vamos*! (Get on
with it!),' repeatedly, whilst I am trying to secure my bicycle in the hold.
Fortunately, his behaviour is counterbalanced by sympathetic, warm
smiles from the kindly woman who sits next to me. At the other end, I
am not sure which is my stop and end up disembarking too early. The
driver continues to be rude and unhelpful, knowing I must be getting off
at the wrong stop, but not telling me so and not helping me with
unloading either. It is a shame. I have had such an upbeat experience in
Spain and now my final take-away impression is of this horrible,
offensive man.

Attempting to re-assemble my bicycle is not straightforward.
Replacing the front wheel is almost impossible. I push hard, but the
wheel resists my efforts to squeeze it past the pannier racks. There is no
one around to help and I am in tears. This worsens when, half-an-hour
later, I am still here when the coach comes back, on the return journey to
Santiago, the same unpleasant driver smirking at my predicament.

Eventually, I succeed, but only through sheer brute force. I know this
is not how it should be done, but by now I am desperate. I realign the
handlebars, replace the pedals on the outside, which also takes ages to

thread them on correctly, until I realise I am turning them in the wrong direction! Lastly, I raise the seat. Off finally, at ten to two in the afternoon, aiming to reach St Palais by the end of the day, some forty miles away, almost a day's cycling in itself.

It does not start well, initially becoming lost, but once on track, the going is good and I arrive at the monastery at eight twenty-five, by now dark, an underestimated fifty-eight miles later. Flavio expresses a perfunctory welcome back, hurrying back to his television for the France versus Italy match. Football? Rugby? Who knows! (Who cares?) I heat and eat someone's leftover macaroni (a hand-scrawled message invites this), after which, I googlemap the location of the home of friends near Toulouse with whom I shall be spending a weekend in a few days' time.

I retrieve my left-luggage mountain, alarmed at where it will all go. Redistributing and repacking somehow does the trick, but, oh dear, my bicycle is sooo heavy I cannot lift it. How did I manage to cycle with it all before? On departure, Flavio provides me with the pilgrim route from here to Rome, as well as a list of refuges. I receive an email from the trailer cyclist inviting me to stay overnight with him and his wife if I am passing through Provence. Oh yes, please.

The noise on my bicycle from four days ago continues, enthusiastically checked out at the refuge in Lescar by two French and two German cyclists, huddling round my front wheel, spinning it, pausing it, deliberating over it. The verdict is unanimous: the noise stems from the front hub. The *office de tourisme* is very helpful, phoning a local cycle shop, that comes back with an immediate response.

'Yes, we can repair the problem. Bring the bicycle in tomorrow morning.'

And that, without knowing any of the symptoms beforehand.

My front ball bearing has worn prematurely, but, *voilà*, is now replaced, thanks to the wonderful Benoit at Vélocité cycle shop. Whilst here, I buy a simpler lock for my cycle security and a roll of blue tape (which Benoit gives me as a present) to replace that on the right handlebar, decidedly tatty from leaning up against rough walls. My benefactor cycles with me just far enough to ensure I am on the right road, before bidding me farewell.

However, after about forty-five minutes, it slowly dawns on me that either the sun has changed axis, or I am headed in the wrong direction. I opt for the latter, execute a self-conscious u-turn and, sixteen miles later, hey presto, I am sneaking by the same cycle shop in an embarrassed sort of way, hoping Benoit does not see me.

I end the day in Marciac, thirty miles short of my intended stop. But does it matter? Where is my timetable?

I am the only guest in the bohemian pilgrim refuge in this eclectic, arty village, seemingly teeming with organic restaurants. I head for the sun-filled plaza in which to sit and down a cold, well-deserved beer after a long day of hot, gruelling hills. The village hosts an international jazz festival each August, which might prompt a return visit.

The following day I cycle along the top of a ridge, unfettered views falling away either side. The road descends through thirteenth-century towns and villages, large, covered market places and ancient churches at their centres. It seems to be the *fête* season, as many are festooned with festively fluttering bunting in the promise of lively weekend celebrations.

I reach my destination, the idyllic hillside village of Beaupuy, the country home of friends who were my neighbours for a few years in UK, before moving to Paris. I arrive by mid evening to be greeted by Didier, who has come alone, the rest of the family having prior engagements. I am my usual sweaty, dusty self, socially in need of a shower; but first a beer. Then, once cleaned and freshened, the evening continues with aperitif of wine and *foie gras*, before sauntering along to neighbours for a garden party. And so the pattern is set for the rest of the weekend.

At dinner the following evening with invited neighbours, we dine outside, drinking in the peaceful pastoral view, as well as the free-flowing, proffered wine. Just as well I am not cycling the following day.

My right foot has been painful and swollen these last couple of days, and my right hand feels weak, with tingling in my little finger. The thought of any injury affecting my trip is disconcerting, but is one of the things that cannot be foreseen or planned for and can only be managed as it arises.

I exert myself to housekeeping duties: wash clothes and bicycle, spray WD40 on all moving parts (at least on my bicycle), update my website journal and photos, post home a parcel of redundant maps and clothes.

Didier is signed up with Skype, of which I have vaguely heard mention, and via which I speak with my older brother. I am bowled over to have a live video conversation with a familiar face and subsequently set up my own account.

Refreshed after my leisurely weekend sojourn, I enjoy a gentle transition back into the saddle by keeping company with the Canal du Latéral the twenty miles to Toulouse. The sun is shining, not too hot, occasional dappled shade. The canal path is sometimes gravel, but mostly asphalt. In Toulouse, I inquire at the presbytery next to the cathedral about refuges. The woman in the office has no knowledge of any, but phones one from my list, which confirms the availability of beds. Situated on the outskirts, much further than anticipated, I eventually find myself at the reception counter of a large monastery-cum-conference centre, greeted by the top of a head, from which comes the words, 'That will be € 12.'

'Good evening,' I respond, smiling, 'I'm glad to be staying in a refuge.'

'First, I need € 12,' he unsmilingly replies, finally deigning to look up.

In the morning, I make my way to another towpath, this time alongside the Canal du Midi. The Canal was constructed in 1681, stretching a hundred and fifty miles from Toulouse to the Mediterranean. Together with the Canal de Garonne and the River Garonne, the combined total of three hundred miles forms the Canal des Deux Mers (Two Seas), connecting the Atlantic and the Mediterranean oceans, from Bordeaux, in the north, to Sète, in the south.

At an ambiguous junction along the canal I meet a party of primary schoolchildren and their teacher and ask directions. They are curious about my cycling trip, expressing surprise when they learn that I am going round the world. The teacher leads the children in a round of applause, followed by 'Goodbye' and 'Good trip' from them all.

After an initial twenty-five miles of smooth, wide asphalt, the canal path changes to a challengingly narrow track, offering an assortment of obstacles to keep my attention focused on the ground directly in front of me. Gravel is surprisingly easy to traverse, mud and tree roots are not, the latter suddenly erupting through the ground in front of me in a deliberate attempt to send me sprawling into the water. Brambles are not keen for me to pass by without at least a brief acknowledgement of their presence and vie with their compatriot, nettles, for the most attention.

I stop briefly in Carcassonne, continuing to Trèbes and a river campsite, easily the most expensive to date at € 11. I presume this to be a foretaste of those to come as I approach the Mediterranean coast.

I spend an uncomfortable night on the hard ground (no grass, only solid, impacted mud), no through breeze in the tent, not enough of a pillow from my rolled-up clothes, lying on top of a sweaty sleeping bag. But in the morning I forget all that at the simple, pure pleasure of camping along a charming river, happy to chat with a couple of French cyclists on the return leg of cycling the Canal du Midi. In the past the young woman has walked the St Jacques Camino and, in September, they both plan to cycle along the *Via de la Plata,* the Silver Route, from Seville, in southern Spain, to Santiago. Maybe the Camino should carry a warning, 'Beware; risk of lifelong addiction to walking the Camino.' Perhaps, one day I too shall become a member of Camino Pilgrims Anonymous.

Later in the day, I meet a cycling Belgian couple, who have heard about me from a lock-keeper, and a Dutch couple impressively negotiating the restricted canal path on a tandem. Narrowboats glide gently along the tranquil waterway until they arrive at the locks, which they attack with amateurish gusto. A group of Brits manage, between the first and second time I see them, to inflict damage to their hire boat by crashing into a bridge. Towards midday and at the suggestion of a lock-keeper, I turn off the canal path to a large lake, selecting a suitably secluded spot for a wonderful swim, then drying off in the sun whilst eating my picnic lunch.

The track is fairly challenging with roots galore, either to avoid or to brake suddenly then wobble slowly over. It occurs to me that all I am doing is looking down at the ground, thus missing the passing scenery. And so I make a conscious effort to lift my eyes and enjoy my surroundings. Which I do for at least ten yards before aaargh . . . bump, bump, thud . . . maybe not such a good idea. I concede victory to the roots.

Being a woman of a certain age, hot flushes are not uncommon, but are totally unwelcome. They switch on suddenly without warning, night or day, instantly bathing me in self-conscious perspiration, the symptoms barely alleviated by madly mopping my face and flapping my damp clothes. At night, attempts at instant temperature regulation have me frantically unzipping the sleeping bag, swinging my legs out into the cool night air, followed almost straightaway by scooping them in again, as I swerve from hot and sweaty to chilling cold. There are not many downsides to being a woman, but this is one of them.

Through Béziers and on to Vias and the local tourist office to find out about the pilgrim refuge included on Flavio's list. It turns out not to exist. However, the woman appears to be in the know about something and phones a campsite, which offers me a camping pitch for free. Why? Simply because I am a pilgrim.

The campsite is perfect: long, lush grass cushioning my tent, amiable staff, hot afternoon sun in need of – a swimming pool. This too is provided; in fact, a rather luxurious one: a soft blue expanse, in the middle of which is a sculpted rock formation with a tumbling waterfall, around the edge a dazzling white terrace of sunbathing heaven, gleaming loungers lined up ready for serious sun-worshippers – or simple cyclists.

I don my sad-looking, 23-year old bikini, dubiously wondering if its flimsy condition will maintain my modesty, and nonchalantly wander over to the edge of the inviting water. I feel self-conscious of my sharply contrasting body markings: dark tanned shoulders and legs, sandwiching a lily white middle section, and so slip swiftly into the soothing depths, to luxuriate languorously in this unexpected blessing, a huge grin stuck on my face. Life is good.

The campsite is out of town and I eat in the camp restaurant from the *menu du jour*: salad, bull stew and *frites*, dessert, carafe of red wine. To top this wonderful day, I have now clocked up 2,000 miles.

On the fifth day I arrive at the last and, I am assured, the worst part of the Canal du Midi. Various people over the last few days have made it quite plain that I must avoid it and go by road for this final section. I arrive at Agde, the beginning of the end. Decision time. Traffic-ridden, smooth, easy road; vehicle-free, challenging, canal path?

I take the latter, confident that I have already successfully tackled some pretty challenging stretches of the Canal du Midi, that Raven and I have stood up to them all with aplomb and that, surely, this last little bit cannot be any worse? I am up for a bit of a challenge (after all, it is the basic ingredient of my trip) and I should like to complete the whole of the Canal du Midi, especially as not many people seem to do this last bit. I realise I also wish to delay returning to the world of roads and vehicles; there is a great sense of being cocooned and apart from the real world travelling along the Canal.

Which is how I find myself cycling easily along one of the prettiest sections of the Canal, wondering what all the fuss was about. Until. . . humph . . . I now realise: the path becomes a track and an extremely narrow one at that. It is right on the canal edge, overhung with tall grasses and predatory, tearing brambles. It is so precariously narrow, that I cannot cycle, only push my bicycle along with my left foot, the redundant foot resting on its pedal. But I am still progressing, inch by slow foot by slower mile.

At one point, the path steers away from the canal up a steep bank. I am forced to remove the back panniers in order to have the strength to push the bicycle up the bank, along the ridge a few yards, back down to the canal path, pumping the brakes in short, jerky spurts, so as not to end up in the water; returning for my bags. Continuing in one-footed scooter fashion, I arrive at the next, steeper bank, by which time I am castigating myself at my ambitious stupidity, but bloody-mindedly refusing to give up and go back. Maybe not the most timely occasion to admit a weakness of mine but, once I have set my mind on something, I am doggedly loathe to change it.

For the second time in a short while, I am unloading my bicycle, hauling everything, one item at a time, up the dusty slope, huffing and puffing, slipping and sliding; then tentatively down the other side and reload. How many more times would this have to happen before arriving at the end? I am dusty, sweaty, dispiritingly exhausted, painfully scratched – and at the limit of my physical capability.

When you are in such a situation, there are limited choices; no Merlin is going to pop up with a wave of his magic wand, no shining bright Launcelot is going to gallop along on his majestic steed looking for maidens in distress to rescue, and, for all I know, it is my guardian angel's day off. I have a pow-wow with God, during which we weigh up the idea of going back (difficult even to turn around on the narrow path) or struggle on.

We decide on a reccy and scrabble to the top of the bank, where, joy of joys, there is a perfectly good track. The only obstacle between it and me is a triple barbed-wire fence. We debate the situation. If it is private land, what is the worst that can happen to me? Least likely, shot at. More likely, shouted at. Most likely, nothing at all. Relieved and happy at this sensible revelation, I struggle up with my possessions, push them under the forbiddingly welcome fence, reunite bicycle and bags, then proceed to trespass along a forest track through a protected nature reserve, eventually coming to a public path; whereupon I begin breathing easily again. It is then a short stretch to Marseillan and completion of the Canal du Midi.

The subsequent release of tension and effort produces a response of tearful relief; an immense tiredness and the sense of achievement are overwhelming. I am worn out physically and emotionally and wish I had someone with me. I remember to send a grateful thank you to my Commander-in-Chief; at least he knows what I have been through.

I stay two nights at the friendly campsite in Loupian, benefiting from regenerative sleep, resting in the shade, gorging on local strawberries and chatting to the roadside stallholder selling homemade apricot and peach jam. She belongs to one of the two oldest families in the village; her husband belongs to the other. She has lived here all her life, is very proud of it and talks enthusiastically of its ancient Roman farm villa with extensive mosaic floors dating back to the second century.

I need an iron – no, not for my clothes; I am not that sad. Holes in my cycling trousers need repairing, for which I have bought iron on patches. The accommodating receptionist offers to bring her iron from home for me to borrow, then forgets, but the thought is appreciated. In the end I hand sew the holes and hem the bottoms.

I seem to be a bit under the weather: a runny nose has become blocked, a cough has become productive, right foot still slightly swollen, right little finger weak and numb – maybe caused by pressure on a nerve from extensive cycling? All in all, it is a good decision to stay put for a day. I hold a d.i.y. Holy Communion service, using the service booklet brought with me from my home church. It is probably not in keeping with liturgical protocol, self-administering unconsecrated bread and wine, but I do not have a sense of God frowning down on me and no lightning bolts come shooting from the sky.

The next morning begins cloudy cool when I set off at six thirty, becoming hot by mid morning. I keep away from the roads, choosing instead a dirt track alongside the 5-mile wide Étang, an enclosed sea that stretches for twelve miles alongside the Mediterranean. This watery landscape is punctuated by long, neat rows of cages, the tops rising above the water; the air resonates with a pungent odour. Oyster and mussel farms, the local livelihood.

The shadeless, searing heat is relentless and I look out for a possible watering hole. Passing by a house with a couple of picnic tables and colourful parasols in the garden, I am hailed by the chap leaning over his garden wall. In response to me saying I am looking for somewhere to have a drink, he waves me in with a welcoming gesture, whereupon I wheel my bicycle into the garden, sinking gratefully onto a shady bench, relieved to have a break from the heat. I order a *café au lait* from the man's wife and the husband joins me at the table. They are from Switzerland, he French-speaking, she from the German side, dividing their time between their two homes.

His wife returns with, not only coffee, but a jug of delicious homemade lemon squash and biscuits. This is unexpectedly generous, I think. They are extremely pleasant and friendly and we continue chatting affably, he acting as interpreter for his wife, who speaks only German. When I am ready to leave and request the bill, they smilingly refuse. It is only then I realise that this is not a café as I had assumed, but their own private home!

The briny lake leads on to the Canal du Rhône as far as Sète, some say the official end of the Canal du Midi. Further on is Montpelier, where I buy a sun visor (better late than never), a replacement bikini (thoughts of Nice and Cannes spring to mind) and tent pegs. On then to a campsite for the night in Grande Motte, the following day, to a pilgrim refuge in St Gilles.

St Gilles is on the Arles route to Santiago, one of the main four originating in France, the others starting in Vézelay, Le Puy and Tours. The large abbey church in the centre of the town acts as a focal point for all things St Jacques de Compostelle. Inside are informative displays of the numerous and varied routes, not only in France, but Spain, Italy and the rest of Europe. During the Middle Ages, St Gilles became the fourth most popular Christian pilgrimage destination after Jerusalem, Rome and Santiago.

The legend of St Gilles is that he became a hermit, living here in the Flavian valley, where he kept a doe, who provided him with his daily pinta. One day, the King's hunting group was about to shoot the deer, but Gilles, stepping in front of her, took the arrow himself. He survived and King Wamba, so touched by this selfless act, gave to Gilles the whole of the Flavian valley, asking him to build a monastery there. After the hermit's death, many miracles were attributed to him; even now, pilgrims still flock to the monastery and the crypt in the church, leaving tokens such as their walking sticks at his tomb.

Opposite the church is a restaurant, *Le Repos des Pélérins* (The Pilgrim's Rest), where I sit at one of the outside tables, the only customer besides a cheery bunch on the neighbouring table. Very soon,

I am enthusiastically invited to join them: Jean, the owner, his wife, Odile, along with their two guests. The ensuing evening is lively, full of *bon vivant*, heady wine and a sharing of dreams, Jean's and Odile's to buy a boat one day and simply sail away.

After a sweltering night, bitten mercilessly throughout – possibly by little creatures in the bed – I arrive the following day in Arles itself. After a quick peek in the cathedral, where I obtain a pilgrim stamp, I arrive in Salon in the early afternoon, heading straight to the tourist office. Following a similar phone call to that of a few days ago, I find myself tootling along to another free campsite. This one does not incorporate such a splendid swimming pool as on the previous occasion, but a swim is a swim, and this pool offers the same refreshing finale to a dusty cycling day. In response to my query as to why he gives free camping to pilgrims, the owner replies simply, 'Because I am a Christian.'

I receive a text from Jean, the trailer cyclist, making arrangements to meet up in a few days, for me to stay the night with him and his wife. After a couple of texts, he follows up with a call, in order to impart directions, delivered at his usual top-speed pace. At the end of the call, I am left with the vague notion that I should be phoning him when I arrive in some place beginning with 'B', from whence we shall attempt to meet up.

In the meantime, I am cycling to Marseille. The very name conjures up an esoteric place, maybe due to its cosmopolitan heritage. Founded by Greeks in 600 BC, it is the oldest city in France, down the centuries a great maritime port. Within striking distance of North Africa and accessible to the diverse countries surrounding the Mediterranean, it is natural that it should attract an eclectic mixture of races: Algerians, Italians, Asians. To add further romance, a mile offshore, stands the Chateau d'If, the famed castle of Alexander Dumas' *The Count of Monte Cristo*.

Entry to this second largest city passes extensively through the slightly unnerving down-at-heel areas, to reach the old port and tourist marina of Marseille. I cycle slowly around the harbourside, past a plethora of crowded cafés, searching for an elusive shady seat. Seeing none vacant, I head out of town and around the headland. A dearth of hard shoulder gives rise to one or two motorists being anything but polite as they rush past with scant regard for my safety.

Looking along the coast ahead, I am confronted by a dichotomy of contrast: bland arid mountains on the one side, a vibrant blue seascape on the other. I squint with dismay at the endlessly climbing, hot, dusty road into the hills, searching hopelessly for any indication of the two campsites as per my map. One will suffice. Nothing. I resign myself to the long trawl to the top and the unknown facilities thereafter. It is slow going, crawling up the 5-mile hill in sapping heat. I pass the locations of the would-be campsites. They have probably evaporated in the heat. Wild camping lends no appeal in this exposed dry landscape, denying me a requisite shower, change of clothes and a cold beer – and the risk of coming face to face with certain creatures that slither and hiss. At the top of the mountain, a day cyclist confidently declares, 'Ten kilometres to Cassis, all downhill.'

And for once a local is right and here I am. The camp ground is stone hard, impenetrable to my tent pegs. Having spoken to other cyclists in preparation of my trip, I realise now one of the main advantages of a standalone tent, the clue is in the name. Unfortunately, I do not have one. I consider just sleeping on my mattress but instead try a simple remedy: inside the tent, place hefty rocks in the four corners; outside, wrap the guy sheets around other hefty rocks (of which there is a supply, presumably from previous campers in the same predicament). Oh and, if trees, bushes and fences are nearby, it is probably preferable to tie the guy sheets to them. It works, of sorts, but the resultant sag is a bit claustrophobic, causing me to hope for no high winds (or, in fact, any kind of wind), as I do not fancy being smothered by my own tent. I am a little disgruntled with myself because, despite careful planning and thought given to the choice of tent, this crucial criteria requiring pliable ground seems a fundamental oversight in my deliberations.

After a shower, I walk down into the quaint town and the ancient fishing port, set in a superbly sheltered natural harbour. It is charming, albeit touristy, fishing boats vying for space with the marina and the sightseeing boats. I stroll along the waterfront away from the crowds, attracted by the softly-lit balcony of a quiet restaurant at the harbour entrance. Here I eat pizza, whilst watching the sailboats manoeuvring towards their moorings, before being absorbed into the dense black night beyond the restaurant's glow.

Back at the ranch, the hope of a still night is futile as all becomes increasingly wild and windy. I try to convince myself that the violent flapping and creaking of my tent probably sounds worse than it really is. In the morning, thankfully intact and still this side of the rainbow, I continue along the beautiful coastal road, to Savary-sur-mer, stopping to relax for a while on a bench near the waterfront, idly people watching. On the point of continuing, a chap on a motorboat raises his wineglass, beckoning me over, whereupon I am welcomed onboard by three randonée cycling enthusiasts. Declining the proffered alcoholic drinks, I accept a pear juice and bitesize *apéretifs* of spicy *saucisse*. Nicholas, the guy who invited me over, when not cycling or entertaining friends (or, for that matter, solo cyclists) in the Mediterranean sun, takes people on deep-sea fishing trips. A simple, idyllic existence. Equally, the men seem just as taken with my current way of life.

It is now time to put my minimal understanding of Jean's instructions into action. We talk on our mobiles as he again tries to impart crucial instructions to me, but talking so quickly, with directions so complicated, that all I can do is grasp the words, 'les plages des Sablettes', and hope that they are somehow relevant.

I arrive in a town and ask various peoples where I might find 'les plages' (which mean beaches and so, I deduce, likely to be near the sea). Miraculously, it works and we meet up. I follow him to his flat in La Seyne-sur-mer, where he and Monique live. After a quick shower and beer, we meet up with friends for drinks and food.

One night extends into an action-packed, sociable weekend, during which we drive to the top of Mount Féron for a spectacular view of the bay of Toulon and La Seyne-sur-mer; spend an evening playing pétanque (throwing heavy balls in the air to land on the ground near other heavy balls) and barbecue with friends. We laze a few hours on the beach and swim – the Mediterranean is shockingly cold!

We visit St Maximin-la-Sainte-Baume and the huge twelfth-century convent and basilica, in which, down in the crypt, is the tomb of Mary Magdalene. It is said that, in order to escape persecution, along with her brother, Lazarus (the man whom Jesus resurrected) and sister, Martha, they fled from the Holy Land in a boat with neither rudder nor sails, which miraculously brought them to the safety of the shores of the Camargue coast. Mary converted the people of Marseilles, then later in life, retired to a cave in the surrounding mountains. After her death, she was interred in the basilica, which eventually became a place of pilgrimage, following various miracles attributed to her.

I shop for quicker-drying shorts and, finally getting around to it, an inflatable pillow; update my journal, and send a photo of the ball bearing to Robin, my cycle man in UK, who readily agrees that it has worn prematurely and so credits my account with the cost of replacing it. I receive a sweet email from Jean-Claude of *Le Repos des Pélérins* in St Gilles, who compliments me on how much they enjoyed my '*sourire délicieux*' (delicious smile). How can anyone not be flattered by such a remark? He also includes an open invitation to return some day (presumably before they sail away in their boat).

An email from Liliane and Huguette informs me that they had arrived in Santiago on 13 June, two days before I had. They are such a spritely pair. And Didier confirms that he has posted the CD of my photos to my older brother, which means that I have a backup of my photos to date (assuming the CD does not become lost in the post. Surely not?). I carry a couple of memory cards for my photos, periodically transferring them to memory sticks in an attempt to ensure that I do not lose any. I do not risk sending them or my daily journals in the post; they are much too precious.

Cacophonous cicadas come out in force every evening, producing such a dreadful din as to make conversation almost inaudible. They have a life span of just a month – and want to make the most of it; it is hard to be intolerant towards them after such a revelation. They are extremely well camouflaged and we have to peer carefully into the trees to glimpse them. We find a delicate, tissue-paper husk of one, which looks like a miniature alien creature escaped from the set of Men in Black.

After the weekend, I take my leave, with grateful thanks to Monique, who generously says it has been a privilege to have someone doing such an intrepid trip staying with her. I am just amazed at the way she readily accepted this cycling stranger being brought into her home, picked up by her husband on one of his many lone cycling trips. She nonchalantly accepts his extensive times away, including next year's project cycling the length of South America.

Jean and I take the ferry across the bay of Toulon, where we pick up a dedicated cycle path, travelling its thirty miles together. After lunch, photos and goodbyes, Jean waves me off, then waits for Monique to pick him up in the car for the return journey.

All partings are emotional. I feel cocooned and safe when with other people, welcoming a break from the subconscious stress of doing everything on my own. On resumption of my solitary trip, I momentarily feel vulnerably alone, uncertain of my ability to cope. However, it is not too long before the mental transfer to solo mode perks me up once more with a buoyant enthusiasm.

I follow the bay road round, chancing upon another cycle route, which eventually turns into a gravel road, but compared with some of the Canal du Midi, this is an A1 road. And thanks to having travelled the Canal du Midi, I am now confident enough to attempt such opportune tracks – and be rewarded with a pleasant picturesque route.

All the way along the coast the views are to die for. I can hardly believe I am on the exquisite Côte d'Azur. Postcards and paintings and tourist propaganda are not wrong: the sea really is a vibrant, rich azure. I cycle leisurely along this resplendent coast, joyfully absorbing the beauty of Cannes, Antibes, Nice.

In Cagnes-sur-mer, sauntering along the promenade, a passing cyclist asks if I am cycling round the world – and is quite taken aback when I reply that I am. It is his dream to do the same. After chatting a while, the guy, Guy (pronounced Gee) invites me to stay the night at his place, where he lives with his son. My gut instinct says that it is OK to accept his invitation. He is now off on a cycle ride and so we agree to meet up at 7 pm. I spend the afternoon in the town library on the internet. Jessica is online and we exchange a couple of emails.

Near the appointed time I head for Guy's hairdressing salon to meet up with him and his son and accompany them to their home. Both seem gentlemanly and harmless and I do not feel uncomfortable in my decision. I realise though, that at any time other than on this trip, I should consider such a thing stupidly risky. I cannot explain my thinking, except in the context of gut instinct being a powerful indicator of danger; plus a measure of commonsense thrown in.

At ten in the evening, normally a time when I would be thinking of going to bed, I find myself on the back of Guy's scooter, whizzing up the coast to Nice for an ice cream. The centre is lively and humming, with people spilling over the café thresholds into the streets – eating ice cream. Nice is very nice at night.

The next morning, I find a cycle route to Nice, then the coast road to Monaco and Monte Carlo. The marinas are full of sizeable luxurious boats. A surprising number fly union jacks; it seems the UK has quite a few wealthy people. In a way, it is a thrill to be passing through these famously rich places, although I find more appeal in the small, pretty fishing villages of Menton and Villefranche-sur-mer. Here I stop and pass the time of day with the local fishermen, push my bicycle onto a quiet beach for a brief dip in the clear water and eat my picnic lunch nestled against a sun-warmed rock.

I have really taken my time today; had numerous stops and kept a leisurely pace. At one point I actually ask myself, why? Then realise that it is something to do with the fact that I am about to come to the border with Italy. Yes? Isn't that exciting? A new country, making progress? Yeees, but – that is precisely it, a new country. It takes a while to get used to a new country, to find the feel of it, to familiarise oneself with basic survival phrases, to become acquainted with the procedure for finding accommodation (the *office du tourisme* is called something else outside of France), to know if the natives are friendly – to wonder if I shall still enjoy travelling alone there. All these things are on my mind as I come up the coastal hill, through a couple of tunnels, over the border – and into Italy.

*   *   *

Italy

9 July – 1 August 2008

*San Remo, Savona, Rapollo, Améglia, Pisa, Marina di Pisa,
Lastra, Imprenuta, Siena, Lago di Bolsena,
Lago di Vici, ROME, Tor San Lorenzo, Lidodi Fordi,
Cassino, Benevento, Bovino, Margharita di Savoie,
Giovanazzo, Costa Marlato, Brindisi*

The first town over the border is San Remo. I am wandering around the centre, feeling as though it is my first day at school, looking vaguely around for the *azienda di turismo*, when a southern hemisphere drawl breaks into my conciousness, asking directions to the tourist office.

Tim is an enthusiastic, fresh-faced, 22-year-old Aussie cycling around Europe for a few months. He navigates by handlebar-mounted GPS and cycles in flip-flops.

We find the tourist office. The nearest campsite being way out of town in the direction from which I have just come, I book a room in the same hotel as Tim. However, between leaving the tourist office and arriving at the hotel, only one room is now available. We go for it. At least it has separate beds. Now, this might seem slightly weird, that two complete strangers are sharing the same hotel bedroom, having met only about forty-five minutes previously. Only the stuff of films, surely? But, viewed in the same light as sharing a room in a pilgrim refuge, it makes complete sense, at least to me – and Tim seems to be unfazed by it.

With nowhere safe to store our bicycles at ground level, Tim and I lug them up six flights of stairs to our room. The following morning, we reverse the process, up at seven thirty, leaving just before eight. This early start is a shock for Tim's system, his normal setting off time being mid/late morning. We travel at my pace, meandering up and down the hilly coastal road, through holiday seaside towns, stopping periodically in the hunt to decide our favourite ice cream from a bewildering array in the numerous *gelaterias*. *Frutti di bosco* (fruits of the forest) rates highly, but, as it seems compulsory to have more than one flavour at a time, I extend my repertoire with pistachio, tutti-frutti, lemon sorbet, double *cioccolato*. The resultant sugar-fix stands us in good stead for the arduous ascents. Pleasure and performance deftly combined.

The roller-coaster road highlights our different techniques, especially on the snaking uphills. I plug away in my lowest granny gear, to tortoise the whole way to the top. Tim's normal tactic is to hare up as far as he can until totally puffed, walking the remainder. However, with me in tow, he forces himself to stay cycling the whole way, 'Cos I don't want to be seen as a wimp.' Arriving red-faced at the summit, after a brief respite, he then shoots off like a bullet downhill. I, on other hand, am too old for such milarkee and do not feel the urge to emulate. At the end of the day, though, we are both equally worn-out.

A couple of days ago, I received a surprise email from GR, in which he suggests possibly coming to Pisa to cycle with me to Rome. A second text now confirms his arrival in three days, enough time for me to cycle a doable daily average of fifty-five miles to arrive at the same time.

The following day we cycle at Tim's pace: voomph, hell for leather, as fast as we can, as directly as we can, along the main road, as per GPS instructions, stopping fairly frequently at roadside filling stations for energy-replenishing, carbonated drinks. Whereas my ambling pace is eleven to thirteen miles per hour, Tim's is a virtually constant seventeen. Twenty-five miles to our lunchtime stop in Genoa is enough for me at this speed, so I am heartily relieved that Tim is staying put for a couple of days of intensive sightseeing. We have had a great time together, but cycling at such different paces is decidedly not for the long-term – for either of us. On parting, we exchange comments of mutual admiration: Tim expresses himself in awe of me doing such a trip – at my age! And I love his enthusiasm – and his ability to cycle in flip-flops. People may come into your life for a specific purpose and then leave. Tim's was to help ease my nervous entry into a new country.

Onwards then, up and down, combining timely rests at the tops of the challenging inclines with full appreciation of the picture postcard views: firwood hills, terracotta roofs, cloudless blue sky, vivid blue sea. Breathless beauty.

In Camogli, I hope for a pilgrim refuge. But talking on the phone to one of the Franciscan sisters at the convent, she speaking no English and I making a futile attempt at pidgeon Italian, I think she takes fright, insisting, 'Oh no, no pilgrims.' Hint taken, I continue to the next town.

At the town railway station in Rapollo I ask for the tourist office, with no result. Back in the busy street, looking around for where to go next, a smiling woman stops, presumably asking if she can help. She is in her seventies, wearing a cheery blue top and yellow trousers, with a flowered mini sarong loosely tied around her waist, flowery flip-flops, large white-framed sunglasses, beneath a blue-ribboned panama sitting squarely on her head, a capacious straw bag over her left shoulder. I mention *azienda di turismo* and straightaway she gestures across the square, indicating that she will walk with me. On the way, she asks if I ever feel in danger, travelling alone, and how far am I going? She speaks no English, but by picking up on a few words, it is possible to understand the gist of her questions and I have learnt just enough Italian to produce a plausible reply. We walk for ten minutes to the tourist office, where she comes inside with me, waiting patiently on a chair, cooling herself with the little fan she carries. After I am provided with directions to a campsite, we go outside, she poses for a couple of photos, tells me her name, which sounds like Estrella, I thank her with a hug and we part. She stands watching and waving as I cycle away; a kindly, mildly eccentric, silver-haired angel.

The following day presents me with a 20-mile climb early on, up which I am easily overtaken by the jovial day cyclists. Being a Saturday, they are out in force, and exude friendliness with their 'Ciaos', hand-waves and toots on their handlebar hooters. Towards the end of the afternoon, I enjoy a glorious freewheeling descent, not expecting any more uphill challenges. Unfortunately, that is just what comes along and, with a distinct lack of oomph in the turn of my pedals, I reluctantly start struggling up it.

A day cyclist passes with a cheerful, 'Ciao', to which I force a less than cheerful response. The next moment though, my pedals are turning on their own and I cannot keep up with them. What on earth is happening? I am flying along at an amazing speed up this daunting incline, laughing euphorically. It finally dawns on me that I am being pushed along effortlessly by a day cyclist – and a mildly handsome one at that. On we soar, his companions one by one, gradually overtaking us, until the last one passes and my guy gives a final extra push, issues a friendly salute, as he too passes by to catch up with his compatriots.

My spirits refreshed, body re-energised, I whizz through my intended stop in La Spezia, on to the small town of Ameglia. From there it is a short day to Pisa and the airport to meet the mid-afternoon flight. The approach road to the airport is a challenge, but I manage to survive intact and unscathed from the mayhem of Italian drivers and the treacherous eruptions of the road surface caused by tree roots. I arrive in good time, in fact, a very safe two hours early. When the tannoy announces the arrival of GR's flight, I wait with some nervousness until, having first had to re-assemble his bicycle after the flight, he is the last to come through the airport door.

I have been unsure how I might greet him; after all, we have not known each other for that long and it has been a few weeks since we last met. As it turns out, we embrace warmly, straightaway feeling at ease just as we were on the road to Santiago, and now on the road together towards another pilgrim destination.

During our couple of days in Pisa, we visit the impressive leaning tower. It is hard to believe that construction of such a building started way back in the twelfth century. The children's song, 'Don't build your house on the sandy land,' comes to mind when you realise that it was ignominiously built on a weak subsoil, gradually causing its distinctive five and a half degrees' lean. It is still sinking, imperceptibly at the rate of a millimetre each year.

We leave Pisa, appreciating the beauty of the Tuscan countryside as we cycle past hectares of hilly vineyards against finely drawn skylines of stately poplars; of golden cornfields sprinkled with giant rolls of harvested crops.

In towns, we contend with the challenging traffic, checking constantly behind as to the other's whereabouts, to prevent us becoming separated. I am in front as we cycle through the centre of Lastra looking for a tourist office. I glance regularly behind, but, on this last occasion, GR is not there. No matter, he will catch me up, so I wait by the side of the road. He does not come. I retrace my steps, but cannot see him. There is no signal on my mobile. Telling myself not to be ridiculous does not halt the rising panic, the thought of us not being able to find each other in this foreign place with no means of communication now dominating my thoughts. I cycle around for a while, eventually coming across the tourist office. I exhale in relief, assuring myself he will come here as this is where we were headed. In the meantime, I can ask about accommodation. As I enter, GR phones my mobile saying he is in the tourist office.

'Where? I can't see you.'

'And I can't see you, so where are you?'

'In the tourist office.'

'No, you aren't!'

It turns out there is another one very nearby. How bizarre. With obvious relief, we meet up; whereupon I am immediately chastised for not doing things properly when you lose someone.

'Immediately retrace your steps to the place of the last sighting; *then* wait.'

There is no campsite nearby and we book into a hotel. Although we share the cost of accommodation, it is still much higher than my daily allowance. I remind myself that I always knew Europe would be in the higher spending category of my budget, that Asia would be much lower and that I was assuming North America would be about even. I also incorporated into my overall funding a small amount for holidays, a portion of which could legitimately be used during this time with GR, as there is (mostly!) a relaxed holiday air when travelling together. For me, the stresses of solo travelling are instantly dissipated with a companion.

We continue on flat roads to fabulous Florence, with its grey, pink and green striated, marble buildings, crowded palazzos and the old Ponte Vecchio bridge over the River Arno. The bridge has shops built on it, interspersed with open archways, affording views up and down the river.

We have not come across many other cyclists on the road so meeting a couple of Belgians next day is a novelty. They are on their way from Antwerp to Rome, approximately nine hundred and fifty miles, following the cycling version of the Via Francigena. We realise we have inadvertently joined the ancient pilgrimage route, which originates in Canterbury.

In Sienna, we find a pilgrim refuge in which to stay, my first since St Gilles. It is run by the Sisters of Charity of San Vicenzo, the same order as the convent I visited in France. We share our dormitory with three Italian pilgrims, walking five hundred miles from Turin and Milan to Rome, probably taking a month to complete. Neither they nor the nuns speak any English and so we all practice friendly smiles and meaningful gestures, throwing in the occasional Italian word to show willing. In the morning, after breakfast, we pay our donativo before departing.

The ten days to Rome takes us through a landscape of mountains and lakes, tough climbs leading to magnificent views and welcome descents, to finish the day at relaxing lakeside campsites. We visit the ancient caves and Roman amphitheatre at Sutri, even acquiring a pilgrim stamp.

Our first 'ROMA' sign on the rural outskirts of the city quickens my pulse and produces a fixed Cheshire grin on my face for the rest of the way into the centre, happy merely to follow my companion without having to work out for myself the route through the city.

Cycling slowly through the Piazza di Risorgimento, a strangely-familiar voice calls out my name. It is Tim. What are the chances of such an encounter, at this precise moment, in such a large, bustling city? He arrived in Rome a couple of days ago, has since been frenetically sightseeing in his inimitable way, prior to catching a train to Munich in three days' time. We make plans to meet up for a meal.

As we cross the final piazza before entering one of the most famous squares in the world, St Peter's, my excitement is palpable, the anticipation breath-stopping.

And here we are. My first impression is, gosh, isn't it enormous! I stand and stare. It is an awesome feeling to be here. GR takes it in his stride, having come here after Santiago. But the overriding thought that is swirling round in my head is, 'I am here, in Rome, in St Peter's Square – and I have cycled all the way!'

Should I be expressing a more spiritual reaction? Well, I'm not. I am bowled over at the mere realisation of what I have done and absolutely proud of myself for having achieved it. In the midst of holiday snaps galore – of me in front of blue and yellow-striped Swiss guards, white-robed nuns, St Peter's church, the Moderno fountain, the Egyptian obelisk – I punch my arms in the air.

'Yes, oh yes. I have cycled all the way from Almondsbury, via Santiago.'

My cyclometer announces 2,986.4 miles.

But the cycling is not over for the day and eventually we set off to cover the last twelve miles to our hotel, bouncing along the bumpy 2,000-year old Via Appia. Pressing through a flock of milling sheep, we savour the history of thousands of ancient footsteps that have polished these cobbles over the centuries. The Appian Way stretches to Brindisi, first

55

built, as with most of the Roman roads, as military roads, then becoming trade and pilgrim routes. We reach the hotel on the outskirts at 9.45 pm, well after dark, tired and triumphant, three thousand miles from home.

We do the sightseeing bit, including the Vatican, the Pantheon, the Trevi fountain, Colisseum, writing postcards and being outrageously ripped off in St Peter's Square to the tune of €25 for two ice creams. We join a guided group for the Vatican tour, which reduces the queuing time considerably and furnishes us with enough information to make the visit more interesting than if we had wandered around on our own. One of the striking exhibits is the Resurrection tapestry, in which Jesus' eyes unnervingly follow you the whole time you are walking by; he just will not leave you alone.

The ceiling of the Sistine Chapel is well worth the visit. The main theme is Man's need for a restored relationship with God, made possible through Jesus. We are herded in and packed tightly into the Chapel for our allotted ten minutes. The loud and officious staff first shush us to be quiet, then paradoxically shout at us all to be quiet and respect the sanctity of the chapel. Despite this, there is still a sense of awe at being there. To stand, gaze, touch something that is hundreds of years old breaks down the boundary of time as it brings history into the present.

St Peter's is a quite magnificent church, everything on a grand scale: the lofty height of the ceiling, the lavishly-decorated interior, patterned marble floors. But, although built to the glory of God, it comes over to me more as a tourist attraction than as an intimate place of worship.

A friend of a friend from Bristol invites us for drinks, at the same time offering me the use of his laptop to update my website journal. I am alarmed to discover that my site is down publicly and locked administratively. I have the heebie-jeebies at the prospect of the demise of my mass communication tool and shoot off a hopeful email to the website helpdesk. As for Tim, we settle for seeing him off at the railway station, as he decides to leave on an earlier train, in order to safeguard sufficient time for the remainder of his cycling tour.

All too soon it is time for yet another farewell. After a beautiful but brief ten days, it is time to say goodbye again to GR. I still have my trip to finish and he has his 'free life' to live, now off to Australia for a few months to build a barn for a Dutch farmer, then possibly to Ghana to continue his involvement in a local building project. We part at the airport and I turn despondently away to cycle off on my own.

The cycling is easy, no gruelling gradients, a comfortable temperature, no humidity and only thirty miles. The road is unattractive and teeming with lorries, but does its job in bringing me back to the sea. This is a popular and expensive stretch of coast. The campsites are either full or charge a minimum of one week's stay, at an alarming €30 per night, more than I was paying for a shared hotel room. The first three sites all quote the same exorbitant price and I arrive disconsolately at the fourth. This turns out to be five euros cheaper, and I am given a discount of a further ten. After putting up my tent, I return to the office to pay, only then to be told there is no charge – because I am touring by bicycle.

The campsite is mostly caravans, but the small, dedicated tent area has the most stunning location, right on the edge of the beach, an unimpeded view of the vibrant blue Mediterranean beyond the wide band of pale, liquid-soft sand.

I swim in the sea, then stroll along the beach to a bar for a beer, joined by a young Belgian couple, Julie and Koen, whose tent is next to mine. They are at the end of their 10-day driving holiday; a delightful couple, in the midst of wedding plans for the following year. The beer turns into a pizza meal together and an evening in the company of their youthful enthusiasm.

Life is full of little delights. The next day, a cyclist passes me on a hill and continues a few hundred yards before pulling over at a bar, indicating to me to stop so he can buy me a coffee. We have no extensive conversation because of the language barrier, but enough for his appreciation of my efforts to be expressed in this spontaneous gesture.

Throughout the day I do my best to ignore the rising Appenines over to my left, as they edge their way towards the coast. At Scauri, I can defer the moment no longer; it is now time to tackle this mountain range, which will take me up and over to the Adriatic coast. GR and I had studied the maps, finding a river route up a valley, a good choice with surprisingly easy cycling for quite a way, until the hills eventually decide to make their presence felt. When I come to a crossroads, I am supposed to turn right but, with no tourist office to ask and not confident about finding any camping, I decide to follow Julie's and Koen's recommendation of a known campsite and so turn left for the five miles to Cassino.

The campsite at first looks uninspiring, but it is quiet and has an unexpected tourist attraction: a mineral water river running through it. I am shown around by the friendly Francisco, the receptionist. He explains that people come here to drink the water for health benefits. It tastes surprisingly good, in contrast to spa places in UK, where the water is reluctantly gulped down more as an act of penance than pleasure. Francisco gives me a lift into town, on his way to his evening job at a local swimming pool, dropping me off at a cheap but good locals' restaurant.

In the morning, having packed up my tent, I am sitting on the ground eating breakfast, when a groundsman comes by and squats down, trying to say something to me. I concentrate hard to grasp the gist of his words, automatically assuming him as friend rather than foe, until I gradually realise his gestures have become unmistakably clear, rendering unnecessary any utterance of his entire English vocabulary, 'Sex.' I look at him with distaste, tell him where to go and suddenly decide I have had enough breakfast to see me on my way.

It is the first time on the trip I have come across this and it leaves a bad taste in my mouth; further similar encounters during the day start getting to me. On three occasions cars slowly overtake me, pull in to laybys ahead, wait until I have gone by, then immediately pull out and overtake me in a slow, deliberate manner. These, and loads of leery toots from vehicles, produce feelings of paranoia. It feels like a really lechy day.

Having said that, I should not forget the positive encounters. A police officer stops, parking his car in the shade of a road bridge, steps out and hails me to stop. I think irritably, 'Oh, what now?!' But he is merely curious as to where I, a lone cycling woman, am going? Later, an elderly chap on a bicycle pulls up beside me at a junction, benignly wanting to ensure I am on the right road. Later I am pulled over by a second squad car, the two smiling policemen doing so out of mere curiosity, in turn attracting yet another one to stop and investigate. All four boys in blue obligingly pose for a group photograph, at the same time informing me that the road will soon turn into an *autostrada* on which bicycles are not allowed, so I will need to come off and follow a parallel road into the city.

Duly arriving at the change of road status, I come off and follow directions, only to find myself heading off the wrong way. I return to the starting point and try again. In the end, I am going round in circles, getting nowhere, ending up losing all sense of direction, panic rising as I watch the sun speeding headlong towards the horizon. In desperation,

I cycle along the forbidden *autostrada* for two hundred yards, before being encouraged by tooting traffic that this is really not a good idea and turn back, coming to a halt on the hard shoulder of a dual carriageway. I am fighting to stay calm and level-headed, in utter bewilderment of *where* do I go now? It is too much and I resort to the biggest cry of the trip so far, overcome by a feeling of total helplessness, stupidly bereft of any commonsense and totally alone. It does the trick. After a few minutes, I stop crying and feel quite calm – and find the right road. It is futile to try to work out how that happens.

In Benevento, the tourist office has long since closed for the day. So how do I now find somewhere to stay? Take a tip from Tim. He purposely roots out a 4-star hotel, on the premise that the receptionist would a) invariably speak English, b) provide a city map, c) advise on cheaper hotels. It sort of works. The 4-star receptionist (€75 per room) speaks English and I come away with a city map and directions to her recommended cheaper alternative. However, the rate is still too high. In turn, a further recommendation brings me to a third hotel which, being now too late in the day for continued searching, I am forced to compromise at €45. It is an unspectacular room, not even with a view – the window having migrated to the top of the wall.

I eat tonight sitting outside one of the restaurants in a *piazza*, dominated on one side by a 2,000-year old arch. It commemorates one of the better-behaved Roman emperors, Trajan, considered wise, just and moral enough to be hailed as a virtuous pagan by the thirteenth-century theologian, Thomas Aquinas. Trajan's adopted son and heir was Hadrian.

The waitress tries out some French with me, mine having improved to some degree since my extended sojourn in France; and the waiter, a rugby player from Bucharest, practices his English. At the end of the meal, he serves me a glass of 'limone', a local lemon liqueur, which tastes, as one might expect, sweet and citrusy.

The next day I meet a couple of young lads, Serbian and French. They started cycling together from Molfetta, a hundred miles away on the Adriatic coast, travelling light, no tents, sleeping in the open air. The previous night they had slept near the town of Bovino, next to a Roman fountain that still spouts (apparently) potable water, and near a small river, in which they swam and washed their clothes. It sounds romantically appealing.

I ask if they have seen any snakes.

'Yes, two big ones in the water!'

Haha, it takes me a few minutes to appreciate their reference. But there is none of the lewdness of my Italian encounters. These are two pleasant young lads, enthusiastic and full of harmless fun.

When I arrive at the foothill of the hilltown of Bovino, I investigate the possibility of my sleeping next to the same fountain, but the ground is unappealingly hard, dry and dusty, with prickly bushes and undergrowth to go through to gain access to the river and to find somewhere discreet enough to sleep. Coupled with the terrifying thought of (real) snakes, I chicken out, deciding on the *sanctuario* up the mountain that the boys had also mentioned.

It is a long, tiring ascent, but the tortuous hill finally terminates with relief on the outskirts of Bovino. I am informed by a helpful chap who speaks some English, that unfortunately I have overshot the mark, not realising the locked building adjacent to the green-roofed church halfway up the mountain was the sanctuary. The man kindly accompanies me back down in his car. He rings the bell at the front door of the building with prolonged persistence, eventually eliciting a sleepy response on the intercom from the padre, presumably disturbed from his afternoon siesta, who then takes an age to come and open the door. He regards me with suspicion, clearly bemused by my presence, but agrees to give me a night's accommodation. The room charge is not pilgrim rates but, on request, he gives me a small discount.

This place is in the middle of nowhere, with no shops, no eating place, no meals provided. The thought of struggling again to the village atop the hill is a step too far for my exhausted body. My evening sustenance therefore comprises unappetising bits and bobs: two bread rolls which have seen better days, filled with sweaty cheese and tomatoes; a mini coffee sponge cake (provided by the padre earlier); a peach. The redeeming feature to this paltry fare is a small bottle of red wine, which I must have bought in anticipation of such a time and now consume as elegantly as possible, sitting alone on an outdoor balcony at the end of a corridor, the unswept floor strewn with a carpet of dead flies.

Later in the evening, I try to break the ice with the padre in a request to take his photo, which, surprisingly, he seems quite pleased about. He even asks me to write down my website address. I leave Raven secured at the bottom of the stairs and go up to my room, to pass a night dominated by a spate of hot flushes.

In the morning, the padre seems more relaxed and issues, 'Good morning,' in English. After retracing my wheels up to the village, followed by a free-fall descent, the remainder of the day's cycling is very flat, but with an immensely strong headwind. This reduces my speed from what should have been a sailing 12-14 mph to a battling eight, producing achingly weary arms and legs by the end of the day.

I arrive on the Adriatic coast and enjoy a celebratory plunge in the warm, salty sea. Just three days earlier, I had been doing the same in the Mediterranean. Relaxing for a couple of hours on a sun-lounger, downing a beer, scrutinising my maps for an ongoing route from Italy to Cyprus, what else could I be thinking other than life is good?

The campsite has a restaurant, in which I enjoy a tasty meal of pasta with clams and hot chilli, followed by whitebait, crevettes and chips, finished off by juicy melon. The owner speaks French, so I am able to have a reasonable conversation for a change. He politely offers to walk me back to the main part of the campsite – on the way deciding to take an opportune lunge at me. Oh, just leave me alone, can't you!

Whereas Mediterranean Italy produced genuinely friendly men, over on this side of the country I have had more than my fill of the leery species. I am now wary and reserved, not wanting to catch anybody's eyes, smile or greet people, as I have been doing up until now. It is not a good feeling. I cannot continue my trip in protective isolation. The trouble is that, however many good experiences one has, all too often, a bad one can cancel them out. Or is it just me who reacts like that?

My website is back on line, thankfully, and I write a journal entry. Technology is great when it works, but stressful when it doesn't, which is when you realise how much you take its availability and efficiency for granted. Talking of which, I have finally been forced to admit defeat with my solar charging, reverting to mains charging for all my devices.

I spend a rest day in Giovanazzo to wash clothes and clean and oil my bicycle. I receive an email from my son who is going through a tough time and all I want to do is be supportive of him, but I am too far away for that. I comfort myself by spending the afternoon in and by the sea but, foolishly careless of adequate sun protection, the result is unnecessary discomfort from sunburn, something I never suffer from when cycling, being always careful to cover up.

In the evening, whilst sitting on a bench waiting for the seaside restaurant to open, a local fisherman comes by with his catch caught off the rocks with a weighted net, a bucketful of beautiful small, yellow-striped fish called solpa. Then a sleazy guy comes by trying to chat me up, from which I am saved by one of the cleaners from the campsite and her grandson, who come and sit next to me, the little 2-year old performing his party trick of animal noises.

Between Bari and Brindisi the main road is sometimes off limits to bicycles. It takes me a while to realise that the signs *Viabiletata di servizio* indicate the alternative, parallel road, used for local access, delightfully almost traffic free and thoughtfully separated from the main road by attractive hedges of pink and white oleander.

My last campsite in Italy is on the Costa Merlato, twenty miles short of Brindisi. It is a very sizeable holiday campground, laid out with specific areas, such as the eating sector, offering a diverse array of food stalls, the young sociables' sector, and well away, the early-to-bed families' and quiet peoples' section. Throughout the campground, a strict noise curfew makes for an amazingly quiet night and even in the morning the use of hushed tones seems appropriate as I pack up and leave.

The final short stretch to Brindisi produces the biggest shock ever. I am merrily cycling along minding my own business, when an unexpected movement ahead catches my eye. Glancing up, my heart gives a jolt and I nearly fall off my bicycle. In the road immediately in front of me, scooting swiftly across, is a black, slithery snake, about four feet long. In shock, I almost cycle right over it, before having the wherewithal, at the last second, to force the handlebars in the opposite direction, passing behind. I do not know who is more scared, him or me. I cycle away as fast as I can, trembling like mad, heart pounding, spending the remainder of the day furtively checking the road in front for warning signs of further intimidating encounters.

In Brindisi, I pull over by the roadside, whereupon a passing chap asks if he can help. He happens to be the owner of a nearby travel agency, from where I now buy my ferry ticket to Corfu. A simple, hassle-free transaction. However, there must be a cultural imperative here that is not mentioned in the guide books, as the guy is now under the impression that I am up for something more than just a drink later on!

Ciao, Italy.

* * *

Greece

2 – 19 August 2008

*Palaeokastritsa, Igoumenitsa, Ioannina, Nikopolis,
Lefkada, Dessimi, Lefkada, Athens*

Corfu (Kerkyra in Greek) is the second largest of the Greek Ionian
Islands, lying off the coast of Albania and Greece. Legend has it that
Poseidon, god of the sea, one day espied Korkyra, daughter of a river
god, Asopos, and a river nymph, Metope, fell in love with and promptly
abducted her. Presumably the gentle art of wooing was not his strong
point. For their honeymoon, Poseidon brought his wife to a previously
unnamed island, naming it after her as a wedding present.

But this is not why I chose to come to Corfu as a stopping-off point
to mainland Greece. I came simply because, as a teenager, I had read *My
Family and Other Animals* by Gerald Durrell and it seemed an enticing
place to visit, according to the free and simple adventurous childhood he
described.

Having done my best to look presentable, somewhat challenging after
passing the night on the lounge floor of the ferry, I nervously disembark
into a new country. It is early, only a quarter to six. I sit outside a café to
study my map of the island. I have no prior Greek, but am equipped with
a phrasebook and the Greek version of my introductory letter. In an
attempt to order a coffee in Greek, I repeat the phrase over and over
again to myself beforehand, so as not just to read it straight from the
book at the waiter. He bears with me – and then, of course, replies in
excellent English.

On the way out of town, I come across the town market being set up,
so stop to buy some fruit and to try out a couple of phrases. I have no
idea what they reply and so I resort to smiling and pointing. I continue

south a little way before cutting up and over the mountains to the pretty west coast, the road undulating up and down, not too arduously, accompanied by beautiful sea views. The campsite at Palaeokastritsas is run by a Scottish woman, Diane, who has been there fifteen years.

During the night, it is too hot in the tent and I sleep out in the open. But this has its drawbacks as I am prolifically bitten despite burning mosquito coils. In the morning, I cycle up to the monastery overlooking the bay, congratulating the founding monks on their choice of such a beautiful location. From there, I make my way back to the east coast, turn north, thinking I might as well take a peek at the coast of Albania. But the road is traffic jam paradise and the beaches a dense patchwork of people, obviously the popular holiday stretch of coast; so I do the sensible thing and turn around, leaving Albania for another time. I manage to catch the early afternoon ferry to the mainland by the skin of my teeth, greatly helped by a cheerful female member of staff, who uses her walkie-talkie to request the ferry doors be held open just enough time for me to scoot across the quadrangle and into the ship's hold.

An hour and a half later we dock in Igoumenitsa, from where I head south a little way to a beach campsite, arriving by 4.30 pm, in time for a refreshing, relaxing swim off the small campsite-exclusive beach. Tonight I do not put up the tent, but hang my mosquito net from a tree, sleeping on my mattress, with my shawl over me during the slightly cooler part of the night. There are quite a few ants around, so I buy a can of spray in the well stocked minimarket to ringfence my mattress from any attempted invasion by the miniature soldiers.

The next day sees me going inland due east. It is tough going, winding up and down three summits of the Pindos mountains. Halfway up one of them, in the middle of nowhere and almost running out of water, I am saved by a passing lorry which, after passing the layby in which I have stopped, reverses his huge artic, stopping a few feet from me. His engine had started overheating on the steep ascent and he had decided to give it a chance to recover. The driver proffers a cup of sweet, cold, black coffee and a large bottle of water, both gratefully received. He also then offers me a lift, which I valiantly decline (after all, this is a cycling trip; but also I am gut-wary unsure of his intentions) and leave him to his cooling off break as I continue up the mountain.

The café at the top is open, radio playing, but no one around for me to replenish my water or food supplies. At the bottom of one of the hills is a small town, but nowhere to stay and the locals are not very friendly. There are loads of bikers, mostly, it seems, from Germany. They are friendly and toot at me as they vroom past. Likewise with the lorries, who also tend to give me a wide berth as they pass. Their country stickers indicate they are from Bulgaria, Slovenia, Romania, Poland, Italy, Cyprus; the majority from Germany. As the day wears on and I am finding nowhere suitable to stay or camp, I am slightly regretting my decision of rejecting the proffered lift.

Towards the end of the 12-hour day, and after the third mountain summit, which I did not think I was going to make, exhausted from the heat, the mileage and the mountains, I now have to contend with the fact that the shadows are lengthening alarmingly with the setting sun. I descend the last few miles to the town of Ioannina, managing to find a campsite easily and set up in the dark.

However, as with many hardships and challenges, it is generally the retrospective that affords the most positive view of an event. I acknowledge a great feeling of achievement from today's efforts.

The campsite is beside a large lake, the tent pitches only a few feet from the water's edge. A young backpacking couple are my immediate neighbours: Domenica, from Poland, and Owen, a British Cypriot, travelling for a month. They are heading for the west coast and I recommend the beach campsite near Igoumenitsa. I spend the following day visiting the island in the middle of the lake and looking around Ioannina, unable to resist buying a large plastic sunflower I see in a florist, attaching it to the front of my basket as a special reminder of my children.

Refreshed after my rest day, I continue south, expecting a short 25-mile day to the next campsite. I take a quiet, picturesque country road, meaning to rejoin the main road just before the campsite. Unfortunately, this does not seem to be happening, as no connecting roads appear, as per my map, and I am in danger of ending up not where I want to be. On top of this, there are no refreshment stops. It is incredibly hot; has been ever since I arrived in Greece. In fact, emails from friends questioning my sanity at cycling in Greece in the middle of summer, seem well-founded. It is really not to be recommended; akin to cycling in an oven, the oppressive heat making breathing an effort.

I stop and ask various people directions for getting back to the main road and they all seem pretty unanimous that I should be retracing my steps – some ten miles. But, I really do not like going back the way I have come and so, more fool me, I persist forwards. I stop to photograph an old woman in traditional black dress and headscarf, herding a handful of sheep across the road. Her husband (one assumes), comes by soon after. We try and communicate; I show him my letter and ask directions. He also indicates going back up the road, then at some point turning off left. On bidding the old man farewell, his voice suddenly becomes *sotto voce* as he indicates that, now his wife has gone out of sight, nudge, nudge, we could go into the bushes for a quickie! Know what I mean, nudge, nudge, wink, wink!? Well, I suppose you have to admire his opportunistic audacity.

His directions prove fruitless and I retrace my steps, feeling like a yo-yo, eventually coming to a junction with a new road heading off to the right. But – it goes down an incredibly steep hill and I know that, if this turns out to be the wrong way and I have to come back up, I physically would not be able to make it. What to do? I stand and wait and think and wait, look at my map and think and wait.

Eventually, a car comes along and I flag it down. The driver confirms that this offshoot links to the main road. So now then, a long and steep, down, down, down. Towards the bottom, as it starts to flatten out, I come to a hamlet. Two cafés, both closed; a third café, this time open. Hurray. The sweet old woman serving gives me a bottle of water; I order a coffee and a chap on another table gives me directions to the campsite, twelve miles along the main road. But I should have accepted by now that the locals do not always get it right. When I arrive at the bottom of the hill and the main road, I should really have turned right and the campsite would have been a few miles up the road. But this guy had said left and, as it is in my direction, I follow his instructions. Nothing appears when I reach the 12-mile mark. On I go, a further twenty miles to the next campsite at Nikopolis. In the end it is another 70-mile day in searing heat.

Time for another rest day. I have made a rather loose rule that, if I go over fifty miles in a day, I have a rest day. In the current conditions, this seems a wise axiom to follow. I am back on the coast and so, after cleaning and WD40-ing Raven, topping up air in my tyres, something I have been meaning to do for ages, and catching up with my diary, I have a glorious swim in the warm sea, just a hop and a skip away on the other side of the road.

I study my map of Greece, trying to plan my route in more detail. I had originally planned to go straight across to Thessaloniki and on into Turkey to Istanbul, then south and east along the coast to catch a ferry to northern Cyprus and on down to the Greek part. But then I was persuaded by GR that I could not possibly travel through Greece without visiting the main ancient and historically important places of the country. Maybe I am too easily swayed.

The next morning, after gazing mournfully in the washroom mirror at my sleep-deprived piggy eyes peering back at me, a result of last night's hot flushes, I continue along the coast road a short way, stopping at some ancient ruins, apparently the largest and best preserved example of a Byzantine settlement. St Paul spent the winter here, during which time he wrote his letter to Titus, one of the books of the New Testament. Groups of men are working on different areas of the site, the excavations funded from government heritage money.

It seems that each country produces its own effective energy-booster for touring cyclists: in France it was cappuccino and sugar; in Italy, ice creams; here in Greece, frappés: lots of coffee, lots of sugar, often made with evaporated milk.

Fortified by my frappé in Preveza, I continue on towards the island of Lefkada. This is accessed by an undersea tunnel, from which I am stopped entering by a uniformed official indicating I should pull over to the side of the road. His walkie-talkie then summons an appropriate escort, arriving in the form of a pick-up driven by a young man in fluorescent orange dungarees. For our short trip under the sea I sit in the open back holding on to Raven. After being dropped off on the other side, I continue to Lefkada, then a few miles further on to a campsite. It is early afternoon, there is a friendly English-speaking proprietor – and a pool.

The next day, the picturesque coast road takes me through small villages, past marinas. I am in buoyant mood, lapping up the scenery, loving what I am doing and wholeheartedly counting my blessings. I overtake a row of parked cars and. . . Wooomph! Suddenly, Raven, my panniers and I find ourselves sprawled in the middle of the road, with me clutching my left knee, shouting, 'My bike, my bike!' All I can envisage is that it is going to be run over by an oncoming car and my trip is coming to a premature end.

The driver of the parked car had opened her door without looking and sent me flying. She is hugely apologetic, saying she had just arrived from Italy with her friend, to meet up with her parents at a campsite up the road. We gather up my bicycle; the handlebar basket clip has broken and the handlebars themselves seem skewed, as do the wheels. And a couple of panniers have come off. A significant crowd has gathered, cooing sympathetic noises. The driver, Federico, speaks good English, for which I am grateful. I am quite shaken and very concerned about my bicycle. She phones her father, who says he will come along with a vehicle to take it to a garage. We wait in a nearby café; I can now feel my knee stiffening up. The father comes along and my bicycle is loaded onto his pick-up to go to the garage, after which I am driven by Federico to the hospital back in Lefkada for a check-up. The hospital waiting area is busy, but I am seen very quickly by a handsome young doctor who expresses great surprise when he realises my age, 'You don't look it.' A nice ego-booster (at the risk of suffering from the sin of pride!). He examines my knee, now swollen and painful, prescribing a week's rest. Federico and I then find a cycle shop to try and get a new clip for my basket, but without success.

I feel very sorry for myself, but am mostly worried about how I am going to continue my trip. I am taken along to the campsite where Federico's parents are staying. They have been coming here for at least the last twenty years for all their summer holidays and so know, and are known by, many others on the campsite, a great many of whom are Italians.

There is hardly anywhere to pitch my tent amongst the hundreds squeezed tightly next to each other. But, with help, I find somewhere and, hobbling painfully, I erect it. I am introduced to Nico, the friendly campsite owner, who says that any drinks I order that day from the camp restaurant are on the house. Federico introduces me to friends and her mother. Everyone is very kind, but I guess I am suffering from the aftershock of the accident and the uncertainty of my immediate future and I find myself crying frequently.

I phone the insurance company, giving them the name of the doctor who saw me at the hospital and his contact details. They will have to receive a report from him before they can authorize more suitable accommodation for me. My bicycle arrives some time later.

The upshot of all this is that I spend the next five days hobbling about the campsite, performing self-prescribed physiotherapy in the warm, blue sea off the white sandy beach, including swimming out to a sailing boat flying a Union Jack and being invited aboard by the four young Brits for a cup of English tea and an hour of English chat.

I chat to other campers, but mostly I am on my own. Although I do take up the invitation from students, Kyriakos and Stavros, to join them occasionally on the beach. They are here for a couple of days, bumming about, rolling joints and generally pondering their lives and their futures.

Using the last of my Italian SIM card credit, I send birthday texts to my older brother. He replies from his sailing boat, enjoying a relaxing birthday breakfast and looking forward to sailing later in the week with my son.

After four days of procrastination, the insurance company finally decides to send a doctor to the campsite to assess my knee condition, following which they agree to four nights' hotel accommodation. I pack up my tent and return to Lefkada by taxi to find a hotel. All turn out to be full because there is some festival going on, but finally, I end up in a flat somewhere in the suburbs. The owners speak no English, but their daughter comes by later who does. I book in for the four nights, with a view to extend, if agreed by the insurance company. Although the flat is away from the centre, it turns out to be a welcome choice, being in the quiet neighbourhood of a small local community.

In the middle of the night, I am awake and wondering what the time is, only to realise that I have left my cyclometer on my bicycle and so get up to retrieve it. Being such a hot night, I am wearing only my knickers, but at least have the foresight to wrap my shawl around me before popping out into the hallway, where Raven is propped against the wall opposite. I take the couple of steps to my bicycle and remove my cyclometer.

But, as I turn around to return to the flat, I watch in horror as the door closes, leaving me stranded in the hallway in knickers and shawl, with no way of getting back in. Heck. What now? Well, I do what comes naturally to most people in times of panic, I pray – for the door to open miraculously. But, for some reason, it doesn't. I go up and down the stairs, switching on the lights, repeatedly (they are on a timer), looking for – what? I don't know, but I need to do something. After a while, I hear a door opening upstairs. It is the owner's wife, who actually does have a couple of words of English, but has no spare key. We try for half-an-hour to pick the lock, but neither of us having been to jail-breaking classes, we eventually admit defeat. I end up sleeping on the settee in the owners' flat, complete with borrowed dressing gown. The following morning, I am invited to join the couple for breakfast, which includes a special bread specifically eaten on the eve of Santa Maria Day.

When the daughter eventually wakes up, she goes straightaway to the front shutters of the flat and opens them, behind which, the glass doors are open and we regain access to the flat and retrieve the key.

The following day, I watch the Santa Maria festival. This takes the form of a lively, colourful procession through town of groups of many different nationalities sporting their national dress and playing the music of their country.

I try to find solace in my uncertain situation by frequenting one of the few internet cafés in town, for contact with home. I am uplifted after a Skype call with my younger brother, but then deflated after speaking with my daughter who is not having a great time in many ways. Unfortunately, long-distance sympathy is not really that effective, frustrating for both of us.

Back at the flat and in the throes of trying to contact the insurance company to discuss my ongoing requirements, the owners suddenly come in saying they need me to vacate within the hour as they have new people arriving! Shocked, having thought I had the option to stay, I am afraid I do not hide my feelings very easily. They respond helpfully, contacting a neighbour who has a flat I can rent for the night. I pack my things, leave my bicycle and baggage in their hallway for the time being, whilst I find a travel agent to book a coach to Athens and a flight to Cyprus, to my father.

When I finally manage to contact the insurance company, it is to be told that they had agreed only the four days' accommodation and that I would have to pay for any more myself, unless there was a need for medical treatment. I am upset and angry; just a few days ago, they had seemed helpful and positive (albeit slow), but now appear quite the opposite, pulling the plug on any further help.

In the morning, I leave the flat, pushing my laden bicycle to the internet café, where I am able to leave it whilst I go to the hospital to see the orthopaedic consultant. I have tried cycling, but my knee feels too vulnerable merely being on the bicycle, let alone to be doing any heavy touring. The consultant examines my knee and writes a letter of assessment and recommendation for a course of physiotherapy, duly faxed to the insurance company. In the late afternoon, I take a taxi to the coach station, relieved now to be having a sense of control and taking action, rather than playing the waiting game.

At the coach station, two eager young guys insist on helping me do the necessaries to my bicycle for the coach journey, saying, 'A woman shouldn't be doing such things.' For the overnight journey to Athens, they continue to look after me, plying me with power drinks, sandwiches and bananas. At the other end, they help me to the taxi rank, waiting until I am safely ensconced in it before making their farewells.

The airport staff give the impression that they have never had a bicycle go on a plane before. What's more, somehow or other, I pay nothing extra for my vast amount of excess baggage and my bicycle goes on the plane as is, no packaging of any kind.

*   *   *

Cyprus

20 August – 29 September 2008

Chlorako, Pissouri, Limassol

My father and stepmother had retired to Cyprus some twenty-five years previously. A few years ago my stepmother developed Altzheimer's, since when my father has been her full-time carer. They have been able to stay in their home, for the time being at any rate, by employing live-in help. This had just come to an end, in timely fashion, a couple of days before I arrived, providing me with a room in which to stay.

On arrival in Larnaca, Cyprus, I am glad not to be cycling from the airport, as the rear brakes have become offset, clamping the wheel, which no amount of wiggling loosens. Other than that and the back light hanging loosely, there is no damage, despite its arrival into baggage reclaim on the conveyor belt. My father has arranged a taxi pick-up to drive me to his home in Chlorako, Paphos, a 2-hour journey.

As we approach the sheltered housing, in which my father and his wife live, I easily identify which is his flat: a large, white sheet hangs over the balcony, on which are painted the words, '*Velbekommen til Clorakas, Astrid, min vidunderly datter.*' My father is welcoming his 'wonderful daughter' in Norwegian. It is exactly what I need: a warm welcome from my father and a partial reminder of my mum, whom I feel I could have done with there and then.

I convalesce for six weeks, during the hottest and most humid time of year in Cyprus. My father and I both appreciate that my accident has provided this opportunity for time together, as well as giving him some respite from his continual caring.

Carers come in twice a day to help with my father's wife; friends and people from church also give of their time to help. My stepmother is away with the fairies most of the time, interrupted by rare moments of lucidity, to which my father clings, the glimmer of a reminder of what was. Their shared passions had been singing and drama, the former particularly standing them in good stead now, as my stepmother invariably joins in once my father starts singing. It is a brief moment of normal interaction with his wife.

I spend a great deal of time with emails to and from the insurance company, with them finally, reluctantly, agreeing to reimburse some of my costs, including a new clip for my basket, efficiently sent from my cycle shop back home. After all, why have I been paying a large insurance premium for my 'risky' trip, if not to cover such eventualities?

As for the stuck rear wheel, this is simply rectified at a local cycle repair shop by removing the wheel and correctly repositioning it!

We attend St Stephen's Church in Paphos, where, on meeting the organist, I realise how small the world is: he is my former music and piano teacher from grammar school days.

Although most visas should be obtainable at a country's border, there are some that need securing beforehand. My prolonged stay with my father, therefore, gives me ample time to organise my Iranian visa. This is slightly complicated by not being able to pay by card. Instead, I am obliged to set up an account with a money transfer company to pay the fee into a bank account in Iran, the location of the visa agency. I have to state where I shall be collecting my visa so I opt for Amman in Jordan. This should allow me sufficient time to reach the Iranian border before the 3-month expiry date.

Eventually I am on my bicycle again, gently easing myself back into cycling mode, whereupon I make moves to organise my ongoing trip to Egypt.

The travel agent does not come up with much in the way of positive news: no ferries, only cruise ships, which do not accept vehicles; my bicycle listed as such. I try another travel agent. Same response. How ridiculous. But I do not give up easily. The alternative to going to Egypt by ship is to fly (not in my remit), or to take a ferry from northern Cyprus to Turkey, leaving me then completely in the wrong place for my ongoing trip, which includes cycling into Jerusalem.

I phone the cruise company directly; same response. I persist, explain what I am doing, and get to speak to the manager. He appears sympathetic to my cause, but is unable to authorise anything before speaking to the captain of the ship. His tone suggests it will be a futile request. The following day he contacts me.

'Good news. On this occasion, the captain has agreed that an exception will be made.'

My father and I take a trip to Limassol to pick up my ticket from the cruise ship offices, and where I am able to meet the lovely staff who have made this happen. I am extremely happy.

At the end of September, Raven is packed and raring to go. Friends of my father come to say goodbye, so that he will not be on his own at the point of departure. After reluctant hugs and farewells and seven and a half weeks since being on a loaded bicycle, I am off again on my trip; thankful that I have such flexibility in my itinerary that this break has not been a problem.

I stop to visit the Sanctuary of Aphrodite and the Palaepaphos museum with its 3,500-year old artefacts casually strewn around the grounds. After lunch at a picnic beauty spot, I stop at Aphrodite's birthplace, pushing my bicycle down onto the beach for a photo opportunity. I stay the night in Pissouri, in a flat arranged by a chaplain friend of my father, the following morning enjoying a leisurely ride to Limassol. I meet up with Mavis, a friend from when I was working as a physiotherapist in the Middle East and who now lives on Cyprus, occasionally getting her leathers out to go on biking holidays with a friend.

The next afternoon, I make my way to the port to join the ship. Raven is secured unobtrusively on one of the spacious crew decks and I think wryly of one of the arguments against my bicycle going on board, 'Where would we put your bicycle?'

In the evening there is a dressy dinner with seating plan. I locate my table, 39a, and become acquainted with my fellow guests: Jan and her chatty, 3-year old daughter, Katy; and a very Welsh-speaking family, Isellte, Swsan and Bobi. After dinner, I join the Welsh trio in the lounge bar for an evening cabaret, accompanied by a nautical brandy cocktail, Dropped Anchor.

I am incredibly excited: not only am I on my way to another new country, but I am leaving Europe, bound for a new continent.

* * *

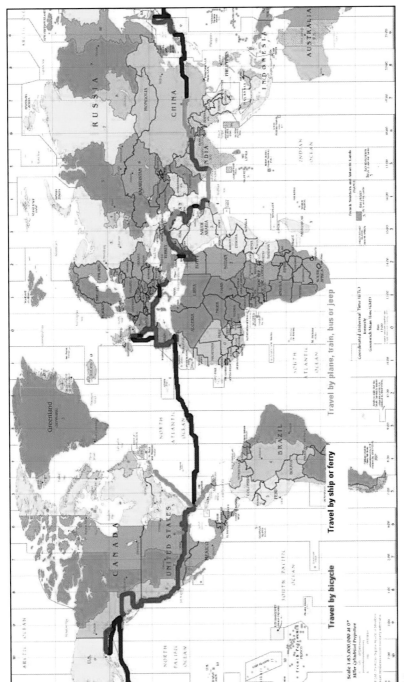

Travel by plane, train, bus or jeep

Travel by ship or ferry

Travel by bicycle

Scale 1:83,000,000 at 0°
Miller Cylindrical Projection

My route.

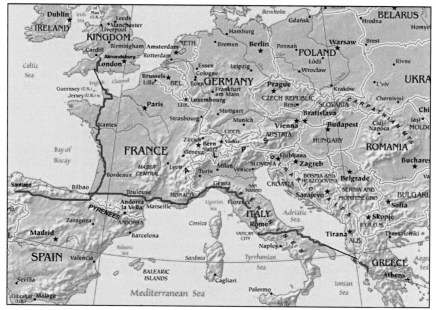

Almondsbury to Cyprus.

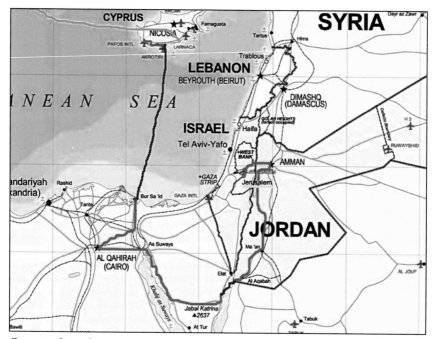

Cyprus to Jerusalem.

Above: *The Scallop shell symbol of the Camino de Santiago.*

Left: *A happy band of pilgrims on their way to Santiago.*

Middle left: *The cycling route sometimes joined the walkers. Thankfully, not for too long.*

Middle right: *St Jean-Pied-de-Port at the foothills of the Pyrenees. A popular starting point for Santiago pilgrims, as well as a confluence for three of the main French routes.*

Right: *Queuing at the Pilgrim Office in Santiago to obtain the hard-earned certificate.*

Above: *The Canal du Midi starts off pleasurably
. . . but (inset) ends less thrillingly.*

Right: *Morale-boosting letter from my children,
secreted by them into my baggage before I left
home.*

Sharing the road along the ancient Via Appia in Rome.

The ambulance station was the only place to camp along the empty stretch of road between Cairo and Suez.

Sinai Peninsula. Not all desert roads are flat.

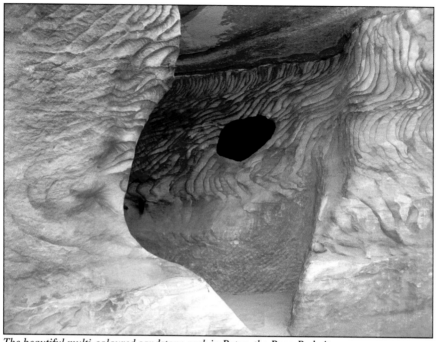

The beautiful multi-coloured sandstone rock in Petra, the Rose-Red city.

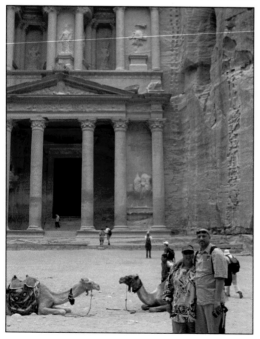

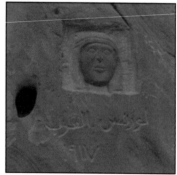

Rock carving of Lawrence of Arabia, Wadi Rum.

The Treasury, Petra.

The church on Mount Nebo, Jordan, from where Moses was able to see the Promised Land.

A well-placed drive-by tea stop at the top of a hill on the way to Amman, Jordan.

Above: *A women's group in Jordan brings together Christian and Moslem women for social interaction.*

Right: *The long haul up from Jericho and the Dead Sea passes through a tunnel . . .*

. . . emerging on the other side into Jerusalem (below), *my third pilgrimage destination.*

Egypt

30 September – 10 October 2008

Ismailia, Cairo, Suez, Ras Sudr,
Ras Abu Rudais, St Catherine's

The Middle East is fascinating, full of similarities and contradictions, of conflict and unity, of separatist fanaticism and inclusive hospitality. Having spent three years working in the United Arab Emirates and Saudi Arabia, I was familiar enough with the culture and with an, albeit limited, knowledge of the language, to be happily anticipating this next part of my trip, particularly the prospect of cycling into Jerusalem.

The telephone in my cabin rings unexpectedly at 5.30 am, the disembodied voice telling me to report to reception by six o'clock. Immigration need to see me before the other passengers, as I am the only one-way passenger disembarking in Port Said. Hurriedly I shower and dress, arrive punctually, only to be told to go to breakfast and wait to be called. Not sure when I might eat again, I decide on a cooked breakfast, plus fruit, pastries, pineapple juice and coffee. As it turns out, I have plenty of time to eat all this, as it is nearer 7 am when I am finally called to be processed, joining the queue with everyone else. It is an exciting moment when I receive my first visa stamp in my passport.

A couple of crew members load themselves up with my baggage and basket, whilst I carry my loyal Raven down the gangplank and into Egypt. I take a few minutes to load up whilst my fellow passengers file past in cheerful anticipation of their day's coach excursion. Once loaded, I go just a few paces to some steps and look around for the ramp. What ramp? What happens if you are in a wheelchair? No option but to start struggling down the steps with my overweight companion, hopeful that help might be forthcoming, but the gaggle of people, including port staff, is quite content to look on as passive spectators. At the bottom of the steps, I run the gauntlet of the persistent street hawkers before escaping into the customs' building to unload for the security inspection. The staff stand by as I hump my bags onto the conveyor belt. I feel irritated, thinking, 'You can help me if you like.' My irritation though is more to do with nervousness, rather than intolerance; my usual uncertainty of how I am going to get on in this new country.

Once through customs, I ask a few people for the road to Ismailia. It is a good way to break the ice and straightaway I feel more at ease. It is the start of the workday and, as I cycle through the city centre, a variety of police are in evidence, the majority being traffic police, one at each street corner and even more at crossroads. I pass tenement blocks adorned with garlands of brightly-coloured washing hanging from the balconies. Litter and rubbish are everywhere. People seem not unfriendly.

My exit from Port Said is accompanied by cheery toots and friendly waves from the excursion coaches on their way to the pyramids or the Suez Canal. The desert road is totally flat and the hard shoulder fairly clean, except for piles of sand periodically forcing me into the main carriageway. I stop first for a coffee, later a coke, only realising at the second stop that it is still the month of Ramadan and the three young lads in the roadside store, Ibrahim, Ismail and Sayn, will not have had anything to eat or drink since sunrise – and here I am drinking a coke in front of them. Knowing that I am a traveller and so exempt from fasting does not totally allay my feeling of guilt.

In Ismailia, with no real idea of where I am going, I head in the direction of what I assume is the centre. After cycling around aimlessly for long enough, I adopt Aussie Tim's technique and make my way up the long, lush drive of an expensive hotel, where predictably the receptionist speaks good English.

'No, I am afraid your map is wrong, there is no campsite nearby, but here is the address of a hotel that even you might be able to afford.'

(He did not really say that; more my perception).

I end up at the Crocodile Inn, politely but firmly insisting that my bicycle comes with me into my room. Later, the hotel manager walks me to a local restaurant on his way home, where he somehow organises a seat for me at a table, despite the place overflowing on this last day of Ramadan with people eager to break their fast and start the Eid celebrations. As seats are a premium, I am soon joined by a chap called

Karim, who claims to be a fighter pilot in the Egyptian Air Force. After the meal, he walks me back to the hotel, presenting me with an Egyptian fifty-pound note (about £5 sterling), having written, 'With my love, Karim,' on it. I am disinclined to accept his invitation to drive out to the Suez Canal and so am safely back in my room by early evening.

In the morning, I go down for breakfast at seven thirty, only to discover that it is only six thirty. The clocks had gone back on the ship by one hour and I had travelled the whole day yesterday without realising this. I remember last night being slightly confused about times at some point, but had not twigged. So, do I leave without breakfast, knowing that shops are most likely closed for Eid, or do I return to bed for an hour? No contest really. In the end, breakfast is served at eight twenty, due to the later Eid opening times for the bread shop.

The young guy on breakfast duty, Ahmed, although impressed by my trip, expresses concern for my health and safety. He tries to give me two large bottles of frozen water, which are dauntingly heavy so I accept only one, grateful for the prospect of cold water during the day's cycling. On a visit to the bathroom prior to leaving, I have an encounter with a cockroach. Yuk. They look so disgusting and have such a sinister air about them they give me the heebie-jeebies.

The desert road is not totally flat today, but the hills are very gentle. About twenty miles before Cairo, I ask at a filling station if there is a phone I can use. In response, the man kindly offers his mobile. As I shall be arriving a day early in Cairo, I need to confirm that there will be a room for me at the Christian guesthouse. For the final dozen miles to Cairo the traffic suddenly increases and it is pretty hairy cycling. It seems the world and his wife are out in force, on foot and in cars, a throng of mayhem on the streets and roads, this first day of the Eid festival. The only way to get through is to cycle with gritted teeth and a bullish attitude. It is adrenalin-pumpingly risky and I am praying like billyo. Ignorance can be heaven sent; it is only later I find out that Cairo has one of the world's highest fatality statistics for road accidents.

Cairo is a large city. I have been told to head for Downtown, for which mercifully there are signs. When I surmise that I might have arrived, it is then a question of repeatedly asking directions, gradually narrowing down the search until, well after dark and beginning to grow slightly frantic, I find myself in front of steps leading up to a locked building with no obvious means of entering. It has been an 83-mile day and I am tired. I am standing on these steps in tearful frustration, when, relief, the person who now comes along happens to be John, the manager of the guesthouse. Soon, I am comfortably ensconced in a cosy apartment, Raven happily and safely stationed on the roof garden. After showering, I meet the staff and other guests, before wandering across the road to the Marriott for something to eat.

The next couple of days are spent as a tourist, including a visit to the Egyptian museum, specifically to see the gold of Tutankhamun. It is stunning! The decorative collars are breathtaking; the intricate, delicate, miniscule craftwork amazing, especially considering it was made 3,500 years ago. I gaze at length at the death mask of the young king, mesmerised by the elegant, finely moulded gold that replicated his features.

I take a taxi to the pyramids and sphinx, surprised by their close proximity on the outskirts of the city rather than in the middle of the desert. Again, my main reaction is one of awe that something so intricately designed and grandly constructed could ever have been visualised and achieved at all, but especially by people thousands of years ago, with much less sophisticated means than we have nowadays.

I manage to get conned into a horse ride to see more of the area around the pyramids and, even though I am careful to agree a price beforehand, apparently there has been a misunderstanding, a higher price being asked at the end. I am upset, but in the end we come to a compromise. I am annoyed at my gullibility, which ends up spoiling some of my enjoyment of the experience. It was fun seeing police patrolling on camels.

The guesthouse occupants are quite cosmopolitan: a family from Pakistan, a group of American pastors; a New Zealand couple and an Egyptian woman as managers. The pastors are newly-returned from Iraq, where they have been ministering to persecuted Christian Iraqis unable to leave their country. They take an interest in my trip, promptly contacting their home churches in America to pray for my continued safe passage round the world and handing me their business cards to contact them on arrival in Alaska.

'In case we can help with accommodation in the States. And, of course, we want to buy your book when it comes out.'

They are not the first people to assume that there will be a book about my trip. I had thought not to produce one, but insidiously the idea seems to be infiltrating itself into my psyche.

I end up staying an extra night, after my ongoing arrangements have been put back a day. The chaplain to the deaf school and deaf community in Cairo, Faraj, had been an MSc student at the Centre for Deaf Studies. It was he who had put me in contact with the guesthouse and who has now arranged my visit to the school. However, I learn that he has been involved in an accident, whilst returning from northern Egypt. Two vans had been following his car since the start of the journey, during which they were constantly 'playing games' with him on the road, eventually resulting in Faraj's car being driven off the road, rolling over and over five times before landing upside down. People stopped and pushed the car upright and helped everyone out. The car was very battered but miraculously no one inside even had a scratch on them. In fact, a person in a car behind commented that, when it happened, it looked as though the car was being lifted up and carried to the side of the road and there placed gently down onto the light, soft sand. Faraj is a Christian and it is not the first time that he has been subjected to such frightening and dangerous incidents. His gentle, firm faith has a strong impact on me.

On the morning of my departure from the guesthouse, staff and guests join together to pray over me for my safety. I am met at the deaf school by Faraj, spending the morning talking to the principal, looking in on the children in their classes and meeting teachers, helpers and parents. There are sixty-eight children in the school ranging from 5-17 years, who come from all over Egypt.

After lunch, Faraj and I walk to a couple of 700-year old churches, via the slum streets of Old Cairo. What an eye-opening sight: huge piles of rubbish as high as buildings, adjacent to, and in the middle of, residential areas; broken, battered shells of numerous abandoned cars; the smell of ordure; distressingly helpless poverty; a haven for rats.

In the evening, the church in the school grounds holds a service for the deaf community and the school children. At one point, as a visitor, I am invited to stand up, so that they might welcome me.

Whilst at the school, Helbees, the housekeeper at the guesthouse, comes to film an interview with me to be used as teaching material for her English course at the British Council.

I stay the night in the school guesthouse, which, although clean and comfortable, in the morning I come face to face with another cockroach, sidling out of the plughole and up the wall of the washbasin. I make a hasty retreat. After seven o'clock breakfast, the whole school goes to church for the daily service. There comes a lovely moment when the children sign prayers especially for me, followed by an invitation for me to sign something to them.

By the time I am loading my bicycle, it is 9 am, later than I had hoped to be setting off on the long ride to Suez. One of the younger lads acts as my assistant, determinedly lifting my heavy front panniers onto the pannier rack. Amidst farewells and much waving, I sail confidently up the road, intent on faithfully following Faraj's instructions to get me onto the Suez road. I should reach it in thirty-five to forty minutes.

Three hours later, I start out on the road to Suez. I think I know where I went wrong, but carried on too far to be able to return to the starting point. It is eighty miles to Suez. I am ever optimistic, but that *is* quite a long way, especially as darkness comes early and quickly in this part of the world – and I am setting off at midday. At intervals along this empty road, new cities are in the process of being built, but are not yet inhabited. Even if they were, no hotels have been included in the plans.

'Because nobody wants to stop between Cairo and Suez.'

In splendid isolation in the middle of nowhere along this empty road, is the Cairo English School, at which I stop, only to discover it is locked for the holidays; so no hope there of being put up for the night.

The cycling is not enjoyable: cars are fast and numerous, the suctioning draft from the lorries is unnerving, the hard shoulder obstacled with dumped cement, shredded tyres, grit, sand and potholes. When it becomes clear I shall not reach Suez before dark, I try hailing minibus taxis, to no avail. I grow concerned; the road is bereft of any habitation or any kind of discreet place to pitch a tent. But I hear my inner voice saying, 'Something will turn up; trust me.'

About thirty miles short of Suez, on the opposite side of the road, is a bright green and orange building, two orange ambulances parked outside.

'That'll do. Thank you, God.'

Six ambulancemen are on duty: Mohammed, Mohammed, Mohammed, Ahmed, Saleh, Abdullah. All are friendly and, although unable to let me stay in the station itself because I am female, they invite me to put my tent up on the hard standing at the side of the building.

'Not on the soft sand, because that's where snakes and unknown insects dwell.'

'Oh, great,' I think, 'and being on the hard standing makes me immune to snake attacks!'

By 5.30 pm and already dark, there is nothing for me to do but go to bed. Three hours later, a knock comes on my tent door with an invitation to join the men for something to eat. A few minutes later, in the throes of dressing, another knock comes, politely saying that they are waiting for me before they can start eating.

Sitting with the six men on the ground next to the ambulances, I have become an honorary man for the evening. I alternate my seating position between 'when in Rome' cross-legged and 'need to return feeling to my feet' side-saddle. Over pitta bread, tinned tuna and other assorted dishes, I spend an interesting couple of hours discussing Islam and Christianity with the chief ambulance guy, via the valiant interpreting efforts of one of the Mohammeds. The chief is a strict Moslem, with a burka-ed wife of the quiet, obedient type. He loves her, 'Like no other,' but also wants to find a couple of other wives, either already with children of their own or a widow.

'I want to look after them because they don't have many rights in Islamic countries. I should also like a Spanish wife.'

(Either he does not expound on this, or he does, but it is beyond Mohammed's interpreting skills.)

The men are all intent on assuring me of my safety, repeating that I can come and ring the bell in the night if I need anything. The main thing I need is for said snakes to keep well away from me.

In the morning, after a cup of tea, I thank them for their hospitality and depart. Up until now I have been wearing shorts, as Egypt is one of the more tolerant Islamic countries. However, I was not particularly comfortable in Cairo on seeing tourists in short shorts and skimpy tops and, although the ambulancemen had not made me feel uncomfortable, a little way up the road from the ambulance station, I decide that, out of respect, I should prefer to cover my legs. I change into trousers, instantly feeling that this is the right decision.

A mid morning stop at a roadside café for breakfast is not the most salubrious of places, clouds of flies honing in on plates of food, to be swiped constantly with one hand, whilst taking a forkful of omelette to my mouth with the other. I do the best I can but, hardly a relaxing meal, it is a short-lived affair. Before setting off, I need to pay a visit to the WC and head in that direction. I pass an old man at a table, a roll of loo paper strategically positioned in front of him; he does not proffer it, merely gestures towards the toilets. I choose what seems to be the least dirty of the three, but still the filthiest, fly-ridden loo encountered to date, the unclosable door providing no opportunity of guaranteed privacy. I am reluctantly and tentatively about to hover precariously above the dirty seat, whilst warily eyeing the gaping black hole of an open drain a few inches to my right, when suddenly, 'Aaaargh! Ugh!' A whopping black rat darts under the door, whizzes past my right foot, before diving down into the murky depths of the open drain. Instantly, I lose the urgency to go and exit smartly. As I pass the table, the old man asks if I need some loo paper.

I do not go all the way to Suez, turning off instead towards Sinai. As this is via a tunnel under the river, I have to wait at the police control post until a pick-up comes along which agrees to take me through. The poor family in the vehicle does not really have any option but to acquiesce to the policeman's demand. My bicycle is lifted into the open back and I climb in beside, holding on tightly as we take our somewhat hairy ride through the tunnel. Once on the other side, we stop and unload and I continue along a single carriageway with no hard shoulder. Fortunately, it is quite wide and what traffic there is gives me a fairly generous berth.

In Ras Sudr, I follow directions for a couple of hotels, on the way passing a small group of teenage boys. As I cycle by, one sprints over and aggressively pinches my bottom. It is done unpleasantly, with an arrogant air, and would not have happened if I had been an Egyptian woman. I continue to the hotels, initially opting for the first one until I am inside my room and see how dirty it is. Neither is there any security, as the door lock does not work. I change my mind, checking into the one two doors along: clean and much more appealing, even though it is double the price.

I wander round the town in search of a suitable restaurant. They all seem occupied by men only, no women or families in sight. I have to eat though and so enter a small, crowded place, first inquiring if it is okay for me to order a meal. The men behind the serving counter are friendly and courteous, making me feel relaxed, and I come away with renewed confidence about the universal acceptance of strangers.

The following morning, after breakfast on the balcony of my seaview room and armed with the hotel staff's certain assurance of hotels in Ras

Aburdies, I set off confidently following the Gulf of Suez. It is a warm, cloudless day and easygoing flat terrain with a tailwind. Turning inland, I encounter hills and a change of direction to a headwind. I feel rather weak and wobbly, and have a headache and nausea, surmising that I am probably dehydrated, so try to ensure I up my intake of water.

Contrary to confident expectation, there appears to be no hotel in Ras Aburdies after all. In response to my inquiries, I receive rather vague expressions and obscure directions that finally bring me to an International Youth Camp. The only people inside are a man and his young daughter, sitting in the middle of a large room watching television. He might be the caretaker. I try to ask if I can stay the night, at which he looks uncertain as to what to do. He makes a phone call, followed a few minutes later by the arrival of a family of husband, wife and two teenage children, who invite me to stay with them in their home. I follow Hela, her husband and two children, Yumna and Ahmed, to their new-build house, as yet unfinished after four years' construction and in the middle of a building site. Hela is a social worker; her husband, a teacher.

In the evening, five of the husband's teaching colleagues come around. They are all men and sit on chairs outside on the building site, chatting and drinking tea. Normally, Hela would stay in the house, being the only woman, but as there are two of us, we are able to join them. A couple of the teachers speak a little English and we talk about education in the two countries and where my trip has taken me so far. At midnight, I am fighting against nodding off and, when asked reluctantly by the husband if I should like to go inside and I accept, he duly disbands the party. I have the distinct impression he was hoping to have continued for a couple more hours.

Before settling down for the night, we discuss timings for the morning. I am invited to stay a few days, including visiting the school, but decide to head on.

'We hope you will like to come again in the future,' Hela generously continues, 'and with your family?'

I sleep on a mattress in the lounge, in preference to being with the children in their room, which is unbearably hot and buzzing with mosquitoes. Forewarned of no accommodation between here and St Catherine's and not much in the way of refreshment stops, I am up at six the following morning for an early start. I try to be quiet in an attempt not to wake anyone, but whilst in the bathroom, the curtain pole falls down with a clatter, waking Hela, who then proceeds to make me a huge breakfast of fried eggs, pitta bread, cheese, tomato, cucumber, tea and dates. She wakes the children, so they can all wave me off at seven o'clock. Before leaving, they pose for a photo, but only after Hela has covered her hair with a headscarf; being dressed in her nightgown does not bother her.

I follow the Gulf towards the junction of Sharm El Sheik and St Catherine's. On the way, the road occasionally veers away from the Gulf and up into the hills. I feel slightly uneasy at the loneliness of this section of road and so am wary when I see a car pulled over by the roadside, a man standing beside it. He watches as I cycle up, waiting until I am level before taking a pee. As I am passing, he comes around the front of his car and says something, which I ignore and carry on. I hear the car drive up slowly behind me; it pulls out to overtake and pass, but then cuts sharply in front of me, running me off the road to a standstill. By now, I am afraid and angry, and shout at the top of my voice.

'Imshee! Go away!'

And he does, making a u-turn and driving away. It leaves me a little shaken, but it could have been worse. Hopefully, that will be my unpleasant encounter for the day.

At the main junction is a restaurant/gift shop where I eat a second breakfast, at the same time making sure to stock up with provisions, drinks and water. Parked outside is a police pick-up with six policemen in black uniforms. A seventh one in a white uniform comes up to me, smiling.

'We shall follow you, for your safety.'

I am a little bemused, but set off. A mile up the road, I realise they actually are following me. I stop.

'For how long will you be following me?'

'About fifteen miles.'

'Oh no, no, there's no need. I shall go far too slowly, especially as this is uphill. You are very kind but please don't stay with me.'

Finally, they are persuaded to carry on. It is the last thing I want, to be followed by a supporting vehicle; far too stressful. I am impressed by the offer, but what a waste of manpower.

The road takes me up the beautiful Wadi Feiran and turns out to be a joy to cycle: clean surface, no potholes, no clumps of cement, no detritus, no rubbish; wide, clean smell, very little traffic. It is the first road in Egypt I have enjoyed cycling along. The big downside though is the incredibly strong headwind, making it difficult to maintain a 10 mph average to reach St Catherine's in six hours.

Further on, in a different wadi, I have my first encounter with an aid-programme village, of which I have heard negative accounts from other travellers. As if on cue, groups of children and teenagers appear, immediately holding out their palms, demanding baksheesh. The most unnerving thing is that they wait until I am level, then suddenly, without warning, run at me with grabbing hands and chase after me. I am afraid of coming a cropper off my bicycle or of something being broken. It is not a pleasant experience and I feel quite vulnerable.

I manage to maintain a good average mileage for the first four hours, remembering to drink frequently to compensate for the accumulated dehydration over the last few days. The final two hours extend to three, painfully slow and hard work, when even the downhills have me changing down the gears and pedalling hard. It is always a mystery why that should be. And why the opposite can happen: that sometimes it is possible to fly up hills in top gear with consummate ease.

The shadows are long when I come to a police security patrol near St Catherine's. I am exceptionally tired and there is nothing definite about my accommodation for tonight, or even how much further I still have to go. Therefore, when one of the policemen says he wants to check my baggage and I need to unload everything, my unequivocal reaction is, 'Don't be ridiculous. You have to be joking.' Sensibly, he relents and lets me through. I reach the monastery just before dark, hoping there is a bed for me.

St Catherine's Monastery was built in the sixth century, as a protection for the monks and hermits living in the area. It belongs to the Greek Orthodox Church and is the oldest Christian monastery in existence.

The only room available is a 5-bedded family room, which I am given (with no single occupancy supplement), situated within the sanctuary of the monastery walls. I meet a Belgian hiker returning from the top of Mount Sinai, where she had arrived at sunset the previous night, remaining there to watch the sunrise this morning. Later, busloads of people arrive all ready to set off on the 3-hour night trek to the top in time for sunrise at five thirty. Visited by hundreds of people each year, this is the mountain on which God appeared to Moses in the burning bush and also where he is believed to have received the Ten Commandments.

The last four days have been fairly gruelling mileages and terrain conditions, covering seventy plus miles each day, the last one clocking up eighty-nine. Therefore, although I am probably missing out on a special event, I cannot summon up enough energy to make the trek to the mountain summit. I spend the time resting.

I have to move to a smaller room for my second night, unfortunately located outside the monastery courtyard. I am subject to hassle from local boys and obliged to keep the curtains drawn to stop me feeling exposed to the curiosities of passing, local people. I discover I have left my universal wash plug in the other room and return to retrieve it, but, although it is only half an hour since I moved out, the plug is no longer in situ and the cleaner has not seen it. I am annoyed at my carelessness, which has left me without a trivial but useful item, not easily replaced.

On my way out of the confines of the monastery for a short walk up the valley, a young tourist policeman stops me.

'You should not be going out on your own. You should have a guide with you.'

I persuade him that I am not going far and he reluctantly lets me continue. I hardly go any distance, literally halfway around the block and down the road a short way before turning back when a car pulls up and stops beside me. It contains a driver and a Greek orthodox priest, the latter making it quite clear that I have no option but to accept a lift back to the safe confines of the monastery.

The same tourist policeman is still at the entrance, but now seems quite chatty, to the point of walking with me up the side of the mountain for a bird's-eye view of the monastery, church, mosque and the site of the burning bush. He also shows me a rock, under which is entombed a small skeleton, covered with the remnants of a shroud. Having had no desire to pay extra at the Egyptian museum in Cairo to see the mummies on display, I have no particular inclination to see too much of these remains either.

Afterwards I go and sit outside the monastery coffee shop to write postcards, asking one of the staff to write a message of thanks in Arabic, to the Egyptian family with whom I had stayed. He offers to post it for me, adding that he knows the family.

I depart early the following morning, after a few miles stopping to layer up against the bitter cold. At least now I can fly down the long descents without freezing to death. By the time it is warm enough to unwrap myself, steep uphills have appeared, some even causing me to walk up. At the top of one is an old man sitting on the ground by the roadside, who beckons me over for a cup of tea. He has a small open fire on which he boils the tea in an old pepsi can, serving it in an unwashed glass, which I gladly accept, having weighed up the pros and cons and deciding that the health risk is minimal. He tries, unsuccessfully, to sell me a piece of quartz rock and then does not accept any payment for the tea.

My travel time is good and I realise I should be able to reach Nuweibah in time to catch the ferry to Jordan that day, instead of camping on this side as planned. According to the timetable, the ferry would arrive in Aqaba mid afternoon. The last twelve miles to the sea is a steep descent. Normally, this would have entailed continual braking but, what has been a curse over the last few days now becomes a Godsend. The strong headwind acts effectively as a virtual brake, resulting in a delightful freewheeling swoop down to the town and the ferry terminal.

There is no obvious entrance to the terminal building, but that is irrelevant for the time being. The first step in the process is to buy my ticket, but not from where one might think, in the terminal building; instead, tucked away in a discreet building nowhere near the ferry point. Once I have tracked down the building and obtained my ticket, which helpfully includes the entry visa for Jordan, I return to the port. The entrance to the terminal building is also a challenge to find, hidden behind a 10-foot high temporary perimeter fence, access gained through a small makeshift gap.

Inside at last, I join the queue for the conveyor belt security check, unload and reload my bicycle, pass through to the room beyond. But then where to go? Apparently out through the doors on the opposite side of the room and across a courtyard to a building a couple of hundred yards away. Here I stand in another queue until I am told I need to fill in one of the forms to be found on the countertops around the room. Once completed, I rejoin the slow-moving line, proudly handing over my form to the official when I arrive at his window. He unceremoniously tears up my paper, rewrites my details in Arabic, stamps it.

I now find myself in a large, crowded hall, people sitting and sprawling on benches, the majority though ensconced on the floor surrounded by their many bags. I weave my bicycle carefully past the staring, curious eyes to lean it up against the far wall. The vast majority of passengers are locals, plus a sparse scattering of Europeans. A young Canadian couple comes over and asks about my bicycle and where I am going.

Considering I am expecting to be sailing at 3 pm, we seem to be hanging around a very long time. I am befriended by a large, formidable Swiss woman called Margitta, travelling with her daughter and boyfriend, who firmly instructs me to join them on board the ferry for the duration of the crossing. You don't mess with Margitta.

Finally, we are herded on board at 3 pm, eventually sailing four hours later, in the dark. I do indeed spend the entire crossing in the company of the magnificent Margitta and family; and am happy to do so. But I am not happy at the prospect of arriving at midnight in a new country, in search of a campsite or hotel. If it had been a weekday, all would have been as I had expected, including arriving in daylight. But this is Saturday and the schedule is different.

*　　*　　*

Jordan

11 October – 12 November 2008

Aqaba, Wadi Rum, Petra, Dana, Al Kharak,
Suweimah, Madaba, Amman

We reach Aqaba at 11 pm, but hang around off the port for two hours, waiting for the pilot to come on board and guide us in, necessary because we are too low in the water, caused by the excessive number of lorries in the hold.

Disembarkation is a joke: a matter of picking our way in the dark across a dirt track, over a bumpy bit of waste ground, peering forlornly into the blackness in the hope of gauging the right direction for the customs building. Once located and inside, a dearth of staff means we traipse up and down the corridor searching for the customs' desk. This eventually turns out to be a small office, into which one by one we enter, are correctly identified, eventually leaving with our passports complete with visa.

Outside, I load up my bicycle and prepare to cycle the eight miles to the city centre, donning reflective armbands and chest strap and my headtorch. I am not happy cycling at such an hour, so scoot along as fast as I can, the lonely, dark dual carriageway filling me with unease. This is not helped when a taxi overtakes and drives slowly in front of me for a while, before speeding away. Maybe he was simply making sure I was okay. Soon after, a car pulls over in the layby ahead and my nervousness increases. But it turns out to be a young couple and their baby daughter with whom I had chatted on the ferry. As I pass them, they call out, 'Welcome to Jordan.'

It takes about forty minutes to reach the lighted streets of the city centre. I have the name of a hotel but, with no idea where to find it,

I stop at the first 4-star hotel. The night watchman at the entrance leads me into the foyer, whereupon the receptionist obligingly obtains the hotel number from the internet, phones to book a room and issues directions on how to get there. Arriving at the hotel, I check into my room, but I am still not finished for the night as the bedding is a bit suspect and I ask for clean sheets and pillow case. Finally, after a brief shower, I am in bed, grateful for the chance to sleep.

I spend a day in Aqaba, but no time for sightseeing. I need a map and information on accommodation in Jordan and on obtaining a visa for Israel; I should write a journal update; I want to buy a SIM card; I should like to Skype my children.

Margitta and Co. are staying at the same hotel, but, not being as accepting as I am of the low standard of the hotel, she has refused to pay the asking price and negotiated a lower one. She duly arranges a discounted rate for me too. Apart from the hotel not being particularly clean, the reception staff are neither friendly nor helpful and I feel more than happy to be leaving early the following morning.

The road begins with a long climb out of Aqaba, not much traffic, hazy views over the Gulf of Aqaba. At the top is a junction, a choice between the Dead Sea to the left or Amman straight on. I choose the latter, along Desert Highway 15, after a couple of hours arriving at a turn-off to Wadi Rum.

'Well that could be fun,' I think, 'so why not?'

A few miles along this road, a seductive sign, 'Last ice-stop before Wadi Rum,' entices me into a Bedouin tent, to lounge on large, comfortable cushions, sipping an iced coke. I am the only customer. The young man serving asks a few unintrusive questions, followed a short while later by a jeep from the desert speeding to a halt outside the entrance to the tent. From here, I am further persuaded by a charming young desert dweller to spend the night in a desert camp. I suspect there has been some collusion to this effect.

The package includes a trip by jeep into the desert for a campfire lunch, ending with a walk back to the camp, on the way viewing a desert sunset. Deal done, Raven and I are loaded onto a jeep and brought to the tented village, whereupon I join a group of eight young students from Haifa University in Israel. Each of them is on a semester placement from universities in their own countries: USA, Korea, Denmark and Azerbaijan.

A couple of jeeps drive us into the desert, depositing us in the shadow of a huge rock, before leaving us to the mercies of our two guides. We forage for fuel for the campfire, on which mince and tomato stew is cooked. This, plus houmous, eggplant dip and pitta bread makes for a delicious meal. I think anything would have tasted good in this location.

Part of the appeal of the desert is the silence. Well away from mechanical sounds of any kind, the still and quiet is beautiful. I remember the first time I encountered it thirty years previously with my father out in the desert in Dubai. To hear the sound of silence is a rare experience, one to be savoured.

On the walk back to camp, camels appear out of nowhere, a couple of the students taking the opportunity to ride them. We walk too slowly to arrive at the recommended point to watch the setting sun, but really it is easy to enjoy the beauty of all sunsets, wherever you are. In the dark, we pass Lawrence of Arabia's camp, a large rock at the entrance on which his face is carved; underneath, Lawrens el Araby 1917, inscribed in Arabic.

Back at our camp, over dinner in the main tent, I chat to Marcus, a young German travelling around Jordan by taxi, having struck a favourable deal with the driver. I accept a lift from him in the morning back to the main junction, but when we arrive, Marcus and the taxi driver are bent on taking me all the way to Petra, fifty miles away, completely bemused that I will not take advantage of this opportunity.

'Thanks, but it wouldn't be a cycling trip, if I accepted all the lifts I have been offered,' I reply.

Cyclists have been a rare sighting in the last couple of months, none in the Middle East and no tourers since Italy. Therefore, it takes a little while to acknowledge that the slowly approaching dot in the distance is in fact just that. As we draw level, we hail each other, park our bicycles by our respective sides of the road and meet at the central reservation barrier. He is a French guy, Patrice, who started in Istanbul to cycle through Syria, Lebanon, Jordan and Egypt, before flying home from Cairo at the end of his 35-day trip. I am the second cyclist he has met in Jordan, the first, also French but on a recumbent cycle, has been travelling for two years through South America, South Africa, Asia and, currently, the Middle East.

On to the junction with the King's Highway, where a lorry driver beckons me over, inviting me to stop for a freshly-brewed coffee. He even has the luxury of a folding picnic chair, insisting I use it. Prior to driving Jordanian Gas tanker lorries, he was in the military for sixteen years. On leaving, he presents me with a couple of home-grown lemons. I'm not sure when I shall use them, but I appreciate the gesture.

The King's Highway is a joy to cycle, through expansive, remote and beautiful landscape. There is not much traffic and I love the solitude of the countryside and the friendly feel of the towns. Until, that is, it is marred by one young man who, walking down the middle of the road, a hostile expression on his face, makes a completely unsolicited obscene gesture at me with his middle finger. The unexpectedness of it shocks me.

In Petra, the backpacking hotels are fully booked and I opt for a friendly over-budget place. Other guests include an elderly British couple, a South African couple, Yousef and Lutvia, and an American, Anne, whose diverse 6-week trip has included London, Scotland, Yemen, Oman and Jordan. Considering her nationality, she has been agreeably surprised at the friendliness of her Middle East experience.

The South Africans and I share a taxi to the entrance of the ancient city of Petra, from there walking out to the furthest point. We climb up rock-carved steps through clefts in the mountains and clamber over boulders, eventually arriving at the top of the last mountain to be greeted, not only with a magnificent view, but with the most impressive sight I think I have ever seen, the Monastery. This is a vast building carved entirely out of solid rock, towering 160 feet to the sky, dating at least from the first century BC. A strategically-placed café/restaurant on a rocky rise opposite allows the viewer to absorb its immensity and achievement whilst relaxing over drinks brought to the café on mule-trains.

The remainder of Petra is equally stunning and fascinating, including another impressively-sized building, the ornate Treasury, and hundreds of other carved-out dwellings of varying sizes. Petra is known as the Rose-Red City, referring to the predominant red colour of the rock, but there are also hues of pink, yellow, blue, grey and black.

Vendors are everywhere, plying their various wares, such as necklaces made from camel bones or from polished stones; or offering their services to transport you from place to place by horse, donkey, camel or horse-drawn carriage.

Leaving Petra behind, the terrain includes long hills, sometimes very steep. In Al Qadissiya, school is out for the day at exactly the time I am pedalling laboriously up one of these harsh inclines. Soon a large contingent of 10-year olds comes and stands in the middle of the road as I am cycling towards them, chanting, 'Money, money,' and throwing stones at me. They flock around and I end up dismounting, struggling to push through them on this steep hill. They press even closer, fiddle with my bicycle, extract the empty water bottle to throw it in the street. I become distressed, even more so when I see adults by the roadside looking on impassively, even after it is obvious I am shouting for them to intervene. One by one, the children eventually lose interest and drift away, in the end leaving two slightly older lads, who walk the remainder of the way with me to the top and who turn out to be quite helpful and pleasant.

I turn off the King's Highway, descending abruptly through the spectacular scenery of Dana Nature Reserve, Jordan's largest reserve, rutted with deep gorges, containing a plethora of flora and fauna: ibex, sand cat, mountain gazelle, red fox, wolf.

The fifteenth-century stone village of Dana is now mainly for tourists, most inhabitants having moved to a new village thirty to forty years previously. Besides the five remaining inhabited homes, two hotels and a guesthouse are located here. A local guide, Jabah, greets me and invites me up to the roof of the first hotel where tea and lunch are served, 'Compliments of the house.' I relax in the afternoon sun, rocking gently on the shaded swing seat, writing postcards bought in Petra. I am told I can sleep on the roof, either on a mattress or in my tent, for just JD3 (about £3). Later on, I am offered the spacious tent that is already erected here. I even arrange a lift back up to the main road for the following morning, the reverse gradient far too daunting for me to consider struggling up it.

Amongst the other guests are Belgians, a young Dutch/German couple and two Norwegians. During the evening, Jabah brings out a hookah to smoke and sociably passes it around for the Norwegians and me to try. The suspect hygiene of a common mouthpiece flits across my mind, but I carry on regardless curious to see what it is like. The taste of apple wood is soft and mellow.

When it comes to retiring for the night, I end up being given a room, normally JD25, at no extra charge.

The landscape reminds me that I am travelling through the biblical land of Moab, the country to which a chap called Elimelech moved with his wife, Naomi, and two sons to escape the famine in Israel. It was there that one of his sons met and married a Moabitess, Ruth, who, even after her husband died, left her own country to return with her mother-in-law to Israel. There she subsequently met and married the lovely Boaz, with whom they had a child, Obed, father of Jesse, who was the father of David, king of Israel and of the line into which Jesus was eventually born. The book of Ruth in the Bible is one of my favourites, a poetically romantic story, as well as being a key event in the history of the Christian faith.

I have a day full of canyons with spectacular views. After passing a friendly police checkpoint, I stop for a drink further up the road in the shade of a tree. Two of the police officers then drive up to me, specifically to ask if I have a problem. I assure them I am fine and they drive back down. Well, it is a quiet outpost after all and nothing much else for them to do.

Much of the day is spent walking slowly up hills. Halfway up one, a car that has just passed me going up comes back down. It turns out to be the Dutch/German couple from Dana, Koen and Lisa, on their way to Al Kharak. When they saw me walking they took pity on me and turned back, offering to at least take my panniers, the car not big enough for Raven and me as well. I appreciate their thoughtfulness but insist that they should not feel sorry for me; I have already gone through that stage myself. I decline their offer, in case I do not make it all the way to the proposed destination, but am more than happy for them to book a room for me in the hotel.

In the meantime, I pass through a town which at first seems friendly when a helpful man willingly gives me directions, but which, is subsequently marred by the unwelcoming and unwelcome stares of men. I am again subjected to stone-throwing but this time unnervingly from adults, rather than boys.

It is dark by the time I reach Al Kharak, so am relieved to spot the hotel quite easily, surprised to be hailed by name even as I am still cycling up the hill towards it. The friendly manager, Samir, has been looking out for me. He offers me a special discount (because I am cycling).

'But don't tell anyone,' he conspires.

The room is grimy and I ask for clean bedsheets, which offends Samir, who insists that they are clean on that day. There is no en suite and the shared shower in what looks to be the cleaning store cupboard, is less than salubrious, definitely a flip flops job. I meet up for a meal with Lisa and Koen, all of us agreeing that the loo wins the award for one of the dirtiest we have seen (but, for my money, not outdone by the ratty one in Egypt). Funnily enough, Samir is from Egypt. His wife and family still live there and he sees them for just two months a year. It must be hard rarely seeing his family, but he does not really have a choice; the money is better here in Jordan, as it was for the two years he worked in Iraq before war broke out.

Al Kharak is perched strategically on a mountain, complete with its own twelfth-century Crusader castle. Many of the rooms are below ground, naturally lit by light shafts in the ceilings bored through from the surface. I meet Lavonne, from the States, who often cycle tours with groups, recently having been on a trip in Austria.

The museum within the grounds of the castle contains pieces of beautiful, iridescent blue pottery, as well as an Islamic hand grenade from Crusader days. It is decorated with flowers, symbolic of martyrdom and paradise. One of the staff, Noorah, accompanies me around the showcases and, with our mutual smattering of each other's languages, enjoy moderate success in an exchange of information. The dates of events are expressed in a mixture of BC or BP (Before Present), the latter striking me as very bizarre – when did the present begin?

When I mention to Samir that I had stopped at the hotel across the road for a cup of tea, he berates me, saying I should only drink tea at his place because it is free. He is also annoyed that I had eaten at that hotel the night before (with Koen and Lisa), after he had directed me to a local restaurant.

'Why do you waste your money when you can eat much cheaper?' he protests. 'Tonight, I shall phone the restaurant, tell them you are coming and they must give you a local price, not a tourist one.'

It seems I have no option but to go. Judging by appearances I cannot think that there is much chance of tourists stopping by this restaurant but, as with most local eating places, the people are friendly and the food is good – and cheap. I have had no tummy problems so far, even from eating at roadside restaurants.

When it is time to leave, Samir is concerned for me, plying me with bread, drinks and a foil-wrapped cake. A group of Israelis, on a trip hiking up a variety of wadis, supply me with their emails to contact them once in Israel.

From Al Kharak, it is downhill all the way to the Dead Sea, braking constantly on the windy hairpin bends. Paradoxically, the uphills are much more enjoyable, those rare inclines when there is no need to pedal because you find yourself flying up them at 28 mph. A brilliant feeling!

I am excited to be cycling by the Dead Sea. There are so many diverse associations with it: lowest sea below sea-level, Dead Sea scrolls, super-buoyant salinity, health properties, geographical and historical context in Judaism and Christianity. I look longingly at the soft cornflower-blue of the water but find nowhere to gain easy access with my bicycle. I pull over on the Mujib bridge for a short break and am quickly surrounded by a coachload of Brits, firing off questions and snapping photographs. They have stopped to look at the newly-built dam at the bottom of Wadi Mujib, the lowest nature reserve in the world, at 1,340 feet below sea level.

Whenever I stop, I am plagued by swarms of flies settling on the bicycle, panniers and me. Taking a swig of water is a risky business as I try not to swallow any of them.

I wonder if I should turn off towards Madaba, where there is known accommodation, or continue along the Dead Sea, taking my chance of finding somewhere to camp at Suweimah. Initially, I go for elevation, but that does not last long, as I realise that twenty miles of this incline in this heat and at this time of day is not going to work in my favour. Back at the Sea, a Highway Patrolman who had stopped me earlier to check I was OK, pulls over and directs me to a beach where I can camp and use the public wash facilities on payment of an entrance fee. Perfect. I change into bathing gear and join the mud-plastered bathers to float in, or rather on the Dead Sea. It is a strange sensation not to be able to swim and to float with no effort. I come out with babysoft skin.

I am the only one with a tent staying the night but there are plenty of others, workmen who sleep in the open, who keep well away from me. I leave before eight in the morning, cycle past luxury hotels, stopping at a truckers' café for falafel wrap and tea, plus taking on water and fizzy drinks for the day's ride. Further along the road and turning left would have taken me to the place where Jesus was dunked by John the Baptist, when the Holy Spirit came down on him in the form of a dove, the voice of God proclaiming, 'You are my beloved son, in whom I am well pleased.'

Instead, I turn right for the long, slow assault up Mount Nebo, an elevation of 3,600 feet above sea level. For the majority of the 3-hour slog it is a matter of getting my whole body weight behind the bicycle to push my heavy load to the top. I decline two offers of lifts. Why? Who knows? On an unnegotiable bend, I am almost resigning myself to set up a relay system to transport bicycle and baggage. Just in time, a binoculared bird spotter above me runs down to give me a push. I stop in the next layby for lunch and the same man brings over a bottle of water to wash my face and hands, after which he pours the remaining contents over my head, under the misconception that I would appreciate being thoroughly soaked all over to cool me down. Disliking the feel of wet, clinging clothes, I do not share his sentiment, but he means well. He then thinks up another good idea: that he should drive behind me, pushing my bicycle up the hill with his bumper.

'That's very kind of you and thanks for the thought, but, no, thank you anyway. No, really, I insist. No thanks!'

Having shaken him off and reached the top of the mountain, I am greeted by a Jordano-Russian family who passed me on the way up. I leave my bicycle behind the wooden vestibule belonging to the tourist police, who promise to keep an eye on her whilst I visit the historic site. As I walk away they are examining her closely. The admission's chap had seen me arrive and waves me in without charging a fee. I walk up to the attractively simple Church of Moses, which looks over into Israel. Nearby stands an unusual and beautiful cross, made from a variety of twisted metals.

Mount Nebo overlooks Canaan, the Promised Land, and is where Moses went to die. He had led the Israelites for forty years through the desert to their new land, a land he did not himself enter.

I return to my bicycle. As I go to leave, I stop in my tracks when a pack of six barking dogs come bounding up. Now, I am not very comfortable with the combination of dogs and bicycles, having heard so many tales of woe from other cyclists, and so am none too keen at their sudden appearance. I attempt to cycle off but stop immediately when they are obviously intending to come with me. I walk the bicycle, but still they come. Hmmm . . . A little further on the road falls sharply away. I decide to make my break, so mount and go hell for leather – which works; the dogs give up after a short distance and I blow metaphorical raspberries at them.

In Madaba, I make for the Pilgrims Hotel, only to find that it is no longer any such thing, but run on commercial grounds. I try for a discount as a bonafide pilgrim, to which the manageress eventually agrees. I stay a couple of nights, eager to take a look at St George's church and the many mosaics, for which the town is famous. Busloads of visitors come to the church to view the many icons and mosaics on show here. But the main point of interest is the seventh-century mosaic map of the world, originally covering a floor area of 1,000 square feet, of which a quarter now remains. Historically, Madaba was an important Christian centre frequented by pilgrims. The mosaic map might have been used by them to plan their routes to other pilgrim destinations.

Sitting in the pews gazing at the icons of Mary and the baby Jesus, I am struck by the look on Mary's face. In each one her gaze is slightly averted from the baby she is holding, portraying such great sadness in the faraway look in her eyes. She seems aware that there is huge sorrow associated with the life of her beloved son, although not yet realising to what extent.

In the Archaeological Park, I view more mosaics, followed by lunch in a small local restaurant: chicken boiled in a lemon and milk soup served with rice, bread and tomatoes.

The road to Amman is busy, the hard shoulder filled with rubbish. At the brow of a hill, I come across a 'drive-by' tea stop, consisting of a table with a couple of tall beautiful pots merrily steaming away, ready to serve tea or coffee to cars when they drive up, plastic cups passed through the open window to the occupants, who then drive off with their takeaway. I have become fond of these stops: they are usually well placed, for example, at the top of a long climb, and I am always treated to a friendly welcome.

Amman was originally built on seven hills, over time extending to nineteen. I am staying with Wendy, a contact via my church at home, and her Iraqi husband, Farkad. Along with hundreds of other Iraqis, he and his family are refugees, having been forced to flee Iraq, ending up in Amman. As refugees, they are not allowed paid employment and so life is naturally extremely hard. For many, Jordan is meant to be a transitional stage, whilst awaiting the result of applications for entry into other countries, such as Australia, America or Europe. The slow, lengthy procedures are a patient, frustrating, uncertain exercise, borne with great fortitude by Farkad and his family, firmly upheld by their deep Christian faith.

Before arriving in the neighbourhood in which Wendy and Farkad live, I had been asked to make sure I am suitably attired, as they are already considered a bit of an oddity, being Christians, without someone as bizarre (or as scandalous) as me, a lone woman arriving on a bicycle, emphasising the fact. I receive a wonderfully warm welcome from them, delighted to be in the comfort of what soon feels a familiar home.

I go along to the Iranian embassy to pick up my visa. Alas, this is not forthcoming, as the consul, the only person able to deal with visas, left three weeks previously and no date has yet been set for his replacement to be in post. They offer to produce a letter for me to take to the embassy in Erzerum, in Turkey, authorising my visa to be issued there. The trouble is, I had not intended to go that far north.

In the meantime, I pack a small backpack and head to the airport, on the way to Bangkok to meet GR for a 2-week holiday. During my wait at the airport, I fall into conversation with a group of four Iraqi women, returning from a conference on education in Casablanca. One of the women is the Minister for Special Needs Education and very interested to hear I work at the Centre for Deaf Studies, wishing to contact the professor there for more information on deaf education. She also invites me to visit her in Baghdad. It is a compelling notion but, from a cycling point of view, I have ruled out Iraq and Afghanistan for the time being.

From a travel perspective, the Asian holiday is a great success, speeding our way by coach and train through Malaysia to Singapore, returning in a more leisurely fashion to Bangkok, by way of a beach hut on a small island in the South China Sea. I'd never have done such a whimsical thing before this trip.

Back in Jordan, I accompany Wendy to a Christian-run women's group, at which Christians and Moslems have the opportunity for social interaction and to talk about health issues, discuss Christianity and participate in shared meals. I am invited to talk about my trip and answer questions. It is a delight to do so, interesting to see that the majority of women are Moslems. Living very sheltered lives, it is not always easy to have someone with whom they can talk freely. This group allows that opportunity, even on a one-to-one basis, when some women end up being surprisingly open in their conversations. After my talk, one of the Moslem women comes up to me to say she has been so encouraged by my trip that she is now fully motivated to go for her dream – to open a beauty salon. This would be quite an achievement, Moslem women commonly are not allowed into such a public sphere; even in lingerie shops the staff would be male.

At my follow-up visit to the Iranian embassy, fully expecting to be picking up my letter for Turkey, I am delighted to be told that the new consul is arriving that evening and I should give him a couple of days before arranging to meet him. I duly take along my passport and a choice of two photos: one with a scarf wound round my head and face (according to instructions from the Iranian visa agency), the second a normal unscarfed version. Bewilderingly, the unscarfed version is chosen, the clerk at the embassy saying I look younger in that one.

Before I can receive my visa, I must pay for it; not a simple matter of handing over cash at the embassy, but of finding a specific bank at which to deposit the money. On the way, I stop by the Hyatt Hotel for a quick loo stop, but this is not quite as straightforward as I had expected. Outside are parked a line of cars displaying diplomatic plates, attended by men in black suits and, of course, dark sunglasses. I am directed to a specific entrance to undergo the rigours of x-ray and a security search before allowed into the hotel foyer. And all for a wee.

Money duly paid into the designated bank, I return to the embassy with the pay-in chitty, at which point I get to meet the consul in person when he comes out of his office to hand me my passport. With a happy grin on my face, I promptly embarrass myself by making the mistake of trying to shake hands with him. He proffers a flat hand, pointing out that it is not the done thing for him to shake hands with a woman. Whoops. Even so, I now have my Iranian visa!

Early next morning I bid farewell to Wendy and Farkad. I pile everything into the school minibus, arranged (and paid for) by Wendy, which takes me to the Seventh Circle roundabout on the other side of Amman, whereupon I set off, eager to be on my way to Israel.

It is good to be on the road again after a sojourn of twenty days. The riding is easy with no hills to speak of for the rest of Amman, after which nothing but continuous downhill all the way to the Dead Sea and the King Hussein border. The rolling hills and deep valleys create a dramatic landscape, heightened by the darkening sky ahead, eventually producing a beautiful rainbow, a sight that never fails to fill me with wonder and optimism.

The darkened sky brings forth rain, gently at first, but it soon becomes heavy enough for me to fish out my cycling cape from the depths of the pannier. I have to brake constantly, but carefully, to control my speed without skidding because the surface is alarmingly ice-like.

The bulk of the traffic is lorries, without exception all descending gingerly-slowly, to the extent that I find myself overtaking one.

As I draw level with the bonnet and pass in front, a powerful gust of wind blows my wheels from under me, the reality of the slippery road surface literally hitting me, as my bicycle falls over and I fall off. Raven and I proceed to slide, slide, slide towards the edge of the road and the chasm beyond, with me thinking, 'Heck, *are* we going to stop?'

Finally, we do; coming to a halt on the hard shoulder. The overtaken lorry stops, then carries on. The one behind stops and waits. I pick myself up, understandably shaken, right Raven and check for any breakages, retrieve the back pannier that has detached itself, and emit a sigh of relief when everything seems intact. It is fortunate I am wearing my cape, as this has prevented damage to clothes, now very dirty but not torn, and injury to my body, bruised head, right arm and thigh, but not scraped or broken. I nearly cry, but manage impressive self-control.

I keep giving the thumbs up to my protector high up in his cab behind, who insists on maintaining his patient wait. After donning my helmet and clambering gingerly back onto my bicycle, I issue another thumbs-up and pedal off tentatively. And what does my protector do? Exactly that: he continues to protect me by driving slowly behind me down the hill, in case I decide to come a cropper again. What an absolute sweetie! After a couple of miles or so, we part company at a junction, this time he giving me the universal thumbs-up, complemented with a big smile. I continue to the border crossing and Israel, thankful for both my human guardian and my heavenly guardian angel.

* * *

101

Israel

13 – 16 November 2008

Jericho, JERUSALEM

The imperative at the border with Israel is to end up with no stamps, visa or any other indication of my time in Israel, if I wish to continue cycling along my proposed route through Syria and Iran. This means exiting and re-entering the same country, not only avoiding an Israeli stamp on entry and exit, but also a Jordanian stamp on exit and re-entry. The aim is to have the four stamps put on a separate piece of paper; apparently, a common request to the border officials, but still requiring a perfectly-timed stay of the stamping hand before the deadly deed is executed.

Arriving at the King Hussein border crossing, I head for the Departures building. Inside, I have a choice of three kiosks, 1st, 2nd, 3rd, which, by some skewed thinking, I take to mean the different options of transport that will take us over the border, and so join the 3rd class queue. Wrong. It actually refers to the order in which we proceed from one kiosk to the next. Perfectly obvious – in retrospect. At each kiosk, I paranoically repeat, 'No stamp in my passport, please.'

'Don't worry, this is not the stamp stage.'

I am through to the other side and on the bus (no cycling allowed) that takes us across No-man's Land. I am not sure what has happened about my exit stamp, the procedures at this point seem a bit hazy, maybe an after effect of my bump on the head yesterday. We stop at a check-point, descend from the bus and file into the office to show our passports.

'No stamp, please.'

Returning to the bus we continue to the drop–off point, directed to wait onboard whilst our bags are unloaded and placed haphazardly in a pile on the ground. We are then allowed off to retrieve our own bags, load them onto trolleys and push them the ten yards to passport control, where designated staff disappear with them under a cordon of tape. My bicycle stays with me.

We each now surrender our passports to an official in a booth to take away to process.

'Please, no stamp!'

The official subsequently passes them on to another official responsible for collecting them into a pile and periodically returning them by calling out loudly the name of the holder. Off again, into the building, to join another lengthy passport control queue. After ten minutes, I am informed by a kindly passenger that I should be in a different line. Well, at least I am not having to start again at the end of a long queue as, happily, it has only one person before me, an American, awaiting the return of his passport currently being scrutinised in a nearby office.

At this point, a uniformed man comes into the hall, shouting loudly to all and sundry, waving his arms in an ushering command for us all to move away from the booths and stand against the back wall. Fifteen, twenty minutes pass – after which we are allowed to resume our queuing as though nothing has happened. No one seems the wiser for the event; the officials in the booths sternly unforthcoming.

As my passport is handed over to the armed female officer, she asks, 'Why do you not want a stamp in your passport?'

'Because I am travelling on through Syria and Iran.'

'What currencies do you have, let me see them, how much is there?'

My passport is taken to a nearby office, returned soon after, no stamps, but not even with a separate piece of paper bearing a stamp.

On through to yet another passport check, at a turnstile over which I must heave my bicycle, then arriving at a strewn mass of bags, dumped unceremoniously across the floor of the hall. I find most of mine quickly, but have to hunt around for the last one. I load up and walk unchallenged past a security-check conveyor belt outside into the bright sunshine.

I expect to have to go on another bus but am told that I can cycle out. Surprised, I mount and ride the hundred yards to the final checkpoint, where, unsurprisingly, the guy makes me wait, letting other vehicles through whilst he phones for confirmation that I too can continue. Eventually this comes through, but with the clear instruction, 'Do not, under any circumstance, stop for the first five kilometres.'

With this directive ringing in my ears and with the barren landscape I am now passing through, dotted with numerous signs, 'Danger. Mines,' set back from the road, the last thing I feel like doing is stopping. I have an insane feeling that there are eyes closely observing me all the way, so that when I surreptitiously fish out my camera and take a couple of covertly-snapped photographs (without stopping), my heart is in my mouth waiting for the challenge from the PA system of a security car speeding up behind me, ready for the arrest. Other than that, it is a pleasant little jaunt.

It has taken two and a half hours to clear the border, a not unreasonable amount of time. At the junction, Jerusalem is to the left, Jericho to the right, I turn in the direction of Jericho. This is under Palestinian administration so, on arrival at the checkpoint, I enter through tall guarded gates, through which Israelis are not allowed.

The way is untidy and rubbishy, having a derelict air about it. When I arrive in the centre, I ask a policeman for hotel suggestions and an ATM. There are two hotels out of town, both expensive, and so I opt for the third, Hisham's Palace Hotel, here in the centre. It is rundown and in the throes of renovation, much of it a building site. The young couple who own it moved in, along with their eight children, two or three weeks previously, the young man's father having built it initially. Apparently, it has some history to it: both Anwar Sadat and Yasser Arafat having stayed here, possibly as students. The place has potential, granted, but in the meantime, the bathroom has not been cleaned, there is no hot water and the air-conditioning does not work. But the couple are friendly and pleasant, embarrassed that the cleaner is not doing her job properly and send one of the young children to clean the bathroom, although this does not produce any real improvement.

On my way to the ATM, a passing taxi stops to see if I need a ride. I do not, but when the driver offers to take me along with another booked fare to Jerusalem I accept, thinking it an opportunity to check out the route for the next day.

We pick up the booked fare, a young couple and their baby. On the lead-up to Jerusalem is a long hill, off which is the turning to the city itself. The taxi driver and his passengers, being Palestinian, are not allowed to go along that road and into Jerusalem. We drop off the family in the Palestinian township of Abu Dis, tantalisingly situated on a hill with a direct view of the forbidden city. The driver takes me to see part of the grafittied, infamous wall, erected to separate Israelis and Palestinians. It is an upsetting statement of the long-suffering state of affairs in this beleaguered Holy Land.

In the morning, I leave leisurely, assuming it will take about four hours to Jerusalem, as it is only about twenty-five miles. Foolishly, I do not stock up on extra provisions or take on more water than the two filled bottles. In the end it takes six hours, and for some reason I make really heavy weather of it: legs weak and tired, resulting in numerous stops every few hundred yards. I can only deduce that it must be a delayed shock reaction from my fall the previous day. A taxi driver stops to check if I need a lift and kindly gives me some water. I take in the surrounding scenery, all beige rock and no greenery, very moonscapey. Part way up is a sign announcing that we are at sea level, an elevation of 1,300 feet above Jericho.

Turning off along the forbidden road to Jerusalem, I come to an Israeli checkpoint three quarters of the way up the long hill. Here, as at the country border crossing, I am surprised at the high number of female security soldiers, fully armed, in combat gear. Their greetings are friendly and I am waved through cheerily, labouring up the remainder of the hill, to a wonderful sign, 'Welcome to Jerusalem.'

There is nothing to see though, until I have passed through a hair-raising tunnel, seeming much worse than it probably is, with the sounds of traffic being amplified ten fold.

Emerging from the dark tunnel into the bright sunlight feels hugely symbolic to arrive thus to Jerusalem. On the downhill to the centre, a sign points to the Mount of Olives. It is so exciting. I have cycled all the way from my home to this amazing and controversial place.

I arrive at the old city, stopping at Damascus Gate. But inaccessible steps make me retrace my way to enter the ancient walled city by way of Jaffa Gate which opens onto a square. Asking around for accommodation, I make my way towards the Jewish quarter in search of a suggested guesthouse. On the way, I meet a procession of cycle tourers.

The group has just this moment arrived from Cairo and, on seeing my well laden bicycle, the frontrunners enthusiastically insist that I will be interested in the guy at the end of the line. This last cyclist is markedly different in appearance to the others: dishevelled fair hair, unshaven face, rugged demeanour, who becomes very excited on seeing Raven.

'You've got the same saddle as me. And the same gear hub as me. Oh, and a Raven Tour, like me. Give me a hug.'

And that is my introduction to Tom. When he tells me the name of his website, The Hungry Cyclist, I exclaim, 'I know you! I've come across your website.'

He is delightful. After chatting exuberantly for more than a few minutes, we catch up with his group, Tom insisting the group leader will be happy to help me with accommodation. Alas, the leader does not share the same happy disposition, bent only on coralling the group to the end of their trip and their final accommodation. Abashed, but undaunted, Tom delves into his wallet and thrusts some money into my hand, commanding me to have a night's accommodation on him. Amidst my protests, he insists, proclaiming that it is little return for the abundance of hospitality and generosity of which he has been continually on the receiving end during his many travels. As we separate, it is with the mutual agreement that on return from my trip we meet up in London for a curry. Blissfully happy at this unexpected encounter, I continue to the intended guesthouse.

In the course of the next couple of days, I meet a variety of interesting people: a Dutch girl here for a year as part of her PhD research, something about the book of Jeremiah and how different groups (Christians and Jews) read it; Jack, from Poland, a nuclear scientist, enjoying a short break after attending a conference in Eilat on nuclear particles; an American couple from Illinois taking this trip paid for by their eight children in celebration of their twenty-fifth wedding anniversary.

I visit the western Wailing Wall, which has segregated areas for men and women. Rows of people stand in front of the wall praying, others sit on chairs set back from the wall, behind them people sit on the ground. I pray at the wall, a poignant moment, afterwards sitting on a chair, casually watching the gentle, hushed movements of the other women and listening to the men praying in the adjacent section. As I leave, an elderly bearded man beckons to me wanting to know if I speak French. Benjamin then decides to show me around some of the ramparts of the wall, past David's tomb (closed to women at the time we go), a Holocaust museum, a garden on Mount Zion and on to Jaffa Gate, whereupon he promptly disappears.

On Sunday morning, I go to the Eucharist service at Christ Church, near Jaffa Gate. I am not particularly enamoured by the American pastor, twenty-eight years in Jerusalem, who makes mocking comments about 'the nutters' he has encountered over the years: the Elijahs, the Jesuses, the Gods. He goes on to deliver a disparaging denigration of Protestant Evangelicals who place far too much emphasis on God is Love, whereas he much prefers God as the judge who calls us sternly to account for our actions. Personally, I am more in the God is Love camp.

After a prayer session with a couple of the pastoral team and homemade lunch in the church hall, I walk out to the Mount of Olives and the Garden of Gethsemane, which turns out to be my favourite place in Jerusalem. Sitting in the olive tree garden on a little bench next to the small carved stone plaque, depicting Jesus in anguished submissive prayer immediately before he is arrested and sent for crucifixion, I read the four accounts in the gospels. The one that does it for me is in Mark, when Jesus prays to his father, 'My soul is overwhelmed with sorrow to the point of death . . . yet not what I will, but what you will.'

Walking through the maze of covered streets in the old city, I am enticed by an Armenian into his shop for a cup of coffee – whereupon, something for something, I am persuaded to examine his merchandise, in this case silver and green malakite (Jewish stone) jewellery. The inevitable result is a purchase: Christmas presents for my children, which I trust him to ship to UK. Sometimes I do think I am disturbingly trusting, but better that than jaded scepticism? When I come to pay, it is disquieting when one of my credit cards does not work, even more so when its debit counterpart later refuses to bring forth cash from an ATM (although I am successful at a different machine). It seems too early on in my trip to have cards quitting on me.

This being a major destination on my route, I have bought a bundle of postcards and now spend a leisurely time in the sun writing them before returning to my basement guesthouse, El Malak, with its gaily decorated front door of trumpet-playing angels. The name has two meanings: the angels and the king; the angels therefore could be heralding the arrival of the king.

*   *   *

Part 2

Jerusalem
to
Lhasa

For I was hungry and you gave me something to eat,
I was thirsty and you gave me something to drink,
I was a stranger and you invited me in.
                                                    Matthew 25

Israel

17 – 22 November 2008

Jaffa, Haifa, Nazareth, Kfar Ruppin

After three days in Jerusalem, I head towards the coast and Tel Aviv. On the way, I stop at a roadside van, rather more upmarket than most, offering freshly-brewed real coffee and homemade cinnamon buns. The pleasant young man serves as a reminder of home (his name is Daniel), and I look on him with a touch of tenderness, uplifted by his warmth and bright spirits. Over coffee and bun he teaches me some Hebrew words, '*Toda* (thank you), *shalom* (hello/goodbye), *bevakasha* (please),' whilst also urging me to pay a visit to a beautiful place half a mile up the road.

This turns out to be the Biblical Landscape Reserve, colour-marked with three themed walking trails through woods, hills and plains. I choose the Blue Trail, based on the passionate Song of Songs, a book from the Old Testament, and the importance of Shabat, the Jewish Sabbath. All along the way, signs identify a specific tree or plant, adjacent to which is often a delightful and relevant quote from this romantic book.

'Torrents of water cannot quench love.'

'As a narcissus among fire thorns, so is my beloved among the maidens.'

'Your breath is like the fragrance of apples.'

Small-group teaching and activity areas are placed strategically along the route, including a small amphitheatre overlooking a lake, as well as displays of ancient millstones and wine presses. The spontaneous couple of hours spent here are unexpectedly rewarding.

A direct approach to Tel Aviv is hampered by being unable to find a non-highway road to the centre. In the end, there seems no alternative but to take a reluctant 20-mile detour, entering from the south into Jaffa (or Joppa), on the outskirts of Tel Aviv.

The first hostel I try is expensive and not particularly friendly; unfortunate therefore that it is a Christian establishment. I pass on staying. The Old Jaffa Hostel, on the other hand, is welcoming, relaxed, exudes character, boasts a rooftop garden and is a third of the price. I stay for two nights, wander around the narrow streets and the old port and scale the hill to the Statue of Faith. This is a concrete monument depicting Jacob's dream, the sacrifice of Isaac and the fall of Jericho, in the form of an intricately carved set of two pillars and a cross-beam. Back down at the sea I walk along the beach and breathe in lungfulls of fresh sea air, delicious after weeks on dusty roads.

Having just spent my last twelve shekels, I go in search of an elusive bank, finally finding three in the same street. After increasingly frantic, failed attempts to obtain money from any of them, using a debit and credit card from each of my two banks, I finally breathe a sigh of relief when I am successful in holding a wadge of money in my hand. The surprise is that as a last ditch attempt I use my prepaid cash passport card, an item I had been wary of purchasing back home as it was a new enough product for the person in the branch of Thomas Cook to be sceptical of its global availability.

'Although, don't worry, it will definitely work in America.'

I loaded the card with US dollars a month before leaving UK, at an exchange rate that was in my favour. Therefore, to gain most benefit from this, I aim to stave off using it until I reach the States. But it depends on how many emergencies crop up in the meantime.

Internet use in the hostel is limited, but I do manage to write a short piece for the Royal Geographic Society's Cycling Workshop at their annual Explore weekend. I attended the previous year as part of my trip preparation and have now been asked to write something to be read out to delegates at this year's workshop, led by the double act of Hal and Al (Hallam Murray and Alastair Humphreys), both extremely accomplished adventure cyclists.

The encouragement received, and the information gleaned, for intrepid would-be cycle adventurers is excellent. However, it seems appropriate to mention that the gender imbalance on the workshop panel might be addressed, as not all the cycling delegates would necessarily be in the twenty-something-year-old male category.

This done, I luxuriate in doing nothing but lounging on a settee on the rooftop garden overlooking old Jaffa town, drink in hand. It's not a bad life.

The road from Jaffa runs seamlessly into uptown Tel Aviv, to join the flat coast road on its way to Haifa. I turn off at Caesarea, happening to come across a kibbutz. It has been my intention to try and stay on one whilst in Israel. However, my confident hope of a night's accommodation is dashed on being informed of the pricey tariff and no option to camp. I am disappointed, having maybe naïvely fostered the impression from the idealism of the seventies (as well as from the encouragement of some Israelis I met in Al Kharak), that the philosophy of kibbutz would be accommodating to travellers, rather than being run on a purely commercial basis.

Continuing towards Haifa, I stop for a break, striking up a conversation with Elan, who was born and grew up on a kibbutz and still lives there working as a security officer. An Arab friend comes by and joins us. He used to work on the same kibbutz as a car mechanic. Seeing these two friends, who are supposed to be enemies (because that is what politics say they should be), illustrates to me the ordinary person getting on with the right things in life, regardless of the dictats of governments.

Situated on a promontory, Haifa has a long sea border which I follow around towards the port in my search for tonight's stay at the Port Inn. Not finding it on the port road I turn up a side street. A voice from on high asks what I am looking for.

'The Port Inn,' I reply to the man leaning over his balcony four floors up.

I follow in the direction of his arm and a little while later a young boy and an old man come up to me.

'Port Inn,' they confirm, indicating its exact location not far away, explaining they had seen me earlier asking for directions. Such pleasant encounters are worth their weight in gold.

The Port Inn's narrow entrance brings me to a young man at reception. Za'ev is very serious, in my experience a common Israeli trait, but appearances can be deceptive for he is also extremely pleasant. My 4-bed dorm has one other occupant, a Polish girl, who in the kitchen later invites me to use the remainder of her spaghetti and pesto sauce. An Aussie woman, Liana, says I am, 'An incredible woman,' before taking my photo to put on her fridge at home to inspire her. I shall claim no false modesty, as I am unashamedly pleased by her comment. My day is further enhanced by managing to elicit a smile from Za'ev, who advises me on the best route to Nazareth that will avoid going up and over a hill.

I take the cable car up the mountain for a panoramic view of the city, which is dominated by the colourful, very formal, Baha'i Gardens, Haifa being the centre for this faith.

The Baha'i Faith was established by Baha'ullah in Persia in the nineteenth century as a development of the Babi Faith (itself an offshoot of Shia Islam) breaking away to form its own religion. Monotheistic, the Baha'i faith incorporates aspects of many religions, declaring a succession of divine messengers such as Abraham, Buddha, Jesus, Mohammed, each foretelling the coming of the next messenger, ultimately leading to the founder of this faith, himself proclaiming to be,'The fulfilment of the one to come in the end times, in order to bring global unity to mankind.'

From Haifa to Nazareth, the day is dominated by heavy rainstorms: big, fat drops of water deluging down, accompanied by significant claps of thunder. I decline an offer of refuge in a man's van, preferring the safety of bus shelters. They have very nice bus shelters here in Israel: clean and not smelling of urine, providing a not unpleasant stopping place until the rains eases, undoubtedly aided by a piece of yummy chocolate cake. At a later restaurant stop, I eat the best falafels I have ever had, unlike previous dry ones, the manager of the shop not allowing me to pay for my refreshments, wishing me, 'Welcome to Israel.'

As I cycle through this rolling landscape, the recurring thought, Jesus walked here, comes to mind, sending a shiver of goosebumps up and down my spine.

After a long, gentle climb to Nazareth, I pass through the new city and arrive in the old. The guy in the tourist office directs me to a couple of suggestions for accommodation, then asks to take a photo of Raven and me, possibly for inclusion in one of their tourist information brochures. I push my way through a maze of narrow cobbled streets, ringing with the buzz of market stalls and tiny shops overflowing their wares into the streets. Finding no room at the Sisters of Nazareth convent, I continue to Fauzi Azar Inn. The small door from the street enters a courtyard from where stone steps walk up the side of one wall into the main communal living area, off which are bedrooms, kitchen and washrooms. These are fully occupied, so my first night is spent in an 'overflow' bedroom in a building in the next street along. The room contains three beds, only one other occupied, by a young lad, Alex, from the UK, travelling around Israel for a couple of weeks. He is a pleasant lad – and does not snore. The second night sees me in the fold of the main building, a much more sociable environment.

I am excited to be in the hometown of Jesus' childhood, even more so staying in the atmospheric, historic part of the city. After visiting the shrine at Mary's Well, I sit quietly in the Church of the Annunciation, the place dedicated to where the Angel Gabriel visited Mary announcing to her that she would be the mother of Jesus. Visitors from all over the world crowd slowly through the church, expressing their own thoughts in respectful hushed tones on the significance of the event that took place 2,000 years ago.

The ceiling and walls are painted in soft blue and orange murals, depicting scenes from Jesus' life. My eyes are drawn to the portrayal of the Annunciation, below which is an inscription in six different languages.

'Hail, thou that art highly-favoured, the Lord is with thee, blessed art thou amongst women.'

And in that moment, it feels as though these words are being applied to all women, throughout the world, for all time.

Onwards to the huge Basilica of the Annunciation, where I sit in on a service conducted in Spanish, by the leader of a pilgrimage group. On the next level up, displayed on the walls are mosaic pictures of the Virgin Mary, beautifully and interestingly created in the hugely diverse artistic and cultural style of the numerous countries from which they come. And Joseph is not entirely forgotten: on a plain glass window in one of the entrance doors is a simple etching of him at his carpenter's bench.

I meet a variety of people during my short stay: a French couple, in Nazareth for a couple of years working to create an interfaith centre; a New Zealander, taking a few days break from working in Jerusalem in an old people's home; and, the one I am most moved by, a young Argentinian Israeli man from Beer Sheba, a city in the Negev desert in the south of Israel, who comes regularly to Nazareth, staying at the Fauzi Azar Inn.

Although thirty-six, he still lives at home with his parents, three siblings and two cousins, whilst he builds his own house. He is not married, does not have a regular job, preferring to live the free life (now where have I heard this before?). We talk about the impact of religious and political divisions that prevent people from being able to come into contact and appreciate each other's traditions and cultures. His ears prick up when he realises that I shall be travelling through Iran. His big desire is to go there himself because he has heard such good things about Iranians and would love to meet them himself. The sad conclusion is that, in his lifetime, he cannot see this as a real prospect because of the chasmic cleft between the two countries.

On the morning of my departure, this young man wishes me continued joy with my trip before embracing me in a sustained, heartfelt, farewell hug before blowing me a kiss, possibly feeling this is his way of sending his good wishes to the people of Iran.

The day is overcast, the going hilly. I pass through Cana, where Jesus performed his first miracle, turning water into wine in order to keep the party going; on to Tiberias and the Sea of Galilee, where Jesus spent most of the three years of his ministry. My intention had been to cycle around the top of the lake to a campsite on the far side, but the rain is now coming down in such buckets that the idea has sadly lost its appeal.

The Sea of Galilee is the largest freshwater lake on earth, thirteen miles by seven-and-a-half miles, 700 feet below sea level, fed mostly by the river Jordan. On its shores is Capernaum where Jesus made his home, as well as many other familiar figures: Peter, Andrew, James and John, all fishermen, and Matthew the tax collector, and from nearby Magdala, a significant woman and disciple, Mary Magdalene.

Two of the most well-known miracles occurred on the lake itself: stilling the storm and walking on water; and it was on these shores where Jesus cooked breakfast for the disciples after his resurrection. Most of Jesus' teaching was carried out here, from a boat and on the hillsides; notably, the Lord's Prayer and the Sermon on the Mount.

At the southernmost point of the lake, I leave its shores, continuing down beside the River Jordan. Just short of a place called Beit Shean, about 4,940 miles into my trip, I experience my first puncture.

Fortunately, I at least have the comfort of a bus shelter to work in. I set about it confidently enough; after all, I had learned how to mend a puncture just before I set off on my trip. I had been five miles into a local cycle ride when I developed a flat. No problems, I thought, I can manage this. Well, having upturned my bicycle, levered off the tyre and pulled out the inner tube, I could not pinpoint the puncture (the nearby puddle was not quite deep enough). In the end I had to accept the offer of the use of a stranger's mobile to call my son, to bring my car, pick up my bicycle and me and take us home. (Unfortunately, I cannot resort to the same measures in this instance.) I then mended the puncture at leisure, after reading the cycle manual's instructions on what bits to detach in order to be able to remove the back wheel.

Now, after so long and having forgotten how, I fish out the manual to remind myself of the procedure. It is slow work, but eventually I set off, or at least try, but there are no gears. Quick panic as to what I have done wrong, it seems that I have not reconnected the gears; so, I undo all the rear baggage again, reconnect – success.

This is my last night in Israel, so when I see the sign for a kibbutz, I decide to have another go; but there is no guest accommodation. However, the woman in the security office phones another one not far away, where they are willing for me to stay as long as I can delay my arrival in order for the room to be cleaned. The reasonable price of 150 shekels (about £20), is an unexpected bonus.

It is dark when I arrive at the agreed time and pass through the security gate. The guest accommodation is laid out in a quadrangle of single-storey buildings of self-contained apartments. I am greeted by Llana, a South African woman who has been here for many years. After settling in and showering, I go along to the recreation centre for the prepared light meal and to collect my breakfast pack – oh yes, and to pay for my stay.

'That will be 375 shekels (£55), please.'

My heart skips a beat as I look askance and stutter, 'How much?'

Apparently, that is the price she had mentioned on the phone – and I had misheard her. There being nothing else for it I have to cough up, although she does reduce it marginally. In the end I see the lighter side: I had really wanted to stay on a kibbutz, but, being pricier than I had expected, this is the only way it would happen.

The kibbutz was created in 1938, initially populated by Jewish immigrants from Germany, Bohemia and Austria. Their main income is derived from fish-farming and agriculture and a plastics factory, owned by the kibbutz but managed by outside contractors. The gardens are open to the public and birdwatchers in particular enjoy staying here. It is on a significant migratory route between Europe and Africa, as well as a bird-ringing station located here.

117

As I leave in the morning, I stop off at the shop for coke and bread, and chat to a customer who invites me to have a coffee with her, but I am in getting-on mode and decline. The manager is equally friendly, taking a good look at my bicycle before issuing a warm farewell.

The Jordan River crossing is just a few miles away. I use the last of my shekels on the exit visa, board the coach to the border, all of a hundred and fifty metres away, and obtain my entry visa back into Jordan. Both visas are on a separate piece of paper. At the third passport stop, I am informed that I shall be obliged to take a taxi at the next one to the final checkpoint half a mile beyond. On arrival though no one mentions the taxi and so who am I to query this? I cycle on.

* * *

Jordan

23 November 2008

Irbid

I follow the valley road north, before turning east, the start of the long haul up from way below sea level to re-surface at Irbid. On the way, a yellow taxi overtakes, stops, reverses back to me. The two women passengers lean out of the window, attempting to coax me into the taxi with them. Their spontaneous invitation, regardless of the practicalities of space, is generous and kind; declining their offer leaving them with perplexed, even concerned, expressions. Further up the slow drawn-out hill, a man and his young son sit on a rock by the roadside, beckoning me to stop as I draw level. We are immediately joined by the the remainder of the man's work cohort eager to take a break from building their rainwater conduit. We enjoy a brief chat of sorts, limited but very smiley.

In Irbid, the tourist police direct me to a rather dilapidated hotel, reminiscent of the one in Palestinian-controlled Jericho. It is imperative I check carefully through all my luggage, discarding anything from, and linking me to, Israel. This includes receipts, paper and plastic bags, sightseeing tickets, postcards, food wrappers, drinks cartons, Israeli coinage – and the large baggage check label on the reverse of my passport, gaily slapped on by a security official on entry into Israel. I peel this off, but there remains a rough, sticky patch. All photos taken in Israel are on a separate memory card which I now remove and hide away in the depths of a pannier, replacing the original card in the camera. I hope I have not overlooked anything.

The border is only four miles away and I arrive shortly after nine the following morning. It is a breeze through Jordanian customs, then a mile

to the Syrian border. The police outside are very friendly and pleasant –
but inside the big cold customs office I encounter Syrian passport
control. I hand over my passport to a rather surly-faced man, who
immediately takes issue with the sticky patch on the back of my
passport.

'You've been to Occupied Palestine!'

Expecting the possibility of some kind of challenge, I had been
considering how to respond without telling a blatant lie. I simply reply
that I have travelled over many borders. This seems enough to satisfy
him and we pass on to the internal contents of the passport. And here
comes the sticking point for him: he sees my exit visa from Amman
airport, then demands to see the re-entry stamp and I show it to him. But
he is not happy.

'You have two passports! Where is your second passport?'

I show him the entry and exit stamps for Bangkok; no, still not happy.
I show him all the stamps, with their dates, between Thailand, Malaysia,
Singapore, back to Malaysia and Thailand but he does not grasp it. It
seems he cannot cope with the fact that I have left during one month and
returned in a different month. Well, with no guilt to impede me, I am
becoming bolshy in frustration and incomprehension as to why he
cannot see what seems to me blindingly obvious. Eventually, he decides
he needs to seek a higher authority and pompously strides over to an
office, followed immediately by a scurry back to his desk to pick up my
passport, possibly a relevant item to show to his superior.

He returns to his desk to deal with more straightforward visa
requests, whilst I sit on a bench against the wall becoming chilled in the
air-conditioned room and envying the quick turnaround for other
passport holders.

Presumably the man in the office is not senior enough to pass
judgement, as the surly officer is duly summoned to transfer my
offending document to the office at the opposite end of the room. More
minutes pass until, beckoned once again, he trots across the foyer,
receives my passport and approaches me with outstretched hand.

'OK.' he relents, with even a fleeting hint of a smile on his face.

In a slightly mollified tone, he then asks me for the fee.

'Fifty-two.'

Assuming he means Syrian pounds I make to pay, but he corrects me.

'Fifty-two dollars. Or you could pay in Euros.'

Having not anticipated that the country's own currency would not be accepted, I now have to dig deep down into my baggage to fish out the required dollars, securely tucked away at the bottom of one of the panniers. Payment of the fee is not here but at a bank, not conveniently located nearby but on the other side of the final checkpoint. I am obliged to leave my bicycle (presumably as surety), cross the barrier, pay the fee, walk all the way back; whereupon – at last – my passport is issued with the visa and stamp, valid for fifteen days. Hurray. Syria, here I come.

*　　*　　*

Syria

24 November – 12 December 2008

Da'ra, Al Jibah, Damascus, M'aloula, Mar Jacob,
Homs, Mahmarita, Mar Elias, Tartus, Latakia, Kassab

The first city over the border is Da'ra. I clock up 5,000 miles.

Traffic police, in the middle of the main crossroads in the town centre, gesture over to the tourist police on the perimeter to provide me with directions to a hotel. Although only early afternoon, it seems judicious to accept the assurance from them of no hotels in the next main town, Sheik Miskin, fifteen miles further on, even though this will mean a long day tomorrow to Damascus.

I try a few hotels to gauge their prices. In the foyer of the third, I strike up a conversation with a woman who is a French teacher in the local college. She suggests another hotel but I have been there already, at which she invites me to stay in her home. The notion, 'There are no such things as coincidences; in everything there is a plan or purpose', comes to mind.

Adele and her family are Christians, living in a block of flats in an area of town predominantly occupied by Christians. But, although there are three churches here in Da'ra, Protestant, Catholic, Orthodox, and even though Christianity is in the public domain in Syria, it seems tolerated rather than accepted. Adele says she has been discriminated against in the workplace, being passed over for promotion in favour of Moslems. In addition, she feels constrained in what she discusses with people, even Christian friends, for fear of reprisals. Conversely, she talks openly with me, a passing stranger, glad of an opportunity to talk freely of her desires and dreams. She would like to move to a freer country but cannot see this as a feasible future, prevented by lack of finances, and the uncertainty of definite work opportunities once abroad. I feel huge chagrin at her situation, but where will helpless sympathy get her?

My hostess prepares a delicious chicken and rice meal which we tuck into mid afternoon, followed by an invitation for me to take a short lie down, only to awake two hours later. It is dark by this time, but Adele wants to show me round the town. I think though it is mainly for us to have uninterrupted conversation, or should I say, she talks, I listen, trying to keep up with my inadequate French. We stop for a coffee in one of the few public places where women are allowed to congregate, unaccompanied by a man.

In the morning, the husband leads me to the old Damascus road, before continuing on his bicycle to his workplace. I make good progress along the flat, straight road; just as well with the substantial mileage to cover today. I also have to contend with some unhealthy interest from one or two passersby; one, a motorcyclist, who draws alongside attempting to converse in a leery way. So, when I see a soldier on duty at the roadside, I stop beside him. The motorbike continues a short way further before executing a u-turn and retracing his tracks.

As I cycle through the littered streets of the next town, there appear to be only men out in public. I am still trying to gauge this new country, despite yesterday's hospitality. This ambivalence though, is soon allayed when I stop at a roadside tea stall. Even as I ask for a cup of tea, a chair is drawn up for me, given a quick wipe accompanied by a smile, a small group of friendly men quickly gathering round, whilst I sip my tea and exchange what words I can. It certainly helps me to feel more relaxed with my surroundings.

Towards the end of the morning, about forty miles north of Da'ra, I stop by the side of the road for a quick snack. A man beckons me over and I raise my hand, 'It's OK, I have food, thanks.' But he persists until I acquiesce. He ushers me into the dappled shade of his enclosed garden, where I am met by a teenage daughter who immediately goes to fetch her mother.

The upshot is that I am invited to stay for lunch, extending through the rest of the afternoon, when I am plied constantly with coffee and assorted aromatic teas. This includes thyme tea, the glass filled three quarters full with thyme and plenty of sugar, topped up with hot water then sipped through a silver 'straw' with holes in the bottom, the thyme floating to the top – really neat.

During the afternoon, cross-legged on the ground, I help the mother and daughter prepare a delicious delicacy of small cooked aubergines stuffed with a homemade tomato paste. Conversation is sparse; surprisingly, even amongst the older daughters, who arrive in the evening from their university in Damascus and from whom I would have thought to hear more English. The family is well used to showing hospitality to passing cyclists, previous guests coming from Russia, Italy and Germany.

Friends and neighbours drop by sporadically during the afternoon and evening; brought in to see the foreign visitor I suspect. The youngest child, Noor, is about eight years of age and a hoot, presenting me with some of his marbles to keep, plying me with carrots to munch, handing me an orange to eat, but only after he has peeled it for me. He and his sister sit close by me on the floor and would like me to stay until they return from school the following day.

The five children wear western dress; the three older daughters have their heads covered. The husband also wears western-style clothes, although on his head is the traditional red and white *keffiyeh*, which instead of hanging down loosely is wound in a neat turban, one corner hanging down over his right ear. In the evening, he prefers to change into the comfortable long flowing *dishdash*. The wife's attire differs from the usual dress, tending towards traditional Bedouin style: a long dark dress, waisted with a twisted scarf belt; the main headscarf is worn over the ears, tied at the nape of the neck, a separate black scarf hanging draped below the chin, tucked under the main scarf at each ear. I like the overall effect, which seems to reflect the quiet elegance of the wearer. The husband and wife seem to have an easygoing relationship, clearly one of mutual respect and affection.

When it comes to me having a wash, the teenage daughter, Hasneh, leads me into the house to a huge, tiled bathroom, virtually empty except for a gas stove in the middle of the floor, on which is balanced an urn heating the water. Provided with towels and soap, I am left to my own devices; after which, before emerging into mixed company once more, Hasneh produces a headscarf, proceeding to tie it round my head in order to cover my hair.

In the evening, the whole family plus friends congregate in the main living room, furnished simply with cushions, television and floor-standing heater dominating the middle of the room and blasting out formidable heat. As it is cold outside this is welcome initially, until it is decided that I should be attired in similar garb to the wife. I am duly dressed in a long, brown velvet equivalent, on top of my own clothes, finished off with the head covering as previously described. Everybody laughs and thinks it great that I no longer stick out like a sore thumb, whilst I am just aware of being boiling hot, turning unflatteringly puce.

Although I am used to seeing Moslems praying in public at the set prayer times, I am still taken aback when the whole family, except the two youngest children who carry on watching the television, form two rows, facing the wall against which I am sitting (the direction of Mecca), to make their obeisances of prayer. I have a quiet admiration for their approach. I often feel I am rather too diffident about expressing my own faith in simple ways – but why? After all, respect for other people's beliefs should be a reciprocal thing.

I sleep in the same bedroom as the three older daughters, all of us on mattresses on the floor. In the morning the girls rise early for school, I am slightly more leisurely, breakfasting with the husband and wife. Despite repeated invitations to stay a couple of more nights, I depart with a warm hug from the wife, who presents me with provisions of *magdoos* (the tomato paste-stuffed aubergines) in bread. There is a noticeable simplicity to their lives: largely the same menu for all meals, their home unfettered by material acquisitions.

Cycling along the flat desert road to Damascus, it seems only natural that I recall the most well-known incident that happened along it almost 2,000 years ago. Saul, a high profile persecutor of the up and coming evangelistic Christians, was travelling along the road to Damascus, hot on the trail to arrest a few more of those trouble-making followers. On this particular day though, things take on a different slant for him when he ends up having a rather dramatic encounter with Jesus himself. The result is that Saul executes a complete u-turn, to become a totally dedicated follower of Christ himself and one of His most fervent advocates. It seems that God sometimes uses the most unlikely people to work for him.

Damascus is the oldest, continuously-inhabited city in the world, dating from at least 3,000 BC. As I approach the distant capital, a grey band of pollution hangs above it.

In the walled city, in search of a Christian guesthouse suggested by a local church school, I chance upon someone definitely not of Middle Eastern origin. Tall, adorned with incredibly blonde hair, Ingunn is from

Norway, here for a month to learn Arabic. She is also a journalist, but keeps this under her hat as she would be ejected from the country if known. In response to my inquiry about accommodation, we approach a queue of people at the small, local bakery nearby.

'Does anyone speak English?' she asks.

A teacher at a local school responds with an invitation for us to accompany her home, from where she will phone around for accommodation. On arrival, we are straightaway served with tea and refreshments by the woman's aged mother, followed by convivial chat, before finally a phone call is made; but no answer. Nothing else seems forthcoming and, as the day is getting on, Ingunn and I thank her and leave.

We eventually locate the Christian guesthouse, too expensive for me, and I end up at the place where Ingunn is staying, a small Christian guesthouse – for a quarter of the price. And what a lovely place. From the street, we enter via a narrow covered entrance that opens up into a small courtyard with a fountain and greenery, the sun peering down from above the parapets of the tall-sided building. The rooms for rent are on the ground floor, the private rooms of the owner and family are up steps to a second floor balcony, from which their various living and bedrooms lead off.

My designated room is huge, plenty of room for Raven. I am delighted at the prospect of a couple of days rest and relaxation, as well as to look around this ancient city. One of the other guests is Anna, a young Spanish woman, also learning Arabic and a journalist (shhh). In the evening, I eat the *magdoos* and bread – and, not liking to waste food, the hard-boiled egg I had brought away from the kibbutz four days ago.

The next day is first spent looking for a new tyre, having noticed a small hole in my back one. I berate myself for leaving my spare in Cyprus. But, no problem, after all I deliberately opted for universal 26-inch wheels. I pop along to a nearby cycle shop I had noticed the previous day but there is only a very knobbly off-road tyre on offer. A second shop can muster nothing at all in my size and so I end up with Hobson's choice, the knobbly one. I try handing over the 1500 Syrian Pounds I think is the stated price, only to discover that it costs only 150 – about £2. Would it be prudent to be dubious as to its durability? My belt and braces solution is to patch the hole in my tyre with gaffa tape and continue to use that for the time being, carrying knobbly as a spare.

There is a prolific number of Christian shops around and I take the opportunity to buy Christmas cards to send to family. I am not usually this organised at home; it is after all still only November.

I spend the rest of the day wandering around old Damascus' narrow streets, twisting and turning and going off in all directions. It is easy to become lost, which I do constantly, but it does not seem to matter as eventually I emerge to somewhere that looks vaguely familiar. It is a far cry from my usual discomfort in similar situations.

My guesthouse is off Straight Street, the road in which Saul stayed during the three days when he was blind. It was to here that Ananias came at God's command to restore Saul's sight. He did so with huge trepidation, as Saul's reputation of his violent dislike of Christians had preceded him. By now, though, Saul was a changed man, re-identifying as Paul to emphasise that fact.

Two days after my arrival in Damascus it is my birthday; a memorable day but not quite as I should have wished. It starts off about midnight with me rushing across the courtyard to the loo. This is repeated every twenty minutes, interspersed with throwing up in a bowl by my bedside, during the next eighteen hours. Nice, eh?! My stomach hurts, it is hard even to walk to the bathroom. I feel like death warmed up and I am cold and shivery the whole time, despite thermals, pyjamas, jumper, socks, three wool blankets, two hot water bottles and a gas heater. The last two items are supplied by the wonderful Ingunn and Anna, coupled with a touching concern for my well being. It is the inevitable and unmitigatingly deserved result of the mind-blowingly, idiotic action of eating a 4-day old, unrefrigerated, hard-boiled egg two days previously.

Ingunn lets me use her phone to contact my daughter to cancel the birthday Skype call that had been organised; there is no iota of a possibility of dragging myself off to an internet café. Things could have been worse: I could have been on the road alone rather than in the comfort of this guesthouse with caring people around me.

Instead of leaving as planned on the day after my birthday, I stay the weekend to recuperate. On Sunday, I wander past a church and enter. There is a service in full swing, the congregation singing unaccompanied, led by a woman with a beautiful voice. After leaving this church I pass an Orthodox church and peep inside. It is much less elaborative, decorated with lighter colours than the Catholic church.

As I am about to leave, a woman calls out to me.

'Welcome. Where are you from?'

She offers me a piece of cake, happy to chat in order to practice her English. Syrians are keen to learn languages. Outside the building in which Anna attends her Arabic classes Syrians are always waiting, hoping to persuade someone to give them practice in English because they cannot afford lessons. Anna herself takes additional Arabic lessons in return for Spanish lessons, interestingly from a young Imam who comes covertly to the guesthouse. He is attending without the knowledge either of his superiors or of anyone he knows because it would be prohibited for him to be taught by an unmarried, European woman.

Fashion is a pretty universal commodity, even in the Middle East, apparent in the diversity of *hijab* styles worn by women. The purpose of this garment aims to make women appear as non-provocative, undefined shapes. However, this does not appear to be the case here, some in fact are quite fitted and figure-enhancing. Head coverings also come into their own. Multi-coloured scarves are the new black and worn in imaginative and creative styles, as displayed on rows of mannequin heads filling shop windows. Quite the fashion accessory.

In the middle of the old city is the Ummayad Mosque, the fourth holiest site in Islam. The site has an interesting history. One thousand years ago the Arameans dedicated a temple to the god of lightning; the Romans outdid this with a massive temple to Jupiter; which was in turn replaced in the fourth century with a church dedicated to John the Baptist. About this time, the church became a popular pilgrim destination. Three hundred years later came the Moslem conquest of Damascus. This did not initially affect the use of the church, as both Christians and Moslems shared the same building for their worship. However, the church was destroyed by the Ummayads in the eighth century, a mosque erected instead. It is a magnificent building, unashamedly including recycled columns from Roman temples as well as from the Church of Mary in Antioch. It houses an elaborate shrine to John the Baptist, in which his head is generally accepted to be entombed. Interestingly, he is venerated by Moslems as well as Christians. It seems strange to see John the Baptist in this context.

Before being allowed into the mosque, I am directed to a building adjacent to the entrance to be kitted out in a long grey robe with pointed hood. I remove my shoes and step through the gateway into the vast ornately decorated marble courtyard. The atmosphere is hushed, people sitting reading or chatting, mostly on the highly-polished floor, some on the marble seating. Inside the vast carpeted prayer hall a number of people are praying or reading, whilst a cleaner vacuums the carpets around them. Taking photos is fine. Surprisingly, there is no segregation of the sexes. Partway down the hall is the large rectangular marble shrine with green fenestrated walls, in which is entombed the severed head of John the Baptist. People touch the shrine, kiss it and pray with their foreheads pressed up against the encasement. As with churches, I enjoy the reflective atmosphere that pervades holy buildings.

Ingunn wishes to interview me for an article, hopefully to have it accepted in a Norwegian magazine. Being half Norwegian should be an added selling point. We carry out the interview sitting outside the oldest café in Damascus, near the steps leading up to the Ummayad Mosque; she promises to send me a copy of the finished article.

I need to extend my visa and Ingunn offers to accompany me to the Immigration Office, as she knows the procedure. It takes just forty-five minutes, despite going from pillar to post inside the building and a short excursion up the street to obtain a photocopy of my passport and a stamp. The whole thing is helped enormously by the fact that Ingunn is tall and blonde, so automatically commands attention. In fact, it is fascinating to watch the reactions to her of passersby in the street. Almost without fail they stare intently and unashamedly, not surprising, as she is also extremely beautiful. It is really quite funny to watch as the men drool over her, especially as she seems completely oblivious to it.

Passing a shop with a tempting window display of sticky, sweet pastries and pistachio and sesame biscuits, I stock up with vital energy provisions for my ongoing travel. Fortunately my tummy has forgiven me for upsetting it.

When I go to settle my bill with Giselle, the owner, I realise she has given me a fifty percent discount. I have appreciated the safe sanctuary of this place; maybe this is due in part to Giselle's habit of burning incense in the courtyard most days, 'To cleanse the house and keep it pure.'

The evening before I leave, she invites me into her small, cramped living room to present me with a small parcel.

'Happy Birthday,' she says, as I unwrap the gift of a pair of hooped earrings. I am really touched. I have brought a bookmark with me from my church at home and give this to her.

The postponed birthday Skype conference call goes ahead the evening before I depart. This is one of the times when the wonders of technology are fully appreciated. It is fantastic to talk with my whole family (unfortunately, excluding my son, who is working) and to hear their homely voices. My father sounds well and I receive a harmonious duet of Happy Birthday from him and my stepmother.

Anna and Ingunn are up to see me off at seven on Monday morning, Ingunn walking with me all the way to Bab Touma Square for a final hug and goodbye.

After a circuitous exit from Damascus, I find the old road, Route 5. The road is busy, many lorries, no hard shoulder. I am constantly squeezed off the road each time lorries in both directions overtake each other. Over to my left in the distance is the motorway, almost bereft of traffic – and most likely containing a hard shoulder. It takes a while though to come across a suitable access track in the scrubland to cut across to the motorway and when I do, I have to negotiate the final bit up a very steep, sandy ridge. It is a real struggle to push my heavily-laden bicycle, which I can barely lift an inch off the ground at the best of times, up and over this final obstacle. But it is worth it, to be on a safer road. Until that is, the hard shoulder disappears here too.

And then, who comes along, but the police. However, they are friendly, merely curious, wishing me a happy journey in Syria. Later, when I stop at a roadside tea stop, a chap with 4-year old twins on a motorbike pulls up. We chat, he pays for my teas, I make the twins laugh and we continue our separate trips. I return to the old road, now deserted of traffic and very pleasant. But when it veers uphill away from the motorway, I swap again, relieved that the hard shoulder has reappeared. Whilst pausing for a snack, a lorry pulls over, the two occupants wanting to talk. It feels better to ignore their approaches and they soon go off.

Cycling is hard work today, even the shallowest of hills. It must be the after effect of my recent period of debilitation. My legs feel weak and tired and everything is a slog. I distract myself by viewing my surroundings, such as the interesting skyline of the Kalamoun mountains, a long, smooth ridge, topped with a ruff of pleated rock.

I arrive in Ma'loula, dominated on all sides by towering mountains. At the locked convent of St George's, the reluctant opener-of-the-gate in response to my knocking vaguely indicates another place further into town. Halfway up a mountain I finally arrive at Mar Tekla convent to a smiley welcome from the nuns. I am shown to a large bedroom and given a secure place for my bicycle.

I meet Mother Pelagia, the Mother Superior, who speaks some English and is very kind, presenting me with a gift of incense and a prayer bookmark with a picture of St Tekla. She also gives advice for my route in Syria, suggesting places to stay, including another convent, Mar Yacob. She takes it upon herself to ensure I have plenty of food: four hard-boiled eggs (hopefully I have learnt my lesson), cheese, 'To strengthen my legs,' and enough bread to last me a whole week. She stamps my pilgrim passport, constantly exclaims, 'Oh, my God,' when I talk about my trip and agrees to have a photo taken with me. She persuades me to stay an extra night for the Festival of St Barbara the following evening.

Mar Tekla Convent is a Christian pilgrimage place, but also well visited by Moslems. The story is that of a young girl, in about AD 45, who finds herself in trouble with her family after having accepted the teachings of Jesus from St Paul. Her father disapproves, to put it mildly, sending soldiers to persecute her and kill her, each time God intervening to save her. She escapes, pursued by her persecutors, eventually finding herself in front of a solid mountain with no way over or round it. Kneeling in dismayed prayer, God comes to her rescue again by splitting open the mountain and providing her with a safe passage through which to escape. And a spring now bubbles up here, thus providing her with a constant supply of water. She spends the remainder of her life here in a cave (situated above the convent), preaching Christianity, converting people, blessing them, healing and praying. She is known as the First Martyr, being the first person to be persecuted for her Christian beliefs. The splitting of the mountain is the First Miracle (post-Jesus).

Ma'loula is one of only three villages where Aramaic, the language of Jesus, is still spoken. Visitors come here just to hear it.

Much of the life of the sisters is spent in prayer. At seven in the morning, I hear singing coming over the discreet PA system, which spurs me to rise and go along to the church with its smells and bells. I sit quietly at the back, listening to two sisters alternating in chanting and reading from a book. One of them seems a likely candidate for a speed-reading competition.

The hospitality here includes breakfast (warm vegetable soup and bread), delivered on a tray to my room whilst I am out washing clothes.

Besides prayer and looking after visitors, another responsibility taken on by the sisters is to provide an orphanage here within the convent. Two of the older orphans now show me the Tekla Gap, walking me through the long, narrow passageway to the village on the other side. Then we go up to the church, from which there is a magnificent view of Ma'loula below at the foot of the immediate mountains, offset by the soft backdrop of yet more mountains in the distance. Atop the mountain directly above the convent, overseeing all, is a whopping big monument of Christ with outstretched arms in blessing, similar to one in Rio de Janeira.

In the adjoining room to me are an elderly brother and sister, Hegmet and Hjobod, from Iraq. They have been in Syria for two years, originally coming for a cataract operation for the brother, extending their stay due to complications, including a detached retina. They had left Iraq when the war started, returned but left again. Now though they do not think they will ever return, as their home has been taken over and it would be virtually impossible to regain it. They have very little money; receiving their pension from Baghdad is a hit and miss affair. The brother still needs eye care in Damascus but hotels are too expensive, hence staying here helped out by the sisters. The touching thing is that they express anxiety for me about the dangers of my trip. But I am far more concerned and distressed at their insecure, homeless situation and prospects for their future.

The Festival of St Barbara in the evening is a re-enactment of Tekla's escape, performed by the children of the orphanage and from the village. They are dressed in costumes with faces painted or wearing masks. I think the painted faces are Tekla in disguise (?as Barbara) and the masks are the pursuing persecutors. The masks are interestingly eclectic, ranging from a gorilla to Munch's *The Scream*. After the performance, refreshments of sweet soup, sweet cakes and oranges are served. Sister Agia finishes off the proceedings by telling three jokes. (And, no, I am unable to repeat them but I am sure they were extremely funny.)

Mother Pellagia kindly offers to have my bags driven to the other side of the mountain by the convent's driver the following morning, so that I can go through the gap with my unladen bicycle. She also exhorts all the sisters to pray for me on my trip.

I am duly woken at 7 am by Sister Miriam, hurrying me to be ready with my bags and bicycle downstairs because the driver needs to leave

132

now. No time for breakfast, although I am glad to manage a perfunctory goodbye to the elderly siblings and to wish them well.

As I seem to have so much food in my panniers, I give my sweet pastries as a present to the sisters, which pleases Sister Miriam. She goes off with the driver and my bags in the van whilst Raven and I make our way through the rocky passage. I am so glad to be doing this, if only for the avoidance of cycling down the steep hill to the village, only then to climb steeply up and out. Let the van do all that hard work. We meet at the small convent of Saints Serge and Baccus, continuing on a little further to the crossroads. My panniers off-loaded, Sister Miriam and I embrace each other goodbye.

The road stretches up a hill quiet of traffic, except when a flock of sheep file past, led by a shepherd on his ass and assisted by his dog, who veer away from the road across the hillside. Once over the summit, I do not cycle far before the freezing cold air forces me to stop and layer up. Scrabbling around for anything to keep me warm, ending up only with my shawl, head-buff and short socks, I decide it is probably time to bring my winter wardrobe to the top of the panniers and relegate the summer one to the bottom drawer.

The hill eventually brings me back down to the main highway, where I stop at a café for a cup of tea, delighted to be allowed to sit in front of a gas heater until I start to feel my feet again. The lovely chap serving does not let me pay for my two cups of tea, even offering me some falafels to take away which I reluctantly decline, full to bursting after all the food pressed on me these last couple of days.

In the town of Qara, I stop in the centre to try and figure out which road I should be taking. A chap beckons me over.

'Mar Yacob?'

I look quizzical. He smiles knowingly, and gestures in the direction I should go. Half a mile up the road, I ask a group of local men sitting outside a house drinking coffee, to confirm this is the road to the convent. Sitting with them is a weather-faced walker, backpack on the ground beside him. He is Jan, an elderly Dutch guy, also on his way to the convent, walking, would you believe, from his home in the Netherlands all the way to Jerusalem. And people think I am mad! So far he has been on the road for six months, following a route described by a Belgian guy called Sebastian Somebody-or-other. We walk together the remaining mile to Mar Yacob convent, greeted by Father Josef, then booked in to our cells.

The convent stands on the site of a monastery dating from the sixth century. The original part of the monastery, including the cells and chapel, is interesting, in that the doorways have been built with extremely low head heights. This is nothing to do with the heights of the occupants at the time but with acting as a protective mechanism against assailants who, in their enthusiastic attempts to capture their victims, do not appreciate the height of the exceptionally low headroom, invariably hitting their heads whilst in pursuit and hopefully knocking themselves out.

The monastery was restored and rededicated in the year 2000, to the Order of the Nuns of the Unity of Antioch. It is a small community of about ten members: nuns, a priest, a would-be brother and a handyman. Currently, also, a Belgian doctor, who seems to come each year for a few months as doctor to the community and to the village. He also happens to be the nephew of the Belgian man whose Jerusalem route Jan is following. The aspiring brother is Stefan, here from Paris to meditate on whether taking holy orders is for him, for which he asks for my prayers. He is young (and very handsome) and this will be a momentous decision for him to make.

Jan and I are persuaded by Father Josef to spend a couple of nights here, 'To savour what the place has to offer.'

The community is French speaking, has a vision for unity of religions and for peace, tries to be self-sufficient in produce, sells its own wine and undertakes the skilled and exacting work of restoring icons. One of the sisters shows us around the workshop to view the breathtaking work performed on these beautiful works of sacred art.

Jan and I are invited to participate in the pre-dinner bible study. I follow enough of it to understand that the theme is, 'Unresolved hurts should not be allowed to fester.'

Dinner is delicious homegrown vegetable soup, vegetable 'compôte', spaghetti, yoghurt, ending with St Barbara sweets. The evening is spent in the common room, chatting and singing whilst preparing vegetables for the next day. This is the warmest room in the whole place and there is a reluctance to leave it for the freezer of the bedroom. However, this is mollified by being issued with a hot water bottle as my comforting bedfellow.

Before we leave, Jan and I discuss our respective routes and exchange specific accommodation recommendations. Jan suggests tips on finding somewhere to sleep, particularly away from cities. His tried and tested method is simply to knock on a door and ask to sleep the night, which invariably seems to work for him in all the countries he has so far journeyed.

On the morning of our departure, a group of school children has come to visit the convent, although Abouna Josef takes time out from them to pray a blessing over each of Jan and me before we set off.

We walk together to the village, where our paths separate; a cheery wave from Jan, admiration from me in what he is doing. There cannot be many like him.

I cycle along pleasant quiet roads for a couple of hours in the warm sunshine. Ah, how enjoyable. I look up and see a handsome young man on the road ahead coming towards me. He is walking. He is not a local. He has a backpack. Amazing. We draw level and greet each other. What is even more amazing is that he is Norwegian and for the second time in this country, I greet a fellow traveller in my mother's tongue. He sees the small Norwegian flag on my crossbar and bends down to kiss it. He is Christian, in both name and belief, who began his walk in Austria and is also following *The Sebastian Way* to Jerusalem. When I mention the doctor at Mar Yacob, he becomes duly excited at the prospect of meeting Seb's nephew.

We sit on the ground by the roadside for the next two hours, chatting and sharing lunch, enjoying our unexpected encounter; all the while looked on by an audience of a passing local who squats on his haunches openly staring at us.

Christian became a believer whilst walking the Santiago Camino, since when he has studied and considered carefully the Christian doctrine, leading him to choose the Orthodox tradition as being purer in discipline and truth than the Catholic way. He recommends *The Russian Pilgrim* as a good read. He travels exceedingly lightly with a small pack, plus a violin, with which he has participated in a wedding in Rumania.

Reluctantly, we discover it is time to move on and so for the second time this day I am waving a fond farewell to a Jerusalem walker.

Homs is my destination tonight, hoping for accommodation with Abouna Jacques, as recommended by Jan. I follow signs for the Old City, pleasantly surprised that city cycling is fairly easy, and come across a Syrian Orthodox Church. I ask about Abouna Jacques from a café-owner opposite, who makes a phone call, only to be told that he is away from Homs at the moment. A further call leads me to the place where Jan himself stayed, the Jesuit centre. I agree with his recommendation of the alternative accommodation, even without seeing it, as this is less than desirable. It is dirty, unwelcoming and lacking in hospitality. I could go on looking, I suppose, but it is late enough.

I get a buzz out of seeing Christmas decorations in public, including a Christmas tree in the café opposite the Syrian Orthodox church and the whole side of a large building lit up with the nativity, intermingled with crosses and bells and candles and stars and trumpet-blowing angels. In fact, the photo I take of this, I use for my website Christmas card.

A young couple and their daughter come and sit on the same table as me, whilst they wait for their takeaway in the small crowded burger restaurant, and who subsequently invite me to their home for coffee. Their flat is warm and welcoming and they are obviously proud of the work they have done to make it so. Theirs is a difficult situation: Dara, the wife, has recently qualified as a teacher and as such must accept her first job placement as allocated by the government. This is in a Moslem school, where she is the only Christian and where the staff dislike her and are unkind to her. She is obliged to stay there for at least one year, possibly two, before being allowed to request a move. The school is far away, involving complicated and lengthy travelling each day because they have only one car between them. Her situation is further complicated by her husband, Amer's work as a civil engineer taking him away from home for a month at a time, followed by a week at home, then away again. This is the pattern for the seeable future.

On mentioning my trip, Amer's comment is that they would never have the freedom of choice or the money to do any travelling themselves. I feel a guilt trip coming on, not least at my insensitivity of waxing lyrical about my trip when they have such difficulties on a day-to-day basis. At the same time, I appreciate the advantages of being born British (or European even), for the freedoms this encompasses. My trip is quite an eye-opener as to how different life can be for so many people.

Dara has made Christmas tree decorations and invites me to pick one for myself; I choose a red and gold glittery star. Amer then insists on walking me back to the Jesuit place; as it turns out, a blessing in disguise as being past midnight, the doors to the grounds are locked, although I was not aware of such a curfew. The bell does not work and banging incessantly and calling loudly does nothing to bring anyone to the gate, only for someone elsewhere to lean out of their window, presumably airing their displeasure. Thank God, though, that Amer is with me, as he phones Dara for a phone number for the Jesuit place, from which one of the priests finally comes, reluctantly unlocking the gate for me whilst grumpily pointing to his watch.

The streets and roads are quiet today, the first of a 5-day holiday for the festival of Eid al-Adha (different from the holiday in Cairo which was Eid ul Fitr at the end of Ramadan). I bowl along on the road towards Tartus, wearing five upper layers against the cold December Sunday. I am aiming for another recommendation of Jan's, Mar Elias and turn off towards Safita, thinking I am on the right road, especially after positive confirmation from many locals that this is the way. Unfortunately, it turns out to be incorrect (something lost in translation, perhaps) and I find myself pushing and heaving my bicycle up impossibly steep hills in the middle of nowhere, at last to arrive thankfully at a huge monastery, St George's, at which I request a bed for the night.

'Oh, no, we can't allow that; we are not licenced for visitors to stay over.'

'In that case, where can I stay?'

And because earlier in the conversation I had mentioned Mar Elias, all I receive from them are directions there and an estimated distance of thirty miles. This is neither helpful nor realistic for me to to arrive there before dark. What upsets me is that this Christian brother is quite happy for me to leave the monastery in the knowledge that I have nowhere to stay tonight. I feel strongly that this goes against the grain of normal Middle Eastern hospitality as well as the responsibility of looking after a lone woman. Reluctantly, I have to acknowledge that this place is more concerned with the economics of tourism than with the compassionate needs of pilgrims. Turned away from the monastery, I stand in the car park wondering what to do, tears of frustration, fatigue and disappointment in the end helping me to decide.

On the opposite side of the road is another St George's, a hotel. There are major building works going on and it doesn't even look to be open, but they offer me a room at a reduced rate. It turns out I am the only guest. The inclusive evening meal is a bonus as I am too tired to feel like wandering around looking for somewhere to eat.

I sit on the balcony sipping a refreshing beer in the hot afternoon sun, waiting for the water to heat up for a much-desired shower. On the distant skyline is the Crusader castle, Crac des Chevaliers, to my right, the impressive structure of St George's monastery aglow in the soft sunlight.

The manager of the hotel, Jacques, is a gentle man, working here whilst his family live in Damascus, whom he rarely sees as they do not often visit. Unlike his brother's family who are here now. I am invited for coffee and special holiday sweets, the name of one translating as 'fingers of the bride.'

Despite his personal situation, Jacques performs his work with aplomb, at dinner and breakfast placing the dishes in front of me with a proud, sedate flourish. In the morning, although breakfast is not scheduled until 9 am, he arranges for the chef to prepare mine for seven thirty. I am presented with, 'an English breakfast', of omelette, cheese, tomatoes, cucumber, olives, pitta bread and jam, and tea, arranged so artistically on the plate I hardly like to spoil it.

The owner, George, suggests my route for today but, as this includes retracing my steps up and down the steep hills of yesterday, I prefer my plan of the downhill route to the autostrade, even though I will re-join it one junction before the one at which I came off yesterday. (I really did go wrong yesterday!)

A fine, misty rain accompanies me to the autostrade, reminding me of a typical Bank Holiday Monday in England. When I stop for a drink, a car pulls up beside me. The occupants ask about my trip, hand me a cup of coffee in a plastic cup and off they go, all the while the young woman is filming me.

I come to a clearly signed turn-off for Mar Elias. The last haul up is steep, as the monastery is atop a pretty high hill. There are only two priests here: Père Georgius, who is about sixty (but looks eighty, probably owing to his substantial white beard) and Père Antonius, in his mid thirties. They are Maronnites who live in rural communities in the hill regions of Lebanon and Syria, affiliated to the Roman Catholic Orthodox Church, but with their own traditions. Historically, they have French connections, hence this being Père Georgius preferred language, although with such a dialect that I find it almost impossible to converse with him. Fortunately, Antonius also speaks some English.

I think they are a little surprised to see a woman roll up on a bicycle but they show wonderful hospitality. Antonius brings a carpet and a heater to my room to try and warm it up a bit. (Jan did not mention he'd had the same comforts.) I am given lunch, even though the two pères are themselves fasting as a lead-up to Christmas. They are vegetarians (in keeping with the diet in the Garden of Eden) and currently not eating milk products, although I am not sure why.

I spend the afternoon replacing my back tyre with the one purchased in Damascus. Why so long to perform this simple task? Well, due to the knobbliness of the tyre, I have to raise the height of the mudguard for sufficient clearance. None of my tools, multitool, Leatherman or spanner is useful, but I am able to borrow an adjustable spanner from Antonius' workshop.

The two men lead a pretty solitary life of prayer and working on the land and with the community. I attend evening prayers in the church.

After dinner, we sit in the 'snug' hugging the heater and conversing about faith. The men present me with a prayer card, on one side a picture of Elijah being fed by a raven, on the other a prayer in Arabic. They make suggestions for accommodation in Tartus, even phoning the Bishop's Palace, but there are no rooms at the inn. A convent is mentioned, but in the end we plump for Hotel Daniel, 'a clean establishment'. The owner is a friend of Father Georgius, so will therefore give me a favourable rate, I am assured.

Before leaving in the morning, I place a donation in the church box for my stay. Rain is falling heavily and the two holy men seem quite concerned for me, saying the conditions are too dangerous. When I reply, '*Mallesh* (no matter),' old Father Georgius laughs. He even asks if I need some money. Bless them both.

I cycle through many little villages, often greeted by villagers, one young man requesting me to stop just so that he can practice his English. In Tartus, I find the Hotel Daniel. After depositing my bags in my room and showering, I go in search of a bank, experiencing a déjà-vu moment as I encounter the same difficulty extracting money from cash machines as I had in Israel.

From Tartus, I take the scenic old road, enjoying a brief respite on the seafront in Banyas for a picnic lunch, revelling in the mysterious draw of the sea. Onwards to Latakia and my second puncture. With only a mile or so to the hotel, I do not repair it at the roadside, opting to stop constantly to reinflate the tyre until I reach Hotel Safwan. It takes me three attempts to repair the puncture, eventually figuring out the leak is coming from an incompetent valve, rather than from my incompetent efforts.

I am persuaded by the owner, Mohammed (who is a Tintin fan) to visit Salahuddin Castle – travelling there by local mad-driver minibus and taxi, cheaper and more interesting than sightseeing by coach. Although there has been a castle on this high mountainous ridge since the first millennium BC, the current restored remains are from twelfth-century Crusader days, obtaining its name following victory by the Muslim leader, Salahuddin.

Back from the crusades and relaxing on the hotel balcony, an elderly Algerian chap working in the hotel brings an array of food to share with me, prepared by Mohammed's grandmother: kibbeh, savoury rice, pickles, pitta bread, cake and cold custard. Later, I find an internet café and enjoy a brief email exchange with my daughter, send introductory emails to friends of friends in Dubai and Abu Dhabi and search for suitable passenger freighter ship routes across the Pacific Ocean.

I eat in a Dixy Chicken restaurant, a table for one being set up for me near the owner's desk from where he and his brother chat to me. Mohammed, the owner, phones his 16-year-old daughter, who duly comes to talk with me using excellent English. She and her friends all prefer to speak English rather than Arabic, and she plans to study film directing at university in England in a couple of years' time.

The road from Latakia is flanked by orange groves and as I cycle towards a roadside stall, the young man watching me, readies himself with three oranges in his hands, placing them into my basket as I am about to go by. I stop.

'How much?'

He smiles and shrugs.

'No money.'

'*Shoukran katir.* Thank you very much.'

The road starts to climb; a strong headwind has developed, forcing me to dismount frequently and push. I take advantage of the plethora of fortifying tea stops and clay-oven pizza stalls along the way.

At the border town of Kassab, I decide to have a last night in Syria. I had thought the town was not far away, but after toiling up a steep hill, hot and bothered, and no sign of one, I take a chance that the distant church with a walled garden at the end of a long downhill lane will be able to offer me a night's accommodation. But it is firmly locked up with no sign of life and I turn to plod back up the hill. However, now walking purposefully towards me, accompanied by a collection of young children, is a middle-aged woman wanting to know if she can help. It turns out the church is only open in the summer for courses.

The woman, Foufou, invites me to stay with her and her husband, Mohammed. (I have now come to the conclusion that you cannot go very wrong in the Middle East if you refer to most men as Mohammed.) The accompanying band of youngsters is made up of their five grandchildren. There are two families, plus elderly mother, visiting from Latakia for the week, returning to their homes this afternoon. It does not seem to matter to them that I am interrupting this family get together for the holidays.

Foufou also has a house in Latakia, which is used in the winter months. In summer, the couple tend to live here in Kassab, but in a small 2-room cottage in the grounds, renting out their main house and an apartment to tourists. Much of Kassab does the same.

We are in apple region and Foufou owns an orchard, the harvest mainly sold in Aleppo. Previously, their apples also went to Damascus, Iraq and Egypt.

During the evening I am able to wash my clothes, we get by with the sparse English and sparser Arabic and we watch most of 'Taxi' on the TV before a powercut announces its premature end.

In the morning, up and breakfasted, I am provided with takeaway sandwiches, Eid sweets and a small bag of apples. I thank them with the baklava I had purchased the previous day. As I leave this delightful couple they extend further open-ended hospitality.

'If ever you are back in Syria, you must come and see us.'

The border takes only a few minutes to reach, I pay my exit tax of $13 and pass under the big blue bilingual overhead exit sign, the English reading,

'Good by. Thanks to your visit.

*　　*　　*

Turkey

13 – 29 December 2008

Antakya, Antep, Gaziantep, Bircek, Şanliurfa, Hilvan,
Diyarbakir, Batman, Bitlis, Erçis, Van

Just beyond the Syrian exit sign is its co-ordinating blue counterpart announcing Türkiye. I pay my entry tax of $20, pass through the barrier to a cheery, 'Welcome to Turkey,' from the security guard.

I cycle along excitedly, immediately struck by the greenness of the landscape, as I straightaway pass through fir woods filled with the sounds of running water from numerous small rivers.

At the bottom of a hill is a crossroads, two vehicles parked by the side of the road and a group of men standing around, two wearing long, dark coats and a couple holding guns. Interesting.

I am flagged down, ordered by one of the long coats to show my passport. I demand first to see some ID from him. Well, it looks official enough, although as it is in Turkish it could be his bus pass for all I know. I show mine in return (which equally could be my bus pass for all he knew). Everyone now content, off I go.

The first town, Yayladagi, is where Jan had stayed in the school house. I try to withdraw money, for the third time failing with my bank cards, only succeeding with my cash passport.

The road climbs progressively higher and out of the protection of the forest. Violent winds blowing from all directions force me to dismount frequently and walk. Reasonable progress is further inhibited by a newly applied top dressing of large stones on the road that is not conducive to easy cycling. As I climb higher, the landscape becomes increasingly exposed and barren and I apply as many layers as I can muster against the cold conditions.

A car stops and two young couples ask if they can help in any way. I cannot really see how they can, although this friendly gesture puts me more at my ease.

The ascent is endless, my progress excruciatingly slow, the dangers of exposure starting to fill my thoughts.

Eventually of course what goes up must eventually reach the top. But even then the subsequent descent requires hard pedalling – the ultimate injustice for any laden cyclist. Happily though, the surface changes partway down to a new, silky-smooth tarmac, treating me to an enjoyable freewheel the remainder of the way to Antakya.

I stay at the same Catholic Church accommodation as Jan, Father Dominic welcoming me into the pretty courtyard and showing me up the outside staircase to my clean and comfortable room – with heater.

Antakya is the ancient city of Antioch, significant in the Christian world as housing possibly the oldest Christian church building, St Peter's Grotto or Cave Church of St Peter, the base for Paul's missionary journeys. Antioch is also where followers of Jesus were first referred to as Christians.

I visit the grotto, a simple room carved into the mountain, in the middle of which stands a marble altar. The cave walls and floor display remnants of frescoes and mosaics. From the rear of the church an escape tunnel runs into the mountain for when it was necessary to flee persistent persecutors.

There is another visitor in the Church, an Australian, a Jehovah's Witness. We go for a coffee and chat about the concept of the Trinity, on which our views differ, and I gather useful travel information. Lindsey has travelled across Turkey from Iran, where he spent three and a half weeks, and reports snow along the route I am now following.

I buy an adjustable spanner from a second-hand tools shop, despite the weight, reckoning it to be a useful addition to my toolkit.

At the early evening service in the Catholic church there is a visiting priest from Syria and Father Dominic welcomes both of us to the congregation. From the couple of words I pick up, I gather he is describing my route as someone who has cycled here from England by way of Jerusalem. I am then asked to stand and give my name.

Partly because it is Sunday and partly because I feel in need of a little more than the basics, I choose a slightly smarter restaurant than is my habit. It is quiet and relaxing, with a cloth tablecloth, shining cutlery and sparkling glasses. My lamb kebabs are served with chips and vegetables (causing 'nouvelle cuisine' to spring to mind: one sprout, artistically spliced in half, complemented by a couple of exquisitely-placed beans). Each course is served with such solemn ceremony that it is really quite comical, but also quite sweet.

The days are now increasingly cold, a reasonable level of warmth appearing only between eleven thirty and three. When I arrive mid afternoon in the small town of Hassa I propose to stop here as there should be a church and a hotel from which to choose tonight's accommodation. However, on arrival I am told this is not the case.

'Try ten kilometres up the road,' someone suggests.

I do but this produces the same negative result. Unfortunately, I think my pronunciation might be the culprit, as, back in Hassa, I might have been thought to say 'Kilisi' (the name of this town), rather than '*kalisé*' (church). And that in fact, here in Kilisi, they tell me there is a church and hotel way back in Hassa. Bother.

Be that as it may, all I know is that it will be dark in an hour and I am in a town which does not seem particularly welcoming or helpful. I ask in the street for *anywhere* to stay (by now I am not being overly picky). I try a mosque, and ask to stay in a restaurant, all responses beginning and ending in, 'No.'

The unexpected disinterest and unhelpfulness is anathema to my experiences to date and to Jan's stories of the friendliness of the Turks. I cycle frantically out of town along an empty road, in the hope of finding somewhere soon. After a few miles, houses appear and a filling station, at which I stop, gesturing to the man inside for a place to sleep. He indicates the adjacent house and, on knocking and repeating my request, I am allowed to put up my tent in their garden. The family (parents and two teenage daughters) invite me into the cosy warmth of their home for a cup of tea. By this time I must seem harmless to them as I end up eating dinner with them.

The meal is a thin stew served with bulghur and pitta bread. The wife, Gülfüroz, ladels the stew into bowls, deliberately picking out the majority of chunky bits for me. I peer politely at what is about to go into my mouth, realising, 'Oh yes, it's stomach lining. Yum.'

I try as best I can to show appreciation for her generosity, whilst politely attempting to decline extra helpings.

There is no running water in the house, only a standpipe outside in the freezing cold, there to wash in freezing cold water and collect water for cooking. Nearby is an outhouse toilet. The family live in a two-room (not two-*bed*room) house, the parents sleeping on a mattress in the second room, (the kitchen area), the children and I sleeping in our clothes on a mattress and settee in the living room. And yet, despite their poverty, this kindly family has taken me in with no fuss and a great deal of generosity.

The girls, Öznur and Emine, show me their English workbooks, but, despite being labelled as grade 7 and 8 English, neither of them have any conversational English at all. I am not surprised when I see the exercises they are meant to do, presented in a dry, complicated, non-functional format. I myself find them difficult to understand and would not impart any motivation or interest in me to learn this alien language.

Early next morning I pack away my frost-rigid tent, departing after breakfast at the same time as the children leave for school.

My friendly encounters continue when a car pulls over ahead of me and stops. A middle-aged woman and her son emerge to offer me a bed for the night. The mother appears extremely concerned about me cycling and, after the son gives me his card indicating to phone him if I should like to stay (although how I would convey this over the phone I have no idea, as he has about two words of English), the mother kisses me warmly many times before getting back into the car and continuing.

Early afternoon and only halfway up a 20-mile hill with still thirty-five miles to the next town, even my optimism realises it is pushing the bounds of possibility to arrive before dark. Therefore, when a passing pick-up reverses back to me and offers a lift, I accept; the heater belting forth is a blissful bonus. Any twinges of guilt at accepting a lift are talked down by the justification that this is my trip and who's to say what the 'rules' are but me. The driver drops me by a 5-star hotel in Gaziantep, from where I obtain directions to the Hotel Yunis, *a Lonely Planet*-listed hotel, to which I arrive with the aid of several passersby taking it in turns to walk with me.

I spend two nights here, recovering from feelings of fatigue rather than it being a particularly significant or interesting place for sightseeing. I manage to procure a SIM card, despite the language barrier putting up quite a fight, and I check out cycle shops for waterproof shoes, for which I have been on the lookout since Syria. I am no more successful here than elsewhere, but take the opportunity to purchase a rare 26-inch tyre.

I receive an email from a reporter in Dubai saying he has been commissioned by *The National* (apparently, the main English-speaking newspaper in the Middle East) to write an article on me. If I am happy for this to go ahead, it will include him meeting me when I arrive in the Emirates and cycling with me a short way.

I make sure to wrap up warmly these mornings. My feet are swathed in a series of layers: knee-high cotton socks, plastic bags, shorter wool socks, sandals. The plastic bags are very effective against the wind, keeping my feet warm the whole day. I am still wearing my lightweight trousers for cycling, with the option to add thermals when necessary.

The cycling is speedy along an excellent hard shoulder. Lunch is processed cheese with flatbread, sticky baklava and chocolates. By the end of the morning I have covered the forty miles to today's destination, Birçek. There is a choice of two hotels. For once I do not go for the absolute cheapest, warned by the locals that it really is not a place I should like to stay in. I take the opportunity of the early stop to replace my knobbly back tyre with the new one.

I am hungry this evening, filling myself up on a banquet of chicken and lamb kebabs, salad, yoghurt, another salad, bread, washed down by Pepsi, water, teas (it is a strict Moslem-run establishment, hence no alcohol). Not many people speak English but I do manage a bit of a conversation with Usman, one of the waiters. He lives and works here whilst his wife lives in London; they have not seen each other for eight months. They have a child and are expecting a second; but I don't know why their situation is as it is.

The next day I send a text my daughter.

'Happy Birthday!'

At the end of today, staying in a cold, cheerless hotel in the town of Şanliurfa, I investigate a wobble in my back wheel and a creaking noise in my bicycle headset (which I have recently learned is the name of the part that connects the handlebars to the frame). It would seem precautionary to sort these before continuing, hence an impromptu rest day.

I print off headset instructions from the bicycle manual that I have on a memory stick and have a go at adjusting it. As for the wobble, I find a car tyre shop to look at it, to be informed that the new tyre is twisted and therefore no good. Fortunately, I have not thrown away the knobbly one, which is now re-instated. The man in the tyre shop tries to persuade me that he should remove the blue tape on the inner rim of my wheel as it is uneven and would cause the tyre to pop out. Instinctively, I feel pretty convinced that this not the right thing to do, but have to be persistent in insisting he leave it in place (when mentioned later to my cycle chap back home, my instincts now are reassuringly correct).

Şanliurfa is considered to be the ancient city of Ur, the birthplace of Abraham. In Primary School, we learned how to remember the name of the town – simply by thinking, 'Er, what is the name?' Dominating the town is a towering rock on which stands a 3,500-year old castle and two enormous columns rising imperiously towards the sky.

A park at the foot of the rock is laid out with a gentle stream flowing into a lake, groups of families and young people picnic-ing and chatting together in the grounds. An adjacent bustling souk lures customers in with their attractive displays of goods: neat rows of cyclindrical sacks of richly-coloured spices heaped high into conical mounds, bunches of dried whole spices strung from hooks on the frame above the stall.

I pause at one stall to look at wonderful fabrics, the owner insisting I take his photo, once, twice, three times, each with more of his friends included. He is wearing the traditional low-crotch baggy trousers, causing me to wonder if this is how the fashion began in UK with young lads wearing their trousers with a dropped crotch (sounds painful). The man gives me his address, so that I can post the photos to him.

As I leave the hotel in the morning, the receptionist, up until now not particularly helpful, seems to have changed his tune; he keeps saying something to me followed by thumbs up and a smile.

A little way up the road, my handlebars are not doing what they should be doing, maybe in protest at my attempts to adjust them yesterday. I stop, rummage for the instructions, untighten something, before tightening something else, remembering to retighten the first thing I untightened; and resume cycling. It seems to have done the trick.

Later, my tyre becomes soft and when I unscrew the dust cap which turns out to be cross-threaded, the whole valve comes out. Pumping up from zero pressure takes a while but, looking on the bright side, it has definitely warmed me up. A little further on and the tyre is quite flat. It is just one of those days. I pull in behind the building of a filling station, unload and upturn the bicycle. Again the whole valve comes out. Thinking (hoping) that this is the cause of the flat, I replace it with a different valve, re-pump the tyre, resume cycling; this time the tyre remains at pressure.

At my first tea stop, I discover the hotel key in my pocket. Attached to it is an oversized fob, designed solely to prevent such an occurrence. The manager of the restaurant, who has come over to chat to me, says he knows the hotel and will return it.

At my second tea stop, the manager makes a phone call.

'You can stay in the Teachers' House in the next town,' he says.

The whole of this area is a windswept, barren landscape. I am wrapped up as much as possible, only my eyes peering out between my protective buff and cosy ski hat. When I stop for a swig of icy water and an energy baklava, two young men on a motorbike pull over and stop just ahead. The bike is very colourful, the petrol tank covered in a red patterned fabric, edged with bright yellow fringing. They dismount and come over to me, asking for some water and quite happy to pose whilst I take their photo.

The Teachers' House in Hilvan is fairly easy to find, turning out to also be the social centre for the local teachers. This afternoon there are about a dozen men playing cards and some other game. Nobody is expecting me, none of them speak English and none of them take any interest in my presence. Floundering a little as to what my next move should be (knowing only that it definitely does not include going voluntarily back outside into the cold), one of the young teachers decides to take me under his wing. He brings me tea after tea to where I am sitting at a table, passing the time with Sudoku and trying hard to warm up by the radiator.

After a while, I am shown upstairs to a room, in which there are three beds and a television, with one occupant, Sultane, a young student teacher who speaks a little English. We chat and end up ordering a takeaway together, when she refuses point blank to accept my contribution towards paying for it. I am somewhat embarrassed, after all she is on student wages. Later, we pop over the road to a café for a drink; even paying for her coffee is thwarted when the young guy serving insists on paying for us. As we part in the morning, Sultane gives me a little pink angel hair band as a reminder of her. I reciprocate with a little pottery vase given to me by a taxi driver in Latakia.

At her suggestion, I accompany Sultane to the school to meet the head teacher. He speaks no English but eventually brings the English teacher, Hande, along to his office, who invites me to visit one of the English classes. The 14-year olds ask me questions about my trip,

148

translated by Hande, but, when then they are obliged to ask questions directly to me in English, the result is rather unimaginative.

'What is your name?'

'What is your father's name?'

'What is your husband's name?'

'What is your brother's name?

Though they do manage to change tack – marginally.

'How old are you?'

'How old is your father?'

'How old is . . . ?'

Is this universal? Were my children's foreign language levels the same and I have forgotten? I visit three more English classes, in one of them being entertained by four young lads who ask to come out in front of the class and perform a little dance for me. Most of the children are wrapped up in their coats, so maybe this also gives the boys a chance to warm up.

At the end of the morning, I gladly accept Hande's invitation to stay the night in her flat. It is comfortable, cosy and warm. We talk about the division in Turkey of west and east, clearly defined as the new and the old, the modern and the traditional, developed and underdeveloped. Hande comes from modern Izmir, whereas her fiancé, a Turkish language teacher also at the school, hails from the backwaters of Hilvan, whose family is Kurdish.

Hande is in a difficult situation as her parents do not approve of the engagement, her father going so far as to say that he will never speak to her again if she goes ahead. It is an unhappy dilemma; she is determined not to give up her fiancé, but at the same time, she does not want to cause a rift with her parents. She and her fiancé have therefore agreed that they will not marry until her father has changed his mind, which they are hoping is just a matter of time. It is interesting that it should be the enlightened western thinker that comes out with such traditional attitudes.

Hande and I stay in the warmth of her flat for the afternoon, she prepares a meal, anxious that I should like what she produces. In the evening, her fiancé comes by and we go off to the head teacher's home along with a couple of other teachers, for tea, fruit and nuts and conversation about the differences in education here and in UK.

In the morning, a substantial breakfast incloudes hard-boiled egg, spicy sausage slices on toast, olives, mince, goat's cheese, tomatoes,

Hande's mother's homemade jam (apricot & strawberry or cherry) and tea. There is no rain today, the weather merely overcast and misty. Having been so cold on previous days, I now sport thermal leggings and long-sleeved, merino wool base layers, thin fleece and down jacket. It is quickly obvious that this latter layer is far too effective and totally inappropriate when cycling for I become soaking wet inside which, as well as being disgustingly uncomfortable, means I become chilled when I subsequently remove the jacket in a café.

It is 23rd December and I need to be sure of Skype access the following day for my son's birthday and to speak to my children before they travel away for Christmas. I make a sensible decision. In Siverak, still with fifty plus miles to Diyarbakir (and internet), I go to the bus terminal and buy a ticket for the early afternoon bus. I have an hour to wait and head for the kebab stall in the station, manned by a really friendly Turkish man, decked out in black wool trousers and brown sleeveless jerkin over a jumper, complete with thick, droopy moustache and a traditional round wool hat. He insists I come round to his side of the counter and sit next to the electric fire, at the same time placing a mug of warming tea in my hands. He tells me he has seven wives and twenty children, one of whom, a young lad, is helping him today.

The bus journey is uneventful and we arrive at Diyarbakir bus station, from there a 5-mile ride into town and a hotel, found without too much difficulty. This is where I shall be spending my first Christmas on the trip. It is clean and comfortable enough and, most importantly, warm, even the bathroom. There is just enough room for my bicycle, which is carefully lugged up the four flights of stairs by Mohammed, who later escorts me, 'For your safety,' up the road to a restaurant. Before I go I hang up my Christmas decorations: the homemade glittery star, carried delicately all the way from Homs, the little pink angel hairband from Hilvan and a hopeful red sack for Santa.

On my return from the restaurant, a young Kurdish guy starts talking to me in the street just outside the hotel, introducing himself as a guide, who would like to practice his English, in exchange for which he would be happy to show me around the sights of Diyarbakir the following day.

The following morning, the first thing I do on waking is send a text to my son, 'Happy Birthday!' He is twenty.

I meet the Kurdish guy in the foyer of the hotel at 11 am, where he is vouched for by the hotel staff before we head off into town. We visit churches and mosques as well as various shops, which turn out to be owned either by members of his family (uncle's carpet shop) or friends (jewellery shop). Naturally, there are attempts to persuade me to buy something which, determinedly, I do not, but I enjoy learning about carpets and watching the jewellery chap create a necklace in jade, jasper and moonstone.

As I am shown around, a particular aspect of Diyarbakir impresses itself on me. Firstly, the jeweller's brother shows me the Turkish Bible he likes to read, even though he is a Moslem. Then, I cannot fail to notice in the shops crucifixes and paintings of Jesus. And now I discover that Jews, Christians, Moslems, Turks and Kurds live and work harmoniously together, mutually respecting any differences of belief and culture.

Although not everything is elyssian. A couple of days previously a car had been found at a military airport containing seventy pounds of explosives and a cache of Kalashnikovs. Also, the Kurds are still fighting for their own identity to be restored. My guide does not know exactly how old he is (he thinks about thirty) because his parents had not registered him at birth as, being Kurds, they did not want him to have Turkish ID.

In the evening we visit his uncle's tea shop, located in an old striped pasha building with lofty domed ceiling, rugs and cushions on the floor and richly-coloured wall hangings. Coffee and tea is served, as is a hubble-bubble (smoking nothing more potent than apple wood).

And so I awake on Christmas morn, alone in a hotel room far away from home and in a strange land. It is still early, barely 6 am, but I am wide awake in childish anticipation of the reward for being good throughout the year. To the accompaniment of *The Messiah* belting away in my ipod ears, I 'find' the presents left by the jolly bearded one in my stocking: a pair of individually-toed Bassett Allsorts knee-high socks, and a diary. I deck myself out in my Christmas tree earrings, brought from home, and partake of a festive breakfast of bread, jam, satsumas and coke, being all that I have in my store of provisions. Then off to St Mary the Virgin Syrian Orthodox Church and to a service so alien in its format that I am unable to glean any Christmas spirit from it at all and come away quite deflated.

The highlight of the day is when I Skype, first my children, then my brothers; unfortunately unable to speak to my father because of his temperamental internet line. Seeing and talking to Jessica and Daniel on this Christmas morning fills me with enough joy to overcome, at least for this brief moment, the inevitable loneliness of not being with them physically.

On Christmas afternoon, I find myself cleaning my bicycle and raising further the height of the rear mudguard against which the tyre has started rubbing. I then meet up again with my guide for a further short tour of the city. We return to the hotel at about 5 pm, already dark. Suddenly, behind us, a noise of firecrackers explodes. Except that they are not. They are gunshots, coming from real guns and being shot by the dark shadows running in and out of the cars just a hundred yards away from us.

The strange thing is I am not frightened; probably because of the calmness of my guide telling me, 'Oh, yes, there are rival gangs in the town that occasionally have moments of shooting at each other.'

What was that about a model city for harmonious living?

On Boxing Day morning, I take the old road out of town, silently cycling along in the frozen stillness of the early morning, a freezing mist hanging above the river, a speckled frost on the iron-hard ground. When I stop mid morning at a filling station for a warming couple of teas, one of a group of lorry drivers offers to buy me lunch. The others remain on the adjacent table, later gathering around ours when they see my camera come out. I am offered a lift to Batman, 'Because it is too cold for you to be cycling and there is snow on the road ahead.' I decline and bowl along at a cracking pace, enjoying the ride, whilst recalling the friendliness of the group.

I arrive in Batman by two in the afternoon, feeling pretty satisfied, both by having covered the sixty-three miles at an average speed of 11.3 mph and by resisting being persuaded to stop cycling because of potential adverse weather conditions. I am not saying I am a stormtrooper, pushing on regardless of the severity and discomfort involved, but neither am I easily dissuaded from doing what I feel confident is the right thing for me.

I leave Batman in thick, freezing fog, disconcerted to see that my back light is not working. I am constantly wary of dogs, particularly in Turkey, having heard reports of their hugeness, as well as of many ferocious encounters with the beasts that often travel around in wild packs. To date, I have encountered just a few dogs, most ignoring me, although some have a mind to bark and advance, only to keep their distance as soon as I look at them. This surprises me greatly; surely they can smell my fear?

Faced now with two massive creatures standing guard outside a police station, first growling, then barking loudly in my direction, I decide it is best not to move. Fortunately, a policeman appears, speaking French, assuring me that they just like the sound of their own voices, that their bark is worse than their bite. I am invited into the cosy warm office for tea, half a dozen officers also preferring the comfort of tea and toast to the icy chill outside. When I come to say goodbye, I proffer my hand to the French-speaker, which he declines, politely prefacing it with, '*Excusez-moi.*' It reminds me of the Iranian consul in Amman.

As the morning advances, the sun melts away the freezing fog, the warm rays cheering me up no end. Passing through a small village, I am beckoned over for tea by a group of a dozen men, sitting on plastic chairs on a piece of scrubland in the sheltered suntrap beside a concrete wall. Other men migrate towards us, curiosity getting the better of them. One of them has a few words of English. I kick myself for not having a Turkish translation of my introductory letter.

I stay for about half an hour, continuing on to a town large enough to be confident I should find accommodation, but come away with nothing. I now have twenty miles to go to the next place for a possible bed for the night. I have given up the idea of camping for the time being. It is far too cold and I have drawn the line between good character-building stuff and downright masochism.

I am offered a lift in an orange minibus, which flies a small green flag. They are Hajj pilgrims returning from Mecca to Uzbekistan. They are also blindingly optimistic in their kind offer for, when I peek inside, the interior has been converted into a bunk bed dormitory, sardining about ten people. They are touchingly insistent but, with the best will in the world, there is no way Raven, baggage and I are going to squash inside.

Not long later, a second offer comes my way in the form of a white van, but this too is fully-loaded with boxes. The third offer comes more realistically from a large lorry. The middle-aged Syrian driver jumps down from the lofty heights and lifts my bicycle up into the cabin; his trousers unfortunately becoming smeared with oil from the chain.

His name is Mahmoud, lives in Antakya and is currently in a convoy of four lorries on its way to the Iranian border. I had planned to try and find a hotel in Baykan and stay overnight, but the weather conditions have deteriorated so much that I remain in the lorry to continue to a larger town.

And it is a brilliant decision as it turns out. Within a few miles we come across a 12-mile stretch of road that has been destroyed by the Kurdish PKK. A sea of freezing mud and potholes, the thought of cycling through it mind-bogglingly abhorrent. Apparently, the PKK is very active in this region. Nonchalantly, Mahmoud points out the two gunslinging men at the roadside as being PKK terrorists. He says I should not be cycling in this area, it is far too dangerous and is why he offered me a lift. Some years ago his lorry was stopped, he was ordered to get out and, when there was nothing for the men to take, they shot him in his ankle out of sheer frustration.

A second reason for being glad to continue in the lorry is that it suddenly starts to snow thickly. I am very thankful Mahmoud came along when he did.

We arrive in Bitlis where I expect to be looking for a hotel but, having pulled up at a truckers' stop where we make our way into the restaurant, slipping and sliding on the snowy, icy surface, Mahmoud says I can sleep in the lorry; he has bunk berths so there is no problem. He is very kind and I do not feel uncomfortable that his motives are anything but well meaning and honourable.

We put my bicycle in the assured safety of a back room in the restaurant, to free up some space in the cabin. In the morning, Mahmoud is up early and, before I know it, we are set to go on our way. He says he has put my bicycle in the back. Four hours later we stop for breakfast – and I see where my poor Raven has ended up! She is not *in* the lorry, but under it, in the place where a second spare tyre would go. She is filthy with dirt and slush. And what about my Brooks? I clean and dry the leather saddle and put on the cover but all in all, she looks a sorry sight.

One of the four lorries has developed a problem, which is still not fixed after two hours. Mahmoud's lorry also needs something looked at. At which point one of the drivers decides to continue on his own. With weather conditions as they are, I am disinclined to follow suit and so hang around, admiring the scenery. It is stunningly beautiful for we are standing on the snow-covered banks of huge Lake Van, rays of winter sun thrusting through the grey clouds to shine spotlights onto the cold watery expanse.

A bus load of Hajj pilgrims come to the water's edge and proceed to remove their socks (those who have them) and shoes, to wash themselves in the icy waters, part of the ritual of their prayers.

A couple of hours later and with the first lorry still going nowhere, the plan now is for the two working ones to continue to a town, pick up the requisite part to be brought back by Mahmoud by taxi. But, the best-laid plans . . . after about ten miles, our lorry starts slowing . . . slowing . . . stop. The revs just die away. After fixing it and driving on for barely a couple of miles, the same thing happens. This time Mahmoud phones a friend, who eventually arrives with a replacement part, but this does not solve the problem. In the end, we take the sole surviving lorry to a town, have a meal and buy some beers and pistachios, before returning to park next to the stranded lorry, drink the beers and nibble the nuts, and sleep in the good lorry, the heater on throughout the night.

In the morning, the battery is flat.

No one is now going anywhere. I hear the two men mention me and realise that I am an encumbrance, as well as it being pointless for me to remain with them. But first I am bursting for a pee and wonder how to do this, with thick snow on the verges and no cover in sight. I go to the back of the lorries, check there are no cars on the horizon and squat down. I can now see a couple of cars far away and so, no panic, enough time to finish. But, I had not anticipated such a volume inside me. I watch the cars advancing at speed and the thought of the embarrassment and indignity of a two-car audience in my current position causes me, as they are coming up the hill now in front of me, to hoist up my trousers, realising with equal embarrassment that I am peeing in my pants. Now is definitely the time for a parting of the ways. I retrieve my panniers and basket from the cabin of the invalid vehicle, unloose Raven from the spare wheel shelf, cleaning her up as best I can, and load her up; profusely thank my companions and depart.

Initially, the road is clear, but this soon changes to a thick and slippery covering of snow and ice, so that it is impossible to do anything but try and stay upright in the car tyre tracks. I am obliged to stop frequently each time a vehicle comes along, pull over to the side and wait for it to pass. It is only five miles to the first town, Erçis, but that is far enough in these conditions, especially when I have to resort to walking.

I am looking for a bus station but am informed by a young shop owner that there are no buses to Dogubayazit (at the Iranian boder) and none today to Van either. He offers to give me a lift which I gladly accept and we pile into his car. On the way out of the town he stops at a municipal building and comes out holding a piece of paper; maybe some kind of permission to go to Van.

After a while, I become uneasy with his behaviour, increasingly so when we stop for something to eat and he makes a phone call, a friend comes by soon after and joins us in the car for the rest of the way. On the outskirts of Van, it finally dawns on me what his intentions are; for some reason, he thinks he (or they?) are going to come with me to whatever hotel room I book into and watch me take a shower! Oh yuk! I cannot believe this is what they have been planning. And I cannot believe that I allowed myself to be entrapped in this way. I order them to stop the car, grab everything out of it, angry with their disgusting behaviour and with my naïvety. When he demands \$30 for bringing me, I furiously throw TYL20 (about £5) at him and they drive off. I realise I had become afraid whilst in the car, as I had been seated in between the two men, making myself vulnerable. I feel sullied and very upset.

My mood is not helped by the cold wet grey weather, a direct reflection of my impression of the town, and in keeping with how I now feel. It is a vicious circle. The next morning, deep snow in the streets and snowing steadily, I slip down to a tourist agency. Heartily glad that they speak English, I ask about the available options for my ongoing travel. They are unable to get through by phone to the train station which means I must go in person. The only buses running are stud-tyred minibuses, but even these slip slide along the road. The one I catch has difficulty making its way to the train station, which is a couple of miles away on the outskirts of town. I wonder how on earth I shall manage to cycle here.

In the end, this challenge is avoided: the 7 pm train is not guaranteed to run on time, if at all, and, anyway, 'You cannot take any baggage on board the train.'

'Why on earth not?!'

'Border control.'

'Uh?'

'But the train in two days' time; then you can take baggage.'

'?'

And so I trudge through the snow to the bus depot, but there are no large buses running to Iran, only minibuses. Thankfully, there is an Iranian medical student who speaks English and booked onto a minibus travelling to the southern border of Iran at Orumiyeh. I book five seats, four of them for Raven. The minibus goes via the hotel to pick up my bicycle and bags, then off to the bus station, to wait an hour for the departure time.

The scenic route takes us up, over, down and up mountains, often with a sheer drop on one or other side of the road. The conditions are pretty dicey; one place in particular causing us to skid badly out of control, when all I am aware of is the precipitous edge of the road speeding towards us, an involuntary exclamation, 'Oh, my God!' issuing from my lips. The driver regains control, the passengers visibly calm down, my heart continues to pound for a while longer.

By the time we reach the police check, forty miles short of the border, it is dark. We continue to the first border and a change of vehicle. Half-an-hour later, we arrive at the border proper and into Turkish passport control. The queue is slow. A Korean reporter is refused exit from Turkey, as he has no Iranian visa (having expected to obtain it here) and so must go all the way back to Ankerra to acquire one. I go through with no problem, but the lovely young medical student, who has been travelling for seventy hours from western Turkey to spend a couple of weeks with his family in Orumiyeh, is refused exit because there is some problem with his passport. His student card is not accepted, even though it has been in the past. His father and a friend are on the other side of passport control and, although the tired young man can see them and talk to them, the Turkish border officials are adamantly refusing to let him through. He says he will have to go to Erzerum, four hundred and fifty miles away, to sort it. I say a sad farewell to him, wishing him all the best, as I enter Iran.

*　　*　　*

Iran

30 December 2008 – 23 January 2009

*Orumiyeh, Esfehan, Shahreza, Saad Sadat, Persepolis,
Shiraz, Mourdak, Delvar, Kabghain, Dayyar, Asaleyeh,
Bandar-e-Bastanu, Chiruyeh, Kish, Moallem, Bandar Abbas*

Iran was always on my itinerary. In the past, not all travellers have
been able to obtain visas for a visit to be an option in the first place,
especially, it seems, entering at a land border (as opposed to flying in).
Even today, although it is currently possible to obtain a 15-day visa on
entry, these are only available at airports. Before setting out on my trip,
there was no certainty that I would be successful in my own application.
Therefore, that I was successful and that I am actually in Iran, is very
satisfying.

Secondly, one generally hears only negative things about Iran, at least
in the western press. I want to dispel those misconceptions, for surely
that is what they must be, because there is no way that the entire people
of Iran would be exceptions to the universal goodness of people. I
remember the young Israeli in Nazareth who expressed such sorrow at
the unlikelihood of ever being able to visit this country which he so
wished to do – precisely because he had heard of the kindness and
friendliness of its people.

I take a taxi to Orumiyeh, in my first town, at my first hotel, on my
first night in Iran, full of excited anticipation. The hotel is *Lonely Planet*
listed but it is a dive. I am shown up to my room by the night clerk, who
proceeds to explain in graphic mime the functions of the various
facilities in the bathroom, including that of the bidet, finishing off with,
'I lock the front door at midnight. We have sex, yes?'

'No,' I reply disdainfully.

At which he departs with a well-it-was-worth-a-try shrug.

The following day, I book a seat on a bus to the city of Esfehan, in the centre of Iran. The overnight journey will take sixteen hours, arriving at 8 am. I shall celebrate New Year's Eve on the bus and on my own; Iran uses a different calendar.

Having been instructed by so many 'well-informed' people about the strict dress code in Iran, I make sure before leaving the hotel, to dress according to protocol. Over my trousers, I wear the only long garment I have, a bright turquoise sundress picked up in Cyprus, that reaches just above the knee. Fastidious to ensure my hair is completely covered, I wear my pink head buff. Feeling exceptionally pleased with the care I have taken, I step out into the street.

The first noticeable feature of the women here in Orumiyeh is the amount of hair on show. And not timidly peering out from under severe black headcoverings either, but triumphantly flaunted from under loosely-draped flamboyantly-coloured headscarves. It is totally unexpected; the first Moslem country in which, when the head *is* covered, I have seen anything but the close-fitting version. The salient feature is that the back of the head is never uncovered. I promptly follow the adage, 'Do as the locals do and you can't go far wrong,' and readjust my buff, relegating it to behind my fringe.

I arrive in good time at the bus station, cold rain falling. The waiting room is full and I sit on a bench outside, protected by an overhang and in good sight of the embarkation bay for my bus. Plenty of people aim curious stares in my direction, the isolation eventually broken when, undaunted by this strange woman, a lively group of fully-chadored women come over and try to speak to me. I respond with the couple of Farsi phrases I have managed to learn, and the ice is broken.

A young woman begins chatting to me in excellent English, talking openly about the politics and culture of Iran: arranged marriages, where a daughter can decline up to three suitors of her parents' choice before she is confined to spinsterhood; that an increasing number of women are choosing the single life, instead of marrying someone under these circumstances. Shabnam, at twenty-one years of age, says she does not wish to marry. She is studying English at university and would like to work in England, under the impression that, 'England is a much happier and freer country than Iran, where the people are sad.' She gives me her phone number, in case there is anything I need whilst in Iran.

My fellow passenger on the bus is very pleasant and, by taking in turns to search through my Farsi phrasebook, we manage to find out a little about each other. She has three daughters, thirty-five, twenty-nine and twenty years of age, and is just returning from visiting her youngest in Orumiyeh. Her stop is well before mine and I am sitting alone when midnight ambles along, the sound of my son singing into my ipod transporting me home, whilst I crack open the remains of a bottle of warm flat coke to herald in 2009.

I watch the sun rise over the mountains of Kurdistan and shiver at the sight of the snow, lying thick on the ground beyond the freezing fog; mercifully, all but disappeared by the time we reach Esfehan. The air is cold as I make my way from the bus station into the centre of the city, to yet another *Lonely Planet*-recommended hotel, the Amir Kabir.

The huge surprise is that here, in the same hotel in the middle of Iran, are not one but a total of six cyclists. The last cyclist I saw was in Jordan. Tomasz has cycled from his home in Poland to here, having set off about the same time as me; Geejun, a Korean, has cycled from India and plans to end his trip in Germany; three decidedly hunky Slovenians are now at the end of their trip, packing up their bicycles to return home by plane. Another traveller is a Japanese backpacker.

The next day, I walk around Esfehan, trying to develop a feel for the city, as well as for the Iranian people. In addition to wearing my buff more loosely, I have discarded the tunic, on the confident assertion by the hotel manager that my long trousers and short fleece jacket are acceptable.

I wander past intricately decorated blue mosaic mosques to the river, then along the bank from one bridge to the next. It is a popular part of the town for people to congregate and socialise on their day off. I sit on a bench in a park overlooking the river, joined by a middle-aged woman, dressed all in black, but with a loose head covering. She had spent eighteen months in England many moons ago, is unmarried and now lives with her brother and his family. She expresses a preference for Tehran and Shiraz, both freer cities than the more restricted Esfehan, and believes that Iran is much better under the more tolerant Ahmedinejad, than the strict Khomeini.

Esfehan, displaying fine examples of Iranian and Islamic architecture dating back to the early seventeenth century, has been described, according to my elder brother, as 'An architectural symphony born out of fusion of the very best in Islamic and Persian aesthetic traditions.'

160

It boasts one of the biggest city squares in the world, namely the Imam Square. Nearby the square, I am rather taken aback at the sight of a man, his face wrapped in a scarf, carrying a poster in front of him, on which is written, 'Down with Israel. Down with USA.'

Further on, police are in the throes of controlling the traffic, that suggests there is, or has been, a demonstration. About what? I have heard no news for months; anything could be happening in the world of which I would be oblivious. Presumably, something has.

I receive an email from the family in Abu Dhabi, describing the benefits of an R&R stay with them: swim in their pool, lounge in deep hot baths with gins & tonics (note the plural), roast meals (only the way the English can do). But on one condition: I tell them about my trip. Life can be so taxing.

The money-changers are closed today, Friday, and so back at the hotel I have to accept a poor exchange rate for my dollars. I was aware before entering Iran that I would not be able to use any cards or travellers' cheques, that I would need to bring enough cash with me for my whole stay. I have a mixture of dollars and Euros, but am unsure as to how acceptable US dollars will be in this anti-American country. Needless to say, money speaks louder than politics and dollars are not only tolerated as a valid currency but, more often than not, preferred to any other.

I postpone my departure by a day, having developed a chest infection a couple of days previously, taking advantage of the extra time to try and obtain an extension to my visa, as I expect to be in the country longer than a month. But I come away from the visa office empty handed, having been told it is too early to apply.

The cycling conglomerate now diminishes: Tomasz leaves to continue heading south, the same route that I shall be taking, and the Slovenians head off to the airport; althought the Korean remains.

To be honest my initial impression of Iran has not been that of an instant liking, as for instance, it was for Syria. I have had some lovely encounters with women and girls, who have been open and friendly and with whom I do not feel any unease; on the other hand, encounters with men have not been that impressive: the hotel clerk in Orumiyeh, the men here in Esfehan.

In the streets, the men behave like adolescents seeing girls for the first time, calling, 'Hello. Hello,' repeatedly as I pass, followed by

161

something else, which I do not catch (maybe I am not meant to), ending with a great deal of sniggering as they walk on.

I want my experience of Iran to be a positive one and so I need to make sure I do not develop a fixed negative mindset. This is helped by a short, but pleasant, conversation with a middle-aged chap.

'Where are you from?'

'England.'

'Ah, do you know Beckham? Have you heard of . . . ? He and Beckham are friends.'

I do not quite catch the name; apparently he is referring to the Iranian national football coach. But this is more like the reaction I was expecting.

On the morning of departure and on the point of leaving, I only then notice the flat tyre, so have to go through the palaver of unloading everything, sort out the flat, re-load, leaving an hour later than planned.

This is my first proper cycling in Iran and I am interested to see how it pans out. The road from Esfehan is mostly flat desert, the hard shoulders narrow or non-existent, varying between smooth and bumpy. Traffic passes quite close to me as the carriageways are not particularly wide. Considering there is a sprawling desert either side of the road, I wonder why the carriageways were built with such tight restrictions.

I stop for a break in a layby, a picturesque viewpoint for a range of mountains. A family taking photographs of them request that they include me in the picture, before thrusting a large bag of fruit and cucumbers into my hands to take away. Cycling resumed, a young man and his wife on a moped travel alongside for a while, informing me that there is a hotel ahead in Shahreza. I even receive a couple of friendly greetings from lorry drivers.

The hotel turns out to be a *mostafarkhaneh*, a lodging house with dormitories and rooms. The dormitory is an open area, occupied by men only and quite unsuitable for me. My room is small, clean and stiflingly hot with no temperature control. There is no shower in the place, only a handbasin in the shared washroom. I am feeling really unwell with my chest infection and very lonely, my low mood exaggerated when I go looking for somewhere to eat, only to be accompanied down the street by the sound of sniggering

The following day turns out to be an interesting one. I am stopped on the road by two young men and a young woman, the slightly older man speaking pretty good English. They have been waiting for me to catch up with them in order to ask if they can each have their photo taken with me. The young woman, Racal, then goes to their car, returning with her favourite small, squidgy tortoise, that she would like me to have. I am genuinely touched and hang it inside my basket.

They confirm there are no hotels in the town ahead, although they think I should be able to put my tent up somewhere. It augures well, therefore, when I arrive at the turn off for the town in question, Izadkjaste, and the first thing I see is a police station, a safe place for my tent and me.

'No,' the police official says, 'you cannot put up your tent here. You must go to Abadeh.'

'But Abadeh is 65 kilometres away. I shall not arrive before dark.'

'Then go to the supermarket or the mosque in town, they will help you.'

I arrive in the centre, a little over a mile up the road, just as a bus to Abadeh pulls up. I try indicating to the driver that I wish to go there but he does not understand. A woman passenger tells him what I said, his response being to issue a derisive laugh and drive off.

The supermarket is immediately by the bus stop and the owner has watched everything but, when I approach him, he is hostile and unhelpful. I cross over the road to the mosque, a man outside looking as though he has some association with it, and ask to sleep there.

'Yes,' he replies, directing me to a room in the far corner of the mosque courtyard.

This turns out to be a women's prayer room (do I really look as though I am looking for somewhere to say my prayers?), but when I ask the man again, his reply is an unequivocal, 'No.'

Frustrated and bewildered, I return to the police station where, happily, they now say I can put up my tent, even offering me cups of tea. I notice a book on the desk that the officers had been poring over when I returned from the village: an American language course book. But they have no English to offer me in conversation.

Half an hour after my return, a senior-looking official enters the office, sits behind the desk, frequently looking at me but not saying much. I ask him about putting up my tent, to which he responds with no words, but plenty of nods. After a while he leaves, the three remaining police officers continuing to ply me with tea. Forty-five minutes later, there is a phone call, the receiving officer listens intently, nodding, then puts the receiver down.

'You cannot stay here. You should go to Abadeh.'

'And are you going to drive me there?' I react, indignantly.

'No. You should go to the hospital in the town. There is a doctor who can speak English.'

I insist they call him, but when they reluctantly do so, there is no reply. I am so angry with them. And I am afraid. I do not want to be cycling along an empty desert road in the dark, nowhere safe to put up my tent. I had not expected this, going from past experience.

In my anger and frustration, I now do a stupid thing: instead of sitting firmly in my seat, letting them sort out the situation, I storm out of the station in frightened disgust, yelling, 'This is not good! I am going to tell Ahmedinejad about you!'

I cycle furiously along the desolate road, an hour before sunset and forty miles short of the next town. The prospect now of cycling for hours in the dark possibly clouds my judgement, as I surmise that my only option is to try and grab a lift from a lorry. In a layby ahead is a stationary truck, but he does not know the place I mention. I continue cycling, then flag down a lorry, a second one stopping just ahead of me. I approach the first one, the driver recognises the name of the town and seems to understand what I want. We load my bicycle and bags into the back, I climb into the cabin and we set off, the driver in the second lorry watching as we pass.

It soon becomes clear that, instead of dropping me off as agreed, my driver thinks I should be going all the way with him to Shiraz, a hundred and fifty miles away. I insist to the contrary, that I just need a lift to Abadeh. Apart from the fact that I have no idea of his intentions, this is after all, a cycling trip. He calls someone on his mobile, hands it to me to say something to the woman on the other end. Is this meant to be reassurance for me or merely to show off to the woman that he has a foreign traveller with him?

We come to what I think must be the turn off to Abadeh but he says it is another town and we need to go on to the next junction. We arrive at a police checkpoint and our lorry is pulled over; he gets out and I wait in the cab. There is nobody near enough for me to confirm the location of Abadeh and I am reluctant to get out, at the risk of him coming back and driving off with everything I possess.

We set off again and soon it is clear that we have indeed overshot my turning. What to do? It is already dark. Each time we come to what would seem to be a reasonably-sized town for a hotel, he declares, 'No hotel, no hotel.'

I surreptitiously check in my bag that my little penknife is to hand (can I really see me brandishing it at him?) and I memorise the emergency police number that is displayed regularly along the roadside (even though my mobile has not been working since shortly after I entered Iran). I am trying to stay inwardly calm and, whenever I speak, to be firm and clear in what I say. But I mostly sound truculent and rude, so then I feel more vulnerable, fearing that he could always get stroppy with me and drop me off in the middle of nowhere. I am between a rock and a hard place.

Totally unsure of his overall motive, I next question his sanity: seemingly from nowhere he produces a gas stove and kettle, balances them precariously between us and proceeds to light the stove to boil water for a drink – all this one-handedly, whilst driving along. Lunatic or what?

After passing many towns, and driven about a hundred and fifty miles, my persistent demands finally produce the result I am after and we turn off the highway into a town. We unload my things in hostile silence, he then driving off gesturing that I am a mad woman.

I ask around for a hotel, each time being confidently directed in the same direction, but nothing appears. I knock on the door of a house, answered by two delightfully helpful men who escort me along the road to the mosque, where I am eventually installed in one of the numerous pilgrim cells, more than adequately furnished with carpeted floor, mattress and, oh joy, a heater. Washing facilities though are outside, a long trough fed by a row of taps issuing freezing cold water; the toilet block a reluctant walk away, but with the bonus of warm water for washing.

Although I feel like death warmed up with the effects of my chest infection, I am now in a cosy room, feeling safe at last. The two kindly men return later with the mudir of the mosque, carrying a blanket and pillow and informing that I do not need to pay until the morning. I cough plentifully and productively in the night, finally convinced that I should start on the course of precious antibiotics I had included in my medical kit.

The next morning, I decide to retrace yesterday's route as far as the ruins of Persepolis, signs for which we passed the previous night. I should take advantage of visiting this ancient site as it is unlikely I shall be in the area again. In the meantime, I look out for Tomasz, surmising that I might well have overtaken him the previous night with, therefore, a possibility of seeing him today. I can hope.

The road winds through a small mountain range, eventually reverting again to desert. As well as Tomasz, I am also looking out for a place to eat, all my supplies being consumed last night, leaving not a morsel for breakfast.

A large restaurant appears on the opposite side of the road, in front of which, loading his bicycle is, joy of joys, Tomasz!

Although I had hoped that I might see him, I did not really think the chances were high and my surprise and delight are cataclysmic. I call out to him and wave. He glances up, gives a half wave and duly returns to loading his task in hand. He has not recognised me.

By the time I negotiate the busy dual carriageway, he is cycling down the road away from me. Well, there is nothing like conviction and desperation to pump the adrenalin into action. Despite my weakened state, there is only one thing on my mind: make sure that I catch up with him. I set off, pedalling furiously.

'Tomasz. Tomasz! Stooooop!'

But he does not hear. I push the pedals as hard and as fast as I can. I keep calling out, 'Tomasz. Tomasz!' ever more desperate for him to hear me. He keeps going; I keep him in sight. After what is probably only a couple of miles but seems for ever, he stops. Now's my chance. I speed up to him and stop. He looks up, a smile spreading across his face.

'I'm really happy to see you again,' he greets.

'And I'm so glad to see you!' I cry in utter relief.

Tomasz, too, has had an eventful couple of days. He was knocked off his bicycle by a lorry, ending up at the hospital in the village from which I had been turned away. He, too, had a poor experience with the local police: they did not let him phone his consulate or submit a report of the accident.

Emerging safe and unscathed from an attempted abduction (well-meaning or otherwise) and resulting in meeting up with Tomasz reinforces my inner conviction that I am being looked after and that sometimes things turn up in the least expected ways. By full mutual agreement, Tomasz and I are more than happy to continue cycling together for as long as we both wish.

We continue to Saafa Shar, where I had spent the previous night, stopping to watch the solemn Muharram procession through the town. Rows of men dressed in black shirts and trousers carry short-handled whips of what appears to be, foot-long bunches of wires, which they swing backwards and forwards in turn over each shoulder, in time with the single beat of a drum. The annual ceremony is one of mourning in memory of the martyrdom of Imam Husayn ibn Ali, after the Battle of Karbala in AD 680.

It seems I was wrong and Persepolis was not back the way I had come but onwards, we duly arriving an hour before sunset, in the nick of time to have a look at the 2,500 year-old ruins of this once fabulous place of Darius the Great. In the soft light of the setting sun, it still manages to command a regal presence of towering columns and delicately-sculpted reliefs.

An Iranian visitor asks me what I think of Iran, anxious that I agree it is a 'super' country and not full of terrorists, as portrayed in the West. Reciprocating, I ask him his impression of England, as portrayed in Iran.

Tomasz and I are able to camp in a wooded area of the grounds behind a security fence. After heating water for mugs of warming comforting soup, freezing conditions force us to retire early into our tents, wherein I quickly become snugly warm in my down sleeping bag and jacket, woollen hat and thermals.

The following day in the town of Marvdasht, we watch another Muharram procession. We need provisions, but all main shops are closed for the holiday and we succeed only in finding a small shop open to buy bread and biscuits. We sit on some steps in the sun eating bread and jam, a crowd of young lads immediately gathering round to stare at us until dispersed by an adult, followed by a young woman emerging from a nearby house inviting us to lunch.

Parking our bicycles safely round the back, we follow Samira into a house and up the stairs to a large room, to be greeted by her extensive family gathered together for a celebratory Muharram meal. A couple of them speak reasonable English and none of them appear fazed to have strangers in their midst. Most unexpectedly, some of the women have no head coverings; even more surprising when photos are taken, there is no prerequisite to cover up first (as was the case in Egypt).

For the next couple of hours we sit around chatting, until Tomasz mentions we should be going, at which point we are quickly brought helpings of food. When we leave, we do so armed with phone numbers for Samira and her parents in Shiraz.

We encounter a couple of mountains. At the first, Tomasz grabs hold of a slow-moving lorry, his drag lift to the top of the long hill. I trudge up under my own steam. At the second mountain, Tomasz commandeers a car to drive very slowly, a training vehicle for me. I cling with my left hand to the frame of the open front passenger window, attempting to steer with my right hand whilst maintaining a steady distance from the car, taking into account the width of my panniers. The driver is very obedient, for as soon as he increases his speed the slightest notch, I gasp, 'Slow down!' Tomasz relays to the driver, 'Slow down,' which he does with immediate effect; bless him.

This process is repeated for probably a mere couple of hundred yards (although even this could be a generous estimation). The whole exercise is excruciatingly nerve-wracking and very hard work for my left arm, until I realise I should adjust it from a bent elbow to a more relaxed straight arm, producing a dramatic reduction in workload on my arm muscles. Disconcertingly, hitching a lift is Tomasz's favoured method of ascending hills.

On the outskirts of Shiraz, we stop at a popular viewpoint overlooking the sprawling city below. Members of a large family group invite us to stay with them, instructing us to follow them the couple of miles to their home. Unsurprisingly, it is much further than stated, a common underestimation by drivers, as is the impossibility of driving slowly enough for cyclists to keep up. Credit due, they persist, stopping frequently to allow us to catch up with them. Tomasz insists that we do not bust a gut to keep up with them.

'It is up to them to keep down to our pace.'

On the way, a young man at the side of the road flags down Tomasz to invite us to stay with him at his parents' house, pressing into Tomasz's hand his business card and urging him to call.

Once in the home of the large family, there is a drastic change of dress code. Gone are all the coverings, replaced with blatant bare heads and bare arms, men and women alike, all except the fully-swathed grandmother. Out comes the hubble bubble (grandmother blissfully puffing on it, eyes closed), the plastic tablecloth on the floor and dish after dish of exotic foods. In the evening, the three younger men take us for a tour of the town, including a visit to the tomb of the fourteenth-century poet, Hafez. Hailed as the father of Persian poetry, most Iranians have a copy of his poems in their house, prone to learning them by heart and quoting them as proverbs and sayings in their daily lives.

We leave our friendly hosts in the morning and make our way to the city centre. This time I am successful at the visa office, coming away with a 30-day extension. We contact the young man from yesterday, arrange to meet him at his office where we leave our bicycles, and just take a few overnight things with us. When we arrive at his parents' house, it is obvious they are not expecting us and the whole visit is really strange. We are given no lunch, only some left-over dessert from the previous day's celebrations and a bowl of fruit; and it is only we two who are eating.

We try to relieve the strained atmosphere, Tomasz showing some of the filming from his trip, I my website; whilst they show us a family wedding video. This awkward desultory visit continues until seven in the evening, at which point the young man tells us that we are not able to stay the night after all. We take our farewell of his parents and follow our dubious host to a bus stop to wait for the next bus to town. Fortunately, a delayed sixth sense in him prompts him to realise that this might not be the appropriate course of action and a taxi is then hailed to transport us back to his office.

Tomasz is fuming by now, unable to be civil to the man; nor am I best pleased, especially when we have to cycle in the dark back to the city centre and start searching for a hotel. The whole event was just so bizarre.

We have no money for food because the money changers are still closed for the holiday; and, boy, are we hungry. Happily for us, although the hotel is very basic the staff are friendly, the night duty manager sharing with us his fried aubergines, rice and bread.

The following day is Friday and the only way to change money is by way of the black market. I use up the last of my cash dollars, euros only from now on. Tomasz and I split up for a couple of hours, he to the castle and bazaar area, I in search of an Anglican church, St Simon the Zealot (one of the Twelve Apostles), successfully found, unfortunately closed.

Reunited, we walk to the outskirts of the centre, ascending a hill for a view of the city. We meet a teacher as he leaves the nearby university, subsequently invited to his home to join his family for a meal. This includes the celebration dessert of rice pudding with cinnamon, reminding me of my childhood and my mum's rice pudding (except that this is yellow), often made for some reason on washday Mondays or as a result of too much milk accumulating in the fridge.

In the evening I pop into a shop across from the hotel, the staff appearing friendly at first, until one of them thinks it is amusing to show me some downloaded porn on his mobile. Oh, please!

Shiraz is deceptively large; only after cycling an hour and a half do we leave the city environs the following morning. Immediately there is an uphill, a long one. Off Tomasz goes, having instantly grabbed a passing lorry.

'Well, Tomasz, that's the last I shall see of you. But, hey, that's OK. After all, it's best to travel with compatible riders.'

In this way, I comfort myself all the way up the long hill, resigned to the inevitable. After an age, I arrive at the summit – and who should be sitting there? Tomasz! He has been waiting an hour and ten minutes in the cold, his lift having taken him the whole ten miles!

From now on the scenery is stunning as we scale a splendid mountain range of bare rock, where deep gullies slash through the solid mass allowing just enough room for a thread of a road to squeeze through them. It is a breathtaking day, the best cycling I've had so far in Iran, wishing it not to end.

I realise increasingly that I am travelling with a mad man; one who keeps veering off the road to cycle precariously right up to the edge of a precipice to take a photo.

By late afternoon, we are over the range and freewheeling down the other side, the landscape changing from rugged rock to verdant pastures.

The first village we come to is Mourdaq, a tiny village of buff, flat-roofed houses accessed by tracks of impacted mud, set against a mountainous backdrop. Here I have my initiation into how possibly to acquire a bed for the night – if unsuccessful, there is always camping.

Stopping at the small shop we buy a few bananas. Villagers gather curiously, stand and stare, until the shopkeeper shoos them away and we continue cycling slowly through the village. As we negotiate the bumpy, stony dirt track, we are followed by an ever-increasing crowd to where the road eventually ends in a field. As we pass the wall of a farm, a trio of heads pops up from behind it, the young women friendly and giggly.

When I ask to take a photo of them, a man on the opposite side of the road objects.

I do not sense a particular friendliness towards us: one man indicates that we should go back the way we have come and a younger man too does not seem particularly enamoured that we have stopped in the field. I try to explain that we merely want to put up our tents and that we will be gone in the morning. Tomasz has already gone on ahead to the far side of the field and I follow.

I start clearing the ground of stones for our tents, whereas Tomasz sits down on a rock, food in hand.

'Don't unpack your tent yet, someone will be along within 20 minutes.'

Sure enough, within a few minutes the younger man, possibly in his mid thirties, comes along, an older woman in tow, saying something along the lines, 'It is too cold to be outside, wouldn't you prefer to come to the house in the warmth?'

No second bidding is required and we follow them both to the house of the giggly girls. And so there you have it – my initiation in how to find a bed for the night, in one easy lesson.

The household seems to consist of five sisters, two brothers, mother and father and possibly another woman, maybe a relative. The older brother, the one who came with the woman issuing the invitation, seems to be the head of the family, whether or not he is married is unclear. None of them speak English but, later in the evening, a friend and neighbour arrives who is an English teacher.

We sit on the floor in the main living room, a large, uncluttered carpeted room, phrasebook in hand. Nobody seems uncomfortable, either with the intrusion of strangers or with the lack of extensive conversation. Hot food is brought in but Tomasz and I are the only ones who eat. The friend asks many questions.

'What do you think of Iran? Of Blair? Israel? Gaza?'

Not quite your afternoon-tea-with-the-vicar type of questions.

As much as it is appreciated to have this dialogue with the friend, that is the problem; the exchange is only between the three of us, excluding the host family. Although I try to encourage him to translate to the others, he only continues talking to us; I feel uncomfortable and embarrassed for them. After he has gone, the television is switched on for the news and we realise for the first time the troubles that have been going on in Gaza since Christmas. Without understanding the words, the opening music to the news conveys the bias against Israel. Even so, the harrowing pictures of women and children killed, of extensive bombing attacks, even of protests in London, all convey that there is a very serious situation in play.

The news over by 9.30 pm, three rolled-up mattresses are brought in. The head of the house, Hamid sleeps in the room with us, placing his mattress between Tomasz and me. In the morning, he cannot cope with the sight of me in a short-sleeved T shirt and my head uncovered, agitatedly indicating to me that I should cover up immediately. I assume it must be equivalent to seeing me in my underwear. We see nothing of the rest of the house, nor, surprisingly, are we offered washing facilities. The outhouse is across the concrete paddock to the rear of the house, cold water only on tap. Adjacent to this is a pen, housing silky long-haired, long-eared goats, whose puckered lips look as though they are about to give you a kiss. We leave with grateful thanks and a ton of smiles, even exchanging email and postal addresses.

Travelling with such a wonderfully laidback companion is enabling me to have a vastly different experience of Iran than if I had remained on my own. It would have been continually stressful to be forced to reach a major town each day and only to stay in hotels, unable to relax enough to appreciate this marvellous country and its friendly people. Instead, I have the confident assurance with Tomasz that nothing is a problem. I am very grateful.

We make our way down towards the Persian Gulf, looking forward to warmer conditions and camping on the beach. En route, we are permitted to erect our tents on a date palm plantation. The night is cold and we are in our tents early, conscious that we have not washed properly for the last three days. As soon as we hit the Gulf, we welcome a dramatic rise in temperature, enough for me to pack away my winter clothing for my summer wardrobe, no more socks with my sandals.

Along a flat piece of road, a lorry comes by, voluntarily slowing down so that we can hitch a lift. I give it a go. It is very hairy holding on and keeping the bicycle steady enough so that I do not end up mashed under its wheels. I manage it for about two miles before releasing my hold. Again Tomasz waits for me further along.

We camp discreetly on the outskirts of Delvar, behind a low sand bank in a date grove. Children playing on the other side of the bank do not bother us but later, three older boys approach us and stand, silently watching. Eventually, we suggest they might like to go away and, when there is still no response, Tomasz takes out his knife, which sends them off. They return but at a distance, carrying lighted date palms which they stick into the ground. A motorbike begins to come towards us, the rider quickly changing his mind as soon as Tomasz stands up – he is quite tall. We have no more disturbances in the evening except for wolves calling in the night.

The water of the Persian Gulf is a beautiful pale blue-green, speckled with white surf, enticing us to swim. Not that I shall be able to do so, at least on this side of the Gulf, unless fully clothed.

We stop for provisions in a small shop and see a whole frozen chicken, asking the shopkeeper if he has half of one. He produces a large serrated knife and begins to saw the rock-hard chicken in half. By the time we are ready to cook it tonight it should be thawed. But maybe we should have held sway as, later, we stop to watch a bunch of cheerful fishermen on the beach, in their sun-bleached, blue fishing boats, emptying their nets of fish, oysters and whelks.

Tomasz strikes off from the road at almost every opportunity, bringing us this time to the middle of nowhere, well away from any habitation, a towering wall of sand dune separating us from the beach and sea. We light a campfire, on which we cook our thawed half chicken. It tastes delicious, but then doesn't food in the open always taste so?

In the light of the setting sun, we clamber over the sand dune down to the sea, paddling in the warmish water, breathing in the intoxicating sea air. Tomasz attempts an experiment with his camera. He chooses a very slow shutter speed and, with a burning palm frond, 'writes' the name of his girlfriend against the black sky. After numerous takes, he eventually manages to time it perfectly, so that he ends up with a photograph of her name in blazing letters. Last year he finished his university course and was 'given' a year off by his girlfriend to go cycling across Europe to Asia, after which they will settle down together.

Although it is not particularly cold, we are in our tents by early evening. Wolves howling in the night seem to be a regular feature, but I still lie in my tent praying that they are content to stay away from us, especially when I remember that we have left the remnants of the chicken in the fire not far away. In the morning, we have a feeling that the wolves had been close to our camp in the night, but not until we look over the ridge of the sand-dune and see a line of multiple paw prints do we appreciate how close.

I am now intent on spending a night in a hotel, in dire need of clean clothes, hair and body, internet access and battery charging. Tomasz does not like to pay for anything if he does not have to and so will find somewhere to camp out of town. As it happens, none of this is necessary, for we are stopped by three men in a car who invite us to stay in their home. They give us directions and shoot off. We reach the town and ask directions of three lads on one motorbike, who willingly escort us to the house.

Family plus friends welcome us. We shower away our sweat, salt and sand; our clothes are washed; we are taken to a friend's house for internet access; fed excellent food and converse with the family via a local English teacher.

'What do you think of a woman travelling by bicycle?' I ask.

'Oh, very good, very good,' both the women and the men reply.

Next day we leave early and stop in the sizable town of Bandar Kangan, but fail to change money for Tomasz from any of the banks. When we start cycling out of town a car pulls up asking if we want to change money. The rate seems favourable and Tomasz strikes a deal.

At the same time, a middle-aged woman stops her car and comes over, inviting us with friendly persistence to accompany her home for lunch. We thank her but decline, wanting to keep going. She drives away and we continue. Half an hour later, she reappears, accompanied by her two young sons, having returned home, prepared lunch and speeded it here to us; which is how we find ourselves sitting in the shade of her car by the roadside, tucking into a tasty meal.

Jasmin is Turkish, married to an Iranian, Ali. Her husband just happens to work in the town to which we are headed. This time we accept the offer of a night's accommodation, agreeing to phone her when we arrive in Asalouyeh.

Off we go, until we are stopped next by a man who presents us with two polystyrene boxes of cooked rice, plus two yoghurts, complete with spoons. Further on in a town, a woman gives me a handful of sweets as she passes by. This random hospitality is almost overwhelming. It is difficult to imagine similar occurrences in Europe.

Having successfully met up with Jasmin and her family, we leave our bicycles safely in her husband's place of work and are driven back to their home for the night. Again we see the difference between the public face and the private; from being completely covered in black except for her face whilst in public, Jasmin immediately discards all when in the home, choosing instead to wear western jeans and short-sleeved top. Being from the western part of Turkey, she finds the restricted life in Iran rather stifling and loves spending the summer in their second home in Izmir, when she can relax in public, wearing whatever she likes.

Her motherly care for us extends to sewing patches over the three holes in my trousers and offering me a cotton overshirt to replace my patchy faded pink shirt (but I am fond of it and politely decline). She is intent on giving me something to take away, settling in the end for a traditional blue Turkish bracelet. I fish out from my panniers a small bottle of perfume that was given to me by the English teacher in Turkey and present Jasmin with it. The following morning Ali drives us back to his office, but not without an attempt by Jasmin to persuade us to stay an extra night.

Often when we are cycling, there is a fair distance between us, invariably Tomasz in front, now and then waiting for me to catch up with him. Much of the time there is scant traffic, many stretches of road usually long and empty. I pass a man standing by the side of his car who, as I come level, jiggles his crotch as I go by and says something.

Seconds later, I hear a car coming up behind me and, as it draws alongside and keeps pace with me, I continue cycling, my head turned away to the right. The man calls out repeatedly, I maintain my fixed position determinedly, only for him to persist with his calling.

Momentarily, I turn my head towards his grinning face, his eyes darting down to his hand, waggling his penis, everything on display. Not a pretty sight, especially just after lunch. I screw up my face in disgust, he drives off gleefully and I catch up with Tomasz to explain what has just happened. He laughs and, when we see the car pulled off and away from the road, quips, 'Somebody likes you.'

Towards the end of the day, we enjoy a beautiful sunset on the beach, whilst watching a group of young children playing tag on the sand. A family carries a picnic down from their car, offer us tea and fruit as well as accommodation for the night, except that their home is way back in Asalouyeh.

Instead we find the local store to buy provisions and be given directions to the police station, a mile along the coast. We pick our way

175

in the dark along the lane to an isolated building and, out of courtesy, ask to camp on the public ground adjacent to the police station.

'No, you can't. Go to restaurant. Only 5 kilometres.'

It is a repetition of the previous police station. I remonstrate at length with the policemen, but to deaf ears. I cannot help a palpable anger rising within me when, on a second occasion, uniformed officialdom belies the overwhelming hospitality of this country.

We return to the store in the village, incidentally run by women, which I find extremely surprising, especially as the Gulf area is much more traditional than other regions in Iran, a high percentage of women wearing burkahs and thick black veils with just their eyes peering out. The upshot is that we are invited to stay in the home of the shop owners.

There is a particularly endearing quality in the women I have met in Iran: their lack of inhibition in standing or sitting in close proximity to me. And so it is this evening when, sitting on the floor, one of the young women puts an arm around me, unabashed and affectionate. This unself-conscious behaviour effectively breaks down stranger barriers without feeling that it is an imposition.

The women are very beautiful, displaying a naturally elegant poise, derived maybe from the loosely draped head shawls flowing gently across their shoulders. The younger women are happy to have their faces uncovered, the two older ones retaining their burkahs, even in the home, although this might be different when there are only family members around. I am subjected to a try-on-my-burkah session, which gives something to amuse Tomasz.

Before linking up with me, the majority of Tomasz's encounters were only with the men of the house, the women and girls hiding away, and he aware of them only by giggling shadows or fleeting glimpses. So for him these are also special encounters.

Cycling in sunshine is the tops and we finally succumb to a swim in the sea when we stop at a remote, secluded beach well away from the road. I change into my bikini and wade into the sea, not necessarily primarily to swim, but as a pathetic act of rebellion – it is unlawful for a woman to be so skimpily attired, requiring to be fully clothed even in the sea. It brings back memories of my time working in a hospital in Saudi when, for the first four months in Riyadh, we stayed in a hotel until our residential compound was ready. The swimming pool looked very inviting. Unfortunately, that was all we women could do, look. The option to sit on the side fully clothed, jealously watching the men in swimming shorts coolly submerging themselves in the refreshing water, was not really an option at all.

Today we cycle along a 20-mile stretch of gravel road which, although rather hard going, I am pleasantly surprised how much fitter I am feeling overall since cycling with Tomasz, because I am pushing myself slightly more than when on my own. He has been suggesting that I cycle with him through eastern Iran and Pakistan to India, but changing my route through the Emirates to India is not one that appeals to me, even though I am enjoying cycling in company. This latter point, of course, has nothing to do with having my ego flattered by his recent comment.

'I have so much respect for you at the end of 100 kilometre days; I could never imagine my mum doing such a thing.'

In Chiruyeh, a timely encounter with a local results in an invitation for the night at the home of Ibrahim and his family. Ibrahim thinks that Farsi should no longer be spoken in Iran and that Arabic should replace it.

'Here along the Gulf,' he says, 'Arabic predominates. Many men go to the Emirates for work, where jobs and money are more plentiful.'

He describes the differences between Sunni and Shia moslems, the former peaceful, as opposed to the more aggressive Shia. He goes on to speak with sadness about the situation in Israel and all the killings going on there.

In the morning, we leave without the chance to say goodbye and thank you, as nobody comes to us, even though some of the women have seen us pack up, ready to go. Maybe it is the protocol of stranger hospitality.

Later, we are flagged down by a lorry driver who gives us tea, even offers to buy us breakfast. His English is fairly good, learnt from working in Dubai and sailing on cargo ships around the world. He mentions Bandar Aftab a few miles up the road, from where we can catch a ferry to the island of Kish. Funnily enough, we had been heading for a place thirty miles further on with the same intention.

As a student of the laidback and streetwise Tomasz, I am learning how to reduce costs of travelling and worry less about where to sleep at night, simultaneously greatly enriching my cultural experiences. Much of his success comes from sheer brash attitude, as witnessed a few times today. After requesting a discount, we are given a thirty percent reduction in the ferry price for the 2-hour trip to Kish. Cycling around the island, we stop to look in at a diving centre, Tomasz's persuasive ways resulting in a 10-minute jaunt on a jet ski, during which I am subjected once more to a sample of his madman persona. But first I have to be kitted out in appropriate attire, a longer procedure than Tomasz's simple donning of swimshorts. I emerge from the ladies'changing room, bikini-ed, yes, but firmly hidden beneath a very fetching set of light blue overalls, the pièce de résistance a lurid green skull cap, sitting tautly on my head, a daring bit of hair allowed to escape in a half-hearted attempt at something that might be called 'chic'. All in vain as Tomasz merely collapses with utter mirth.

We mount the jet ski, me riding pillion, naïvely relaxed, he well and truly in the driving seat. Any normal person might be thinking, 'OK, this being my first go on such a machine, it's probably a good idea to take it easy at first; get a feel for it, see how it works.'

Tomasz, on the other hand, thinks, 'We only have ten minutes. Let's make the most of it.'

He presses the 'Start' button, launches into full throttle and heads straight out to sea. Suddenly, he veers ninety degrees left, then right, left, right, le.., no, right, in fact, let's do a full 360°, no need to let up on the throttle. I hang on for dear life. Apparently, my vital role is to make sure I lean opposite to the swerve, otherwise, we are likely to end up in the drink entering at speed, not a compelling option in my humble view. They say your life flashes in front of you on the brink of death. Memories of a particular rollercoaster ride in Sweden twenty years previously shoot into my mind, the whole ride spent with a terrified grip on the restraining bar, mentally yelling, 'Help! I'm going to fall out. I'm going to fall out. Help!'

Tomasz loves the ride.

Further round the island we come to and gain free admission to the Dolphin Park, before ending the day camping right by the sea on the 'Women's Plage'. We make sure to arrive after dark, in the morning just missing the arrival of a group of workmen as we leave.

The return ferry to the mainland takes two hours for our passage to be sorted, in an attempt to obtain the best deal to one of the three ports to which the ferry sails. At length, the manager of the shipping line succumbs to Tomasz's charms and gives us free passage to the furthest port, Bandar Lengeh.

Back on the mainland, we continue along the coast. An inky sky later in the day does not bode well for camping but, stopping to watch a bunch of young lads at their football practice, we are befriended and subsequently taken to the community centre for the night. In the evening the 'owner of the city' brings a meal on a tray for us. In the morning, as we are leaving, children walk by on their way to school. We try and photograph them but they are very shy and turn away. A solitary young girl carries a baby goat, maybe it is 'Show and tell' day, and we try to photograph her, thinking that from a distance it will be alright. Spotting us, she stops dead and begins to cry, poor thing.

Currently the mornings begin cool but soon warm up, each day tempting us towards the alluring sea, if only access points were not so elusive. In the meantime, we stop at a small village shop, Tomasz to buy his customary can of condensed milk and sit on the steps of the store to eat it, neat, sweet and thick; yuk. A woman, unsolicited, offers me a wash (do I really smell that bad?), leading me by the arm through the back of the shop to the courtyard behind, indicating a toilet and shower area in the far corner.

We end the day camping in open country about quarter of a mile from a village. We are in full view of the village, there being no cover, so it is not surprising then that we are susceptible to visitors, duly arriving in the form of a man on a motorbike bearing four young passengers, plus three youths on their own motorbikes. They hang around for a while, watching as we pitch our tents. Later in the evening, the man returns, lights a campfire and sits on the ground with us. There is no real conversation, but I don't think that is important to the man. I think it is part of the general attitude towards strangers, an attempt to make the outsider feel welcome. He leaves when we indicate we want to go to sleep.

Our campsite is on thorny ground, resulting in an instant puncture in my back tyre as soon as we set off in the morning. I replace the innertube whilst Tomasz mends the puncture. A motorbike zooms over, a father and young daughter asking if we need any help, returning a short time later with a handful of fruit and vegetables. The man from last night comes by, returning my Pink Panther lighter he had used to light the fire. Further random gifts of generosity are bestowed on us at a kiosk when, having made our purchases, the young shopkeeper comes out to where we are sitting eating snacks, presenting us first with bottles of water and a few minutes later, two packs of orange cakes.

So far along the Gulf coast, traffic has been light, but now approaching Bandar Abbas, it increases markedly. Not only the roads, but all hotels are full except for one, but at $40 for a single room, it is not an option. One might think that, having had to pay for only one night's accommodation during the last sixteen, this could be construed as being extremely tight with my money. It would seem that Tomasz's influence is having an effect. Accustomed now to travelling cheaply, coupled with my own attempt to ensure I have enough funds for my two years, there is a begrudging reluctance to spend more than required.

At the port we find out information on ferries to Sharjah, my next port of call. The next ferry is three days away and I wonder what to do in the meantime, considering there is nowhere to stay in Bandar Abbas.

I am glad we have not found a hotel for me (Tomasz was always going to find a place to camp out of town), as it gives us one last camp together before he sets off on his way north, then east, to Pakistan. On the outskirts of town we ask to pitch our tents in the grounds of a local business. Initially, the man is unwilling for us to do so.

'Dangerous. Snakes.'

It is dark by now and we persist, eventually he relenting, even bringing us oranges later and being quite friendly.

I am not looking forward to the next couple of days, on my own again, out of the safety of the cocoon of company, uncertain about accommodation, midnight arrival on the other side of the Gulf.

In the morning, it is difficult to say goodbye to Tomasz. We have been cycling together for sixteen days, virtually twenty-four hours a day in each other's company, looking out for each other in a land strange to both of us. We are both reluctant for the final moment of departure to arrive. Eventually, though, after photos and hugs, we cycle together for the last time, me accompanying Tomasz a couple of hundred yards up the road, until a U-turn, for me to head back to the city centre. As I am about to turn, Tomasz slips something into my basket, we bid each other a final farewell and cycle off in opposite directions. I am unable to prevent myself from blubbing like a lost child. When I have calmed down, I peep into my basket to see what Tomasz's parting gift has been; a small spray canister of C-S gas glints back at me. I hope I never have occasion to use it.

One of the first buildings I see on returning to town is a large ornate mosque. Outside its perimeter wall on the pavement is a village of tents.

Inside, women in the courtyard clean the floor and steps with rhythmical sweeps of their long palm branches. I take photos, expecting the woman who is now coming towards me to tell me off and shoo me away. On the contrary, she invites me to bring my bicycle into the courtyard, where she will safeguard it so that I can visit the mosque, which I now enter swathed in the voluminous, flowery chadour she hands to me. I inquire about the possibility of sleeping here that night, at which she indicates the open-fronted cells against the inside wall of the courtyard, nodding and smiling that I can sleep there.

Relieved at having tonight's accommodation sorted, I can now relax and enjoy my visit. I enter the women's section, to sit for a while on one of the large rugs, watching the women, mostly solitary. Some are performing the prayer ritual: standing, kneeling, face to the floor, kneeling, standing; others sit, presumably reading the Qoran; one feeds a young child. Back outside in the bright sunshine, I watch as one of the black-shrouded courtyard sweepers laughs gleefully as she plays a game of frisby with a child.

I cycle to the port, on the off chance that I might be able to book myself onto a cargo boat across the Gulf, the cost of the ferry determines I should at least try (prices on the internet, vastly lower than the actual fares, have turned out to be a couple of years old). It is nothing more than a half-hearted attempt and so am not the least surprised when I find myself on the way to the ferry offices to buy a ticket. I suggest they might like to give me a discount, but sadly I am not able to display the same natural ability of my erstwhile companion and they decline. As they will not accept my euros (I have no more dollars), I return to town to change money, buying my ticket instead from a travel agency located conveniently near the money exchange.

I am in an internet café for only half an hour, when the woman tells me to finish soon as she is about to close at one o'clock. I proceed to pack up my things and am on the point of paying when another customer comes along and pays my dues, then invites me to lunch. But a young man who had helped me hoike my bicycle up the steps to the café, now comes out of his computer shop opposite to help me down the steps. He starts chatting to us both, says something to the other man who goes off, after which he invites me for lunch at his house, where he lives with his mother, sister and other family. He says he was concerned about the man who had been with me as he, Salim, had not seen him around before. He proceeds to warn me about going off with strangers. I have to laugh, especially as he does not see the irony of his words. But my gut instinct reassures me and I leave my bicycle in his computer shop, taking a few essentials with me. We drive to his sister's flat, although not entirely without some reservations on my part.

'Am I being totally naïve and misguidedly trusting? I have no idea where I am going and I shall have no idea how to get back to my bicycle, if everything goes belly up.'

We stop first at Salim's parents' house before continuing to the home of his sister, her husband and 4-month old son. Everyone is delightful. I am fed, able to shower (the first in four days) and made to feel extraordinarily welcome. On the Friday morning, Salim takes me sightseeing around Bandar Abbas including re-visiting the mosque, where the same chadoured woman recognises me with a smile. There are no churches but we stop to see the renovations in progress of an old Hindu temple.

I am included in a family outing to Genoa hot-water springs, a sister, a cousin and I the only ones to don swimsuits to take to the spa waters in the segregated hot-springs swimming pool. My bikini is rejected as inappropriate and I am obliged to buy a less than flattering homemade swimsuit and bathing cap, both discarded afterwards. Many women come up to me in the pool and we exchange smiles and the odd word. I am challenged to a race by one woman, which takes me aback, but soon realise that she is one of the few women who can claim to swim in any way and is proud of it. I admire her, especially considering the limitations of opportunity for learning, fully clothed in the sea is hardly conducive to anything but drowning. The visit to the baths is followed by a family picnic seated on rugs in the car park, finished off with puffs on the portable hubble-bubble.

After my couple of days' stay I am reunited with Raven and cycle to the ferry terminal, meeting up with Salim who wants to wave me off. We sit in the waiting room, the place slowly filling up with other passengers. Approaching the time of departure, a man whom I recognise from the ferry office the previous day comes in and announces something. He sees me but makes no attempt whatsoever to try and explain anything to me.

'I expect he's telling us that there is no sailing,' I quip.

'Yes,' replies Salim.

Apparently, the weather is too bad on the other side of the Gulf. The next ferry is not for four days. As if he has not done enough already, Salim now comes into his own. He obtains my refund for the ferry ticket, drives me to the airport for me to buy a plane ticket and takes me back to his parents' house to rest before the evening flight to Dubai.

During a conversation, Salim describes the difficulties that young people in Iran have meeting people of the opposite sex. I feel very sorry for him, as the regime is such that it is virtually impossible to meet socially in any way, illegal even to talk to each other in public places. Special police patrols look out for such activities. It is why visiting people in hospital is so popular with young people, as a social meeting place.

Soon we return to the airport for my evening flight, Salim supervises the wrapping of my baggage in clingfilm, whilst I do the necessaries to my bicycle. I declare to the airport staff that I should not be paying any excess costs – and I don't (maybe I do have some of Tomasz's ability after all). We are told, very late in the day, that my bicycle needs to be packaged in cardboard, the two of us then scrabbling around to find something suitable.

Salim waits with me right up to the point of departure, during which he falls into conversation with another passenger, an Iranian with a business in Dubai who, impressed with Salim's behaviour towards me, gives him his business card and the possibility of offering him a job in Dubai. Salim is very happy, having previously mentioned to me his wish to work in the Emirates, and takes this as an (unsought) reward for his actions.

The flight is called and we bid farewell to each other, with me trying to express the huge gratitude I feel towards him. It is the best ending I could have hoped for after a truly positive experience of Iran.

*   *   *

United Arab Emirates and Oman

24 January – 11 February 2009

Dubai, Abu Dhabi, Al Ain, Suhar, Al Habaiah,
Muscat, Al Qurum, Muscat airport

My father had taken early retirement in his mid fifties, within a year finding himself out in Dubai as Solid Waste Manager for Dubai Municipality. During his time there he became known as Mr Tidyman, the result of him introducing the widespread installation of public litter bins sporting a green tidyman. Throughout the eight years in the Emirate, my father attended Arabic language classes three times a week, feeling strongly that this would give him a more satisfying and enriching experience than if he had not bothered. He saw massive changes in the country during the short time he was there, not least the extensive building and spreading of the city far into the desert; into the sea came after he had retired to Cyprus.

The brief, 30-minute flight impressively provides passengers with refreshments, a drink, sandwich and cake, before landing at Dubai International. Part-way through the flight, my heart gives a resounding jolt, at the sudden thought that I might be responsible for blowing us all up or at least my tyres. I suddenly remember there is a camping gaz canister in my baggage and I have forgotten to deflate my tyres. Well, it is late, after all, and I have had lots on my mind.

Traipsing through passport control and into baggage reclaim, my spirits lift. Arriving in Dubai is like a breath of fresh air, the atmosphere so different from Iran. Although traditional white, ankle-length dishdashes abound, which could seem anachronistic in this contemporary place, not only does everyone speak excellent English, they deliver it in a relaxed and friendly manner. I have not appreciated it until now but, in Iran there was an underlying sombreness in the people, whereas here, there is an energetic enthusiasm.

The beaming staff show a great deal of interest in my trip, coming into baggage reclaim to examine my stalwart companion located at last on the far side of the carousel in a recumbent position. I restore Raven to a cyclable state, taking longer than necessary until I realise I am trying to screw the second pedal against the thread (Spain obviously taught me nothing).

Emerging at last from the arrivals building, I press through the customary crowd of waiting families, lack of barriers preventing an unimpeded pathway for weary passengers. A bystander asks about my bicycle and if I have any television coverage arranged. My confident reply that a commissioned reporter has things in hand does not prevent Yousef from giving me his contact number.

'In case I can be of any help,' he says, adding, with a cheeky grin when he realises I am not married, 'I am available.'

Initial plans for the press interview, made whilst travelling through Turkey, in the end could not come about and I am now waiting to hear from the reporter about revised timings.

The four miles to the city centre are along brightly-lit roads; no lights on my part required. Neither is there a dearth of people of whom to ask directions, even though it is one in the morning. After many diversions from road works, I finally arrive at the flat of friends of my father, later than anticipated at 2 am. Reluctantly I wake Labid and Pat who issue a warm greeting of welcome, followed by, 'Food? Drink? There's the bathroom; here's your bedroom. Please excuse us if we return to bed. Goodnight.'

I stay in Dubai three days, fully exploiting the convenient opportunity for internet access on my hosts' computer and enjoying my first wine since Damascus. Raven goes for an essential pampering at wonderful Wolfie's, a German-run cycle shop. When I pick her up at the end of her visit, she is hardly recognisable: a brand spanking new model, even having undergone a thorough and meticulous clean.

'In order to be able to see any underlying problems,' they say.

She has had a full service, essential oil change, the knobbly rear tyre replaced with a new smooth tyre.

I am informed by Robert, the store manager, that the only road to Abu Dhabi is a six-lane motorway, in each direction.

'On which bicycles are definitely not allowed – unless with special permission, unlikely to be granted, especially at short notice.'

I am duly pointed in the direction of the police station, from there directed to the Roads and Transport Authority. About to hail a taxi to take me there, I find myself on the opposite side of the road to Dubai Municipality, where my father had worked thirty years previously. I had promised I would go and see if there were any staff remaining who had known him, so cross the road and enter the building. As soon as I mention his name to the receptionist, a security guard nearby jumps in with, 'Is that your father?'

'Well, yes, but how do you know?' I exclaim in amazement.

'Your features resemble his.'

This is immediately followed by a lengthy discourse on what a good man my father was, after which I am propelled upstairs to the Environment Department to meet two more former colleagues, both obligingly called Mohammed. One of these had worked directly under my father, as a 20-year old, taking over when my father retired. These two men also wax lyrical about what a good man he was and how much he had done for Dubai.

The one who had worked directly with my father now escorts me into the office of the Assistant Director of the Environment who, although he had arrived a year after my father's departure, knew him by reputation, and adds his praises. I am sure the ears of the person in question must be glowing with pride and pleasure.

My trip comes into the conversation, including my current quest, at which point the Assistant Director pens a letter to the Director of the RTA, requesting permission be granted for me to cycle along the motorway. Mohammed happens to know the person in charge of that department and willingly drives me to the Right of Way Department and the office of the Acting Director, unexpectedly a woman. But why am I surprised? After all, Dubai is more liberal than other Middle Eastern countries. I put it down to having been four months in the Middle East and this is the first time I have come across a woman in high authority. She is an extremely pleasant and helpful person, having no hesitation in writing a letter of authorisation for me to travel the Sheik Zayed road. She throws in a police escort for good measure.

'No, please don't do that, there is no need. I shall be fine on the hard shoulder.'

'But that is not safe because lorries use it regularly to undertake other vehicles. It is my responsibility to keep you safe.'

She then introduces me to Abdullah, the person who will be in charge of the mission.

My favourite place in Dubai is the Creek, bustling with water-borne traffic of all sorts, the small local water taxis, *abras*, more interesting than the larger touristy ones. Here it is possible to be reminded of the intimate, village atmosphere of a former Dubai, before its exponential growth and onset of ostentatious affluence. The resultant overbearingly high cost of living engenders a feeling in the local population, what is left of it, of having been supplanted by overwhelming numbers of foreigners who poured in during its heyday. Pat and Labid, expats who have lived here for thirty-five years or so, also mourn the vast changes, unsure whether they wish to continue living here indefinitely.

During my couple of days' respite, Pat and I attend a cultural festival on the creek. Arab horses and whirling dancers are in action, there is a plethora of local dishes for the tasting, a variety of arts and handicrafts on display. We also sit on the sun terrace of a hotel overlooking the creek, sipping white wine spritzers over a light lunch.

Saying goodbye to my hosts, I cycle alongside the softly-misted creek, the air still and peaceful in the early morning. Only a few people are about, unloading cargo from boats or making their way to work. I am heading for the distinctive sail-shaped Burj Al Arab Hotel in Jumeirah, the pre-arranged meeting point for my escort. It takes me longer than anticipated to arrive and I roll up forty-five minutes after the agreed time. Shortly after, my escort pulls up behind me, in a socking big 4-wheel drive monster, orange hazard lights flashing. As it happens, Abdullah and his co-driver, Abdullah, have been following me for the last three intersections.

'Oh dear,' I think guiltily.

After a brief discussion on how we are going to play this escort to Abu Dhabi, we set off. At the first intersection, they pull alongside me.

'It might be better that you do not go through the red lights; too dangerous,' they remark politely. I smile sheepishly.

The thought of being tailed for a whole day by a police vehicle forced to keep down to my speed, knowing this is anathema to just about all drivers, has filled me with a large degree of discomfort. It will be difficult not to feel under pressure to push myself at a faster than comfortable pace. However, they both display a smiling, relaxed demeanor which puts me at ease, giving the distinct impression that they are more than happy to be spending such an easy day pootling along behind me. Despite this, I cannot help but push myself slightly more than I would have done if on my own. The good thing is that the terrain is very flat, the cycling therefore not particularly arduous.

I have to admit that being so effectively shielded from danger along this fast-running highway is a wonderful feeling. Traffic coming up from behind participates in the occasion, firstly by taking an interest in the escort vehicle, secondly, by showing their amusement at this laden cyclist with jolly toots and thumbs up as they slowly draw level, before speeding past.

Abdullah uses the PA system to good effect, his voice booming out over the tannoy to suggest strategic breaks at services. The two of them then go for a McDonald's special, whilst I sit on the kerb outside with refreshments from my pannier.

Shortly before the border with Abu Dhabi, when Dubai jurisdiction ends, we pull over in a layby beside a parked police car, the hand-over team. My new escorts are not as smiley as my Abdullahs and their English is nowhere near the same, but as there is not much opportunity for any conversation anyway, this is almost incidental. So now I have a 2-car police escort; at least to the next intersection, when, with a pip of the horn and a good luck, the Abdullahs swing off and u-turn onto the opposite carriageway back to Dubai. It is only now that I see atop their vehicle three giant, orange, flashing arrows. There really was nothing subtle about this event.

I am feeling quite tired by now having covered a stonking eighty miles, but eventually we arrive at my turn-off for Khalifa City. The police car stays with me and would accompany me all the way to the door of the house, except that I convince them I can manage on my own from here, thanking them gratefully for their safe company. As the car doubles back to the motorway, it emits a friendly beep. An average of 12.9 mph for the day is not bad.

I spend a week basking in the cosy comfort of a family home with Andy and Julie, and their children, Lucy and Daniel. I am treated to a much anticipated real roast meal; luxuriate in the bath with g&ts; make the mistake of diving into their pool, gasping for breath on re-surfacing at the unexpected freezing temperature of the water. I manage to give my party outfit an airing at Andy's birthday party. I am even let loose in the kitchen one evening to cook a meal: a homely cottage pie and apple crumble.

I discover a little lump in my armpit, which concerns me enough to pay a visit to a clinic for the peace of mind that it is nothing serious, coming away with a tube of antibiotic cream, as well as a replenished supply of broad-spectrum antibiotics.

For the first time in four months I wear shorts in public, at first feeling exposed and uncomfortable, before slowly becoming accustomed to it. We drive around Abu Dhabi past various sights, including a newly-built mosque in brilliant white marble, gold-leafed spikes adorning the pinnacles of the domed buildings and minarets. In garish contrast is the richly-decorated Emirates Palace Hotel, its huge, ornate foyer ceiling, clad completely in gaudy gold leaf.

We visit the fishing port, where traditional dhow fishing boats rock gently, gunwhale to gunwhale, their white upturned prows proudly cocking a snook at towering, ascetic glass buildings stretching across the skyline behind.

It is only now I realise I need a visa for India before arriving in country. It comes as quite a shock. I was sure I had checked this before leaving home but maybe I had arrogantly assumed that, with Britain's strong historic links, it would be a simple matter of collecting a visa on entry. In alarm, I ring the Indian Embassy, to be informed that the turnaround for a visa is ten days. When I arrive in person to begin the process, I discover that, on payment of a fee, it can be done in four days.

By the time I leave the Embassy, having discussed my trip with the obliging official, this has been shortened to two days. And I am not even required to leave my passport with them. On my return two days' later, I am invited into a back office for tea and a chat with two helpful embassy staff, whilst my visa is inserted into my passport.

I am now ready to leave the luxury of my week's R&R, hopefully not having outstayed my welcome by too much.

As for the article for The National newspaper, as the reporter says, when he finally responds to my emails, 'Welcome to the uncertain world of journalism.'

It transpires that, when it did not work out that a reporter would meet me at my point of entry and cycle with me, the editor of the paper decided to pull the story.

'It would not now have enough colour,' she said.

So, a lone woman cycling round the world, making a detour to stop off in a prominent Middle Eastern country where her father had worked for the government thirty years previously, is not enough to appeal to the local reader.

It makes no difference to me or my trip whether or not I am interviewed along the way. But having been approached so enthusiastically, I was well up for it, and it would at least have given me an opportunity to promote my chosen charities. Are the press always this whimsical?

Abu Dhabi to Al Ain is a long stretch, which I had thought to cover over two days. Pushing on in one go, I arrive at my next hosts' house at the 105-mile mark. It is the first time I have covered more than a hundred miles in one day and results, for the first time on my trip, in my thighs feeling really stiff and aching the following day. I stay for a couple of nights with Peter and Heather, friends of the couple in Amman. I am party to another birthday celebration, this time one of the children's coming of age thirteenth, complete with a murder mystery game and chocolate cake. Heather and I visit an Emiratee neighbour, a young woman who speaks good English, keen to improve further through conversing with Heather.

Peter and Heather are rigorous in observing Middle Eastern protocol and so, just as with their friends in Amman, when Heather is not present but Peter is, I am not able to stay alone in the house with him, even if their three children are around. Which is how I find myself cycling along in the rush-hour traffic of a busy main road whilst it is still dark, on my way out of Al Ain.

A crippling headwind reduces my speed, from the glorious 14-16 mph from Abu Dhabi to a pathetic 6 mph to Oman. I pay the exit fee of 25 dirhams at the border a few miles away, cycle through no man's land for the next thirty miles, then 60 dirhams for the privilege of entering Oman. The first notable sight is the attractive and distinctive way the men wear their headgear, not simply hanging down, but intricately wrapped around their heads, a short tail hanging down the nape of the neck.

I have a choice of two roads, through mountains or along the coast. I choose the latter, arriving late afternoon in Suharr. In my search for accommodation, I stop a man to inquire where I might put up my tent.

When he finds out that I am English, he instantly comes out with, 'I hate the English.' Thinking I have misheard him, I say, 'Pardon?'

'I hate the English. More than the Americans and the Israelis, I hate the English!' He speaks vehemently.

'Oh,' I reply feebly.

He is a Palestinian, forced to leave his country to find employment, ending up here in Oman. He sees his family every two years in Jordan, as he cannot return to Palestine; sometimes his wife visits him in Oman. He blames the English for his situation, pouring scorn on our part in the agreement that brought about the creation of Israel on 14 May, 1948. Having expressed the strength of his feelings in no uncertain terms, he then unfathomably proceeds to offer me a bed for the night.

'But why are you offering me accommodation?'

'Because I want to change my opinion of the English.'

No pressure, then.

He is on his way to an appointment and so we arrange to meet in a café in a couple of hours. It is by now dark and so, when the appointed time comes and goes and no sign of him, I begin to feel a little stupid that I have been taken for a ride. But Abdulrahman has given me his number and so I use the phone box outside to call him. I think he had forgotten about me, but confirms that his offer still holds. I follow his directions so far, stopping a passerby, Michael from Ghana, to help me with the last bit. He phones Abdulrahman, who arrives quickly from his house nearby. Michael is visibly concerned for my safety, giving me his number to phone him if I need any help. I appreciate this gesture, although I do not sense that I am about to be murdered in my sleep. Abdulrahman, who shares the cramped flat with another man, talks at length about the Israeli/Palestinian situation, bringing maps out to show the redistribution of lands, putting forward his side of the Palestinian cause.

I understand when he wishes me to leave early in the morning, mindful of neighbours' reactions to a woman in his house overnight, again setting off in the dark. I follow the road along the coast all day, occasionally having to head inland for a while before returning to the sea. I do not think I shall ever tire of cycling by water. I stop to chat with a large family sitting on rugs under a makeshift awning against the wall of their property, shaded from the heat. They invite me to stay the night, but it is only morning, a little early to stop.

On one of my inland forays along a lonely, traffic free, country road, a car sidles alongside, a young man trying to say something. I assume his interest is in my laden bicycle, until a gradual dawning that he is suggesting we go back to his place. I ignore him and try to carry on but he cuts in front of me, barring my way whichever side I try to pass him. He starts demanding money, persistently and increasingly aggressive.

'No!' I shout.

And I bang my fist down on the roof of his car to let me by, at which point he dramatically draws his right index finger across his throat, before driving off. I stop, my voice by now quite hoarse and I am trembling from the emotion of the brief but scary encounter. I know I have to continue, but do so with trepidation as I do not know if he will have stopped further on. After a few miles, with no further sight of him, I allow myself to relax a little, remaining wary, my spirits not as buoyant as they were.

Towards evening, I enter a small village, hoping to find accommodation for the night or a safe pitch for my tent. The houses on the edge of the village are enclosed with high walls, at one a group of chatting women are gathered at the open gate. After an initial offer to stay is subsequently retracted (too many people in the house) and approaches to three other groups of women meet with a negative response, I move onto the neighbouring village, Al Haba. After my encounter, I am not keen to put my tent up in an unprotected spot away from habitation.

I am given the okay to pitch my tent amongst the houses, quickly followed by an invitation to stay in one of them. After a shower, I am installed in the 'guest room', in which various members of the family, children, grandmothers, adults, take it in turns to entertain the visitor throughout the evening. Later, a tray of food is brought in, everyone then disappears, leaving me to eat alone. In the morning, with no one in evidence, I leave a thank you note in Arabic.

Partway through the morning, an initial speck in the distance gradually manifests itself into a cyclist, the two of us embracing in reciprocal delight when we meet. Peder, a Swede, has been travelling with his trailer cycle for the last seven months, having set off in July 2008. His route has brought him through Europe, Turkey, Middle East, North Africa through Sudan, Eritrea, and across to Yemen, whose friendliness and hospitality he particularly enjoyed. I had considered this direction myself, but thought the North African section was too unstable politically.

We exchange information and stories over the next hour and a half; he outlining his ongoing plans, funds permitting, that would take him to Iran, Uzbekistan, China, Japan, USA. He had fifteen punctures in Turkey (Tomasz had about the same. I had none).

Muscat is somewhat isolated from the remainder of Oman, separated by a mountain range, the main approach road to the city therefore prefaced by a long uphill to the cut-through in the mountain, after which a freewheeling downhill to the ports. I head straightaway to the main port, hoping to find information about ships to India, joining a group of American passengers as they return to their cruise ship. The port officials direct me to a booking office which deals only with cruise ships, but they give me the whereabouts of a freighter company, even making phone calls to check their opening hours, thus saving me an unnecessary journey as they are now closed for the day.

I ask about the two huge ships moored just outside the small harbour, which turn out to belong to the Sultan of Oman. Maybe I should ask him if he would like to visit India.

Muscat is too built up for me to camp anywhere, forcing me into a hotel. I am pleasantly surprised to find that a couple of guests, a father and son, happen to live in my home area of Bristol.

Amongst my emails this evening is one from a different reporter on The National who has seen my website and would like to interview me if I come back through Abu Dhabi. In my reply, I suggest Peder as an alternative interviewee (I know he would be up for it as he had mentioned he was always looking to be interviewed, having experienced a few already).

I spend the entire next day going from one shipping agent to another in the hope of passage on a freighter ship, finally giving up when the repeated reply is that passengers are not allowed on container ships due to immigration controls.

The options now before me seem to be: ferry up the coast to Khasab then cycle back to Dubai and try for a ship to Bombay; fly to India from Muscat; cycle back to Dubai, if no ship, fly to India.

With nothing more to gain from staying in Muscat apart from a hefty hotel bill, I retreat back up the mountain and down the other side to Al Qurm, intent on finding a beach site or similar for tonight's camp.

Everywhere is very built up and the beach seems uncomfortably public, so when I find myself in a bread shop responding to a customer's queries about my bicycle and my search for somewhere to pitch my tent, I suggest straight out that she might like to offer me a small place in her large garden (of which she had boasted). In the end, she invites me to stay in their guest bedroom.

Su is Malaysian, married to an Australian, with two teenage children and a live-in housekeeper. The next day, she kindly drives me to a local business area for me to try more freighter companies. At one point it seems there could be a chance that I might be able to sign on as crew; this tenuous hope is eventually dashed when the owner refuses permission.

I have decided it is probably fruitless to return to Dubai and expect a different result, thus dolefully resigning myself to heading off to the airport the following evening to catch a flight to Bombay. Michael Palin did not have such a problem when he wanted to sail by dhow across the Indian Ocean.

On the way to the airport, I am cheered by the appearance of Barry, a British sports cyclist, who accompanies me as far as the entrance of the airport. He is a helicopter pilot for the Omani Royals, government and visiting dignitaries, yesterday flying the French President Sarkozy.

I have five hours to kill before my flight. The airport staff are able to produce the promised cardboard for wrapping my bicycle but can only offer masking tape to secure it in place, which breaks as soon as look at it. I become agitated, due in part to stressing out that things are not running smoothly, but, mostly, if I am honest, because I am in a filthy mood at being forced to fly when I so dearly wanted to cross by sea. A money-changer comes to the rescue, producing a roll of parcel tape. A kindly duty officer helps me through to check-in, where I end up once again paying nothing for my baggage excess. Finally on the plane, the journey is spent chatting to an Indian Professor of Pathology working in Oman with her husband.

I fly away from the Middle East, four and a half months after arriving in Port Said.

*   *   *

194

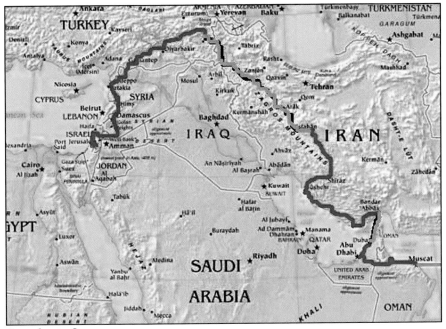

Jerusalem to Oman.

India to Kathmandu.

Kathmandu to Lhasa.

Middle Eastern hospitality in Syria.

Interior of the Umayad Mosque in Damascus, in which is entombed the head of John the Baptist, acknowledged as a prophet by both Moslems and Christians.

Dutch pilgrim, Jan, walking to Jerusalem, takes tea with locals in Syria.

English class in Turkey.

Cold Turkey.

Freezing fog is cold, but cyclable.

Twenty miles of freezing mud along a broken hill road in Kurdish PKK area of Turkey.

The sunny snow is beautiful . . .

. . . but I don't do cycling on icy snow.

Time for a bus from Turkey to Iran.

Five of the six cycling tourers in the same hotel in the same city in the centre of Iran. A Korean, a Pole, a Brit and three hunky Slovenians all together in Esfehan.

The sixth cyclist became my travelling companion when we happened to meet again later in Iran.

On their way to school. The women in Iran were friendly and curious. The men didn't know how to handle me: a woman, travelling on her own, and cycling.

*The ruins of ancient Persepolis, 400 miles
south of the present capital city of Teheran.*

*Camping in the grounds of ancient Persepolis. Bitterly cold temperatures
meant an early night, dressed in as many layers as possible.*

A hookah-smoking grandmother in Shiraz.

Convenience store in Iran.

The obligatory 'lone cyclist on a lone stretch of road in the middle of nowhere' photo. Persian Gulf, Iran.

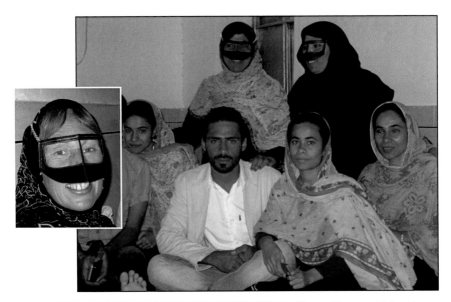

Above: *Women with burkhas were much more common at the Gulf than in the middle of Iran.*

Inset: *Does it suit me?*

Left: *Crossing Dubai Creek by abra (water taxi).*

'One cheese pancake to go, please.'

My Dubai police escort hand me over to their Abu Dhabi counterparts.

The Taj Mahal, Agra. A stunningly beautiful and romantic edifice.

Deaf School in Navsari, India.

A mistake to be on the road during the Festival of Holi.

Nepali roadside restaurant.

Freshly prepared and cooked to order.

Physiotherapy for a leprosy patient at Anandaban Hospital, near Kathmandu.
Inset: *The Leprosy Mission Nepal logo.*

Standing on the Roof of the World in Tibet was awesome.

Middle left:
Prayers on the go with a prayer wheel.

Middle right:
Buddhist monks in philosophical debate.

Left: *Potala Palace of the Dalai Lama, Lhasa.*

India

12 February – 20 March 2009

Charoti, Navsari, Ankleshwar, Baroda, Ahmdavabad,
Himatnagar, Kherwara, Udaipur, Iiwer, Bhim, Pushkar,
Bagru, Shahpura, Jaisinghpur, Delhi, Hodal, Agra, Etah,
Budaun, Pilibhit

We touch down at 5.30 in the morning. This is my third continent and I experience the usual mixture of feelings: excited anticipation, mostly overridden by nervous trepidation.

The first concern is that there is no ATM at the airport and no money changers open.

'You'll have to go into Bombay itself.'

Neither is there tourist information, for maps and accommodation.

'There's one in the south of Bombay.'

As the airport is on the outskirts of north Bombay from where I shall continue up-country, neither of these bits of advice are particularly helpful to me. I notice that bottled water is more expensive than in the Middle East.

Exiting the airport, I ask an airport employee the way to the road to Ahmedabad.

'Follow me,' is the instant reply.

He dons bike helmet, revs up his scooter and off we go. Talk about hairy. Firstly, I am concentrating on keeping up with my guide, who does not appear to appreciate that I am on a human-powered pushbike. Secondly, I realise shockingly quickly that I am on a journey of self-preservation. Anarchy rules the roads here, everyone taking their own precedence as the Highway Code. The roads are broken, there is no consideration for others, vast numbers of vehicles overtaking

dangerously close, cutting in. The main thought pounding my head is,
'I'm going to die. My daughter was right. I am going to die!'

I do not, but in the first thirty miles I witness the worst driving of my
trip so far. And then there is the poverty. So many street people, whole
communities living with no accommodation. Other communities risen
up as longterm makeshift shanty towns. All amidst litter and filth and
demeaning, desperate squalor. The assault on my senses is overbearing. I
don't want to be here; I want to get through India as fast as possible.

Away from the sensorial brutality of Bombay, the traffic lessens
slightly, the hard shoulder is reasonable, the terrain flat, air hot. I have
now calmed down enough to feel slightly more positive about my ability
to cope in the days to come. More surprisingly, I am sufficiently
confident to grab the tailgate of a slow-moving lorry up a hill, until it
tries to run me off the road, maybe offended at my refusal of the
proffered can of beer. (I only have a limited number of hands.)

As I pass through the countryside, the striking feature that
immediately presents itself is the vivid contrast of the vibrant colours of
women's saris against a neutral buff landscape.

By mid afternoon, I am thinking about accommodation for the night,
pulling off the highway to check out a clean-looking hotel/restaurant. As
I park outside, a Luton accent directs itself at me from the top of the
steps leading up to the restaurant. Nick flew into Bombay this morning,
on his way north to his parent's home in Navsari to attend a friends'
wedding. He invites me to stay if I am passing.

'How about tomorrow night?' I respond promptly.

As for tonight, Nick recommends this place and I end up agreeing
with him. My room is clean and pleasant, my evening meal and beer on
the house. Afterwards, I wander around the shops and stalls, finding
somewhere to buy a couple of small bolts to replace a lost one on my
pannier security system. This incurs no cost, 'Because you are a visitor
to our country.'

On balance, my first day in India is a good one.

I wear shorts the next day, peculiar after four months of covering up
except for the couple of days in Abu Dhabi. However, I stop feeling too
exposed on seeing the guy walking in the middle of the road in front of
me, completely starkers. I assume he is a Naga Sadhu, a holy man;
respected as such and supported by the community at large for the
perceived benefits from his spiritual activities.

Sadhus are not the only ones on the roads who seem to command respect and immunity from injury by the traffic. Animals also enjoy that privilege, such as the tall, black goat pausing obstinately in the middle of the road for a moment's reflection, cars and lorries steering adroitly around it.

The bright colours of yesterday are augmented today by the elaborately painted lorries trundling by. And the reason why India is such a cacophony of sound is made transparently clear on reading the tailgate instruction.

'Blow Horn!'

Local restaurants abound, providing cheap, tasty dishes, such as the *masala dosa* I sample this morning: spicy potatoes in a large paper-thin rice bread, served with coconut paste and curry sauce.

After a long day's ride of ninety miles to reach Navsari, I am given a warm welcome by Nick and his parents. They are kindness itself, inviting me along to the evening's 'do' on this fourth day of the 5-day Hindu wedding celebration; a double wedding, the grooms are cousins.

A whole contingent from Luton is in town, spread around the three adjacent apartment blocks. These are local people who left their country for better prospects, now wanting to share their success with those in their home town.

Arriving at the evening's venue, we enter via a decorated marquee tunnel that emerges into an open arena to a display of traditional wedding Gerber dancing. Seating is in formal rows but the protocol is very informal, guests watching the spectacle, interspersed with milling about and chatting to each other. The women are splendidly adorned in their finest, most beautiful clothes and jewellery, the men likewise in their elegant three-quarter length embroidered coats. Later on, more dancing displays on stage, followed by a singing group, then speeches. I am introduced to many of the guests, including the bride's father, who, I think, foots the bill for the whole event.

During the speech by the bride's father, he makes mention of the guests who have travelled far distances to be at the wedding.

'And we are privileged to have someone who has cycled here especially, all the way from London.'

At which point I am called upon to ascend the platform and impart a few appropriate words into the microphone. Rather stunned, I wend my way through the applauding crowd, up onto the stage, blurting out with,

'Hello, India,' as my opening gambit, quickly followed by a few brief words about my trip and charities, finishing off with expressions of hope for ongoing joy and blessings for the two couples at the start of their new lives.

Speeches finished, the dancing begins, everyone enjoying a raucous time in the 'stick dance', trying not to maim too many people in the process. One of Nick's friends, Neishaa, has a contact in Delhi for the magazine, *Time Out*, with whom she offers to try and set up an interview.

In the morning we pay a spontaneous visit to the local deaf school. I am fascinated to learn that, when it was established in the 1950s, children were taught in sign language. Whereas at the same time in the UK the prevailing teaching method was through oralism, where use of sign language, even outside of the classroom, was actually banned, to the point of punishment if caught in the act. This is a residential school for 5–16-year olds, boys and girls segregated; founded on Gandhian principles of love, truth, non-violence. I am in my element, chuffed that I can communicate with the children, spending time mostly with the girls, who are bubbly and beautiful.

Nick's father's life makes uplifting listening. As a young child, he and his family moved from India to Africa. At the ages of sixteen and fourteen, he and his brother, finding themselves alone and penniless, hitched their way to the UK to find family. They worked hard, did well for themselves and their families and have a second home here in their hometown, in order to be part of the local community. Contributing to its welfare out of a sense of duty, they do so imparted in a spirit of cheerful willingness. They have paid for improvements in the school and adhere to the custom whereby, when a family member dies, all children's school meals are paid for on each anniversary of that day in perpetuity. Such altruism is accompanied by great humility in Nick's father, for he would not talk about these things, Nick being the one to inform me, justifiably proud of his father.

The wedding celebration continues on the fifth day with a street procession leading to the marriage ceremony. Dressed in our gladrags, saris are sumptuous, hands henna-ed, hair intricately styled, adorned on the back with sparkling beads. Neishaa wears a large, ornate, bejeweled pendant in the centre of her forehead, framing her face with matching earrings and necklace.

We take a taxi into town to the starting point of the wedding
procession. An elaborately decorated horse-drawn carriage transports the
two bridegrooms, another carries elderly family members, on which
children take it in turns to ride (a grandmother even invites me to join
her at one point). Behind these carriages process the brides' fathers and
families and all the wedding guests, led by a lively band marking the
route. The two brides are nowhere to be seen, waiting at the wedding
arena to make their appearances later.

The streets are crowded, not only with the wedding party, but with
local people, vehicles and cows, everyone in good humour, enjoying the
spectacle, not bothered at the delays from this fourth procession of the
day; a fifth waits in the wings. It is the wedding season, similar
processions repeated in villages and towns throughout India. Progress is
slow because people are enjoying themselves so much, making the most
of the occasion. Even so, the wedding procession behind is forced to
tread water for rather too long and we must speed up a notch.

After four hours, we arrive at our destination, once again emerging
from the tented tunnel into the wedding arena. On the stage, two domed
pink and white canopies have been erected side by side, decorated with
borders of flowers. Under each, a pair of thrones in rich red and silver face
each other. The wedding ceremony was supposed to have started at six,
but it is seven o'clock by the time we arrive and fill up the rows of chairs.

The two gorgeously-attired brides now make their long-anticipated
entry, carried high on the shoulders of brothers and friends, then lowered
gently onto the dais to sit opposite their respective grooms on the
thrones under the canopies. And now, surprisingly, the informal protocol
of yesterday evening continues as, rather than wait for the marriage
ceremony to be completed, it seems acceptable for us to leave the
ceremony in full swing to make our way to the numerous buffet tables,
laden with over forty dishes of regional specialities, and to pile our
plates with delicious food. No alcohol is on offer; this is Gujerati, the
only 'dry' state in India, declared so since India's independence, out of
respect for Mahatma Gandhi who was born here.

We return to our seats with our laden plates, talking and laughing,
intermittently pausing to glance over at the ritualistic activities, maybe
even wandering up to the wedding group to see what is happening.

A religious overseer, dressed for the occasion in T-shirt and jeans,
conducts the proceedings, which are divided into different sections,

involving at one point an embroidered screen with a hole in the centre suspended between the couple, so that they cannot see each other. Each places a hand through the hole whilst prayers are incanted as they are joined together as man and wife. Bowlfuls of rose petals are passed around the guests, handfuls scooped and thrown in the air to flutter down onto the couples. It is fascinating to watch the whole proceedings and to be a part of it.

The next day is Sunday and I go along to a local church. The distinctive cross atop the building and a statue of a welcoming Jesus gives me a moment of homesickness for the familiar worship of my church back home. The main gates are locked and a prominent sign reads, 'No parking or standing in front of gates.' It is not a great welcome. I go through a side gate, but now the church itself is locked. A priest comes out, introduces himself and leads me in through the unlocked door on the far side of the church. He informs me that mass is at noon (it is now ten), then leaves me alone. I look around: it is an open space layout, traditional rows of pews, paintings on the walls of Jesus at the different stages of the cross. Christmas decorations still adorn the walls at the altar end (it is mid February). I sit in a pew enjoying the silence. After a while the priest returns, prepares the sacraments, ignores me, goes out and leaves on his motor scooter. I leave also.

I spend a couple of hours at an internet café. When I come to pay, I discover Nick has already paid for me. We go to a pizza place; he will not let me pay. Not all the pizza is eaten and he asks for it to be boxed up, offering it to one of the beggars in the street outside. He does not give money to them, but even giving food to one means others then come along wanting the same. It is a real dilemma, never a comfortable situation to see those in such dire straits. I admire and respect the innate altruism that stems from this family and their cultural inheritance. It certainly makes me think about my own attitudes towards these social issues.

The majority of Indians are Hindu, the associated activities being an important element in their daily lives and whole way of living. There are numerous temples everywhere, attended frequently to fulfill the ritual of regularly praying. Often people pop into a temple on their way to and from work or shopping, an automatic activity, ingrained in the culture. Often in Sikh temples in particular, food is cooked daily for anybody to eat free or with a donation, depending on personal circumstances. This outward giving and caring attitude is demonstrated by the rickshaw driver used regularly by Nick whenever he is here.

Rickshaw drivers are not the wealthiest of people but he refuses payment and in the past he has dropped Nick at an internet café, still there an hour and a half later because, as Nick explains, 'He did not want to leave me there at night.'

Before I depart, Nick plies me with provisions: protein bars (which he sells from one of his online businesses), cheddar cheese brought from UK, miniature fruit and nut chocolate bars, shortbread biscuits. I am also supplied with contact details of other family members with whom to stay in a couple of days' time.

Back on the road, I am fascinated by all there is to see along the roadside. I stop when I see a rope-making contraption in action. It is a very simple affair, strands of rope suspended a hundred feet between two wooden frames, a man at one end turns a wheel, which twists three strands, a woman guides them to twist into a final thicker rope.

A crowd gathers around me, all women and children; the usual being men and boys only. I take photos of them, and they delight in seeing themselves on the camera screen. They are so beautiful in their richly-coloured saris, some adorned with large, gold nose rings, all are smiling and friendly.

I arrive in Ankleshwar and find a clean, reasonably-priced hotel, the Highway Inn. The manager needs some soft persuasion to allow my bicycle into the room with me. I shower, wash smalls, lie down and read for a couple of hours before eating in the restaurant, the food tasty and not too spicy. The next day takes me through extensive stretches of roadworks along Highway 8, lovely for me as it means empty roads for much of the time. A police motorcyclist flags me down to offer refreshments at the next restaurant, even paying for my lunch. Throughout the day, other motorcyclists draw alongside asking if they can help in any way.

Much of each day is spent in my own company, giving rise to ample time for my own thoughts. It is a humbling experience being on this trip. I realise how privileged I am to be British (even European), for I can go just about anywhere in the world, with no real problem obtaining visas. I have been able to find money and opportunity to do this trip; I speak English. As I have found during so many encounters thus far, not all people in the world have the same freedom of opportunity to fulfill their preferred life choices. I felt this most strongly in Syria, the guilt of having such freedom, denied to others, could easily have resulted in returning home. But what would be the good of that? Would it have helped anyone? Would I have felt any better about myself? Maybe sharing it as now is a more positive response.

I stay the night with Nick's relatives, Shefila and Sumil, escorted to their house by a passing motorcyclist. The children's bedroom is given over to me, whilst all four of them sleep in the parents' room. In the morning, Shefila tests her daughter in readiness for an IT exam and after breakfast we all make our respective departures.

Cycling along the main highway, a motorbike draws level, attempting some kind of conversation but he has no English. It is soon obvious what he is indicating, nothing to do with my bicycle. I indicate for him to go away or I shall call the police. Undeterred, he stretches out and gropes me. I push him away with a yell – and instantly fall off my bicycle. He rides away as I shout angrily at him. Crying, I pick myself up and examine the grazes on my forearms and legs. The bicycle is undamaged, just needing a pannier re-attached. A lorry driver travelling by in the opposite direction has stopped and comes over, attempting to call to a vehicle going in my direction about the motorcyclist; and telling me I should report the incident to the police.

I continue, shaken and bruised, physically and emotionally, considering the best course of action for when it happens again. Whatever else I do, the crucial thing is to stop, in order to prevent injury to myself. In the meantime, the day continues in a similar vein: whilst re-adjusting my saddle, a man asks if he can help, at the same time fingering his nether parts. Later, another cyclist propositions me. By the time I deal with a flat front tyre from a damaged valve and have to settle for a grotty room, in a grotty hotel in grotty Ahmdevad, I have not the heart to be stared at in a restaurant. Instead I sit forlornly in my room, munching on biscuits, protein bars and an orange.

On the way out of town the next day, I stop at a church, the pastor unlocking it for me to have a look. As before, it is open plan and light-coloured. Again, Christmas decorations are still in place. I am invited to the pastor's home next door, meet his wife and teenage son, and offered tea and roti. Amazingly, there are thirty-five churches in Ahmdevad alone, denominations including Methodists, Baptists and Irish Presbyterian Missionary Society.

Further on towards the outskirts of town outside the front of a building is a man sitting at a handloom weaving cotton fabric. Inside are bales of the different quality cottons they produce, a book of samples displaying the range of patterns and colours available to order. Basket weaving is another roadside industry I pass today.

My new tactics against unsolicited advances are tested today when it becomes obvious that the driver of a rickshaw is not merely wanting to pass the time of day. I suggest he might like to go away, he persists, I stop on the hard shoulder; whereupon he pulls over, climbing out gleefully thinking, 'My luck's in.'

I turn to face the oncoming traffic and flag down a large lorry, which actually does not stop. I try flagging down a motorbike carrying a whole family, and a car with an elderly couple. They too carry on. No matter, for by now the rickshaw wallah has caught the gist and decides to scarper. And when I turn round to resume my cycling, there in front, lined up single file on the hard shoulder, are all the vehicles I had signalled to pull over. I go to each in turn to thank them, trying with gestures and facial expressions to explain my action, for none of them speak English, but am left with the definite impression that the phrase, 'Mad dogs and Englishmen,' might be passing through their minds.

Even though these incidents have happened on main roads, I decide I am probably safest to stick to them, on the whole possibly less vulnerable than on lonely country roads. The validity of this is emphasised when I pass a Border Security Forces station, a reminder that Pakistan is just two hundred miles to the west. On his journey through Pakistan, Tomasz was obliged to travel all the way in a bus as part of a police convoy, too dangerous to cycle any of it.

I eat a cooked meal during the day, so that I do not have to go out in the evening. Himatnagar does not strike me as much of an improvement on yesterday's destination, adding grimy to grotty. At these times particularly I long for a travelling companion. I have invited GR to join me in America, but part of the problem, for me at any rate, is that his 'free life' does not allow him to commit to anything. In this lonely frame of mind, I go to sleep, awoken at 1.30 am by my daughter unexpectedly calling on my mobile. I laugh at her wonderful timing.

By the end of the next day though, the negative aspects of India are insidiously overwhelming me. For the third night on the trot, I am staying in a dirty hotel, but this one in Kehrwara is the worst so far. For one thing, the room rate is way higher than I have been paying, although the manager eventually comes down to the going rate. The sheets are dirty and I have to ask for them to be changed. The towel is dirty so I use my own. I have to change rooms because this one does not lock. The light does not work in the bathroom. There is no shower; I take a bucket bath back in the first room. The electricity for the whole place cuts off: no lights, no fan, it is stifling.

In the last three days, I have had to contend with unsolicited attention and incidents with men, the pervading poverty and squalor, grimy hotels in which I am imprisoned in the evenings, too uncomfortable to go out alone. I am stared at, contact with home is scant because my SIM card does not work properly, English is not nearly as widespread as I had expected and neither do the locals cotton on to what I am trying to convey in as simple and clear a way as possible.

And I feel I am being a typically arrogant Brit abroad.

The way I feel is no one's fault but my own. I am responsible for my own attitude. I can wallow, if that is what makes me happy; I can be acceptingly tolerant, if that is as much as I am able to muster; or I can give thanks in whatever the circumstances I find myself in. One good thing today is that I have crossed the border from Gujerat into Rajasthan – the prospect again of a beer at the end of the cycling day.

In the morning, I eat an Alpen bar and orange before setting off, stopping after ten miles for tea and biscuits, only to discover the room key in my pocket. The shopkeeper says he will return it to the hotel, at the same time asking me what the accommodation was like and the cost. I reply that it was dirty, although the manager had been friendly, but he had also told me there were no other places for fifty miles, whereas I had passed one (cheaper and cleaner) soon after leaving the town. Beware helpful advice from those with a vested interest.

Looking at it objectively and in retrospect (always a time of great wisdom), I ask myself, 'Has there been any stretch of road more than twenty miles, if that, without accommodation? No? Remember that for next time, then.'

I like the undulating terrain of the hilly countryside of Rajasthan. Everything looks tidier, more ordered, than in Gujerat, even the natural countryside. I pass distinctive-looking trees that only bear orange flowers, no leaves, the only living feature amongst areas of burnt landscape. Arriving in Udaipur, having only had biscuits, tea, pepsi and water during the fifty miles, I feel faint and wobbly, glad to find a hotel pretty quickly. This relief is soon dispelled however when, after confirming beforehand that I can keep my bicycle in the room and lug everything up the steps in relay, the hotel chap then says, 'No bike!'

Frustrated, I repeat the tiresome operation in reverse, and continue towards the centre. I come across a genial Dutch couple, Floris and Marieke, perusing a *Lonely Planet*, who point me in the direction of an ATM and the hotel area. I end up in the delightful Pleasure Guest House. Despite its possible connotations, it is strictly above board, a family-run establishment, cheap and clean, homely and relaxed, tucked away in a quiet side street just off the tourist area. I have a large room, ample space for Raven, a shared bathroom; there is also a restaurant in the pleasant, arboured garden.

I like Udaipur. There is a buzz and excitement about the place and, despite large numbers of people, which is not my preference, I enjoy wandering the streets, a riot of colour in the shops and temples. A string of donkeys plod by, weighed down by their bilateral cloth panniers bulging with boulders of hewn rocks. I meet a French cyclist, Justin, touring India for three months and, meeting the Dutch couple again, at their invitation rendezvous with them for lunch at their plush hotel, Raj Palace. Back at the Pleasure, amongst the guests is a Brit, Darren, from Northampton, six weeks into touring India for a year on a Royal Enfield motorbike, which he bought in country.

After the discomfort of the previous few days, I make the most of this relaxed oasis, remaining here four nights. The front man at the Pleasure is G2, in his forties, a wiry, amiable host, supporting ageing parents who also live here, helping with cooking and cleaning. Sitting in the garden is both relaxing and lively: two chickens make their presence known jumping up onto tables and chairs, amongst which dart umpteen little chipmunks, eating any scraps left them, holding them deftly in their tiny paws whilst they nibble away, keeping alert eyes on their surroundings.

Darren has the run of the kitchen for a while, in order to make tomato soup as taught him a couple of days previously by G2. It is deliciously simple, and simply delicious, blended tomatoes, generous crushed garlic, garam masala, splodge of water, salt, sugar, boiled vigorously. For the evening meal, the main course on offer is tasty goat mutton curry. Afterwards, I attend a Son et Lumière at City Palace, a beautiful backdrop for recounting the history of the Mewar region and India.

I visit the City Palace during the day. It now stands on five levels, instead of the thirteen in the original design. Maharana Bhupal Singhji was ruling at the time of Independence in 1948. He was disabled, in a wheelchair and a lift was installed in the palace. I like his simple apartments. And paintings displayed on the walls are interesting, those showing a ruler illustrate him with a nimbus around his head, green on gold, or gold on green.

Udaipur is built on seven main lakes, each able to overflow into each other to keep the levels uniform, apparently quite an engineering feat when it was begun in the fourteenth century.

There is no escaping the strong cultural influence of the Hindu religion throughout India. It is all pervasive and forces one to absorb some of its detail, including the plethora of gods, of which there are thirty-seven million, unsurprisingly some more well-known than others. G2 and his family favour the sporty, monkey god, Haroman. Krishna is the playboy god, Ganesh the elephant god of good fortune, the camel god is for love, the horse for power.

It is often said that Indians can take anything and mend it, so it is with great confidence that I take my party sandals for re-heeling (prematurely worn down by the 4-hour wedding procession, no doubt). But I come away disappointed with a poor job, a nail banged into the heel sitting proud in the centre of a rough-shod heel.

Passing a 'beauty' shop, I go in for a haircut and manicure, during which time the electricity goes off and my pleasant manicurist invites me to her home to meet her children. The 16-year old daughter has a smattering of English, although really not much more than my knowledge of Hindi.

The electricity returns after an hour, whereupon tea is made, accompanied by chapatti with lime pickle.

Later, I take coffee and French apple tart in a rooftop restaurant overlooking the palace lakes, at the same time realising the difference in lifestyle and opportunity between the manicurist and me.

A cousin of G2 hennas the back of my hands, a design of flowers and stars, into which I ask to be incorporated my children's names 'Jessica' and 'Daniel', one on each hand. Emailing a picture to my family, my daughter responds, 'Oh, Mum, it made me cry at work.' And my older brother, presumably reminiscing back to his youthful hippy days, replies, 'How groovy.'

I browse a couple of secondhand bookshops, picking up copies of *Slumdog Millionnaire*, the film of the book recently receiving rave reviews and awards at the BAFTAs and Oscars, and a Paulo Coelho, *The Kahir*. Darren lends me his laptop to view a film he strongly recommends, *Into the Wild*, based on a true story of a young man who leaves everyone and everything to live on his own in the wilds of Alaska, but lacks the wherewithal and means to survive, and dies. He leaves behind his written account of what he was trying to do, amongst his last words a resonating realisation that, 'Happiness needs to be shared with someone.'

These words in mind, I reluctantly take my leave. I have stayed four days already; the more familiar I become with people and a place, the greater the loneliness on setting off once more, back to my solitary happiness. I am waved off by Darren and G2, the road out of Udaipur unexpectedly turning into a bumpy, dirt track through small, friendly villages, then back onto the main road, to bypass Jaisalmer, heading towards Pushkar.

Spoiled from the last four nights' pleasurable accommodation, I pass over three possibilities of accommodation for tonight as too expensive, too dirty, too grotty. I decide on a different course of action. Cycling well clear of town, I pull over to the side of the road, check up and down to ensure I am not seen by anyone before veering well away behind a hillock. I follow a stone wall until I am able to hoike everything up and over it, a couple of protruding stones in the wall acting as steps.

I am now in a field, a wide open view before me. I pitch my tent to face the setting sun, revelling in the sweet, fresh air on my face as I sit and write my journal and listen to the soft sounds of nature around me. Eventually though some far-off animal noises unsettle me enough to drive me into the psychological security of my flimsy refuge. Restless during the night (I wish my Thermarest was a tad thicker), I continue to hear various noises.

'Ooh, that sounds rather near. Is it a snuffling?'

Or is it merely the imagination of the night? At least I manage not to freak myself out by them.

My dread on this trip is to be injured sufficiently to impede my progress. Mid morning the next day, I stop for a picnic snack by the roadside. Whilst crossing a trench between the road and the bank, I step on a stone which topples and sends me a cropper, twisting and banging my left ankle against the stone. The pain is excruciating and I sit there, tightly hugging my leg, with repeated self-admonishments.

'How stupid! What a careless fool! What a stupid thing to do!'

A police jeep stops, as does a lorry, the three occupants checking to see if they can help. It hurts but I can walk and move my foot.

'No, I'll be fine thanks. But thank you for stopping.'

I cycle on, encouraged that it is comfortable whilst cycling, but concerned how painful it is as soon as I bear weight. I manage a reasonable distance for the day, arriving in Bhim and a hotel. My foot is swollen and wincingly tender at the slightest touch. The hotel manager ferries me on the back of a motorbike to the nearby hospital, an x-ray revealing no fracture. My foot is swathed in a crêpe bandage and I am returned to the hotel, in the company of strong painkillers, hoping fervently I shall be able to continue the following day. With elevated leg, I pass the evening on the hotel balcony, loudly entertained by a cacophonous choral symphony, a rousing performance from hundreds of green macaws in the adjacent trees, with a lengthy encore at dawn.

Although my foot is painful and I should rest it, this is not the right place, despite the kindliness of the manager. The hotel and the town are all rather grey and depressing, so the next day I continue.

I stop at a small roadside restaurant, the home of a young couple and two children. I am invited to sit under the latticed wooden awning, watching as my food is made from scratch: dal fry and chapatti. Sitting on her haunches, deftly kneading the dough in a large shallow metal bowl, the wife is an elegant picture of vibrant gentian and saffron, the border of her sari a wide red band embroidered with white, swirling chainstitich, loosely-draped around her head neatly framing her petite face. Her two young children are dressing for school, husband supervising, whilst looking on is an aged father sitting on his haunches atop a low wide wall, wrapped in a striped shawl, his head sporting a loosely-wound orange turban.

My second stop is a rather more upmarket tourist restaurant and gift shop, where I eat a tourist cheese sandwich and coke, surrounded by touristy souvenir nicknacks. As I leave, a plum-voiced English couple kindly offer me a lift to Pushkar in their smart, chauffeur-driven car, but my foot is bearing up enough for me to be able to decline.

I arrive in Ajmer, emphatically rejecting it as a place to stay for it is just as Darren and G2 had said, dirty, smelly, polluted. From the town, a long, slow mountain road brings me up and over to the next valley and Pushkar. By the roadside are hundreds of monkeys sitting intimately de-fleaing each other, or lording it at passersby, their benignly confident facial expressions assuming ownership of their mountain.

Pushkar is a popular destination, visitors flocking to the holy lake, entering its waters from numerous ghats associated with the four hundred and fifty temples crowding the lakeside. I find the guesthouse G2 recommended, in a quiet suburb away from the hubbub of the centre, paying a little more for a light, double-aspect, upper room with balcony as I plan to remain a few days to recuperate.

The next three days are spent in the room, leg elevated. Bunti, one of the sons of this family-run guesthouse, buys books for me from a secondhand bookshop in town, a couple at a time, taking the read ones back in part-exchange for the next on my list. And so I work my way through *Slumdog*, Paulo Coelho's *The Zahir*, *The Fifth Mountain*, *By The River Piedra I Sat Down And Wept*, and Rushdie's *Midnight's Children*.

My foot remains painful, particularly at a small, deep, puncture hole. I clean it as best I can, apply Savlon and a sterile dressing, pain balm on the foot and ankle, wrapped in the crêpe bandage more to aid absorption than for support. All three of the men of the guesthouse, Bunti, Maneesh and their father give their common opinion of the required treatment: a procedure of warm water poured over the leg, pain balm (Iodax) rubbed in, bandage applied, three times a day. By the end of the day, there is a significant improvement (oh, the power of suggestion). But the puncture wound becomes infected, to which I apply an iodine-based lotion supplied by Maneesh.

A yoghurt drink called Lassi, taken either sweet or sour (with salt) is frequently listed on menus. Here at Natural View Hotel is the first time I have seen Lassi Special and I order a mild one after my evening meal. The 'special' part consists of weedy leaves, the effects from which are supposed to produce a feeling of well being. I however experience no change in my usual demeanour. The next evening I try a strong one, double the quantity of leaves. Not only does it have no effect on me whatsoever but it tastes absolutely disgusting, requiring to be washed down by large drafts of water, eventually discarding the last of it. At least I can say I tried it.

In the afternoon of the third day, I walk to the centre for the first time.

Taking things easy, I relax with a drink on the balcony of a restaurant overlooking the lake, falling into conversation with a young Israeli backpacker. She is travelling around India, Nepal and Thailand for four months, before returning home to try and find work, although jobs are scarce in her field of plastics engineering. Her father cycles and so she makes a note of my website, hoping it might encourage him to fulfil his longstanding dream of a long distance trip. An American couple, Shirley and Harry, come from a place called Truth or Consequences in New Mexico. The town was originally called Hot Springs but changed it in 1950 in order to appear on a TV show of that name.

The centre of Pushkar is one big shopping bazaar, in which I could have a field day if I had not decided to limit my purchases to zero. The lake is very pretty, the many temples leading down to the water's edge via steps filled with people in and beside the water, bathing and washing their clothes. Some ghats charge extortionate fees to unsuspecting tourists to allow them down to the water, but I find one with open access, going close enough to have a peek without being intrusive.

The centre of town is frenetic with motorbikes, motorscooters, rickshaws, cows, dogs, people, fresh dung. I am standing amongst this mayhem, looking around and minding my own business, when suddenly I am knocked painfully sideways, almost falling over, having been head-butted by a cow! I feel somewhat affronted at the unprovoked injustice of the cow's action. The peace and quiet of the guesthouse beckons.

On the sixth morning, I am waved off by the whole family: Mum, Dad, Maneesh, Bunti and wife, supplied with directions to Jaipur that negate the need to return up arduous monkey mountain and smelly Ajmer. Away from the NH8 and along tranquil country roads through villages is enjoyable, especially the friendly spontaneous greetings from the women.

In the middle of nowhere on a lonely stretch of road, I arrive at a junction, where a small crowd is gathered. A group of policemen stop me from continuing along the road, the reason at first a mystery. Eventually, though, it becomes clear that there is a competition about to start and I shall have to wait for it to finish.

'How long, do you think?'

'An hour,' proffers one of the policemen.

'Er, no, twenty-five minutes,' amends another.

'No time at all, they come now,' declares a third.

And here they are, a large bunch of policemen with numbered bibs racing towards the tape. It is the local police sports day. Once they are all over the finishing line I am let through and the road is all mine. Presiding police officers line the road every few yards, white powdered chalk lines mark one and two kilometre distances. I come to the other end of the race track, a long queue of traffic waiting patiently for the all clear from this direction.

Shortly after, I rejoin the NH8, grabbing hold of a slow-moving lorry for a short distance. On release, I find myself with a puncture from a huge nail in my rear tyre. When I examine the tube, three substantial holes wink up at me. That was some nail. I do not repair the tube, hoping to be able to buy a new one in Delhi as this is now pretty well patched up. Whilst replacing the wheel, I manage to strain my back, my right sacro-iliac issuing forth sharp stabbing pains. I feel a real decrepit with my four areas of pain: left lower leg, left thumb, right thigh, right back; but an oddly pleasing symmetry in their distribution.

Another puncture next day attracts an audience of would-be helpers. I hope there will be no more as I have no intact spare tubes. It is, after all, an unusual occurrence for me to have any, let alone this many.

It is not only the women in India who liven their surroundings with colour. Tonight's motel in Shahpura is highlighted with a spectrum of pinks and oranges from the prolific bougainvillea against its walls. I have seen amazingly-coloured birds, especially when in flight: bright petrol blue; black and white-striped. Monkeys are all over the place, swinging leisurely, wandering languidly, sitting cockily. Most are the grey and white-faced variety; only one has been the more aggressive red-face.

I clock up 8,000 miles.

During a bout of homesickness, I recall the forlorn words of a friend, 'I am alone and unhappy; worse is not possible.' And that is how I have been feeling of late. If I was at home, I could talk to someone. Here in India, I write in my journal. In two months I shall be midway through my journey of self-discovery. Five weeks after that will be the anniversary of my arrival in Santiago, a special memory. Up until now, I have been on a cycling trip; henceforth, I feel I am on a pilgrimage.

The purpose for me of this pilgrimage is to become the person I should be, rather than being the person others think I should be, or even the person I think others think I should be. Ah, the intricacies of self-perception. By being away from the familiar where I am known, my thinking is that I would have the opportunity to be myself and gain a clearer picture of who I am. And by finding out who I am, maybe then I shall see clearly my future direction in life.

The following night, I land on my feet in glorious style, in the brand new Sangrila (aspiring to Shangri-La?) Hotel, opened four months previously. The place was recommended by last night's hotel, but at 2,500 rupees is way out of my Asian budget, my normal room-rate a fraction of that (hence the high level of grottiness). I state my budget and they offer me a hefty discount to 500 rupees. Not thinking too straight (bearing in mind this is about £6) and keeping fixedly to my mental budget, I decline and prepare to move on.

They then offer me a room for 350 rupees (my maximum), situated away from the main hotel on the other side of the grounds near the swimming pool. I laugh when I see it. The room to which I am escorted is the right half of a 2-roomed small square building, the room on the left displaying a Gents sign above the door, mine, a Ladies. I am sleeping in a converted loo block. Nice. There are no windows and no bathroom. I am allowed to use a bathroom in one of the rooms in the hotel. However, when it is discovered there is no electricity and so no lighting, they let me stay in the hotel itself, for only an additional fifty rupees. And very nice it is too, to be sleeping in such a plush hotel in a spacious ultra clean room, in a bed with fresh, pristine sheets, pillowcases and duvet – all matching. Divine luxury. And all topped off by sitting in the soft evening sun, near the pool, sipping wine and writing my journal.

I am expecting the ride into Delhi to be fairly harrowing and adrenalin-flying, if my experience of Bombay is any indication. But my fears come to nothing. There is none of the squalor of that initial onslaught, and I am now more used to the traffic. People are helpful with directions and I have the useful city map pages from *Lonely Planet*, donated by Darren. On the outskirts of the city centre is the New Tibetan Colony, fenced in for security, accessed via a couple of entrances. I locate Wonghden House hotel down a narrow side street.The rooftop view overlooks a peaceful landscape of neat, well-maintained, vegetable plots, the River Yamura separating them from the forested skyline beyond.

Amongst my emails I am relieved to have confirmation that Tomasz is safely through the troubled areas in Pakistan, as I have not heard from him for a while. He is currently in Pokhara, Nepal, on his way to

Calcutta, a flight to Singapore booked for three weeks' time. He makes sure to give me an important date for my diary: 4 April – Formula 1 Grand Prix! Very thoughtful, Tomasz.

A planned visit to The Leprosy Mission hospital has been arranged and I am duly picked up by Arun Kumar from TLM and taken to the hospital, meeting with Dr Abraham, the Director there. Later I spend time in the physiotherapy department, watching the Head Physiotherapist, Indranil Ghosh, at work and discussing the status and future of leprosy and its victims and families. A down-to-earth, kind and dedicated man, Indranil has worked for twenty-five years with leprosy patients, post-surgically rehabilitating their deformed limbs to achieve as much functional movement as possible for an independent and productive life.

But his work does not stop there. He is constantly trying to encourage hospitals to refer leprosy patients to him on the same day of diagnosis, for assessment of total needs, rather than being returned to their villages unsupported, in the misguided supposition that they will successfully complete their course of MDT (multi-drug therapy), which often does not happen but which is vital for their cure.

Indranil keeps records of each patient, reviewing them regularly, assessing their needs and ensuring they receive whatever is appropriate in the way of appliances or support in the local community, including monitoring completion of their MDT-course. The whole tragedy of leprosy not yet being eradicated is that, *if* diagnosed early, it can be successfully treated through a simple course of drugs, thus preventing all deformities. This then avoids the ensuing loss of employment or becoming an outcast from home, family and community. The main contributing factor why leprosy still flourishes is the accompanying stigma of having contracted it in the first place and the long-carried fear it still instills in society. This prevents people going for early diagnosis, hence the development of totally preventable disabilities.

A newly-confirmed leprosy patient, still in the infectious stage, comes into the physiotherapy department for assessment by Indranil. Patients are not isolated because there is only a five per cent chance of becoming infected and, anyway, the MDT course easily cures it. It is akin to taking a course of antibiotics for a chest infection.

Arun and I visit one of the leprosy colonies nearby. He grew up in one as both his parents had leprosy. He is afraid for his daughters' prospects of marriage because of the related stigma by association. A new project called *Shalom* is based in this colony, where most of the project workers are residents. It aims to raise public awareness of the truth about leprosy in an attempt to reduce stigma and to work with local schools, both private and government, to accept children from the colonies into the schools, from which they are so often barred, again due to the associated stigma.

The colony is a well set-up, clean village, with tiny one-roomed homes, one or two also serving as a shop. This comes in the form of a small three-shelved unit in the room, displaying a few jars and packets of biscuits. I see the activities of this community: a husband dressing a wife's ulcerated feet, three men sitting on the ground outside a front door playing cards, a group of women seated on the ground in a courtyard, one combing another's long black hair. Another, a young girl, sits cross-legged holding a sleeping baby in her arms; yet another woman squats at a standpipe washing dishes. It is a cheery, welcoming, supportive community, offering purpose, hope and fellowship.

Time Out magazine interview me over the phone, asking me for my impression of India as a whole, and Delhi in particular, as the article will go into a local edition. A photographer is arranged to meet me the following day. At the end of the call, my mobile is empty of credit, even though I have a local SIM card and incoming calls should not be affected. It turns out that each Indian state has its own SIM card, so that when calling to another state, it is treated as an overseas call and charged accordingly.

I am bitten to death in the night, from the resident bedbugs and by mosquitoes. I check out in the morning, cycling into the busy centre in search of a cycle shop. The only inner tubes on offer have large valves, unlike my thin delicate ones. The option now available to me is to have some sent out from UK to a known address. I do not like the other option: to drill the valve hole on the wheel rim larger, in order to accommodate the large valves. Who's going to drill them and what if something goes wrong?

I now stay in a hotel in the Pahar Ghanj area of Delhi. The *Time Out* photographer eventually arrives, just three hours later than the appointed time (this is not UK, I remind myself). Anshika has me cycling slowly up and down the road a few times, clicking away for that one photograph. The article should appear within a couple of weeks and she agrees to email me a copy. She asks that I send her the two photos I have taken of her.

It is the eve of the festival of Holi, the streets bursting with parties, heralding tomorrow's peculiar celebrations. These will consist of throwing handfuls of coloured powder paints over as many people as possible, often accompanied by a bucket of water to make sure of an even coating. I had been informed of this forthcoming event, emphatically advised not to be cycling at night (something I always endeavour to avoid anyway).

In the morning I cycle confidently out of Delhi in the direction of Agra. It is not long before I see people walking around with clothes, hair, faces and bodies already an adornment of primary colours. And it does not take them long to regard me as an obvious target. I am obliged to run the powder-paint gauntlet, obligingly happy to rise to the spirit of the occasion with as much gay abandon as I can muster, as I look increasingly like an artist's palette.

And it *is* fine, initially, because it is all done in good humour. But, as the day wears on, I become aware of the lack of vehicles and people on the road, the only ones now groups of young men who, like these dozen or so strung across the road ahead of me, are becoming increasingly drunk. I approach with trepidation, looking for a bolthole but not finding one. As I draw closer, they crowd around me; one man advances purposely with a handful of powder, but rather than the usual throwing, rubs it roughly on the front of my shirt. I am angry at this rude intimacy, shove his hand away, shouting at him to leave me alone. They keep pressing in, I dismount, and try to push through them. I look around to see if there is by chance a vehicle coming by. There is and I hail it, but it drives by, the occupants an elderly couple. I can't blame them for not stopping. I continue pushing through, my angry shouts by now intermingled with tears. At last they break the posse and let me continue. I am badly shaken and know that I must retreat from the road as soon as possible.

A few miles on, I stop at a tourist bungalow holiday centre, relieved to be off the road and in apparent safety. The centre is not yet fully prepared for the holiday season; the room rates are extortionately high, especially considering the dusty dirty state of them. I ask to camp in the grounds.

'Yes. But only after dark.'

There is nowhere to shower; I do what I can with the cold water from the tap on the filthy washbasin (what kind of holiday place is this?) but, after pitiable attempts, I am forced to remain in my painted state. And, although I assumed this to be a safe haven, I am being stared at by a man standing just a couple of yards away who seems unable to grasp the idea that I want him to go away. He starts to make sexual gestures, even following me when I make my way to reception hoping to enlist support from staff, sadly unforthcoming. I can do nothing but tolerate his presence until he eventually decides to depart. This is by far and away the most unpleasant and miserable day of my trip.

Surprisingly, I have a peaceful night, even fairly comfortable, even sleeping some. In the morning I leave soon after the gates are unlocked (at least it is a safe haven at night), noticing after a few miles that my cyclometer has stopped working; after a few more miles, that my mobile is not working; after the next few miles, that I do not like motorcyclists drawing alongside; and that I am morose and negative. But I do not wish to be this way. I dislike not greeting anyone; and when this morning I have smiled at the occasional woman, it does not feel right because I am not smiling inside. I stop at an upmarket hotel-restaurant, thinking to treat myself to a 'normal' breakfast, something I can relate to, in a sterile atmosphere, away from the flies. But there is not much on offer, not even an omelette, as this is a pure vegetarian establishment.

Later on though, the response to a heartfelt prayer comes in an unexpected form, the shape of a big yellow 'M' at the roadside. And I think, 'Why not? Something familiar – *just* what I need. Thank you, God.'

I order veggie burger surprise (curried) and iced coffee, delicious. I eat it outside in the shade. I go back for soft scoop ice cream with chocolate sauce and filter coffee, perfect. I read the letters from my children, taking a photo of them with Ronald McDonald as the backdrop and sending it on my (now working) mobile to my children. A reply from my daughter sighs, 'How sad, that Ronald McDonald saved you!' Sad, maybe, but I am now in a much more positive frame of mind, no longer feeling the victim. Yo.

I arrive in Agra, a much larger place than I had anticipated. Cycling past Agra Fort, I look over to my left – my first view of the Taj Mahal. Even at this distance it is beautiful.

The Maya Hotel, recommended by another traveller, is within walking distance of the Taj. The staff are amiable, the premises clean, set in pleasant, shaded grounds. My favourite place is sitting on huge cushions at the low tables on the blue and white crazy-paved tiled balcony, surrounded by trees inhabited by monkeys and chipmunks. As my foot is still troubling me, I spend the next couple of days mostly resting on these cushions, from my vantage point watching the bustling street below, market stalls, cycling street vendors, cycle rickshaws, horse-drawn carts (further south these were pulled by camels, oxen, donkeys); an opera of colour, sounds and smells.

I clean my bicycle and panniers and do my best to remove all trace of the Holi experience, but my linen shorts obstinately retain remnants of red powder paint. Next door to the hotel is a telephone exchange from where I call my daughter and son, receiving updates of their love life (oh dear) and work (oh good).

Looking ahead to Tibet and China, there is a possibility of not being able to pass through the former because of the current protests and uneasy situation. Poring over maps, there appears to be no feasible alternative route from Nepal into China via India. But I am determined to find some kind of overland route, although desperately hoping to be able to travel through Tibet itself. I must wait until Kathmandu before any final decision can be made.

It is dawn. I walk through the courtyard, up the steps, through an archway . . . my eyes follow the length of the still watery avenue to the building at the far end . . . the Taj Mahal.

It was built in the seventeenth century by the Mogul Emperor, Shah Jehan, to entomb the body of his beloved favourite wife, Mumtaz Mehal. He chose to lie alongside her after his death.

The morning is slightly hazy, the sun slowly rises making subtle changes of light on the marble edifice. When I finally make my way to the monument itself, punctuated frequently by pauses to gaze, it is to marvel at the simple intricacy of the building, decorated in delicate floral designs with precious and semi-precious stones, emerald, lapis lazuli, yellow marble, jasper and jade. The tomb is enclosed by an intricate fretwork screen featuring stems of plants from which flowers of hearts appear; love growing and blossoming, I presume.

I spend five hours there, totally mesmerised by the romantic vision.

My sixth and last day in Agra, ankle still painful, I prepare to depart the next morning. Advice from the Foreign and Commonwealth Office in Nepal is to beware of Maoist activity and not to go out at night. I register my details on their LOCATE register. I finish writing thirty-seven postcards (after all, I am at the Taj) and part exchange my two Coelho paperbacks for Eric Newby's, *A Walk InThe Hindu Kush*. I like his humorous writing style.

As I leave Agra, I see that my cyclometer is not working again. Silly me not to have bought new batteries when I had the opportunity. I may well have to wait until Kathmandu. It is very tiresome as I rely on it heavily for timings and distance as well as for my overall distance.

For only about the second time in India I am cycling along a quiet, country road. It is very pleasant, clean-looking villages and countryside, no nostril-crinkling smells or pollution. After twenty-five miles the smooth asphalt deteriorates in a trice to potholes, stones and sand, bumping and shaking me mercilessly for the next twenty-five miles. How the one-gear bicycles with passengers or huge loads manage to keep going fills me with admiration. The concluding twelve miles for the day are a return to asphalt and the odd leery rider alongside.

In Etah, I pass a few Christian schools and churches, trying one of them on the offchance of being able to find accommodation, but there is no reply to my knocking. The first hotels I check out either have no vacancies or they are expensively filthy. One of them tells me I need a letter of permission from the police station before I can stay in a hotel; a new one on me. In the sunny courtyard of the police station, I queue at the wooden desk, behind which sits a uniformed official issuing hotel permits. Whilst I am waiting for mine, a couple of journalists appear, one from the local paper, the other from the American news agency, CNN, expressing an interest in interviewing me. They come later to my hotel, accompanied by a film cameraman and a couple of assistants. During the filming there is a powercut so we finish the interview in dusky gloom, after which I exchange contact details with the CNN reporter and a request for him to let me know if anything comes of it.

I am properly saddlesore, the first time on the trip, probably from the constant chafing from the bumps. The next day therefore I am not at all happy that the first twenty miles are a repeat of yesterday's off-road conditions. In Kasganj, I stop to buy fruit from an enticing market stall, a crowd gathers close, restrained and respectful, from which there emerges the usual one person with a smattering of English. I think they are just surprised to see someone like me, or rather *any* visitor passing through and stopping. Animals pulling carts are diverse: paired-oxen, water buffalo, camels, donkeys. Many carts carry eight or more people pulled by slender horses which nonetheless prance along at a fair pace, presenting an amusingly unbalanced picture.

The road leads onto a bridge to become incorporated into a railway track, traffic and trains taking in turns to cross. The traffic extends back hundreds of yards and I cycle gaily past them all to the front of the queue. Fifteen minutes later, the train passes and we have the all clear. The challenge now is not to become ensnared in the grooves of the track, as I did once in Dublin on the way to the ferry port, coming a cropper when I fell hard onto the concrete surface. Successfully reaching the other side, I take out my camera and snap a picture, instantly followed by the sudden appearance of a policeman who insists I should accompany him to the police hut nearby. I can only assume I am being told that I should not have taken the photo, although I do not know why. After showing him the picture on my camera and asking, 'No problem? OK?' he lets me go, the gathered crowd entertained by the spectacle.

In the hotel in Budaun (pronounced Bad-eye-oon), one of the owner's young sons is willing to go on an errand for batteries for my cyclometer. I am dubious whether he will return with the right product; it just seems too straightforward. But I am mistaken, the young lad returning promptly with exactly what I need. I have to re-set the cyclometer, including the miles since Agra, which is a complex process, pleased therefore that I remembered to bring the instructions with me from home.

From Budaun to Pilibhit is by far the best and most enjoyable cycling in India: smooth-rolling surfaces for the most part; scant traffic; clean, attractive countryside and villages; amiable people; alongsiders, yes, but manageable; and, at the end of the day, a reasonably clean hotel, where I opt for an 'ordinary' room (as opposed to a 'deluxe'). The difference is cold running water only in my room, hot water being brought to me for a bucket bath; rather than a shower as per the 'deluxe' room. The television even has a choice of non-Indian channels, my last evening in India spent watching the second half of the film *The Search for Eagle* and the Flintstones in *Rock Vegas*. And I do not pass up the chance of a final helping of Bollywood musical soaps.

The next morning is a repeat of yesterday's pleasurable ride. A middle-aged couple on a bicycle pass, the woman, as usual, nonchalantly riding pillion side-saddle, the ends of the blue and pink flower-patterned sari flowing behind, somehow escaping the would-be clutches of the back wheel. They are Christians; interestingly, there are four hundred in their village alone. They invite me for *chay* in a small tea house in the next town, where they have a hospital appointment for the woman's slowly mending broken foot.

At the border town of Banabas, the original plan of staying here tonight is overturned as I cannot locate any money changers and there seems to be no internet. It is only two in the afternoon and so I might as well continue into Nepal.

I have been heartily glad of these two pleasant days at the end of my stay in India. At least I am exiting the country with a favourable last impression. Except that India decides to deliver me a parting shot. A bridge over the river separating the two countries is the border over which I must now cross. As yesterday, this too is shared with a railway track. Partway along, my wheel becomes embedded in a groove of the rail track – and I fall off. The bicycle is undamaged, but I sustain a knock to my left knee, a bruised left arm, and my left ankle is none too impressed with this further setback.

But I still love your colourful saris, India.

*   *   *

Nepal

21 March – 13 April 2009

Mahendranegar, Chisalpani, Shamsharganj,
Lamahi, Butwal, Bharatpur, Mugling, Kathmandu

As soon as I cross the bridge and enter the fertile lowlands of Nepal, my shoulders lose their tension and my spirits soar. Over on my left is a peaceful pastoral scene of soft green fields, gentle blue rivers, misty mauve mountains; Nepal's way of saying, '*Namaste*. Welcome.'

Mahendranegar is just a few miles over the border, where I stay the first night; the next day continuing through the flat lowlands.

A building project in the late 1990s resulted in the erection of twenty-two bridges along this stretch of road. The road itself was then built up to the same height as the bridges, so that it now runs on top of a high ridge, dropping abruptly away on either side to level out as open fields or to curve up to the same level on the other side. The resultant chasm is bridged at intervals by wooden planks, giving access from the road to the small gatherings of scattered dwellings.

The Nepali people are small in stature, with round, smiling faces and sparkling eyes. I pass many of them transporting huge bundles of twigs, either walking upright with them balanced on top of their heads, or stooped forwards, a band of cloth across their foreheads, taking the weight of the heavy load on their backs.

I feel relaxed and carefree, so different from the majority of the time in India. I do not know why it should seem so different here; all I can say is that I feel safe from hassle. My mood is enhanced when I am able to call home from a public phone, my daughter wishing me, 'Happy Mothering Sunday.'

I am allowed to put my tent up in the grounds of a project calling itself 'Hindu Integration', although I am not sure what that is all about.

One of the staff is Christian and there is a group of Chinese here who have been searching the river for gold for a year. I am none the wiser. I do know the river in question is not the one just across the field. It is obvious it used to be huge, but has completely dried up since its diversion to another river at a lower level. It is a sorry sight, especially as I watch the slow, lonely walk of an individual to the middle of the vast arid wadi, lower his brace of buckets in turn into the deep borehole well to draw up this precious, scarce commodity, returning with them, yoke-style, to his home with his day's supply.

In the evening, I sit outside my tent looking upwards to an amazingly clear sky of bright stars, my ipod aptly singing, 'All heaven declares the glory of the risen Lord.' Life is good.

To wake up in the outdoors to a sunrise and fresh, clean air is a joy and a delight. To break the ice with local people in roadside restaurants by simply showing them themselves on the screen of my camera are happy moments. To pace myself leisurely along stretches of roads virtually empty of motorised traffic is idyllic.

I leave my bicycle at the top of the ridge to nip down to a crystal clear bubbling brook, cooling myself with splashes of water, freshening myself with a perfunctory wash. Butterflies, yellow, black and white striped, flutter by.

Local cyclists do not bother with the wooden bridge crossings, preferring to launch themselves nonchalantly down the wall of death, the momentum of the descent carrying them effortlessly up the other side by.

In the evening, I camp on a grassy bank by the side of the road on the edge of a small village, unfazed by the large crowd of its inhabitants standing around whilst I pitch my tent and sit to write my journal. So far nobody in Nepal has hassled me or been unpleasant; here we all smile at each other and mime a few things. Even so, I am grateful when a young man finally disperses everyone to leave me in peace. The only mar is the mosquitoes, forcing me prematurely into my tent.

I do not think I am eating enough. The next day's cycling is hard going, with me feeling weak and lacking in energy and so I make a conscious effort to fuel myself properly and to take extended breaks in the heat of the day.

At one point, four beefy motorbikes ride level for a while, two girls, two guys, Swiss, Russian, South African, Swede. They recommend going to beautiful Pokhara, the roads are quieter, the uphills winding, rather than steep. I bear in mind this possible diversion.

This pleasant encounter is followed by one from a moronic motorist. He overtakes me, stops, reverses in a wild zigzag, smiles inanely out of the window and grunts something incoherently, before proceeding to run into me, completely oblivious of the fact that he has done so. Apoplectic, I storm off, leaving him wondering, 'What did I do?'

In towns, bicycles outnumber cars, invariably passing by with a passenger perched on the pannier rack. Men walk down the middle of the road, young in western trousers, old in traditional sarongs, all ages sporting the familiar pastel pink and blue wedge-shaped caps. Women are loosely-swathed in glorious technicolour and hold aloft cheery umbrellas against the sun.

I hotel it tonight, to charge my camera and ipod. One of the other guests works for a government-subsidised bio-gas company involved in a highly successful government scheme, which received an award from the UK (presented by Prince Charles). Households are provided with bio-gas plants, their cow and buffalo dung, even their own poo, used as fuel to produce methane gas for cooking and lighting.

'Although this is all good,' the man says, 'the government is corrupt; most people feel there is little hope of changing the system.'

The hotel is noisy throughout the night. A large party of travellers are awake and up at one in the morning, showering, talking loudly, banging doors, TV at full volume. At the end of three hours, blissful silence. Only to start up again an hour later. I am on the road by seven thirty.

Stopping for breakfast later, I talk with a Nepali English teacher who reckons the road towards Butwal is flat. My map suggests it is a long hill climb. In the end, my map wins. The ascent is a precursor to the dramatic change of scenery once I head away from the lowlands into the mountains, a landscape of mountainsides tumbling down gorges to raging torrents below.

In the evening, away from habitation, I take advantage of the dense forests to find a suitably discreet entry point, duly making sure the coast is clear before scooting off along a small track deep into the thickly-wooded forest. I wait before pitching camp, to make sure I am undisturbed. Tonight's campstove menu is macaroni tossed in tomato soup, chocolate and fruit for dessert. The campstove is burning with an unsteady flame and I notice how sooted-up it is from the petrol, the dirtiest of fuels (but the cheapest and most available).

I use my torch sparingly, to ensure the security of my solitude. It is very quiet so far away from the road, almost eery, no animal noises, the only sound is of leaves falling.

In the middle of the night I awake from a bad dream and peep out of the tent to check on my bicycle. With alarm, I see crouching shadows creeping around a few yards away. I peer intently.

'Heck,' I think, 'what on earth do I do? If I call out they will know I am a woman, making me a vulnerable target. What if they come closer? Why did I stupidly put myself in this situation? How am I going to get out of it? Lord, you *are* still keeping an eye on me, aren't you?'

All the time this is going on in the front of my mind, in the back, logic and rationale are trying to be heard.

'If there are people moving around, why is there no noise from the dry, rustling leaves?'

It is only when I see a shadow moving towards my bicycle and I shout out, 'What are you doing?!' in the deepest, most strident and forbidding voice I can muster, that the delusional spell is broken. Recovering gradually from scaring myself witless at my fearful imagination, I allow myself a modicum of pride to have camped wild in such a location, regardless of my fear of spiders, snakes and ne'er-do-wells.

After the hilly interlude, the remainder of the way to Butwal is indeed flat. Decision point at the main crossroads leads me straight across towards Bharatpur on the way to Kathmandu, rather than the detour via Pokhara; the road now busier, noisier, more litter-ridden and mountainous. It is hot and I feel shaky and faint, plying myself with biscuits and fizzy Mountain Dew to raise my sugar levels.

The air is thick with the acrid smell and stinging sparks of large areas of burning vegetation, controlled conflagration carried out by small groups of boys and young men as part of forest management.

I stop at a clifftop café for Pepsi, tea and panoramic view, before negotiating a long, dysfunctional descent of broken road surfaces strewn with fallen rocks, met at the bottom by a routine police check.

My subsequent forest camp is handled slightly differently to the previous night, reasoning that, a) if I am accosted, I am hardly going to run away and leave my bicycle and belongings, am I? b) if I do not hear anyone coming, I shall not be afraid. Solution: to go deeper into the forest and, when in my tent, listen to my ipod for the first hour, then insert earplugs for the remainder of the night. Anticipated result:

unaware of any untoward noises to cause me unnecessary concern that someone might be in the vicinity. And it works. I have a better night's sleep. Simple deception for a simple mind?

The turn off at Bharatpur bids farewell to the lovely lowlands. The now mountainous road wends its tortuous way to a higher altitude, alternating between dipping steeply down to river level and ascending to hundreds of feet above. I peer down into the depths of the canyon and the tiny river, slung with slender suspension bridges that sway sickeningly as figures tread their way across the hundred metres or so above the shooting rapids. Adventure centres offer river rides, exciting experience guranteed.

I arrive at Mugling, having found no obviously discreet place to camp and so plump for a hotel. In the evening, I wander past colourful market stalls, down to the road suspension bridge (seemingly sponsored by Oranjeboom Lager, judging by the number of posters plastered on the vertical struts), where I meet a woman and her young son on their way to a church meeting. She shows me her hymnbook, written in English, in which I see many familiar hymns. This starts us off singing hymns together, in the middle of a bridge, looked on by a couple of bemused passersby. My children would have squirmed in their shoes and walked away in embarassed disownment.

Although hotels appear cleaner than in India (bathrooms at least look as though they have been cleaned), I continue to adopt the same procedure as in India regarding sleeping; I spread my shawl over the sheets and pillow and sleep in my sheet sleeping bag. Unfortunately, this does not prevent me from being bitten by minute intruders, from which I distance myself as much as possible with layers of duvet and sleeping bag.

Steep climbs and dramatic gorge-ous scenery are enhanced by traditional decorative art on buildings and elaborate archways. Children play on the road with simple toys, such as rolling a hoop along with a stick.

As the day wears on, it becomes clear that I have been misinformed that the going will level out once I reach the T-junction with the Pokhara-Kathmandu road. Instead it continues to climb steeply. It is going to be a struggle to reach Kathmandu, but I have hardly any cash on me, there is nowhere to obtain any more and there is nowhere to put up a tent on these narrow mountain roads. And in contrast to the lowlands, I do not feel the same relaxed safety as I wind my way

225

through the mountain villages. Attempts at hitching a lift fail; I have no option but to press on.

Night falls. Lorries often do not often have their lights switched on and the edges of the road are uneven and full of potholes. My headtorch gives off inadequate light, I feel horribly vulnerable and at risk, unlike any other time on the road.

I am really frightened as I keep on going. My heart is in my mouth every time a lorry comes along, hoping and praying I will be seen. At least when they do have their lights on, it helps me to pick my way momentarily, but then plunged into dense darkness once more. It is not just a few miles, more like twenty, that obliges me to keep cycling under such dangerous conditions. Added to this, it starts to rain.

Finally, with profound relief, I arrive in Kathmandu. The designated meeting place with my forthcoming host is outside The Bakery Café on the Jawalakel roundabout in Patang. I phone Mary from the café, who soon whizzes up on her bicycle with a cheery greeting, inviting me to follow her, with difficulty (she goes so fast), through the intricacies of the streets to her home, where she lives with husband, Huw. It has been a long thirteen hours and seventy-one miles but it ends with a warm welcome, food and chat, candlelight and torches (powercuts for sixteen hours each day being the norm.)

Huw is a doctor, here primarily to set up a medical training programme. Mary is Personnel Director at UMN (United Mission to Nepal); she is also in the final throes of writing up a thesis. They sold their house a few years ago, now working in such places as their skills and experience allow and their hearts take them. Now that sounds familiar.

The church they attend is KICC, Kathmandu International Christian Congregation, unable, for political reasons, to be called a 'church'. On Sunday, I am amongst the newcomers and visitors invited to stand up to be welcomed and to say a few words about ourselves. It is through this congregation that Mary and Huw arrange a house-sitting for my second week in Kathmandu, with an Australian family off trekking for a week. It is an excellent reciprocal arrangement, recent numerous break-ins causing people to increase security of their homes.

I visit Durbar Square. Many of the temples are constructed from red bricks and tiles, their roofs an assortment of shapes, the windows in dark fretwork and carvings. Pairs of stone-carved lions guard entrances to the temples. A procession makes its way through the square: the all-male band wears the traditional pink and blue-striped cap, white trousers and tunic, black waistcoat, their instruments comprising flutes, drums and small flat bells, like cymbals. The women follow, colour co-ordinating the men in blue and pink patterned, long-sleeved blouses, black skirts with red-frill trim, large white stoles wrapped around their waists and draped diagonally over the opposite shoulder. Some carry large, flat platters of white sweets. All this is the forerunner to the main attraction: carried on the shoulders of a small posse is a highly-decorated throne bearing a squat, cross-legged, turbaned holy man.

Despite internet blogs and forums expressing the unlikelihood of cycling from Kathmandu to Lhasa, I am ever optimistic. Initially, signs are encouraging, both from a travel agent and the Chinese Embassy. The main stumbling block is that the border is currently closed, has been for a few months and no certainty as to when it will re-open, although there is hopeful talk of an imminent date.

My first visit to the Embassy encourages me to think there is a likelihood of cycling to Lhasa, bearing a visa that will also take me cycling into China. My second visit a week later dashes all such expectations. At least the border is now open.

Similarly with the travel agent: at first, encouragement that my plans to cycle might come to fruition, then dashed in bitter disappointment. Not only can I not cycle solo, but there are no cycling group tours for me to join. They only ever cycle from Lhasa to Kathmandu, apparently it is too hard in the other direction. (Well, there's a thought for the future: organise my own group tour). In the end, I am forced to accept that my only option is to travel with a group in a convoy of jeeps. The first travel agents are far too expensive at $2,500; the second, Tashi Delek, coming in firm favourites at a fifth of the price. We leave at 6 am on Tuesday, six days away.

I receive an invitation to visit the TLM Anandaban hospital, ten miles south of Kathmandu. Dr Hugh Cross, the national administrative leader for TLM Nepal, is on a visit, unfortunately in the unhappy role of assessing where cutbacks can be made, the global economic climate adversely affecting their resources and income.

He shows me around the hospital, introducing me to staff and patients, the latter mostly here either for surgical procedures, such as amputations, tendon transplants, release of hand contractures, or following reactions to the multi-drug therapy. Most of the leprosy victims come from supportive families and communities, but there is one young man, just thirty years old, whose leprosy has left him with no family, no friends, no home, no means of work (below-knee amputation of one leg; forefoot amputated on the other; virtually useless clawed hands), whose life prospect is to return to his region and continue to beg and to sleep under whatever shelter he can find. His eyes brim in his utter distress; it is impossible not to feel the depths of his anguish. How can anyone live with such bleakness?

After we leave him, Hugh reassures me that he is not going to be discharged to such conditions. A self-help group in his area is now up and running and will provide him with the support he needs, including training for some kind of occupation, such as painting (the Christmas cards of the intrepid and skilled foot and mouth artists instantly spring to mind).

The desperate plight of leprosy victims is not easily alleviated here in Nepal, where they are reliant solely on charitable funding, for there is no government help. The official line is that leprosy is eradicated and so there is no requirement for funding. And yet, two thousand new cases were diagnosed in the first three months of this year in the Anandaban hospital catchment area alone.

On a happier note, there is a lithe, spritely, elderly man recovering from an amputation on his second leg, the first one performed twenty-five years previously. He is well-supported by his family and community, leading an independent life as a vegetable farmer before this second amputation, with high prospects of retaining a good quality of life on his return.

I purchase a neat little netbook from Mary, who bought it just a couple of months ago as a back-up to her main computer during the powercuts, but it does not have sufficient battery charge time to be as useful as she had hoped. For me though it is fantastic; the slightly extra weight and space it takes are more than compensated by its enormous advantages. I now sit happily in my choice of pleasant surroundings (rather than the gloomily dark interiors of internet cafés), working offline, sorting photos and writing website journal entries; online, uploading my work, regularly checking emails, gathering trip information so easily.

One of its best features is the integrated camera and microphone, working in tandem with already-installed Skype. One morning, I speak with my daughter whilst she continues to apply her make-up and dry her hair in readiness for work. The nearness and level of normality of being there with her feels almost surreal and is great fun. My son has just woken up and I hear of his plans for the weekend (driving with friends to a racetrack in Germany – as one does! And that he might be going sailing with my older brother in the summer).

During the week's house-sitting, I enjoy being able to bake bread and cakes. I take breakfast on the roof, my chair positioned in the direction of the Himalayas shyly peeping above the Kathmandu skyline. I watch *Slumdog Millionnaire* (quite different from the book) on the house laptop, read *A Thousand Splendid Suns* by Khaled Hussein, attempt to watch *The Kite-Runner* by the same author, but forced to give up halfway through when the DVD stops working properly on the laptop.

A delightful Nepali couple, Ramchandra and Maya, look after maintenance of the house and live in a small house in the grounds. They invite me for a meal with visiting friends, all whom speak English. Maya has impressively prepared a whole array of tasty dishes, solely on a two-burner stove.

Palm Sunday at home involves my church processing around the village following a donkey and carrying palm branches. Although this does not happen here, and the liturgy is unfamiliar, the hymns are well-loved favourites. Afterwards, I take my original hosts for a thank-you lunch at the SingMa, a Singaporean/Malaysian restaurant serving up tasty main meals and memorable desserts, mine being apple crumble cheesecake.

After the sombre Good Friday service, I attempt to make hot cross buns, but instead of the success of my recent bread bakes, I can only manage a sad result of lead weights; in fact, my usual result when at home.

Easter Sunday, of course, changes the mood into one of great relief in its outpouring of resurrection hope and joy. Unfortunately, this has to be without the aid of chocolate eggs as there are none to be purchased anywhere.

Housekeeping activities include replacement of zips on trousers and a bag at a local tailors. I restock my medical kit with a savlon equivalent and insect bites' cream, adding a new item, tablets against giardia (caught from contaminated water). Googling the infection, I come up with a graphically evocative description.

'Giardia can be asymptomatic, but symptoms often include loose, watery stools, with a certain foul-smelling greasy, floaty, frothy je ne sais quoi. Flatulence, cramps, bloating, and malaise can also be present.' Too much information?

The morning of my departure from the house-sitting, Maya presents me with a multi-coloured, striped pouch she has crocheted. It is a memento to treasure, and perfect for keeping safe my memory sticks.

I stop to say goodbye at The Bakery Café where I have whiled away internet hours with my new netbook. It is one of a chain throughout Nepal, run by signing deaf staff.

I now return to hotel grottiness, in the hectic Thamel area of Kathmandu, near the pick-up point for the trip to Tibet. I begin to wonder if there is a danger of my having developed a kind of inverted, masochistic snobbery by insisting on going for the cheapest possible accommodation in each country I visit; or am I merely paranoically thrifty to ensure my funds will stretch the full two years?

For some reason, I am told by Tashi Delek that my bicycle needs to be boxed. It is going on a jeep, for crying out loud! But the only box on offer at the cycle shop is too small for the usual basics to be removed or re-positioned. When the chap in the shop begins to dismantle my bicycle, way beyond anything I would have the know-how to rebuild it at the other end, alarm bells sound. A feeling of panic begins to well up from the pit of my stomach, until I request he put it back together. I shall find some other way to package it. After a fruitful trip to the market, the end result is Raven wrapped in wide sheets of thin polystyrene packing material secured with parcel tape.

In the street, I meet a single mum, Fiona, and her two-year old daughter, Rosa, looking for accommodation. Undeterred by my description of the hotel, she books in. Her outlook on life is quite admirable, especially taking into account that the two of them have been travelling around Asia for the last seven weeks, buggy and backpacks notwithstanding.

I am up with the dawn chorus, the tour rep commandeering a cycle rickshaw to carry my parcelled bicycle to the waiting coach (we join the jeeps at the border), whilst I ride pillion on his motorbike. Despite the travel agent's confident assurance, 'We have put boxed bicycles inside the bus in the past; two on one occasion,' we do not manage it this time, tied on the roof instead.

I take in my fellow passengers, comprising Greek, German, Italian, Swiss, Belgian, Dutch, Canadian, fifteen in total, spanning a broad age range.

We drive clear of Kathmandu, before climbing up into the mountains, winding along twisty roads, hugging the cliff face on one side, precariously near the edge of head-spinning gorges on the other. In a village, a particularly muddy stretch of oozing sludge allows me to appreciate the comfort of the coach, in preference to the alternative if I had been on my bicycle. A motorbike has similar thoughts, pausing to reconsider continuing through this mire.

After breakfast in a hilltop restaurant, we arrive at the border. A quarter of a mile uphill trudge is necessary to bring us to the passport office. There are porters around but I have no Nepali money left. How annoying that my bicycle is incapacitated as it means we now have an easy job made difficult. Whilst I carry Raven (who is not light), my bags are distributed to various of my companions to hump along with their own packs. They are remarkably good-natured.

We are quickly through passport control, excitedly making our way to the Friendship Bridge; no pausing, no photographs allowed. I have heard cyclists say they have crossed this border under cover of darkness in order to be able to cycle through Tibet, but it also means they do so without a visa, pretty risky with the tight controls the Chinese impose on traveller checks. I had thought of doing the same, but decided my bravado does not extend nearly far enough. And seeing it now, I know I made the right decision (but have a sneaking admiration for those who have done it). As we cross the gaping chasm, we see our four jeeps lined up on the other side, one with a roof rack.

*   *   *

Tibet

14 – 20 April 2009

Nyalam, Shigatse, Gyontse, Lhasa

Our Tibetan guide and the driver of the roofrack jeep are not happy to
see my bicycle. It seems to have slipped the mind of the tour office in
Kathmandu to inform them of this extra load. The driver is demanding
that I pay extra; whereas I refer him to the office in Kathmandu. There
seems to be something of a standoff but, unable to delay longer and with
both of us in a disgruntled mood, we hoike Raven on top of the jeep and
secure her. The rest of the group sort themselves into the jeeps, four in
each. My companions are Evanthia (Greek woman), Klaus-Peter and
Jürgen (both Germans). Jürgen is a cyclist, his eighteen months
travelling in Asia coming to an end after this side trip to Lhasa, when he
will fly back to Kathmandu, from there to cycle home. I appreciate his
moral support with the current situation.

As we drive along I make a mental note of the terrain and road
conditions, with a possible view to future cycling here. The first section
is a head-banger of a ride over bumpy, unmade road until we reach
Tingri, the point at which the newly-built road from Lhasa has so far
reached. The gradient seems excellent for cycling. We stop at the first
border town for mid-afternoon lunch, running for cover from a sudden
deluge into the small pre-arranged restaurant for steaming noodle soup.

Nyalam is our stop for the first night. Although it is 8 pm, it is still
light; the result of a massive two-and-a-quarter hour time difference with
Nepal. I already have a throbbing headache and nausea; not particularly
surprising considering we have gone from 4,500 to 12,000 feet in one day.

We enter the courtyard of a brightly-painted building; overhead
flutter rainbows of triangular flags, strung in rows from roof to roof. The

picturesque exterior belies the freezing interior; no heating, no hot water. Our guide assures us that hotels will improve further along.

I have to insist that my bicycle comes off the roof rack at night so that it can stand upright. Manufacturer's instructions say that it should not be laid horizontally as the oil will leak out; topping up is not as simple as for cars. In the morning, the driver vents his displeasure, by roughly-handling my bicycle, whilst I pray that it will survive intact, wincing when the unhappy man kneels on top of it whilst securing the ropes. Fortunately, Klaus-Peter's quiet calm spills over to me and we set off in good spirits.

We are now travelling China National Highway 318 that extends all the way to Shanghai, this Tibetan section to Lhasa more commonly known as the Friendship Highway. The landscape is spectacular, unlike anything I have seen before, razor-sharp, snow-covered mountains, huge, wide plateaux. We are travelling on the Roof of the World in the Himalayas, traversing numerous passes and marvelling at the (albeit distant) view of Everest. That I am here is an awesome feeling.

The highest pass stands at 17,000 feet. Wow! Merely standing still is a breathless occupation, the slightest exertion exacerbating one's breathing many-fold. I wonder if, at the slower pace of cycling, altitude symptoms would lessen substantially. Only one way to find out, I guess.

Each of the passes are heralded by the iconic, multicoloured, triangular prayer flags flapping in the wind, sending off requests on the 'wings of a prayer'. We are well above the tree-line in a bleak, barren landscape, where windswept sand skims silently across the surface of the road.

We compress two days' driving into one to arrive a day early in Shigatse, on the grounds that it is a much nicer hotel than the one in the itinerary's second night. The tour involves quite a few visits to monasteries, starting with Tashilumpu monastery, the spiritual home of the Panchen Lamas (second-in-command to the Dalai Lamas). The current Panchen is a 7-year old boy but, because of China's repressive rule over Tibet, he is not allowed to reside here, held by the Chinese authorities 'in protective custody' in an unknown location and in unknown conditions. The Dalai Lama himself was forced to leave his country in 1959, to live in northern India. From there he administers the Central Tibetan Administration, most commonly referred to as the Tibetan government in exile. Politics and spectacular scenery aside, the telling aspect of my short time in Tibet is the peaceful nature and simple, religious piety of the gentle Tibetan people. This is one of the highlights of my trip.

There are four main Tibetan Buddhist groups, of which two, the Yellow Hats and the Red Hats, are most referred to in talks from our guide, Chougak. Shigatse is the primary centre for the Yellow Hats.

Most Tibetan people are seen carrying prayer beads; interestingly similar artefacts to other religions, notably Catholics and Moslems. Rows of prayer wheels are everywhere, set gently spinning by a delicate touch of the hand as the person passes, praying whilst they continue walking. Many also carry handheld spinning wheels, quietly incanting their prayers whilst on their way to work or shopping.

In the monastery grounds, a shrine invites pilgrims to circumambulate it three times, slowly, some pausing every few steps to bow and prostrate themselves flat on the ground. As one might expect in such a place, the atmosphere is hushed. Until that is, a sudden hubbub is heard and we go over to investigate. Scores of red-robed monks are gathered in a courtyard in small groups of two or three, actively and vociferously entering into philosophical debate with each other, often accompanied by graceful, sweeping gestures of the arms ending in a decisive clap of hands as the point is made. This intriguing sight is a competition between the eight hundred monks, to find the champion debater.

This monastery also boasts the biggest Buddha in the world: 85 feet (26 metres) high, in solid bronze, 100 years old.

Traditional Tibetan dress is worn by many and is as colourful as the decoratively-painted buildings and prayer flags. The many beggars though are a less cheerful reminder of the realities of life.

We cannot ascend any higher and now enjoy a day of flat terrain (perfect for cycling) with views to die for, just out of this world. A sprinkling of snow produces an ethereal scattering of icing sugar on the rounded hills. At one point we stop at a tempa factory, where barley is ground into flour in the dusty millhouse, the millwheel turned by the stream. We all buy bags of roasted barley as a tasty snack. Traditional farming methods are still used here: yak and horse-drawn carts and hand-ploughs; scattering seeds by hand. The houses are built for the prevailing weather: numerous large south-facing windows; scant, small north-facing ones.

We arrive in Gingatse, another monastery visit. Wandering from room to room, each filled with different Buddhas, we arrive at the Buddha of Protection. A monk is seated, gong and cymbals in his hands, from whom emanates an incredibly deep bass chant. He has a cheeky sense of humour, enjoys pulling faces, at which we laugh, more so when he himself cannot help but laugh also, whilst endeavouring the almost impossible task of continuing his chanting. His natural showmanship obviously relishes the way he is playing his audience.

The next day, a lone cyclist, from the direction of Lhasa, approaches and passes. Half a mile on, a jeep (with guide and driver) follows; in a further half mile, a second cyclist brings up the rear. It is great to see them. The cost of such a venture for just two people, though, must be astronomical: at least two weeks with driver, guide, jeep, accommodation, food, plus flight to Lhasa.

The final pass at 16,300 feet is dominated by a glacier, Nojin Kangtsang, where we are subjected to icy hailstones pelting us for a brief spell. This is followed by one of the best outlooks of my trip, Yamdroc Lake, the Turquoise Lake, breathtakingly, vividly Mediterranean blue.

A long, snaking descent now brings us back down to the treeline and verdant valley – and an uninspiring entry into Lhasa past functional, bland Chinese buildings.

Happily, our final hotel is set in the Tibetan quarter of Lhasa and is a delight, definitely the best saved for the last. We enter through tall gates into a luxuriant courtyard garden, enclosed on three sides by a brightly-painted building of traditionally-decorated wooden beams, green-painted balconies underhung with white frilly pelmets and rows of terracotta plant pots vibrant with blooms.

I cycle to the Potala Palace of the Dalai Lama, the iconic white and dark building sitting high against the cloudless blue skyline. I take a photo, a voice behind me saying, 'Welcome to Lhasa.'

It belongs to one of two young Tibetan women, both studying English here in Lhasa. They walk me to a cycle shop (my tyre is flat), to buy a valve adaptor, thus enabling me to use car pumps on my tyres. I invite them for a drink and we go to a tea shop for milky Nepali coffee and sweet tea, the latter served in a tall glass, with tea bag, an assortment of fruit and large lumps of sugar, drunk through a straw and frequently replenished with hot water. At an adjacent table is a group of five bubbly teenage girls, all attending English classes and all eager to speak English with me.

One of the young women is a nun, now twenty-six years old, having entered the nunnery when she was twelve. After the troubles associated with the Buddhist monks in Burmah the previous year, she has had to stop wearing her nun's habit, donning normal street clothes instead. She lives in a convent in Shigatse, her hometown. The other woman, Sonam lives in a remote village in the mountains, three days' travel by bus, motorbike, horse and cart. She aspires to become an English teacher for her village, no English currently being taught there. Due to be married this year to a Nepali Tibetan, she will then acquire a passport (normally difficult and expensive for Tibetans), enabling her to go to Nepal, thence to India for her teacher training, at the end of which she would like to return with her husband to her village. Sonam walks back with me past the palace, insisting on pushing my bicycle. We give each other a hug, as I wish her all the best for her personal goals and vision, including her forthcoming marriage.

The group tour includes visits to Potala Palace, the huge Jokhang Temple with its golden roofs, the most important pilgrimage destination for Tibetan Buddhists, and Drepung, about five miles from Lhasa and the largest monastery in Tibet, formerly housing up to ten thousand monks. A fourth monastery is on offer, which I forego, monasteried-out by now.

Sadly, the Potala Palace is now a museum, unable to be used by the exiled Dalai Lama. The original building dated from the seventh century as a red building, replaced in the seventeenth century by the current much larger, distinctive white one, in which many of the Dalai Lamas are entombed. The Dalai and Panchen Lamas head the fourth of the Buddhist groups, the Yellow Hats. Each of the many rooms in the palace are given over to different activities, for instance, the Blessing Room, the Meeting Room, individually furnished with a throne upon which the Dalai Lama would sit to conduct any business. Each throne is now displayed with a symbolic arrangement of clothing, a poignantly sad reminder of Chinese rule over these peace-loving people.

Throughout our week's tour, Choedak emphasises and constantly reminds us of rules regarding topics of conversations and taking of photographs. We must in no way mention the current Dalai Lama, nor should we take photos which include any hint of police or police buildings. The consequences would be against Choedak rather than us, a threat to his livelihood. One of our party inadvertently photographs some policemen, resulting in quite an issue being made of it when the police complain, although no further action is taken on this occasion. We are very fond of our guide, especially because of his remarkable patience with our various foibles which keep him on tenterhooks as to what we might do next. Consequently, we collect a substantial donation for him at the end of the trip.

As I shall be leaving by train from Lhasa to Chongqing (pronounce 'q' as 'ch'), I cycle to the station a couple of days before my departure to verify its location and to find out how my bicycle will travel. But the station is only open when a train arrives and departs (one a day is busy). At all other times it remains tightly closed, Chinese security guards assiduously preventing anyone approaching nearer than a hundred yards.

Following my reccy, Choedak informs me that I will have to be taken in a vehicle to the station, it is forbidden to go alone. He adds the same proviso, rather late in the day, for cycling around Lhasa. I have seen many police whilst on my bicycle, none reacting adversely.

The young Swiss guy, Paolo, is a Buddhist, leading us to have lengthy discussions on Buddhist philosophy and Christianity. He sees his main focus in life as living in a way that does not cause upset or disharmony to others.

It is time for our group to disband, thirteen of the members leaving early in the morning to be taken to the airport for the return flight to Kathmandu. From there, Jürgen will resume his cycling through Pakistan, Mongolia, the 'Stans', northern Europe, home. Evanthia has five days in Kathmandu that includes a whitewater rafting trip. Klaus-Peter, extremely unwell for most of this last week, poor man, has come to the end of his whole trip, which has included a 15-day trek with guide and eight porters (just for him) as a fifty-eighth birthday present to himself. The Canadian, Cliff, is going on to China, Mongolia and back to Canada, thence to Prague to teach English as a foreign language. Paolo and I remain behind together until it is my turn to depart. He leaves the following day on a train to Beijing, in the meantime hastily trying to change his ongoing plans having just realised the journey takes forty-eight hours, not twenty-four.

At the appointed time, after goodbyes to Paolo, I pile into the minibus to be driven away from the gentle lure of Tibet.

Part 3

Lhasa
to
Santiago
(and back home)

*Love the Lord your God with all your heart and
with all your soul and with all your mind.
Love your neighbour as yourself.*
Matthew 22

China

21 – 28 April 2009

Tibetan Plateau, Chongqing, Yangtse River, Yichang, Shanghai

On arrival at the station, barriers prevent vehicles driving all the way up to the entrance, entailing a lengthy walk. The driver is not allowed to come with me into the station, to help sort out arrangements for my bicycle, because the Chinese forbid Tibetans from entering the vicinity of either the train station or the airport, at risk of them leaving the country.

I sit in the waiting room, anxious to know when, where and what I should be doing. Eventually a member of staff comes to me, followed by another, until there is a group of four, all speaking incomprehensibly to me, none in English. Finally, they bring someone who has a smattering.

'Problem, bike. No baggage car. Train doors too narrow bike through. You need fold up, pack. Best you fly Chongqing.'

I force my instant dismay to subside. There is no need for me to stress; it is for them to come up with a solution. In a moment of enlightenment, they realise that the panniers can detach from the bicycle. Good, we are getting somewhere. But now they insist that I take them off there and then, remove the front wheel and inline my handlebars, refuting my suggestion that this is done once we have reached the train. No, they have committed themselves to this course of action. My entourage of four work up a healthy sweat as they lug my various bits of baggage and bicycle on the lengthy, unwieldy walk, up stairs, down stairs, through doors and along corridors, down more stairs and onto the platform. They even conjure up an inadequate bag in which to pop my bicycle. Once on the train, bureaucracy remains on the platform and I find a neat little niche for Raven, in the corridor just an arm's length from my sleeper compartment, where I replace her front wheel. Mountains and molehills come to mind.

My fellow occupants in the six-berth cabin are three Chinese, a young couple and a slightly older guy, the latter possessing about ten words of English, five more than my Chinese. Along with my Mandarin phrasebook, which ends up being a point-and-read tool (one word can have five different meanings, depending on the intonation), I manage to glean that he is a salesman of car engine cleaning substances, he has been working in Lhasa for the last eleven days, he lives and works in Chongqing.

There are few stops en route, but on each occasion most passengers take advantage of a break from the train, disembarking to stock up on provisions form the platform sellers. My companions insist I try this dark, chewy thing, which turns out to be pig's ear. I also have a go at yak meat, which is quite tasty, but I decline the chicken's feet. I am the only non-Chinese on the train; great, except that I balk at one aspect of the experience. The habit of the male partner of the young couple is to clear his throat and emit a veritable gob onto the carpet before grinding it in with his shoe. It is totally disgusting. Eventually, at his companion's instigation, he changes to gobbing into a bag. Imperceptibly less disgusting.

I sit for hours on one of the fold-up corridor seats, staring out of the window at the vast, open plateau against a backdrop of snow-glazed mountains, rare scatterings of cattle and men briefly interrupting this wilderness.

The train is clean and comfortable; the berths have mattresses (even though they are classed as 'hard' when buying a ticket; a more expensive 'soft' option also available), duvet and pillow. After twenty-four hours and still in the middle of nowhere, I discover that my 23-hour journey is actually forty-five, although not according to Tashi Delek at the time of my booking. So then, a similar situation to Paolo, except that I do not have any firm ongoing bookings that need changing.

We pass tented villages housing railway workers. The landscape changes to mountains, valleys and gorges. A town occasionally pops up, nestling at the foot of one of the valleys, alongside a river. I like the symbiotic relationship of road, river and rail, particularly when they harmonise each other's movements with matching contours. I finish reading *Like a Flowing River* by Paulo Coelho.

Chongqing is wet and misty when we arrive at 9.30 am. I receive help from a young woman who speaks English, with directions to the ferry office. There is a cruise boat leaving at nine o'clock tonight. The booking assistant, Yam-me, confidently informs me that I shall be able to obtain an extension to my 16-day visa from the Bank of China. She enlists the help of the office driver to take me to one – two – three – four branches of the Bank of China, plus a couple of Banks of Somewhere else. Unfortunately, there is no visa extension as a reward for our efforts. Neither is cash forthcoming from a couple of my bank cards; thankfully, a third comes up trumps. It always produces a few palpitations when I do not have ready cash in my hands.

Despite assurances by the wise and ignorant from Kathmandu to Chongqing that I will be able to procure a visa extension, I do not, for the simple fact that I entered Tibet on a group visa, which they cannot (will not?) extend now that I am an individual, even though I am allowed to travel as an individual on the group visa. Work that one out. The only way would be to exit China and re-enter, as long as it is not from Nepal. I am now on a tight schedule to be on a ferry out of Shanghai before my visa expires.

Once again, I am the only non-Chinese on the cruise boat. It's what I want. Those carrying foreign tourists would not give me the same local experience as this one will. But they are also way out of my budget.

I am sharing a cabin with two young women who are part of a large group, and an elderly man, the rest of his party next door. The cabin is cramped, the shower emits only cold water, and we have a smoker in our midst. The same person also owns a loud and irritating mobile phone tone, which goes off frequently at all times of day and night, into which she speaks loudly for long periods, even at two in the morning.

Cruising down the Yangtse has always been high up on my must-do list. I have a real buzz being here, hardly believing that I am.

Included in the 3-day cruise are shore tours, kicking off with a visit to Ghost City. Walking through the town in the dreary rain, we are confronted with static scenes, lavishly depicting hell, torture and the underworld. The evening's shore excursion to a floodlit temple is far more congenial.

During these side-trips, I try to keep fellow passengers in sight to ensure I am not left behind. I now discover a young Slovenian couple on board. They too have had trouble with the ATMs, leaving them short of cash for this river cruise, thereby limiting extra side-trips, such as the Mini Three Gorges.

For this, we pile into a flotilla of small boats, vertical cliffs towering heavenward either side, as we progress up the first gorge. We crane our necks to follow the guide's finger indicating a holy cave high up, a depository for dead bodies. Access to it looks somewhat precarious. The guide relates information about the river, tagging on a song. It is unintelligible to me but I do my best to join in the song's taught response. His finale is to produce a wide-brimmed hat and mantle made from straw, and a long bamboo boat pole, along with invitations for passengers to don them and pose on the prow. It comes as no surprise then, when the *gweilo* (the foreigner) is encouraged to do just that, so that everyone can photograph her strutting her stuff.

The Dragon River jaunt involves long, narrow, blue and yellow dragon boats, with slender, elongated, gold-painted bows ending in brightly-coloured, maniacally grinning dragon heads. We are obliged to work our passage. Each wobbly dragon boat seats twenty team members, paddles included, with which we do our best to outrun the other boats. We paddle competitively away from the start line, but when the boat on our port side threatens to overtake us, we simply switch on the motor and speed away. Our dastardly cheating comes to nought, as the engine of the following boat trumps us to the imaginary finish line.

We moor the boats alongside a pier and stagger in single file along a watersnake of wobbly pontoons, slithering up a creek to a walkway of steps cut into the rockface. We wend our way along the path to the ethereal sounds of singing ringing out from the forest surrounding us, part of a dramatic re-enactment of the life of a famous poet. A high wire across the gorge features an impressive cycling and acrobatics display, the warm-up act for the exciting saga, staged in the auditorium below.

At the end of our river cruise, we disembark with our luggage, transferring to a coach for the concluding excursion: a tour of the gi-normous Three Gorges Dam, part of the Three Gorges project. After the visit, the coach deposits us in Yichang, where I find a clean and comfortable hotel for the night, the following afternoon catching the overnight sleeper bus to Shanghai.

This does not come without its trials, the driver immediately complaining about my bicycle. The baggage compartment is out of bounds for passengers' baggage, the driver requiring the space when he later takes on a cargo of boxes. We therefore have to squeeze all our baggage in between the bunk berths. Raven ends up on a bunkbed, heavy cases piled on top of her, and I end up having to pay extra for the berth. The duvet and sheets look like they have never been cleaned since the bus was commissioned and the loo is something to stay well clear of it. This is all such a surprise as, until now without exception, China has been extremely clean.

The seventeen-hour trip, with one meal stop, ends in Shanghai at seven the following morning. I would like to have stayed a while in this lively city; it has an amiable feel to it, the attraction enhanced by the abundance of cycle lanes. At a junction near a bridge, I ask for directions and realise that I am being filmed by Shanghai TV for something or other. In response to my query, the young assistant helpfully indicates what it is all about, by swivelling round to show me the explanation on the back of her sweatshirt – written in Chinese.

I arrive at the ferry terminal at 9 am; the next sailing to Japan is in two hours, another one not for four days (my visa runs out tomorrow). Cards not accepted, I leave my bicycle at the terminal and rush off to find a bank. Again only my HSBC card works. I buy enough currency only for the ferry ticket; plus a token amount of Japanese yen. I sprint back to the ferry, arriving in timely fashion to pay and hurry immediately on board. I deposit my bags in the 4-bed shared cabin, no ensuite; the second cheapest option. The cheapest would have been on the floor of a large room with fourteen other passengers. Maybe next time.

Frenetic activities accomplished, I stand quietly on deck. Moorings cast, we slip gracefully away from the dock. I now briefly savour my surroundings: a skyscraper skyline on the east bank, dominated by the double-sphered needle of the Oriental Pearl Tower.

We glide away, my encounter with China frustratingly fleeting, urging a return in the future.

*　　*　　*

Japan

29 April – 6 July 2009

*At sea, Osaka, Kyoto, Lake Biwa, Eigenji, Nagoya, Yidashi,
Iwata, Yidashi, Fuji City, Fuji Area, Kamakura, Tokyo,
Lake Kasumigaura, Hitachi, Shimaiko, Kashima, Sendai,
Kumatsushima, Oshima, Ichinoseki, Morioka, Ninohe, Noheji,
Aomori, Hakodate, Unoma National Park, Lake Toya-ko,
Sapporo, Sunagawa, Furano, Nagunama, Sapporo, Chitose,
Lake Shikotsu, Chitose, Mukawa, Tomakomai ferry,
Oarai, Tokyo, Yokohama*

We are two days at sea. My cabin companions are a Chinese mother
and daughter. The daughter, Yue, has been studying Economics for three
years in Japan and speaks very good English. I do not see much of them;
most of the trip they are seasick and supine in their curtained bunks. On
deck, I meet a young English woman, Sophie, travelling around Asia for
three months, having jacked in her government job to become an
animator. I chat to a bright-faced young Japanese guy, Toru, who lives
on the northern island of Hokkaido, from where I hope to catch a ship to
Alaska. On one of the quieter decks, a French backpacker plays his
clarinet. In the women's hot bath, waist high in the hot water, I sit naked
beside a naked stranger. We stare out of the blindless window at the
passing ships, a sublime smile on my lips at this surreal scene.

I love being at sea. It is mesmerisingly soporific to gaze at the flat
divide between sky and sea, life and death. I like the not-too-large ferry,
where it is possible to be sociable or solitary, as desired.

I should like to have had time before departure to buy provisions;
food on board is expensive, to be expected, but more importantly, not

freely available, the restaurant being open for only an hour and a half for each of the three meal times. The tiny shop, with only very limited stock, is not open much longer. Breakfast is included in the ticket price: two air-light rolls, a hardboiled egg, slice each of tomato, cucumber and pineapple, a sachet of cherry jam, butter, coffee. A pot noodle carried over from the Yangtse cruise is my lunch on one of the days, augmented by a packet of biscuits grabbed just as the shop is about to close.

On arrival in Osaka, the ferry is immediately boarded by a team of masked, white-coated, briefcase-toting officials, requiring all passengers to queue in an orderly fashion. Laser thermometers are shone on our foreheads in quick succession, at the same time as we are asked whether or not we have been to North America in the last few weeks. The latest global flu epidemic is on the advance, emanating apparently from North America, and we need to be clean in order to be allowed into Japan. Having passed the test, Raven and I now find ourselves for the first time ever on Japanese soil. At the risk of repeating myself, the realisation that I have cycled all the way here is a stupendous moment.

After a not-very-friendly welcome into Japan from the slightly sarcastic customs officer, I cycle out of the port with a tremendous heart-pounding excitement at the thought of cycling in this exotic country of tea ceremonies, tatami mats and golden pagodas. Yue, recovered from her nautical nausea, has written the name of the Municipal Youth Hostel in Japanese on a piece of paper. By this simple show and point method to people in the street I find the hostel without too much of a challenge.

And what a youth hostel it is: clean, modern, light, hot baths (I am beginning to have a penchant for these), *heated loo seats,* push-button control bidet, antiseptic dispenser for cleaning the seat, supply of paper. The contrast to most of the conditions during my previous seven months is marked. Sheer luxury. In the foyer, shoes are removed and left in cubby holes, exchanged for slippers; the process further repeated on entering the toilet.

But I am shocked at the price of a bed, considering it is a youth hostel, breaking out into a cold sweat at the fright of wondering how on earth I am going to afford to stay in Japan for two or three months. Later in the evening, however, I realise I have been using an exchange rate of 140:1, instead of 70:1, thus restoring my inner equanimity.

My 6-bed dormitory is empty but for me, other guests also being given their own dormitories. In two days' time though, this will change when the hostel becomes full at the beginning of the week's national holiday, Golden Week.

At the email suggestion of my cycle man, Robin, I replace my noisy chain. In the cycle shop, I have a choice of regular or heavy duty, so clearly opt for the latter. But touring chains are longer than ordinary road cycles, so I am obliged to buy two chains for the extra few links. Rather than replacing the chainwheel, as would be normal practice with a new chain, it is merely flipped over, the less worn backs of the cog teeth now bearing the force of the chainlinks. But the end result is disappointing: the chain is still noisy and feels rough when pedalling. I email a photograph of the chain to Robin, who suggests loosening it a little (working with the cycle manual, I manage this for the first time, pleased at my achievement), adding that it could also be noisy because of new chain against old chainwheel.

One of the other hostellers is a young Canadian, Alex, who also carries with him a netbook, but has downloaded an alternative, much more user-friendly desktop interface. He admits there were problems when the built-in mic stopped working, but this was sorted with the help of a computer friend reconfiguring it over the phone. I should like to do the same with mine, but only with a computer-savvy person in tow.

Rather than buying section maps en route, I purchase a road atlas from a bookshop, the only one they had with any Roman script place names. I dissect and discard the pages I will not need (all those south of Osaka) and ask the hostel manager to translate additional place names for me to write on the remaining pages. For each day's travel I shall cut a page from the atlas to be placed in the map holder on my basket.

A striking accessory I have seen used by Japanese people so far is the widespread wearing of facemasks. Even indoors, the hostel staff wear theirs permanently; except once when they remove them prior to me taking their photograph. Another sight, which tickles me rigid, is that of the women sedately cycling along the pavements on their sit-up-and-beg bicycles, shaded by sun parasols clipped to the handlebars.

On the morning I leave Osaka, the chain is embarrassingly noisy and I return to the cycle shop, the man insisting there is nothing more he can do; it probably just needs wearing in a bit. All the same, and despite the weight, I retrieve my old chain, just in case.

I cycle through the grounds of the castle and well-laid out park to join Route Number One to Kyoto. Here, I am expecting to camp, but on arrival realise that the campsites are way out of town, up in the hills. Tourist Information recommend a hostel in the city, a pricey affair (a parking fee even demanded for Raven), but with friendly international fellow guests and the shared dormitories are only three-bedded.

Although I have arrived in Japan having just missed the cherry blossom parties, Golden Week abounds with festivals of all sorts. I am delighted to pass a beautiful and traditional Japanese water garden. The lake is edged with pink oleander bushes and soft-leaved acers; spanning its banks, a gently-curving, orange-red bridge, on which stands a woman in traditional kimono.

Stalls offer freshly-cooked finger food, such as small round shrimp-filled doughballs, which must, of course, be sampled. I follow a crowd to the theatre pavilion to watch *mibu kyogen*, Buddhist mimed morality plays. Before we enter the theatre, we must remove shoes, plastic bags available in a box at the entrance in which to hold them on our laps.

In the first two plays, the spectacle of masked men in long dresses is interesting to watch, but the action is very slow, emphasised by a simple, constant, slow rhythm from a trio of flute, drums and gong. As this would appear to be the structure of the plays, I decide I have seen sufficient inaction to call it a day and so leave. However, a young man makes a point of coming after me to say that the third play is the most popular, something about Spiderman. Sure enough, it is not long before the baddie, bedecked in grotesque mask and menacing black cape adorned with a spider's web, reveals his secret weapon. As he flings out his arms, endless streams of white spider's thread are released into the air, successfully ensnaring his opponents in a tangled web. It is startlingly unexpected and very exciting and the audience loves it. The baddie of course, does not triumph in the end. The name of this play is *Tsuchigumo* (Spider).

Kyoto is a pleasant city in which to cycle (unlike the majority). Trundling along by the river, I pass random individuals incorporating their lunch hour with a music practice. Here is a sax player; further along a trombonist; then another sax; and, finally, an ensemble of six school children seated side by side along a low wall, playing clarinets, trombone, French horn and tuba.

The city is safe enough to leave my bicycle discreetly behind a building whilst I visit Kinkakuji, the fabulous Golden Pavilion Zen temple. The top two storeys of this pagoda are covered entirely in gold leaf, seen at its dazzling best in the afternoon sun. The grounds in which the temple is set are extensive and beautifully laid out; the Golden Pavilion itself set on the edge of a peaceful lake, edged with soft acers and blue irises.

Back at the hostel, I meet a group of six cyclists, newly arrived from Tokyo, the Brit leader, Kevin, giving me useful low-down for my ongoing route. He also teaches me a very useful phrase in Japanese, 'Where am I now, please?' to be expeditiously followed by, 'Please show me on the map.'

After two nights, I decide to transfer to Kyoto Cheapest Inn, cheaper but also the staff much friendlier and the atmosphere and facilities more amenable. I discuss with the hostel owner's wife my exit road out of Kyoto and possible ongoing routes. She suggests one that would take me through the important Ninja region, in her mind a preferred alternative to my proposed scenic rural and lake roads, which she dismisses as not very interesting. My interest in all things Ninja being somewhat limited, I decide to risk the scenic option.

Initially, this proves to be unpleasantly busy, including countless screeching 2-stroke motorbikes passing close by me, whilst weaving in and out of the cars. One driver even suggests it is too dangerous for me to be cycling here.

I have been forewarned of the abundant tunnels in Japan, today getting to grips with four of them: a very long one, but extremely well lit, and three shorter. Maybe I am more used to tunnels now, but these seem infinitely safer than the pitch-dark Italian ones.

Gradually the traffic lessens and I look out for signs to take me off to the right and over the bridge at the south end of Lake Biwa. I approach what I think is my likely junction, but do not turn off for lack of signs. Immediately past the turn-off, I am startled by a loud voice from a tannoy.

'You. You. Stop now!'

A police car overtakes and pulls onto the hard shoulder, followed by a second – and a third, all lights flashing. Two smart officers from the first car jump out, indicating that I should also pull over; as if I had not worked that out already! We have a very useful conversation.

'You must get off. This is the 161; it is a freeway.'

'When did it become a freeway? There were no signs. I am looking for the 477.'

'You must go down to the road below; that is the 477.'

By now we are down to the one car, which escorts me down the up slip road to the roundabout and the 477. Safely away from harm, they take down my passport details, before urging me, 'Take care; Japan is not safe.' (They seem the only people in Japan who think this.)

I continue happily along, thinking, 'Now that was well-timed!'

I cycle over the bridge and follow the lake around, passing an attractive-looking campsite. It is too early to stop and there are two further sites marked on the map. On the way, I stock up on provisions when I come to a shop; just as well as there is nothing at the campsite, when I eventually find one. On arrival, they try charging me an extortionate 1900 yen (it was only 1200 at Kyoto Cheapest Inn). In the end, I am not sure how or why, I pay only 200. It is by now raining miserably, no let up when I pitch the tent, although in the morning it relents for half an hour for me to decamp.

Today is the 6th May, the first anniversary of the day I left home. I am halfway round the world, 9,151 miles putting me on my estimated total target of 20,000 miles.

I follow quiet country roads past acres of paddy fields. I have always wondered how they sow rows of rice seeds in ankle-deep water; my question now answered as I watch a small tractor plough furrows, four abreast, simultaneously dropping in seedlings from a conveyor belt attached behind the plough.

After a couple of hours of incessant rain, I decide enough is enough. Stopping at a restaurant and gift shop by a canal, I drip in to dry out, ordering coffee in phrasebook Japanese, conversing with the woman serving, who is married with two sons in their mid thirties. My inquiry for internet access results in her making a phone call, marking my map with directions for an internet café five miles away and not charging me for coffee.

The internet café requires completing an application form and a payment of a membership fee before I am allowed to pay for a session of thirty minutes. It seems a rather convoluted system. I write an anniversary journal entry on my website and pick up a handful of congratulatory emails, including from Liliane, the spritely elderly cyclist from the Camino.

The rain continues as a heavy downpour, persuading me to take refuge in the World's Kite Museum. I am greeted by the three staff in the empty museum and installed in front of a fascinating video to learn about Giant Yocachi Kites, their history and how they are made.

The size of kites is measured in tatami mats: the largest kite ever made being equal to two hundred and forty; the usual size nowadays is the equivalent of one hundred mats (forty-three feet by forty feet). It takes six hundred people one month to make a kite of this size; twenty people to carry it; one hundred people to pull it along the ground to launch it.

Afterwards, the staff ask me about my trip, then on departure formally present me with a head bandeau, a pin brooch and a 1956-birthday monkey badge.

The rain increases, the distant cloud-wrapped mountains do nothing to dispel the prospect of continued discomfort. Wishing to mitigate this as much as possible, I stop at a restaurant on the outskirts of a small town, my entrance accompanied by a dripping path of puddles as I make my way to a table. I gingerly divest myself of sodden clothes whilst eagerly awaiting my steaming bowl of noodle soup.

I ask the whereabouts of a campsite, the owner makes a phone call, swiftly followed by the arrival of Suzuki, speaking excellent English with a Canadian accent, the nationality of his former wife. He mentions a local campsite.

'Or you could come and stay at my place,' he offers.

He gives me directions and goes off. Soup finished, I follow suit, arriving at the restaurant in a few minutes. Hardly have I entered than I am introduced to a couple of friends, owners of a restaurant in a nearby town. They speak some English and we pass the evening in easy company, sitting at the bar, drinks and snacks to hand. The noodle soup restaurant owner, a sushi chef, joins us after his place has closed for the night, bearing a platter of sushi that he has prepared specially for me. Octopus tentacles are recognizable and salmon, others of which I have no idea. I only know that this is high quality sushi, and it is delicious.

Later, Suzuki's girlfriend, Masai, returns from work and now it is just the three of us, drinking beer and saké, and dancing about, generally having a pretty riotous time. Suzuki has been running the restaurant for thirteen years, meals by reservation only. The next reservation is in two days' time. I have no idea how he manages to keep going on such a scant clientele.

A mat is rolled out for me in the guest bedroom. I luxuriate in a hot tub, afterwards sitting by the sliding window overlooking the river, listening to the rain pattering. In the morning, Masai brings in tea and toast, one topped with chopped tomatoes and onion, the other with maple syrup, before driving off to work. It does not take much to be convinced by Suzuki that there is, 'Too much rain to continue cycling,' in order to accept his offer of a second night. This presents a further opportunity for me to sample more gastronomic fare; the couple from last night are owners of a soba (buckwheat) noodle restaurant, our lunch venue for today.

Our group is augmented by more friends, and we sit, legs dangling, around the edge of a carpeted well in which stands a low table and to which our speciality noodles are brought. Lunch finished, we transfer to the other friends' large, traditionally-built house to continue the party. More food, saké and wine appear as we sit and chat over the next few hours. The heavy rain continues; a good decision to have stayed put, at the same time giving me an intimate insight into the lives of local people.

In the morning, in damp and low cloud, I bid farewell to Masai, who has prepared a takeaway lunch for me: rice balls with some spicy stuff in the middle. Goodbyes and heartfelt thanks to Suzuki follow on the arrival of a friend, June, who is transporting me in his pick-up to the top of the mountain road. Their well-meaning insistence, 'It is too much for you to do with your heavy bicycle,' obliging me to acquiesce graciously.

The route is picturesque and, yes, if I was cycling, it would be taking me most of the day to reach the top. And, yes, there is a long, poorly-lit tunnel; and, yes, there is low visibility cloud. Reluctantly, I have to admit that, in a way, I am glad to have this easy ride up. June speaks no English and much of the drive is conducted in silence interspersed with phrasebook conversations, or rather, questions in phonetic Japanese responded with smiling unintelligibles.

When it becomes obvious that June's intention is to take me all the way to Nagoya, my destination for today, I put my foot down, firmly persuading him to pull into a layby on the mountain descent. He is very reluctant to leave me in the middle of this forested nowhere, presenting me with a keyring with a well worn tiny Snoopy attached, looking for all the world like the giver's favourite talisman. I hang it on the inside of my basket.

The views are beautiful, traffic minimal and I enjoy the cycle down. The mountain eventually levels out to the plains, the road passing through, oh so quiet villages, my still noisy chain embarrassingly heralding my passage. The road atlas pages are working well, the scale big enough to show the majority of small roads, which are easily equated with the road number on the frequent roadside signs.

On the outskirts of Nagoya, I head for the centre along a traffic-strewn Route 23. Overtaking lorries display displeasure at sharing the road with a cyclist; cyclist no happier to be here than they are to have her here, but there is no option, the pavements broken, overgrown, rubbish-filled.

I head for the university to meet up with the daughter of the soba noodle restaurant owner, but find myself in a professor's office at the wrong university, waiting for Yumi to come to pick me up. The intervening minutes are filled with an enthusiastic demonstration of the robotic mechanical gripper the professor is developing.

We meet up with a couple of Yumi's students in a restaurant for a lively chatty evening. Yumi picks up the whole tab, forbidding me to contribute.

'You can return the favour when I come to England,' she smiles.

She helps me map my ongoing route, identifying more place names in my atlas. When I set off in the morning after a cooked breakfast, I am armed once again with a packed lunch of rice balls enclosed in seaweed, wrapped in clingfilm and neatly parcelled up in a square of material. Yumi cycles with me to the beginning of Route 1, which then brings me to the coast.

Ah, the sea. But a short-lived pleasure, stretches of road along which bicycles are not allowed force me to double back along alternative roads inland. The weather has now transformed into glorious heat and sun, my healthy packed lunch requiring to be balanced with a McDonald's chocolate milk shake to counter the effects of the rise in temperature.

I come to a river, a track alongside leading to a campsite. These commercial sites are really only geared up for all-singing, all-dancing campervans, one levy for all, so there is no point in me paying for what I cannot use: electrics, water, waste disposal. I cycle away intent on finding somewhere more reasonable, even though dusk is now falling. I ask at a nearby park and restaurant to camp in the grounds, but am refused. I cycle around the lanes, ask a shopkeeper, no joy. Finally, I knock at a house, inquiring of the woman who opens the door if I can put my tent up on the piece of grass opposite her house. Initially, she does not seem to grasp what I am asking and miming, but when I go over to the patch of grass and start unpacking my tent, she becomes agitated, the only recognisable word, 'Police!' making her meaning quite clear.

It is now dark as I resume cycling hopefully along this quiet country road. And a small clearing in the trees just off the road provides me with the perfect spot. I sit and have something to eat, wait until I am fairly confident that I shall not be disturbed, then set up my tent. Nobody at all comes by during the night.

The next day I discover the Pacific Coast Bicycle Route, a dedicated cycle path along the coast and on forest trails. The cycling is delightfully picturesque and pleasant. The day is meant to end with a night's accommodation on a beautiful peninsula, but both the two campsites and the youth hostel, all featured on my map, fail to materialise. I am forced to continue a great deal further than intended for the day, to a stretch of coast with possibilities for discreet camping. In the process of looking, I meet an evening stroller, Azuma, whose greeting is, 'You sleep my house?'

Even I am somewhat wary at such direct hospitality. Having ascertained that he has a wife and children in his house, causing him great amusement from the implications of my questioning, I follow him to his home half a mile away. His family does not seem unduly surprised to see an alien in tow; little surprising when I learn that the son, Hiroki, is a member of International Friendship Association, an organisation set up entirely for this sort of eventuality.

After a much-needed shower and hot bath, I am welcomed to the family meal table to be well fed with fish and chicken dishes and potatoes, followed by *manju*, a sweet aduki bean paste, washed down with saké and beer. Tomorrow's route-planning sees Hiroki on the internet attempting to locate open campsites.

After a sumptuous breakfast the next morning – fried eggs, sausages, miso, slices of avocado, grapefruit wedges, rice and green tea – I am stocked up with the usual rice picnic lunch, prepared by the daughter. Red pickle provides a variation on the theme for the centre filling of the rice balls. This time, the balls are wrapped in a green cloth tied at the corners. As I pack my bicycle, neighbours come by, one presenting me with a jar of the red homemade pickle, and an elderly man with a jar of jam and a gift bag of coffee candy.

Cycling along the coast continues joyously, especially when I am on the cycle paths. But, as yesterday, I keep losing the poorly-signposted trail. Today I realise why. What I have been taking to be signs for the cycle route turn out to be warning signs at awkward junctions saying, 'Be Careful.' So that is why they are always attached to a post with a mirror!

At lunchtime, I manage to confuse my tastebuds when they discover that the jar of jam is, in fact, seaweed relish.

In the environs of Fuji City, I ask at a petrol station for the whereabouts of a campsite, pointing to its location on my map. The owners make the usual phone call and within a few minutes Airi arrives with an invitation to stay in her home. Her English is fluent, having lived in Australia for three years. We stop off at the family business where I leave my bicycle, to be brought later to the house by the husband in his pick-up. We shop for the evening meal at a supermarket, where I buy drinks as some contribution towards my stay.

Meal patterns seem standard in homes throughout Japan: an array of dishes appear at each meal, leftovers are carried over to the next meal, supplemented by new dishes. This rollover effect continues with each subsequent meal, causing minimal food wastage. My first uncertain reaction to rice and fish for breakfast is followed by the realisation that it is not culturally strange to the English, kippers and kedgeree being traditional dishes in the past.

Before I leave the next morning, I accompany Airi and the two children, Yutsuki and Roti, to their school. Inside the entrance, the first thing we must do is remove our shoes, placing them on shelves. As soon as the children enter their respective classrooms, they don a protective uniform of green smocks. When I leave, I am assailed by the class with the usual 'V' sign that is prevalent by adults and children alike throughout China and Japan. As someone commented to me, it seems slightly bizarre that the victory sign that hailed defeat for these countries is now used as a form of friendly greeting. The interesting phenomenon of language mutation, I suppose.

I try following Airi's directions onto the right road, but end up convoluting this way and that along busy roads. I realise I have made no progress when I have a déjà-vu moment back at the same place, at least enabling me to pinpoint where I am.

I keep to quiet roads, at one point climbing slowly up a mountain, eyes bent on the ground immediately in front. Eventually I pause for breath and look up – and almost fall off my bicycle at the unexpected sight of Mount Fuji towering above me, seemingly so near. What an amazing view, albeit short-lived when my current mountain soon obscures it as I continue upwards.

The road takes me through a forest landscape, sunlight tentatively picking its way through the trees, my bicycle now reluctantly submitting to being pushed up this extremely steep hill. According to the map, we will eventually reach the summit, after which it will be a glorious cycle ride directly in my intended direction. What could be simpler?

The only trouble is that the road and the map have not colluded in this exercise. Deep in the forest the road ends with roadworks, in the throes of creating an asphalt surface. I pick my way through the gang of men and machinery, wondering if I am being stubborn with my fixed route. Beyond, the way looks hopeful for a short distance, but then reverts to a tricky trail to cycle. By which time, the sun has disappeared into a thick and eerie fog, leaving me feeling very alone and vulnerable as it closes in on me. I retrace my steps, attempt to obtain a sensible response from the roadworkers, but am only met with one of them finding it highly amusing that I should have to go all the way back down the self-same road I have just spent two hours crawling up. This being good character-building stuff, I nonchalantly laugh in the face of such hilarity.

Back on the main road, traffic is scarce, probably everyone prefers to luxuriate in warming hot baths than experience the pleasure of cycling in damp pea-soup. There is little surprise when the usual mapped campsites fail to appear; even so, I stop at a coffee sign to inquire. Inside the coffee and gift shop, the owners end up offering their holiday property behind the shop as a place for me to stay as their guest.

Raven stays in a shed at ground level, I am in the living/sleeping area on the first floor. A huge picture window dominates the room, framing a spectacular view, for there again is majestic Mount Fuji. Currently, partially shrouded in cloud, she still manages to maintain an aura.

A friend of the owners who speaks English, and his wife drop by, thus extending the conversation beyond the contents of my introductory letter. Food is cooked at the table and I am treated to bamboo shoots, some kind of edible grass, miso soup, cow's heart, pork, accompanied by *sho-chu*, potato wine with hot water added. The wine encourages us all to relax and laugh a great deal.

I happen to be awake at 5 am, when Mount Fuji displays herself at her best, as the pale hues of a cold, pink morning glow reflect off the snow-covered mountain.

I am invited to stay a second night. The day includes a trip to see a particularly special azalea just coming into flower, which bears smaller flowers and more stamens than most other azaleas. In the evening, the two couples invite me to dine with them again, a unilateral bring-and-share buffet, including *sukiyaki*, for which we cook our own thin strips of beef, mushrooms, spinach dipped in raw egg. When I ask what I can contribute they merely reply, 'It is enough that if ever we come to England, we might be able to stay with you.'

Takao presents me with one of his wood crafts that are for sale in the gift shop: a beautiful, small, wooden-handled razor knife (perfect for cutting out the pages of the road atlas).

The friendliness of the Japanese is further encountered the next day when I am packing my bicycle with provisions just purchased at the Family Mart and a voice greets me in perfect English. Uta, who lived in Malaysia for some years, hence the English, was told by the shopkeeper that I am cycling around Japan (well, he did ask). She writes down her phone number in case she can be of any help.

Views of Mount Fuji accompany me through the morning. I take the tortuous route through mountainous, wooded areas up the Ashgirawa Pass. At the top is a tourist area with an information board, giving the height of Mount Fuji as 3776 metres (12,388 feet). Gazing again at the grandeur of this mountain, it dawns on me that I have actually stood on a pass nearly 5,000 feet higher than the mountain at which I am now looking!

The long, slow, winding descent takes me past paddy fields, and a row of little grey shrines, each wearing a red crotcheted hat, tied under the chin, and a child's bib. A large teddy bear is placed on the ground nearby. These shrines are dedicated to the god, Jizo, who is, amongst other roles, the patron saint of motherhood and the guardian of unborn, aborted, miscarried and stillborn babies. In Japanese folklore, red is the colour for expelling demons and illness, inevitably becoming associated with the ever present battle between good and evil, and therefore dedicated not only to deities of sickness and demon quelling, but also to gods of healing, fertility and childbirth.

I follow a pleasant cycle path along the coast, frequently dismounting to push through deep patches of slippery sand blown from the beach, nonetheless enjoyable. In Kamakura, I meet a day cyclist, Humaiyaki, who has cycled and camped free all around Japan, saying it is very safe and possible to camp virtually anywhere without any problem. He illustrates this by pointing out a car park with a small patch of grass and a scant three trees at the side.

'You can put up your tent there. It is very safe. No one will bother you or tell you to leave.'

'Ohhh, no. Fine for you, maybe, but far too exposed for me!'

Instead, we go to a very large park, keep well away from the section where the homeless and drunks hang out, and find a perfect pitch amongst a scattering of trees near the early-morning jogging track. It is 7 pm, dark enough to make camp. Humaiyaki (at least I think that is his name) takes his leave to cycle the twenty miles home. I feel a bit sorry for him; he seems sad he is not yet married and currently is without a job.

'But,' he says, 'I am a free man, not a robot, which is what most Japanese men are. So much pressure to conform to society and work long hours. They do not have control over their own lives.'

The advice and comments I receive from this young man have given me enough confidence to start worrying less about where I shall sleep at night, encouraged by repeated comments on how safe Japan is.

Early risers jogging by at five in the morning propel me to be up and away an hour later. As I leave, a man on the other side of the park fence sees me, says something, indicating a cigarette; I indicate I have none. I do not understand his reply until he blurts out in English, 'Give me money; give me 100 yen.'

It is strange; he does not look like a beggar or homeless, his attire being quite smart. I say, 'No,' and walk away.

The coastal cycle path near the town is wide and well maintained. I arrive at a small park, the security man just finishing his night shift, the park warden arriving and opening up the main gates so that I can wheel my bicycle through. I go over to a picnic table to brew a hot chocolate. The security chap comes along, looks at my stove, and wishes me well on my trip. The smiling park warden comes over with a banana for me. A member of the public passes by, looks disapprovingly at my stove and tells me I should not be using it. Surfers cycle by, kitted out in wetsuits and flip-flops, carrying their boards on special racks on the side of their bicycles.

Kamakumara is famed for its Big Bronze Buddha, a hefty fifty-two feet high, set in beautiful gardens of acers and azaleas, pagodas and lakes. In the same gardens are myriad other shrines, including a large wall against which hundreds of little Buddhas are lined up, eyes closed, standing in peaceful meditation.

On then to Tokyo, arriving at the Visitors' Information, with minutes to spare before closing. Awaiting my turn, I chat with an American backpacker who previously lived in Alaska. He is impressed at my trip, but not half as impressed as I am when he mentions that he runs Iron Man competitions *barefoot*.

The recommended hotel is six miles away, but still near a vibrant part of the city. My room is too tiny for Raven to share with me, so spends the night in a garage after I insist she cannot remain outside. The room is vacant for this night only and I transfer to a different hotel for the second and third nights. Here, the rooms are traditionally laid out with tatami mats and roll-up mattress. It happens to be the weekend of the *Sanji Matsun* (Three Shrines) Festival.

I join Julia and Vincent, a couple of backpackers I meet at the hotel, to walk to the Asakusa Temple, the oldest temple in Japan, dating from AD 654, as well as the most colourful, making it an extremely popular visitor attraction. Our route takes us past numerous street processions, delaying our arrival at the temple by about three hours, as we stop to watch the heavy, ornate shrines carried on the shoulders of large teams of pall-bearers. Fresh teams periodically take over throughout the eight hours or so it takes to complete the assigned routes. The bearers adopt a rhythmic, bouncy movement, accompanied by chanting. The teams comprise mostly men, but a few young women, even children, take their turns. The common attire is short, patterned kimonos in team colours, mostly worn over dark, plain trousers or leggings, although a substantial number of men prefer the kimono on its own, exposing legs (some of them not bad), and in quite a few cases an array of bare buttocks. This last sight takes me by surprise for its sheer unexpectedness; the Japanese being such polite, reserved people, or so I thought.

The next day I am caught up in yet another procession, this one bearing each of three shrines along different routes, between them visiting all forty-four temples in Tokyo, stopping at each one for a short ceremony of prayers and blessings. It is fascinating to watch, but means I arrive at the Imperial Palace Gardens ten minutes after closing time. The rest of the day is spent catching up on website journal, emails, sorting and uploading photos, with a relaxed interlude for a complimentary cocktail in the hotel's Ocean Bar.

Leaving Tokyo, I aim for Lake Kasumigaura, hopefully to find a campsite. I encounter my first Japanese snake, in the middle of the road, a six-foot green thing, head floating four inches above the ground, sticking its tongue out as I go by in shocked panic, valiantly controlling myself from overbalancing. It could be a Japanese Rat Snake, harmless.

Cycling is a joy along tranquil country roads in rural Japan, well away from busy highways. The main drawback is that I have become accustomed to the frequent convenience stores; along these roads there are none. They have become my main service providers: for provisions, ATM, Skype subscription top-ups, water bottle refills, fast food takeaway, sweet pastries, freshening-up washes (especially after wild camping), heated loo seats. Village shops, on the other hand, are tiny, not much on offer and quite a rarity.

Finding a suitable place to pitch my tent turns into a challenge, so much of the land is under a few inches of water in this rice-growing area. However, I come across a park on the edge of a large lake, a picnic bandstand serving as my dining room. Once dusk diminishes my visibility to passersby, I feel confident enough to put up my tent amongst a patch of trees.

The next day takes me the length of the lake, for the most part past rice and vegetable fields, often divided into small individual holdings, a bonneted, solitary figure steadily progressing along the rows in stooped cultivation. Returning to the coast road, I arrive in Hitachi as darkness falls, eyes alert for a suitable tent pitch.This turns out to be a quiet spot up a track at the end of a street, next to a small discreetly-placed shrine. Whilst eating my evening meal of minestrone and chicken vegetable soup with added noodles, washed down with a beer, a woman comes by walking her dog; we exchange greetings. A little while later a man comes by; the dog looks familiar; we also exchange greetings. He seems about to say something more, decides against it and continues his walk.

After a noisy night from the constant traffic, I have breakfast of bread with peanut butter and jam (separately), banana and currant buns. I write up my journal and read some Bible. Total time, plus packing up and loading onto the bicycle, an hour and a half, leaving by seven thirty – unusually prompt for me.

I take a calculated risk on the steep hill leading to the road I wish to be on, Route 1, clenching the brakes the whole way down – only to puff my way back up again when it turns out to be a dead end. In fact, when I finally make it to said road, it is to discover that I am on Route 6, further along the coast than I had thought.

The weather is consistently fabulous, gloriously sunny; impossible not to run down the beach to the sea, kicking and paddling and jumping about in the Pacific Ocean, ecstatic to be alive – and to have cycled all the way from Almondsbury to here, the Pacific Ocean, Asia. I remove the panniers in order to carry Raven down to the sea, asking an elderly man to take a photo of the two of us, wheel and toe dipping, with thoughts of doing the same on the other side of the pond.

After a while, I leave the pounding waves and continue my sandy cycling. In the evening, I camp in the grounds of what looks to be a campsite, but there is no one around, although the gates to the site are unlocked. In the morning I am up at six, taking just twenty minutes to pack up and away – gosh, I'm getting good. Along the seafront is a loo block and showers (sadly, the latter do not work), where I manage a good all-over wash in the handbasin, as well as rinsing through my cycling clothes, draping them over a nearby bench to dry, whilst I brew up hot chocolate for breakfast.

The cycle path along here is well laid out with small paving blocks, periodically widening into flowing rivers of grey, blue and pink. At intervals along the seashore, large, strange-looking monuments have been erected. It is all very pleasant and soothing, although slightly incongruous to see this along such a desolate stretch of beach in the middle of nowhere.

As well as continuing to be embarrassingly noisy, my chain now insists on slipping off the rear sprocket, usually when I am back pedalling before pulling away at junctions, thus punctuating today's progress in an annoying way.

Away from the sea, the road takes a slightly inland direction. I stop and check on my map for the (supposed) whereabouts of tonight's campsite, when a voice in English comes from behind.

'Where have you come from?'

Karfori (pronounced Karfolly) is married to a Polish guy, whom she met whilst working in England. In their early days, thinking he was English, she could not understand why he was constantly mentioning Poland. By the time she realised, she had fallen in love with him, thereby scuppering her plans of acquiring an English husband. The couple live in Poland, but now in the final stages of pregnancy, Karfori has returned to her mother's home to give birth. In the village in Poland, no one speaks Japanese, or even English, nor are the locals particularly friendly towards her; having her baby on familiar territory, therefore, is rather more desirable.

Karfori had seen me earlier when I had stopped for a drink. She had wanted to speak to me then, but felt reluctant to delay me in case I was heading for a particular place for the night. She waited twenty mintues along the road, until she saw me again, inviting me now to stay with her at her mum's in Kashima, about twenty miles further on. I am very tired, glad therefore to persuade Karfori that it is quite possible to fit my bicycle into her compact car.

We arrive at a house undergoing extensive building work, reinforcements against future earthquakes. Currently there is a high-risk warning of imminent occurrences. Karfori forewarned her mother of a stranger in their midst and I receive a warm welcome. The customary shower and hot bath are followed by a diverse array of dishes (I love the way Japanese people present their food), including d.i.y. food cooked at the table in seaweed bouillon. Mariusz, the expectant father, phones in the evening, checking out my website whilst we chat; we extend mutual invites to each other's homes.

Karfori presents me with packs of Polish soups, cake and chocolates to supplement my supplies. She also helps me identify a few more place names on my atlas pages. It is raining today, but a temporary ceasefire is called at the time of my departure. Karfori cycles with me a little way to ensure I start off on the right road (my reputation precedes me). We even hug in farewell; she is not your average Japanese.

Contrary to the weather forecast, the day turns out splendidly sunny and bright. I stop in a layby, attracted by posters in the window of the building, hinting at the possibility that succulent strawberries might be purchased inside. The staff are such fun, inviting me to sit down for a chat, even phoning someone who speaks some English, who subsequently comes to the shop. One of the men presents me with what seems to be his packed lunch, a large seaweed-wrapped rice ball. The wife of one of the shopkeepers slips home for ten minutes, returning with two punnets of strawberries for me (I don't know why she just didn't take them from the shop). When I finally leave, the stock of gifts includes a pot soup, preserved banana, packet of nuts – oh, and along with the strawberries is a brown paper bag, in which I discover a 5,000 yen note (about £40!). I am overwhelmed. I have the woman's card and address written in English, to send a postcard from Alaska.

Before setting off, I decide to have a go at tightening my chain, with an impressive result: no ratchet noise, no clunking, no falling off. I have my beautiful bicycle back again, lost, but now found. Late in the day, I know, but I now remind myself that new chains loosen in the first few hundred miles and need to be tightened. Mine must have been too loose to begin with. I am over the moon with relief. My joy knows no bounds. (Maybe a slight overreaction.)

In the Youth Hostel in Sendai, a girl from Quebec shows me photos of Okumatsushima, where I am headed the next day, off the coast of which is an archipelago of islands with unusual rock formations, worth a visit. When I arrive, I book onto a 40-minute boat trip around the islands of wind-carved rocks rising out of the sea, in company with a group of seven middle-aged motorbikers on a week-long trip from Tokyo.

The next day, I meet a Turkish guy, who greets me in English. Serkan is married to a Japanese woman, hoping one day to return to Turkey. For now though, he imports Turkish jewellery and nicknacks for his stall. I buy a bracelet in pink, the same design as the blue one given to me by Jasmin in Iran, to send to my daughter, and a blue wrist band for my son. The kindly Turk gives me his mobile number in case I need any further help.

The weather, bored with its recent cheery outlook, aims now to dampen my spirits. Well, it does not work. Although it has been wet and drear for most of the day, my discreet camping ground along a quiet track gives me a delightful panoramic sea vista, and sufficient time to brew, drink and eat before the rain comes down to nudge me into my tent for the night.

The dampener is not the rain, but that my ipod is not working since yesterday, after plugging it into the netbook to listen out loud to my son singing, rather than through the earphones. I remembered too late reading something on an internet forum that this particular netbook, an ASUS, has a penchant for this sort of social sabotage. Bum. I like to listen to music on my ipod, my spirits so often lifted after a song or two. The screen ipod says something about needing to be reconfigured. I try resetting but nothing changes, and now I can access nothing.

The following day is my younger brother's birthday. I purchase an international phone card, plus pay for credit on my Skype account, which must now be registered online to activate it, but I am unable to find any online by which to do so. I am confident though, that, in this land of advanced technology, I am sure to find a phone or internet somewhere today.

Oshima Island, the Green Pearl of Japan, is reached by a short ferry trip and takes no time at all to cycle around. A field ablaze with poppies causes me to well up nostalgically at this association with travelling the Camino a year ago, when the same flowers were in as much evidence and I had the pleasure of my lovely companion.

I leave my bicycle at a coffee shop and walk to the lighthouse along the well laid out wooded clifftop trail. Afterwards, rejecting the landscaped cliffside campsite with showers and toilets, I opt to wild camp beachside in a small grove of trees, romantically attracted by the vision of lolling on the sand, beer in hand, gazing up at the star-studded heavens, the gentle lapping of the sea later lulling me to sleep. This idyll is somewhat marred when I am beset by an onslaught of midge-type characters, successfully destroying my attempt at reverie.

Neither has it been a good day on the telecommunications front, having to admit defeat when I discover there is no internet on the island and the phoneboxes do not accept international phonecards. And so much for being lulled to sleep by the gentle lapping of waves; throughout the night, the rhythm and volume change constantly, from lapping, to crashing, and splashing in between. Even so, the bay is very pretty and the beach is very white. Life could be worse.

I return to the mainland on the morning school-run ferry that includes an extra stop to deposit one set of schoolchildren near their school, the other group disembarking at the main terminal. They are a cheery bunch, either leaning against the cabin wall in a line of sombre, bowed heads of concentrated thumb-texting, or grouped in giggling gangs, flashing the v-greeting when I click my camera in their direction.

I send a small parcel home from a post office before cycling on moderately flat terrain beside a rail track for most of the day. Later, spurred on by locals' confident assurances that there is indeed a campsite up this inordinately steep hill now before me, I persevere almost to the top, finally raising the white flag and retreating halfway down, parking myself discreetly behind an elaborate shrine, hoping there will be no more visitors here in a forest in the middle of nowhere.

The next day is a significant one. At 11.45 am on Wednesday 27 May

2009, cycling along Route 28 between Ichinoseki and Morioka, I watch my speedometer change from 9,999.9 to 10,000 miles. How about that?

Just as twenty-one days ago I had a milestone day with passing the halfway time mark for my trip, today I arrive at the halfway distance mark. My first thought is that I am a very long way from my children and home. The second is that I have cycled this very long way from my children and home.

In Morioka, I book into a *ryoken*, a traditional Japanese inn. The luxury of a shower is welcomed by my neglected body, just as my clothes appreciate becoming more sociable once more. I use a whole phonecard on a brief two and a half minutes, 'Hello. How are you?' to my children.

I discover on the internet that the rules for a US visa seem to have changed since January (or I could have misunderstood them; unlikely) and I shall be unable to obtain one on entry but must get it beforehand. Having passed through Tokyo and the chance of visiting the American Embassy there, I am banking on the Consulate in Sapporo.

Morioka boasts the famous Rock-Splitting Cherry Tree, the English inscription reading, 'Ishiwarizakura is one of Morioka's most famous symbols of the spirit; endurance against all hardships, even the impossible; a cherry tree growing from solid granite.' Currently standing at 350-400 years old, the tree cuts a fairly impressive figure.

I leave the *ryoken* at a leisurely hour in the morning, but not until the manageress, dismayed by my unspeakably uncomfortable-looking saddle, brings me a cushion to attach on top of it. It takes some persuading to leave it behind.

Keeping to quiet, hilly roads, I pass acres of neat rows of polythene-covered ridges, the green broad-leaved crop bursting through the ground into the light and warmth of the sun. By mid afternoon, I start thinking about where to sleep. Nowhere seems accessible or suitable, until the church spire in the small village of Ninohe invites me inside. No one is about and I sit in a pew for a while, looking around at this small cosy church; it has a good feel to it. As I emerge, a woman walking a dog stops. I say that I am looking for somewhere to sleep. It turns out she is the pastor's wife, speaks English very slowly, but unhesitatingly says 'yes' to my request.

She and her husband have been here for six years; the building is twelve years old, but there has been a church here for over a century.

We put two pews together as my bed, seat cushions as my mattress. The building also houses a meeting room, a kitchen and WC. I have a kettle at my disposal and food and drink in my panniers. What could be better?

In the morning I meet the pastor, Michikaru Higashiyama, who speaks no English and is a very gentle soul, as is his wife. He knows the pastor at a church a day's cycle away and will phone him to expect me. I meet their cat.

'His name is Bread,' says the pastor's wife.

'And is the dog's name Wine?' I respond.

'No. That was the other cat (now dead).'

The weather first thing is the usual overcast low cloud with sunny spells, but I have a confident expectation that this will improve as the day goes on, as it has been recently. Instead, conditions deteriorate, plummeting from 22°C to 12°C. I am only in shorts and sandals. The weather closes in as a thick, damp, cold fog. I stop at a roadside restaurant to warm up with their set menu of rice, omelette and *soba miso* (noodle soup).

I arrive at the church in Noheji by mid afternoon, to an anticipated welcome by the pastor and his wife, who in turn phone a young couple from Alaska, in the village for a couple of years teaching English. In the evening, Julie and Tailor initiate me into the experience of a floating sushi restaurant, food served by way of a conveyor belt that continuously passes your table, from which you pick a plate with food of your choosing. At the end of the evening the number of plates determines the size of the bill. There are two variations to this: soup is not served in this way, deeming safer to arrive by conventional waiter, and special orders are intercom-ed through, the order arriving by Shinsen bullet train on a second conveyor belt at eye level, stopping adroitly at your table. It is great fun.

In the morning, I am invited to their flat for a hot shower, internet and breakfast: American pancakes with maple syrup, bacon, apple and carrot jam, coffee. Delish. Tailor tries to rectify my ipod, but is reluctant to do too much at risk of obliterating my music and photos. Julie gives me some maps of Alaska and Oregon and tips for dealing with bear encounters.

'On no account scream in a high-pitched voice or run away.'

Well, er, no; of course not. No problem.

Being a wimp when it comes to the current combination of grey, wet, cold conditions, I half hope to be invited to stay the weekend, especially as I am also feeling a tad lonely and miserable, the weather reflecting this (or the other way round?). I remind myself, though, that this is normal and will pass. The weather cheers up slightly and the twenty-five miles to the incredibly windy town of Aomori are covered easily.

Once again I have directions to a church but on arrival I find it is locked. The Tourist Centre's suggested *ryoken* is pricey and, strangely, the youth hostel even more so – as well as being situated four miles out of town. I return to the church, this time finding the young pastor, his wife and daughter. They are rather taken aback by my request, probably the first time it has happened but, reluctantly at first, allow me to stay. I lay out my sleeping bag in a small office adjacent to the church, my accommodation providing me with all the comforts I need: warmth, kettle, toilet, electricity. When I leave in the morning the young family gathers to wave me off, standing at the top of the steps by the main door, the 8-year old daughter posing proudly when I take a photo of them. They continue to look somewhat bemused that they have put up this *gweilo* traveller in their church.

All three churches I have stayed in are in immaculate condition. I tried finding out how they are supported; it seems from donations. But all three churches have such small memberships, the one in Noheji with only four families. Only one percent of Japanese are Christians, yet there are three churches here in Aomori. The situation seems unsustainable, and yet somehow, it is able to support well-maintained buildings and pastors.

Before catching the ferry to the northern island of Hokkaido, I take time out to photograph the elegant gold-coloured bridge I had seen earlier, and to visit the prepossessing triangular, blue-glass building that dominates the seafront and harbour. It turns out to be an arts and cultural centre, displays in the foyer focusing on local industry. Apples are big in Aomori, here presented in such choice delights as apple and cream cheese turnovers, preserved dried apple slices, bottles of cloudy juice, all demanding to be sampled. On the way to the ferry is a ship museum, a varied collection of vessels that includes a Viking ship.

On board the afternoon ferry, I could go up on deck and continue battling with the raging winds that prevail in Aomori, or I could experience the Japanese way of travelling on ferries. I go below decks to one of the two spacious carpeted rooms, removing shoes at the doorway.

There are no seats, instead long bolster cushions along the walls, to lie or sit against for the three and three-quarter hour journey. It is a comfortable and relaxing way to pass the time, all the harder to leave though, when it comes to disembarking into the driving rain of Hakodate.

I cycle to the train station where the Tourist Centre comes up with possible port contacts for a sea passage to Alaska, and recommend the Hakodate Yama Guest House for accommodation. This is located on the outskirts of town and boasts an unimpeded view over the large bay, as well as en route to Tachimachi Cape. Sasa is the friendly laidback owner, three ebullient Thai students the other guests.

I cycle to the port, to the address supplied by the Tourist Office. It is a small government building with no English, but staff direct me to a tall building close by, which has. On the fourth floor are the offices for HAFEX (Hakodate International Trading Incorporation), where one of the staff, Rumi, explains that there are no direct passages to Alaska from here, routes only going via Tokyo. She and a colleague, Tetsushi, will look further into possible options for when I return the following day.

Reminding myself of the lack of success at my previous attempt to obtain a sea passage, I decide this is the time for my secret weapon, in the hope it will aid and abet the efforts of these valiant philanthropists. With an understated flourish, I produce The Letter. Typed on House of Commons-headed paper by my local MP, the contents first testify that I am of good character, before launching into the main thrust, along the lines of the this-trip-is-unusual-enough-to-warrant-special-consideration ploy. Well, it seems a waste to have carried it with me for it never to see the light of day.

I now search for an elusive cycle shop; the first one does not exist, the second almost does not. But the elderly man within does manage to replace my threadbare rear tyre, and we jointly succeed in replacing the brake pads. It seems about the right time to have new pads, after all I have covered 10,200 miles on the same set. Unsurprisingly, the old ones are paper thin. We undertake this procedure together, finally succeeding only when I point out to the man that he has put the pads on the wrong way round (according to the enclosed diagram).

Hakodate is situated on a hill, the port-directed streets looking as though they could be in San Francisco. Of the three churches on the tourist list, the Roman Catholic one appears too austere, the Episcopal is locked, and the Russian Orthodox is a welcoming smell of incense, soft music and a volunteer handing me a 'presento' of two postcards.

A neat, well-tended park makes its way down the hillside, Escher steps ascending and descending amongst the blazing azaleas. A pale grey and yellow American colonial-style building, the Old Public Hall of Hakodate ward, stands in the middle of the grounds. Nearby, a group of four sombre, important bronze men oversee a solemn ceremony, contrasting further down with a scene of two lively children, a playful pig and a serenely-smiling somnambulant bear amidst slender, stylistic trees.

In the evening, Sasa drives me to the top of the mountain for a night view of Hakodate.

'One of the three best sights in the world, alongside Naples and Hong Kong.'

He informs me that there are bears on Hokkaido; perhaps then, I do not have to wait until Alaska for a grizzly glimpse.

After much telephoning over the next couple of days, Rumi and Tetsushi come to the firm conclusion that all trans-Pacific sea routes originate from Tokyo. My best option therefore is to return to the capital, which is also a flight departure point, if it comes to that. They produce a cruise route, Otaru to Cold Bay, but at sixteen days for € 12,000 it is slightly out of my league. I come away with a list of four companies in Tokyo that ship to Vancouver and Seattle. Maybe the best chance is to make contact in person, despite my previous experience in Oman. The Letter unfortunately, has not had the desired effect. But worth a try.

I visit a public onsen (hot baths). As I do not have my own washing set, I pay a small additional charge for one, most of the other women obviously regulars with their own. Leading off from the ultra-clean, warm changing rooms, glass doors open onto the washing and showering area, beyond which are three pools of various temperatures. My initial self-conscious feelings of being a European *gweilo* wandering freely naked amongst strangers, are quickly dispelled by the helpful assistant guiding me in the right direction and by the unobtrusive smiles of the other women. I make my way to a vacant stool, sit at the low-level basin and shower and proceed to wash myself thoroughly and meticulously all over, slowly and deliberately, following the actions of those near me. Some women wash and scrub themselves for ages, in particular one woman, already sitting on a stool when I arrive, still there washing herself when I leave forty minutes later. To my uncultured eyes, it almost seems to border on the obsessive, but maybe it becomes more of a meditative activity than solely functional.

Many women are alone, but others are in pairs washing each other, even a family group of three generations having this sociable time together. I move from the washing area to the different pools, but am unable to remain too long in the oppressive heat without feeling unwell. I finish off my experience lying for twenty minutes on the floor of the tatami-ed lounge, with low seating and bolster cushions for post-pool relaxation.

After three nights in Hakodate, I head towards Sapporo and the American Consulate to obtain a visa. I detour through Unomi National Park, following the shores of a huge lake, the skies lowering, once again bringing rain. A campsite is signposted but, expecting high prices, I also look out for potential alternatives. Sometimes, as now, things happen in threes: the rain stops; the campsite is free; its location is beautiful. I sit outside my tent, contentedly inhaling the peaceful scene before me: soft, still surface of the lake, hush of the evening air seeping into my soul, mellow smoke from my campfire, a pan of water for my nighttime hot chocolate coming to the boil. Another perfect moment.

It rains all night, ceasing at eight in the morning and no point in leaving the tent before then. A group of excited teenagers arrive, launch their canoes with lively rocking movements, before ordering themselves in single file behind their instructor and heading towards the middle of the lake for waterskills' lessons.

The road continues towards the coast through a couple of National Parks. Along the way, as there have been almost since I left Hakodate, are regular signs indicating evacuation routes from various volcanic mountains, here Mount Komagatake.

Japanese have a great sense of fun. Take their speeding warning signs at the roadside: a large white board painted with the bonnet of an approaching police car, above the board (the roof of the car) a pair of real red siren lights, triggered to flash at speeding vehicles. Or take their roadworks' bollards; instead of orange plastic cones, rows of green frogs or orange monkeys mark the roadworks' area.

The day is unpleasantly cold and misty and I am grateful to be warmed on the odd occasion when the sun, reluctant to be contaminated by such drabness, tentatively emerges through the hazy veil. I camp in a park, surrounded by water features and pom-pom trees, in an adjacent field, a bronze statue of a kneeling woman, sister of the Little Mermaid in Copenhagen. I camp in what appears to be a designated camping area, although it could just be a picnic place. Even though it is a visible, open area, all is well and the night passes undisturbed. The next morning I eat breakfast in a small arbour, exchanging a few words with an inquisitive local.

On reaching the coast, the pungent smell of shellfish pervades, the area littered with fishing pots. At times the road ascends on elevated bridges through densely-wooded pine forests, disappearing into well-lit tunnels, each a mile in length. I look out for indications that this is indeed Milkland, as Hokkaido advertises itself, but see only one dairy farm, the cows in sheds, devoid of any sign of grazing pastures.

On Lake Yoka, I come to an official campsite and proffer my translated letter to the young assistant, who completely disregards it, merely stating the campsite fee. I repeat the proffering, asking her to at least read it. An elderly man nearby takes the letter, reads it carefully, nodding every so often, and instructs the young woman to let me stay without charge. I smile widely in appreciation and utter inadequate thanks. Wooden chalets on the site are a reminder of the wooden wigwams in Tyndrum in Scotland, which we have stayed in as a family on the way to or from Drimnin on the Sound of Mull.

During the night, violently-loud explosions wake me up. Initially, I think they are fireworks, but nothing appears in the sky. The noise continues at length. Suddenly a big, red flash of light explodes behind the trees, fire drops now raining down. At this point, with the mountain evacuation route signs instilled in my mind, I convince myself it must be a volcano woken up and spewing out its insides. I go to my neighbours who, by means of the dictionary on their mobile phone, reassure me that it is nothing more than firecrackers.

The next day worsens: cold, rain, wind, fog, perpetual climbing. I am feeling exceptionally tired and very low in spirits, wanting to make Sapporo for warmth, comfort, cosiness, cleanliness. After a warming miso soup near the summit, the down side produces nine miles of almost continual braking, coping with a blustery wind, accompanied by memories of my Dead Sea descent and coming a cropper. The gradient gradually eases to a gentle downhill and easy cycling to and through Sapporo city centre, arriving at Ino's backpacker hostel.

Amongst other guests here are two Australian cycling couples, one pregnant, one with a baby, just arrived in the country for four weeks touring on Hokkaido. I hope the weather cheers up for them, although they seem a hardy bunch.

My experience at the American Consulate is not without its challenges, initially advancing no further than the front door security foyer, with instructions to apply via the internet for an interview in Tokyo. I am nothing if not persistent and I stand my ground, intent on not leaving until I have seen someone face to face. In the end, my insistence unheeded, I am afraid I throw a tearful wobbly, the only thing fixed in my mind being that I need to get my visa sorted here and now. It is only then that an English-speaking person is called, who admonishes me for not having carried out better prior planning. He informs me that there are only two interview days each month here in Sapporo. Pressing him, he reluctantly confirms there is one next day.

'But,' he hastens to add, 'it is full.'

'Please can I be fitted in?'

He goes away for an eternity, returning with an agreed squeeze-in at eleven thirty in the morning. I spend the remainder of the day completing the application form, purchase the requisite Expack 500 envelope for them to post my visa to me. I try to pay the fee at the PayEasy ATM, but it is having a bad hair day; I fare better at a Post Office counter. I mistakenly acquire black and white ID photos (I brought a plentiful supply from home, but they are not the obligatory size for the US, not big enough) and am obliged to repeat the process for colour photos.

Back at the Consulate the following morning, I relax with my book for the two and a half hours' wait, having completed the substantial form, noting one of the questions with amusement, 'Are you a terrorist?'

Now that I have run the gauntlet of consular staff, it is a pleasure to find the consul, Ian, amiable and helpful, even suggesting I contact Hokkaido University and the Marine Sciences Division to find out if there is any likelihood of joining a research boat going to Alaska. My visa should take about seven days, to be posted to Ino's, as I plan to travel around for a few days and return there.

On my way back to the hostel, I witness an ironic sight: standing outside a hospital is an inpatient wearing a protective face mask, lighted cigarette in his hand.

Things continue to look up as I receive a reply from a passenger-freighter agency confirming an available passage from Yokohama to Prince Rupert in Canada. It is due to leave on or around 8th July, taking about nine days to cross the Pacific. The only berth available happens to be the owner's cabin. I think I can cope with that. There is no reply from the University.

Lightening my load by leaving some luggage at Ino's, I head off for a soggy week on a north-south circular route. It is fowl weather, loved by them no doubt but, try as I might to embrace it, I do not really succeed. After a damp camp in a park, I arrive in Furano and a hostel, more than happy to accept a generous discount for three nights, my letter (not to be confused with The Letter) working its charms. I welcome the shelter and cosiness of the hostel, warm shower, hot bath, steaming coffee.

In the same dormitory as me is a young woman, Aya, and her 3-year old son, Shou, who has Down's syndrome. They live on the east-side of Hokkaido, periodically attending a rehabilitation unit for Shou, here in Furano. Later, she meets up with another mother whose son has the same condition. They are all very sweet and, as all children with Down's, the two boys have glorious smiles. The following day, Aya presents me with a beautiful card she has made, incorporating photos of Shou and me taken the previous day, and lovely words, which she must have asked someone to translate for her. I am very touched.

Technology is great when it works, fantastic to be able to deal with so much at the click of a mouse whilst on the move: managing bank accounts, communicating visually with family, ordering gifts, uploading journal updates. But it is equally frustrating when things do not proceed smoothly. It is Saturday and I have until Tuesday to pay for my freighter passage, an easy transaction with today's bank cards, universally accepted – except for Iran. And Canada. Instead, I must arrange a Swift wire transfer, which can only be arranged by taking a completed form to my bank branch in UK. So, quick flight back home then?! I also need a recent medical certificate, no older than seventy-five days, the clean bill of health brought with me from home therefore null and void. I email the form to my GP, requesting they print off and fax the completed form directly to the freighter agency. Ticking that off my list, I spend a couple of hours looking for a printer to print off other forms that for some reason must be completed by hand and faxed to the agency. The hostel, a hotel, the Tourist Centre do not have this facility, until I am inspired to ask at the latter if it is possible for them to use the staff printer.

Reluctant to leave the comforts of the hostel after my three days, I force myself to venture forth into the pouring rain, up into the hills: lush, forested, river torrents and waterfalls, low cloud shrouding the tops of mountains and forests. At first, the rain falls in large, fat, wintry globules, later, as fine rain, still falling heavily, sometimes cold, occasionally less so. There are many lakes on Hokkaido; all exude expansive tranquility.

For most of the day, there is no shelter from the rain, although a covered picnic area at a beauty spot offers temporary respite. My feet are numb with cold and I belatedly wrap them in plastic bags; it makes all the difference, feet eventually warming up nicely. These and my cycling poncho must look a bizarre sight as I walk down to view the reason for this being a beauty spot: a gushing torrent cascading over a stepped waterfall.

I have one more night camping in the damp before glad to return to Sapporo and Ino's Place, its familiarity placating my sense of dreariness with the weather and my emotions. My American visa has been waiting for me for the last three days. I am genuinely impressed with this efficiency. Moreover, having at last located an Apple store, my ipod is successfully reverted to its former working state, although some of the music titles appear in Japanese hieroglyphics.

Ino's seems to be a place to which guests return. Vin, a Korean French guy is back, and Hiroshi, a motorbike tourer returns after a couple of days, not keen on the rain. I even have the company of a Scottish couple, Sheena and Adam. As for payment to the freighter company, when push comes to shove, I am allowed to use my credit card. Except it is rejected. At which point, I can use PayPal! So easy, but why not offered before? Aaaargh!

I repair an alarming tear in my trousers, highly dubious that they are going to last intact to the end of the trip; such a shame, as they are perfect and any replacement is likely to be a poor substitute. Contact with family mainly leaves me feeling ineffectual towards helping them with their various challenges.

Juggling is a favourite pastime for Ino, practicing most days in the street outside the hostel, competently keeping the four truncheons in the air. His children participate in a festival street procession, the small team of eager beavers dressed in bright blue and white kimonos, carrying a gaily-coloured homemade shrine atop the parallel poles.

I receive confirmation of payments and paperwork now received by the freighter agency, and an email from the Alaskan couple in Noheji offering to arrange accommodation with friends in their hometown of Valdez. All in all I am feeling very upbeat with how things are panning out.

After final goodbyes at Ino's place, I set off to while away a couple of weeks before returning to Yokohama for the freighter ship. On the outskirts of town, a woman flags me down. She had seen me further back and wants to give me a Japanese doughnut she has just purchased from the supermarket. Her English is the remnants of having lived in Wales thirty years previously.

My thoughts turn to where I might go these next couple of weeks. I am not very comfortable with wandering for the sake of it, preferring to have some kind of destination in mind. Neither am I too thrilled at the thought of cycling and camping in the incessant rain. There must be a better way to fill in the gap. Suddenly, I remember the two separate people recently who told me of their WWOOFing experiences. WorldWide Opportunities in Organic Farming allows the pairing of travellers willing to do a bit of work for an unspecified time, and hosts offering board and lodging in exchange for work on their farms. What a brilliant idea. Instantly, I change direction to Chitose, the nearest likely town for internet access, register with the organisation, contact a potential host, arrangements confirmed two days later, to arrive with them two days after that. What could be easier?

Whilst all this is happening, I camp in a big park in Chitose, follow a cycle path to Lake Shikotsu, another of those tranquility views from my tent; in the evening invited for drink, food and cherries by a family camping along the beach. I return to Chitose for two drenching days in the park. My request to sleep in a local church is refused, but I am grateful for the warm, dry library in the park grounds, in which I am able to pass the time in comfort. I am also on the receiving end of the park camp officer's kindness: free camping; banana and carton of coffee, and numerously repeated, 'Good luck. Take care,' on my departure.

I arrive at the farm in the late afternoon, to a handwritten sign, 'Welcome, Astrid! WWOOF host family, Yamaya's home,' pinned on a wooden shed next to a giant painted yellow bear licking his lips, a pawful of honey scooped from the jar he is holding.

Naomi is the only one who speaks English and is the driving force behind the farm. She lives here with her husband, Kazi, and their three young children, Hero, Asaku, Sato, and Kazi's elderly mother. The farm grows various vegetables, particularly cabbages, and runs a dairy herd. I live with them for the next nine days, my first task each morning to muck out the cow stalls, for which I cover up as much as possible, in green overalls, white wellies, pink head buff and cap, mask and gloves. It is pretty disgusting shovelling and brushing sloppy poo about. At least I know now not to become a livestock farmer.

Other acitivities include feeding the curious cows, plus rounding up the occasional escapee before it nibbles too many of the seedlings; sowing spinach seeds and Chinese lettuce; hoeing and banking up rows of young sweetcorn, with the satisfaction of watching their significant upward progress over the ensuing days. I spend many days hoeing a dauntingly vast acreage of cabbages, occasionally alleviated by weeding in the greenhouses.

Living with the family at close quarters is fascinating. One noticeable difference with many other homes in which I have stayed is that this is extremely cluttered and untidy, until now anathema to my experience of Japanese culture. In a way, it is a bit of a relief; aspirations of perfection overruled. One of my favourite times is when Naomi joins me for a beer; not a regular habit with her as it makes her sleepy. Suddenly, she is up on her feet, dancing and singing around the garden, visibly relaxed and enjoying herself. It is great to see, especially as she bears the weight of responsibility for the success of the farm and does not always feel able to let her hair down.

The children attend a weekly calligraphy class on Saturday mornings and I am invited to join them. Half a dozen children attend the class, each greeting their diminutive teacher with a great deal of respectful bowing. We all sit on the tatami floor at low tables, paintbrush in hand. After being taught to write my name in two different Japanese languages, Hirugana and Katagana, I spend the rest of the time practicing to perfection, or as near as I can muster.

Later in the day, the children dress in kimonos and paper crowns, a streak of white paint on their noses, to participate in a street procession with a lively group of about forty children, pulling a cart carrying a white elephant representing Buddha, in celebration of his birthday.

On the way to the children's judo, Naomi drops me off at the local onsen. It has additional pools to that in Hakodate, a couple of outdoor ones, which instantly become my favourite. It is really odd walking naked out into the cold, but once in the hot water it is a fantastic feeling, deliciously warm as far as the neck, cold air wafting over my face. And when the constricting heat in my stomach becomes too much, a simple rising up to perch on the side of the pool quickly alleviates this. It is surprising how long you can remain sitting comfortably out of the warming water. As before, there is a post-pool relaxation room, and a choice of floor cushions, massage chairs or settees to rest and read for forty-five minutes before rejoining Naomi. In the car on the journey home, the children and I swap our respective ipods to listen to each other's music.

I receive joining instructions for the ship, now due to leave Yokohama a day earlier on 7th July, taking only eight, instead of nine, days to reach Prince Rupert. This will give me four days there before catching the monthly ferry to Whittier in Alaska, a passage I now book via the internet. There will be just two other passengers on the freighter ship. I need to be leaving the farm in six days' time to catch the ferry from Tomakomai to Oarai on the mainland, two hundred miles north of Yokohama. I am childishly excited at the prospect of this mini adventure.

On my last morning, I go with Naomi into school, to sit in on Askar's Social Science class, one of the regular Class Observation Days to which parents are invited. The children are curious about me; one young lad examines me closely, concentrating on my face.

'You have a long nose; we all have short noses,' he eventually concludes.

In front of the class and parents, each child presents a picture they have drawn of something they have found or seen where they live, explaining briefly what impression it has made on them. The children are obviously used to this, most of the short talks delivered with a fair degree of confidence.

I have enjoyed my short stay with this family. They have had quite a few wwoofers over the previous few years, ranging from stays of a few days to a few months. It is a set-up with benefits all round and occurs worldwide.

The ferry from Oarai has not long docked when I arrive. A couple of cycle tourers disembark, one a Brit, Nigel, living in New Zealand for the last twenty-five years, and about to inaugurate his Kiwi girlfriend into the joys of cycling for a month on rainy Hokkaido. She does not look too excited at the prospect.

Queuing for the ferry are many motorbikers, including one rider with a sling pouch on his back, containing a fluffy, four-legged bundle of dark, downy fur, demurely watching the activities around her.

This time on the overnight ferry, I go for the communal sleeping room. I am glad to see there are only four of us in the 12-futon sleeping cabin; if full, we would have been touching noses. It is a very simple and relaxed way of travelling on a ferry and feels much more civilsed than dossing down on the floor of a public lounge.

After the 24-hour trip, we arrive in Oarai and I cycle away in the misty rain. I find a delightful campsite, mentally warning myself not to become too blasé at the tranquil locations that constantly pop up, for, yes, it is another softly-lapping lakeside tranquility affair. These basic municipal picnic/camp sites all have ultra-clean toilet blocks, but this one raises the stakes by providing wooden-soled sandals at the doorway. In the morning, a man who seems to have some duties on the site, walks over saying something to me, but I can only shrug politely. I do not hear any mention of yen or see any indication that he is asking for payment and, when I say, 'Wakarimasen (I don't understand),' he shrugs and walks off. The day is hot and sunny and the terrain kind; that is, until I encounter the steepest hill I have yet come across.

I slog up it for a while, unable to recall seeing an alternative road. Even so, part way up I decide, 'Blow this for a laugh, there has to be a different way.'

I u-turn and whizz back down, retracing my steps a few miles, only to find no roads leading off after all. Dispirited, I return to the herculean effort of scaling this mountain. I put all my weight and strength behind pushing my bicycle four steps at a time, then rest the pedal against my shin to stop it from going backwards, four more steps, pedal against shin, four more steps. I hardly have the strength to make any progress and contemplate the possibility of unloading everything, relaying them to the top one bag at at time. I am glad there is little traffic as, for the most part, I am in the middle of the road, with no chance of sprinting to the side to make way for vehicles. When a car does come along, I resent its ease of ascent and wonder in amazement that the occupants can possibly glide by this sorrowful sight without even a thought to give me a lift.

'Oh, stop whingeing!' I scold myself, 'You've chosen to do this. Get on with it.'

Three-quarters of the way up, I welcome a refreshment stop: a cooling stream splashing down the jagged rocks. And as with all things, there is an end, eventually. The struggle crosses the finishing line at a crossroads on the top of the mountain. I stop to try and work out which is now the right road to take, when a couple of day cyclists veritably sprint up from the road to my right. We are equally shocked: they, that I have scaled the hill.

'We *never* go up there! Far too hard.'

And I on learning there apparently was an alternative. But where?!

The view on the downhill is of dense pine forests and distant mountains. I camp in the grounds of a leisure centre, it could even be a private club, but the grounds are big enough for me to hide away. In the morning it is time to de-camp when a baseball team arrives for training at six o'clock.

A cycle path leads me onto a ridge, possibly an old railway embankment, following a river. After a section back on busy roads, I follow a cycle route all the way to a northern suburb of Tokyo. Remembering that Japan is safe to camp everywhere bar the centre of Tokyo, I seize the chance encounter of a huge park to investigate the camping potential. It does indeed have a designated camping area, but it is very remote and overgrown and, seeing a couple of men in one of the covered picnic huts, I do not feel comfortable enough to pitch my tent in such a solitary spot. Instead I return to the main populated area by the lake to bask in the sinking sun, beer and food in hand. A couple with bicycles stop for a chat, he Japanese, she American. They are really interested in my cycling trip and make a note of my website, whilst I attempt subliminal messages regarding overnight accommodation. They though, fully endorse my proposal to camp in 'their favourite park.'

I cycle around for an hour and a half in search of a spot, but not happy with anywhere, increasingly wondering why, if so concerned to be inconspicuous, I am drawing attention to myself by cycling aimlessly now that it is dark. In the end, a park bench, semi-discreetly positioned behind an attractive fretwork screen, beckons me to place my sleeping mattress, pillow and sleeping bag on it, optimistically promising a state of somnolence for a few hours.

Let's just say, it is an interesting night: mosquitoes and other insects are curious to find out more about me and a friendly frog (or toad?) keeps sentry duty directly under my bed, occasionally croaking, 'Who goes there?' Adolescents wander noisily through the park, even past my bedroom, into the early hours. Then barely a couple of hours quiet solitude before walkers, cyclists and joggers commence their fitness programmes at 4.30 am, at the same time that dawn declares the end of the night and I feel too conspicuous to remain abed. Up from bench and down to lakeside by 5.30, and a hot chocolate brew-up. Later, my daughter will exclaim in shocked abhorrence, 'Whaaat?! My mum, homeless, sleeping on a park bench!!'

Cycling through Tokyo, past plush 'Designer Row' fashion houses at this hour of the morning is easy peasy. Straight on to Yokohama and the Yokohama Porto Hostel, friendly, new, cheap. Even though I have paid for a dormitory bed, I am placed in a single room.

'We have plenty of free space.'

Without me asking, they put my bicycle in secure storage inside.

'Because your bicycle is important to you.'

I am allowed to use the office computer to upload two large batches of photos for my website. Breakfast is included in the room tariff: two fresh, warm rolls, butter and jam, omelette, salad, coffee++. The hostel is a lovely last experience of my two and a half months in Japan.

As usual with hostels, there is a cosmopolitan clientele, English being the predominant communication language. Chatting in English with the Israeli, Australian, German, Canadian travellers and Japanese staff, I realise how much I have missed easy-flowing conversations. I have to say that, after ten months in non-English speaking countries, I am looking forward with a tinge of relief to arriving in North America, no phrasebook required (I hope).

*   *   *

Cruising down the Yangtse.

Japan in festival season.

Half way! Just another 10,000 miles to go.

The art of displaying food.

Approaching Prince Rupert after 9 days trans-Pacific from Yokohama.

30-foot bighead in Valdez, Alaska.

Plenty of trees and lonely roads in beautiful Alaska.

Look out! Logging trucks speeding south.

Wild camping in Canada.

Along Route 101 on the stunning Oregon Coast.

Inset: *An encouraging sign in Washington State.*

Above: *A motley collection of Pacific Coast cyclists – and not a pair of padded lycra shorts in sight.*

Left: *Arizona and New Mexico produced plenty of punctures from tough thorns and metal filaments from shredded lorry tyres.*

Right: *Christopher Columbus on Miami waterfront.*

Left: *Semana Santas festival in Seville. Processions take 12 hours to complete.*

Middle right:
The Bombeiros (Portuguese Fire Department) offer pilgrims accommodation . . .

. . . as well as fix their bicycles. (Inset middle left)

The path of light of the ongoing pilgrimage.

Did you miss me, children?

Pacific Ocean

7 – 14 July 2009

Hanjin Madrid

The three of us meet for the first time in the foyer of the Navisio Hotel near the port in Yokohama. Krista is an American teacher at the US Naval Base on Okinawa, one of the southernmost islands in Japan; Elliott a geophysicist, made redundant, now taking a year out to travel around the world flightlessly, before setting up his own consultancy business.

The port agent arrives and we pile into the minibus, to be transported through the security gates of the port and processed by the various immigration and customs controls. We head past towering cranes adroitly loading huge metal crates onto enormous ships, in a few minutes pulling up at the gargantuan *Hanjin Madrid*, the only one to flash a grey-green light, indicating she is larger than large, at 60,000 tonnes. Her port of origin is Hamburg, German built and owned, currently leased for ten years to a Korean company, Hanjin. Germany specialises in container shipping, claiming a sixty-five percent monopoly of the global market.

We stand at the bottom of the daunting steps leading up to the deck far above us, before wobbling our way up the steep and shaky gangway. Krista, in front, momentarily pauses at the top, causing Elliott and me to follow suit, until Elliott, in a strained voice, urges us to keep moving. It is only now we are aware of his fear of heights. I admire his gutsy attitude. One of the Filipino crew lithely hoists Raven on his shoulders, nonchalantly stepping up the gangway, depositing her gently in her very own cabin.

We are shown to our respective abodes. Mine is the Owner's Cabin. From the doorway, a small vestibule leads into a spacious room. Straight ahead, a desk beneath a porthole looks out towards the bow, a second desk at 90 degrees against the wall on my right. My eyes move to the left to a second porthole above a three-seater settee, in front of which is a coffee table with bowl of fruit and bottle of water. A second settee and a pair of armchairs face each other over the table. Completing my 270° sweep, a widescreen television and DVD player come into view. Off from the vestibule on the right is a double bedroom, also with two portholes and with plenty of storage, a further door leading to the compact ensuite shower and toilet.

I stand in the middle of my lounge squealing with excitement, pinching myself to confirm that I really am where I think I am. From my many cabin portholes, I watch mesmerised as giant cranes grab huge containers, swinging them effortlessly and efficiently, up, across, down, into computer pre-assigned positions, according to the port at which they will be unloaded. I watch this slowly evolving landscape of red and blue as it rises ever upwards towards the level of my cabin, names of Hanjin, Kline, Senator, Cosco identifying the cargo transportation companies. As with icebergs, what is seen above deck is only a small percentage of the total cargo, the bulk of it hidden from view in the depths of the hull.

Krista is staying in the Purser's Day Room, also a large cabin, similar to mine; Elliott in Super Cargo cabin, a spacious single room.

We meet Captain Schmeling, charming, easygoing, with a dry sense of humour, who allows us to go anywhere on board ship, even encouraging us to visit the Bridge, the ship's nerve centre, whenever we wish.

'But you must remember that this is a working vessel. Officers and crew have their duties and responsibilities, which do not include entertaining the passengers. Although,' he adds hastily, 'we are all happy to help out with anything.'

Adrian is our steward, responsible for cleaning our cabins each day, unless we request otherwise, serving us our meals in the Officers' Mess, in which as passengers, we have our own table, separate from the officers. The Filipino crew have their own Mess (and menu) on the other side of the galley. The food is tasty; the officers (mostly German, one Polish) and crew, amiable.

Loading finally completed, we are ready to manoeuvre away from the dock, the miniscule pilot boat now about to perform its vital role. Talk about David and Goliath. This tiny vessel effortlessly pulls the giant stern, pushes the massive bow, to point the ship in the right

282

direction, guided by instructions from one of two visiting pilots on the Bridge. Manouevre completed, this first pilot must now descend the trembling gangway to transfer precariously to a wobbly rope ladder, descending hand over fist to the heaving pilot boat on the bumpy sea. The Bay Pilot now takes over directing the tiny tug boat to lead us through the shipping channel to the open sea, whereupon, in the windy darkness, he repeats the same disembarkation manoeuvre as his colleague earlier, returning to port as a thick eery fog descends.

And now begins the routine of ship life, geared around meal times: 7.30 am Breakfast; 10 am Coffee and Biscuits; 12 noon Lunch; 3 pm Afternoon Tea; 5.30 pm Dinner. The early dinner means that we become hungry during the evening, raiding the fridge de rigeur; although the first night we do not realise this is a legitimate activity, feeling very much like naughty children as we tiptoe our way to the galley.

The deck levels comprise: Upper Deck, decks A-G, Bridge. Krista and I are on level F, Elliott, one down, Captain, one up. When in port, the strict rule is that all doors on all levels, except the portside door on Upper Deck, are kept locked – against the possibility of pirates boarding, a very real threat in some waters. This is also the deck that enables us to circuit the whole ship, Krista and I doing so on a daily basis to breathe in lungfuls of healthy fresh air. After a couple of days, we persuade Elliott to come with us, walking in the middle. It is a massive achievement for him, but once is quite sufficient, thank you very much. Even outside the Bridge he can only venture so far.

The stacked containers create a constant creaking from their inevitable movement, no matter how calm the sea might be. The resultant sound is rather alarming at first, but your senses gradually become accustomed to it. Fog invariably falls at night, but often clears away by mid morning, leaving a warm, humid air.

The Bridge is great. It certainly has an air of importance: its elevation and uninterrupted views, radar screens blipping away mapping our progress and indicating other ships in the locale. We hone in on individual vessels, whereupon their vital statistics pop up on the screen: who they are, what they are, how big they are, their destination port, whether or not they are carrying hazardous waste. Daily chart printouts of our progress are issued by the Second Officer.

To compensate for the time zone differences as we move eastwards, we advance our clocks each day by one hour. By the third day, the loss of an hour's sleep each night begins to take its toll as I have to drag myself out of bed for seven-thirty breakfast. I could of course just take a leaf out of Elliott's book and stay in bed, but routine is routine.

Halfway across the Ocean, we have to accommodate the International Date Line: not only advancing one hour, but also turning the clocks back one day. On the first Friday evening, we attempt to get to grips with the fact that, although the next day will be Friday, 10 July again (forward one hour, plus back one day), it is during the second Friday evening we will actually cross the Date Line, when the clocks go forward one hour and back one day. This does not sound right, because isn't that what we are doing this evening, if it is going to be Friday again tomorrow?

In the end, we merely obey instructions to report to Bridge at 8.45 pm on the second Friday evening to witness the date change. Alan, the Filipino Third Officer is on duty. Whilst we are waiting, he takes the ship off automatic pilot, permitting me to steer the ship, course 072. I grip the tiny steering wheel, eyes locked onto the digital compass, the weight of responsibility heavy on my shoulders as I take control of the vessel. It feels akin to sailing, when it is easy to push the tiller too much one way, then overcompensate the other, resulting in a zigzag path rather than a direct line. The scale here is a thousand times greater, taking a minute or so for the rudder to respond to the turn of the steering wheel and then for the ship to respond to the rudder, by which time you know you have over-steered and perform a reverse correction, which is just as extreme; result: a drunken 66,000 tonne container ship on the loose. The stress for us all lasts just a few minutes, after which I am more than happy to relinquish my bid for control, power, world domination, and return to the business in hand.

The date change is scheduled for 2114 hours. As the time approaches, we steadfastly fix our eyes on the digital compass, the figures advancing towards 179°59', after which it will show a second 179°59', but diminishing. There is no 180°.

When the actual event happens, it is a bit of an anticlimax. We are concentrating so hard, we manage to miss the change, then it is a few minutes before we realise that the numbers are now diminishing. It is still special though, certainly sufficient to continue breaking open the bottle of sparkling wine to toast the occasion. Even though we have now officially crossed the Date Line, we have already done the one step forwards, 24 back routine and so it is Saturday. It seems you can do what you like at sea, the Captain has control. For some reason, it is better for the routine of the ship to have made the change a day earlier.

Following dinner each day, we usually adjourn to the Officer's Lounge. Elliott joins forces with the officers, all furiously intent on some computer game, 'Just for the boys.' Thinking about it, are there *any* computer games just for the girls? Just because they are alien to me, it does not hold that it should be for the rest of my sex.

Each of us has substantial time in our own cabins: Krista reads and falls asleep over *Pride and Prejudice*; Elliott is writing a book about his trip; I attempt to create a powerpoint of my trip aimed at Primary School children, something Krista might like for her schoolchildren. However, I come to a point when the presentation does not save, the capacity of the little ASUS obviously has its limitations.

The onboard gym is equipped with a static bicycle, positioned to look out of the window at the static view for, let's face it, grey sea, horizon, grey sky do not equate to a moving landscape. We take advantage of the other main piece of equipment, table tennis, becoming fairly aggressive at times with our shots. On the other side of a partition window is a small swimming pool, filled with sea water once the ship is out of port, emptied before re-entry. The Chief Engineer uses it regularly, fitting himself with a harness to swim static lengths. We wimps decide it is too cold and never actually get round to taking the plunge.

The Chief Engineer takes us on a tour of the engine room. We don ear defenders, looking like Mickey Mouse in the process. Confidently assuming the engine room is going to be big does not adequately prepare us for its mind-blowing proportions. The ten 10-feet high cyclinders and the propeller shaft of at least 100 feet in length say it all. And forget grease-grimed engines, think pristine pistons. Discard the notion of filthy boiler-room stokers, replace with squeaky-clean touchtype computer operators. Everything is gleaming and orderly, even the tools arranged as a wall-mounted art exhibit. It is absorbingly interesting – and the most animated we have seen the Chief Engineer.

A farewell party is held for Jakob, the Polish Second Officer, who will be leaving the ship in Seattle; as will Captain Schmeling and, so it seems, all of the crew. So, really it just seems a vague excuse if one is needed, for a boozy knees-up. We gather in the Crew's Lounge, most people bringing drinks, the officers providing food and cocktails. The TV screen shows pop concerts as background for the evening, subsequently followed by BeeGees karaoke, the Filipinos particularly singing along with great gusto, although, by this time, most of us are in a suitable state of inebriation to give it a go.

Early on the seventh morning, I glance out of my porthole. Where is my wall of fog or flat horizon? Mountains and land loom instead. They are the first of the Aleutian Islands: Akutan and Akun. Wildlife makes an appearance: blow sprays from whales off the starboard bow; a humpback off the stern jumping completely out of the water; dense flocks of birds flying low over the surface across the bows. This brief interlude ends abruptly, when fog descends; no more view for the rest of the day, as we glide silently through Unimak Passage in the Gulf of Alaska.

A freighter ship has to time its arrival in port precisely, to coincide with its pre-booked berth. As we are ahead of schedule, the engines are cut on two days, when we drift aimlessly in perfect peace from noise and vibration, one day for six hours, the next for twenty-four. Back on course, we enter Dixon Passage, officially now in Canada and on my fourth continent.

*   *   *

Canada

15 – 19 July 2009

Prince Rupert

Dixon Passage marks the maritime boundary between the US and Canada, the entrance to the strait indicated by the sighting of Dall Island off the port (left) side, followed by Prince of Wales Island. The pilot comes on board at 1300 hours, accompanied by an observer trainee; our docking time is at 1500.

The grain plant at Prince Rupert is sighted in the distance and, as we pass the archipelago of pale grey islands that stretch out on our starboard side, the sun triumphantly breaks through the mist and cloud. Out come sunchairs and sunglasses, their first outing on the voyage, and clinking cans of cold beer. Forty-five minutes later the soft mist once more descends; a sweet interlude nonetheless.

A small fishing boat bravely steers a course across our bows, only to bottle out, stop, thrust into reverse, in prudent respect of this colossus. We turn left at the grain plant, our next landmark the tall red and white unloading gantries of Prince Rupert port, jutting upwards on the headland far ahead. Drawing ever closer, we make out Prince Rupert itself, sitting at the head of the bay beyond.

Hanjin Madrid sails up the narrow passage, past the port towards the bay beyond. Pilot requests the ship be stopped. Much to his surprise, this happens instantaneously, his expectation was to have carried on a bit further. Despite this, there is enough room to swivel 180°, returning to the port alongside the gantries. Gently and skilfully, now pushed by two tiny tugs fore and aft, we approach the docking berth, arriving with a virtually imperceptible touch at exactly 1500 hours. The dockworkers far below look miniscule.

Port officials board. They have no clue what to do with our trio, so phone a supervisor who says he will come to the ship, but never appears. Bidding farewell and au revoir (Krista will return the following day) to the captain, officers and crew, the three of us wobble down the steps on our sea legs, our baggage lowered by hoist in a sturdy net. Being a hard-hat area, we wait for a port pick-up vehicle to take us on the thirty-second trip to the perimeter gate. Our names are there checked off on the list by the security man in his little box, who gives us the all-clear to go. But we are slightly perplexed; it is too easy, too uncomplicated; and we have no entry stamps in our passports. There appears to be no customs control anywhere and this man knows nothing, merely shrugging his shoulders.

The security man phones for a taxi, my companions wait, I depart up the hill, having arranged to meet the others in town. Halfway up, I pause to take photos. Krista is waving and calling, I return the wave and continue; I have no idea what she was saying. A beefy four-wheel drive roars up behind, toots his horn a couple of times and I respond with a merry wave. He draws alongside; it is Customs instructing me to return. Elliott happened to notice a building, knocked on the door and, hey presto, Customs lurking anonymously. They are not pleased that we left the ship without clearing customs! But they still stamp our passports.

I return up the hill, to be greeted by a cheery blue and yellow sign:

Welcome
The Best Place on Earth
BRITISH COLUMBIA
CANADA

Successfully meeting up with the other two at the Information Centre, we make our way to the Black Rooster Hostel. I book into a four-bed dorm, the others, on a different budget, in an apartment next door. We return to town and to Cow Bay, check out Cowpuccino's Café, where live music is about to start but there is no food on offer. We head for Smiles across the road.

After a less than great meal, Elliott and I have our first encounter with the double taxation and compulsory tipping on just about everything. The latter is given very grudgingly, as the salmon was overcooked and service not up to much. At a hefty fifteen to twenty percent, it increases the cost of a meal significantly.

The next morning, Krista and I send parcels home from the post office. Afterwards we visit the Museum of Northern British Columbia, learning about First Nation History, building of the North Pacific Trunk Railroad, the Alaska Marine Highway. We meet up with Elliott for a final goodbye, as Krista heads back to the ship for her final four days to Seattle. The three of us talk of a possible reunion in UK the following summer.

I take my netbook along to a computer shop to try and sort out a problem. They confidently suggest a particular course of action and I agree. However, on my return later to collect it, things have not gone smoothly and they are trying to resolve it, needing more time. I try not to panic; but this is my main means of communication with my family. In the meantime, I go for a walk to find the ferry terminal.

On the edge of town I pause to consult my map as to which path to take through the forest, when a voice breaks in on my deliberations.

'Hi. Can I help?'

Joe has lived in Prince Rupert for many years and we chat for a while. He walks with me through the wooded park, pointing out the lake frequented by a particular family of bears, continuing with useful tips on how not to surprise a bear.

'Sing as you walk along. And if you do encounter one, try to be with someone else at the time, but make sure you are wearing the better running shoes. And definitely do not climb trees; bears are extremely competent climbers themselves.'

I happen to mention my computer, whereupon Joe whips out his mobile and calls the shop, telling them to put the bill on his tab! My protestations are merely waived to one side.

Back in town, I bump into Pilot John, just returned from guiding in the *Norwegian Star*, a 2,000-person cruiser, this voyage specifically made up of gay families. We go for a beer, he tells me about his twenty-three years at sea before becoming a pilot, experience and in-depth knowledge of local waters being the pre-requisite for this crucial job.

Elliott is looking to buy a vehicle which he can adapt for sleeping in for his travel through North America. We check out a couple of local car lots, but in the end he decides to try and book onto the same ferry as me to Alaska and continue his hunt there.

I retrieve my computer, the situation in the end only able to be resolved by reinstallation of the operating system. Disappointing, but better that than not working at all.

A couple of women arrive on bicycles at the hostel. One, a French woman from Whitehorse, arrives on the early morning ferry from Skagway, planning to take a train to Prince George and then cycle back to Whitehorse. The second, a newly-qualified graduate, has just cycled from Washington to Port Edward over sixteen days and proceeds to make us all a load of cookies before continuing her trip.

In the evening prior to my departure, I happen to notice that there is a hostel noticeboard, pinned to which is a piece of paper bearing my name. It is from Joe, dated the previous day, inviting me to go with him to watch salmon jump. Such a shame it is too late to take up the offer.

I have to be at the ferry terminal at 6.15 in the morning. I set the alarm for five o'clock; it does not go off. I awake at 5.49. Help. Up, dress, bags outside (*so* glad I packed everything bar my toothbrush last night), haul bicycle up from the basement, load bags, on the road by 6.01, arrive a bit breathless at the ferry terminal at 6.15. No panic.

At check-in, there is a mix-up regarding my roomette booking and I end up paying extra for an outside berth, which is what I thought I had already paid for. The next step is to go through American immigration (more convenient to do it now as we leave Canada, than when we arrive in Alaska). I am issued with a white card, valid for six months.

'But I have a visa for ten years.'

'Yes, but that is different from the white card.'

'But I need longer than six months to cycle the length and breadth of America.'

'Well then, you will have to go out of country at some point and come back in.'

I am becoming somewhat agitated until the immigration officer makes a parting comment.

'When you enter the lower 48 from Canada, you should ask a supervisor at border control for an extension.'

Next time maybe say that at the beginning?

I push Raven onto the ferry, looking forward to the coming three days through the Inside Passage. To all intents and purposes, we have already arrived in Alaska; ship time is an hour behind Prince Rupert.

* * *

Alaska/Yukon/Alaska

20 July – 7 August 2009

*MV Kennicott, Valdez, Tickel, Willow Creek, Gakona,
Slana, Tok Junction, Deadman Lake, Beaver Creek,
Lake Creek, Kathleen Lake, Haines, Alaska Marine Highway*

Roomettes are a brilliant idea. They are tiny little cabins; a table in
between two seats convert into a bed, above which is a foldaway second
bed. It makes for affordable, comfortable accommodation. During the
three-day voyage up the beautiful Inside Passage, we stop at Ketchikan,
Juneau (learning with surprise that this is the capital of Alaska, not, as I
thought, Anchorage) and Yakutat. These towns nowadays exist mainly
for cruise ship tourism. During the season, seven ships, each carrying
two thousand passengers, descend on Juneau each day at the same time
for just a few hours. The visitors are then cajoled and enticed into the
tourist shops, ninety percent of which are owned by the cruise
companies, the remainder proudly displaying notices that they are First
Nation owners. The mass departure empties the place instantly.

Sea planes frequently taxi on and off the water, no road access is
available. Our visit to Juneau coincides with Sarah Palin stepping down
as governor, comments about her from the locals being far from
flattering. It rains heavily and almost constantly for the three days of our
voyage. On one day the sea becomes so rough, the ship billows so much,
that half the passengers and crew are flat on their backs in their bunks.
Elliott and I pride ourselves that we manage, by superhuman self-
control, not to succumb to throwing up. Sitting in the lounge, it is
hilarious watching anyone attempt to walk the length of the room, their
drunken gait staggering back and forth with the swaying ship.

Daily in the lounge are 20-minute talks on the history of the three towns we visit and on whales, bears and salmon. Whale-spotting is a popular pastime for many of the passengers, and I delight in the sight of the dorsal fin and back of an Orca whale. At the National Park centre in Yakutat, the ranger talks through the different protective tactics to adopt with bears, depending on whether it is a grizzly or a black bear with whom you are having an encounter. I just wonder what sort of presence of mind he truly thinks most people will have when face to face with one or the other, to be able to adopt enough of a calm, collected manner to ascertain the appropriate behaviour for the occasion.

We arrive in Whittier at half six in the morning, disembarking into an Alaskan scene of cold, windy, torrential rain; a dark, dire, dismal welcome. I remain in the terminal waiting room for six hours before my bay trip across to Valdez. Elliott leaves in a minibus taxi for Anchorage, intent on buying a vehicle in which to drive to the Arctic Ocean – to swim in it. Brrr.

I try chatting to a German cyclist; his third time in Alaska and never had any problems with bears. He reckons that campsites are within a day's cycling of each other. He returns to reading his book. A cycling German couple, who have been on the road for a year, discuss how they are going to negotiate their bicycles through the two-and-a-half-mile tunnel between here and Anchorage.

The view as we cross the bay to Valdez is fully appreciated from the snug warmth of the ferry. I peer through the rivulets of rain running down the windows at the mountainous backdrop, semi-obscured by a blanket of cloud. The six-hour trip across Prince William Sound brings us to Valdez, not a large place, low-rise, wooden buildings laid out spaciously, straddling wide streets. A 30-foot wooden carving of the head of a native American towers above the roof-line.

I make my way to Rogue's Garden, a coffee shop run by friends of Julie and Tailor, relieved that I shall be staying in the dry, not camping. Kathy and Bruce welcome me, despite there being a full house, plus another house guest.

Whilst here I try to find out why my mobile is not working, the helpful shop-owner trying out various permutations between my mobile, his mobile, my SIM card, his SIM card.

'Possibly, it is due to there not being a very good signal here. Maybe, you should wait until the lower 48.'

I check out an outdoor clothing shop for replacement trousers, opting instead to buy patches. I try unsuccessfully to contact the children for a Skype call; write a mound of postcards; bake an apple pie (like my Mum used to make) for my host family. I enjoy the easy, open hospitality here in crime-free Valdez, where you don't need to lock up your house whenever you leave it.

By the time I depart, a phone call has already been made to arrange for me to stay with a family down the line. The rain graciously disappears, and now, 'The sun has got his hat on, hip, hip, hip hooray.'

After nineteen days of no cycling, my soul and body are more than ready to be on the road again. I have had a thoroughly enjoyable experience with the various sea passages over the last month, but now fully refreshed and raring to go on this next leg. I cycle out of town in buoyant spirits along a flat road, hardly any traffic, except for the occasional loud-engined RVs (Recreational Vehicles). Each time I see one advancing, I think it is a coach full of people, and am always surprised when it turns out to be an RV with just two occupants.

Adopt-a-highway roadsigns appear at various intervals, each one sponsored by different local organisations, such as American Legion Post 2, committing themselves to keep that particular section of the highway clear of litter.

As in Japan, so here, warning signs, 'STOP, tsunami evacuation area; in case of earthquake stay on high ground or inland.' A third type of sign particularly catches my eye: a yellow diamond-shaped warning sign, picturing a mummy duck leading three baby ducklings. Aaah.

After nineteen miles of flat tundra and staggering mountain views, a slow, six-mile climb to just over 2,600 feet summits at glacial Thompson Pass. On the descent, I see several more beautiful glaciers.

A campsite after forty miles is closed, as is the second at fifty-two miles, a small, nondescript place called Tickel. I am beginning to realise that there are not going to be many provision stops in this part of the country, so best to stock up whenever there is. At this second campsite, I meet the German cyclist, Robert, who turns out to be more sociable than implied at the ferry terminal in Whittier. We continue a couple of miles up the road, turning off along a track in search of a hut he had used three years previously. We find it, but it is derelict and we return to the closed camp, installing ourselves near the river. Mosquitoes and flies pay us a visit en masse.

I have been nervous all day about camping alone. What if I meet a bear? Much as I have been eagerly anticipating such an encounter, my enthusiasm of late, with everyone's dire warnings of the risks and dangers, wanes at the very thought. Therefore, having Robert around on this first night is perfect. I go off into the bush, singing away, feeling more upbeat than I would have on my own. Robert is well set up with his camping gear, even rigging a water bag fitted with a shower nozzle high in a tree to take his daily shower (in swimming trunks, I hasten to add), inviting me to follow suit afterwards. I pass, washing face and hands is enough for me, far too cold.

We take water for cooking from the flowing river, my culinary effort involving the last of my sachets of Polish soup given to me by Karfori in Japan, peanut butter and cheese rolls. I have a length of rope, a carabina attached to one end, to which I attach my black rolltop bag, filled with all my smelly things, which I hoist about ten feet above the ground, out of paws' reach.

After a rainy, but uneventful night, Robert and I cycle together along the remote roads. The previous day I had seen a sign indicating the TransAlaska Pipeline Terminal. Today we see the pipeline itself, on elevated supports, making its long journey through the trees carrying its precious fuel. It reminds me of the ancient aqueducts I had seen in Italy, transporting to Rome over great distances their precious commodity, water; both impressive achievements.

Robert turns off into Wrangell-St Elias National Park, I continue along the lonely highway, the landscape an endless expanse of trees stretching as far as the eye can see, broken only by this one swathe of road before me. Lakes and rivers of gushing, glacial torrents are to the side of me; beyond, the four Wrangell-St Elias mountain ranges in the distance, hiding behind patchy clouds. I love it. I look out constantly for the promised wildlife: bears, moose, caribou. None yet; oh well.

In Willow Creek, I head for the five-acre homestead of friends of the family in Valdez. Doug, Marnie, daughter Taylor, they also have a full house of family guests, from whom come offers of accommodation when I come to the lower states.

Just as guitar-playing and singing was evening entertainment in Valdez, so it is here. Doug is prevailed upon to strike up on his guitar, choosing one of his own compositions, a protest song bemoaning the effects of the Exon Valdez oil spill a few years previously.

The homestead is virtually self-sufficient in vegetables. Catching and home-smoking salmon and hunting for meat is still very much taken for granted. The hunter/gathering, living off the land way of life seems prevalent in both Alaska and Canada; which certainly has a romantic appeal to it, although whether the year-round realities would hold up for me, I have my doubts. I have chosen the narrow window of opportunity of favourable weather conditions to be in Alaska during July/August, most other months riskily too extreme for me.

I sleep reasonably well, Taylor kindly vacating her bed, so dispensing with the need for me to erect my tent. I leave in the morning armed with a package of home-caught, home-smoked salmon, three large home-grown corn-on-the-cob, a mass of praline chocolates from Marnie's mum, contact numbers for the 48-ers and for tonight's hosts in Gakona.

The road surface here is covered with numerous large cracks, the visible effect of the permafrost melting, a result of global warming so I am told. The effect is also seen in Arctic ice and bergs, which have decreased in size and number causing a reduction in the number of polar bears; although there is evidence that some are learning to adapt, at least one bear having been found a hundred miles inland in Yukon.

Copper Centre boasts an interesting little museum, describing the history and culture of the area and the extensive mining of copper creating the railroad to transport the ore between Juneau, Cordova and McCarthy. The mines are all closed now, maybe to be opened up in the future as a tourist attraction. Wishing to learn more of the history from a first-hand point of view, I buy a book from the museum, *Penny In My Shoe,* an account of an eighteen-year old girl's time in Alaska in these early mining days.

On to Glenallen Visitor Centre, where Debbie, an assistant there, lends me her car to drive to the supermarket a couple of miles away on the Anchorage road to stock up on provisions, the car making it quicker and easier to negotiate the return uphill. Duly supplied and back on the Tok road, I pass a German cycling couple (what is it with the Germans and Alaska?) camping for free in the grounds of Gakona Lodge.

At the top of the next hill, I arrive at the 160-acre homestead of Bruce and Kari, their two-year old daughter, Grace, and black labrador, Scout. Once again on the receiving end of another warm welcome, I hope that I shall be as forthcoming and hospitable when I am back home.

I have my own sleeping quarters in the loft of a separate outbuilding, where the family lived whilst they were building their palatial log house. The majority of their acreage is wooded, the rule for a homestead being that ten to twenty percent of the land is to be cleared.

Each Alaskan resident is permitted to work their own fish wheel to catch salmon for their own use. In the evening we drive down the thickly wooded track to the river to check the catch for today. It is not uncommon for there to be forty to fifty salmon at a time; this family's record an incredible ninety-one! In a year, one fish wheel can catch a thousand salmon. Residents are not allowed to sell them, only give them away. It is a far cry from when I was a child, when we had salmon just once a year as a treat.

The next day starts out flat, becomes undulating, with a couple of long hills. A yellow diamond warning sign, topped with two red flags, announces, 'Rough Road.' Underneath, a yellow square sign, 'Next 112 ml', (I take the 'ml' to be miles!). At the foot of the post a red and white striped bollard stands to attention, to its left more red and white diagonal stripes on a board. The road shortly becomes loose gravel, often slippery, not made for easy cycling.

My first possibility of a stop is at Chistochina, a small sprawling settlement with one shop. I sit outside at a picnic table, my lunch before me, when a pick-up pulls up, the driver jumps out and comes over to sit on an adjacent bench and proceeds to ask me questions in an aggressive way. Not caring much for his manner, I do not engage in conversation. Maybe provoked by my disinterest, he then comes and sits at my table. Fortunately, a woman with whom I had chatted when I first entered the village, now arrives and enters the store, coming out to sit on the front porch with her ice cream. I go over and talk with her and her little dog, Plato. They are from San Diego, way down on the west coast of America. Since taking early retirement, they have been travelling in their Winnebago motor home for seven months.

The disagreeable man leaves, thankfully in the opposite direction to me. I set off, lapping up the sun and warmth. But then the same pick-up overtakes me, the man shouting something out of the window as he passes. Further up the road, there he is parked by the roadside, standing by his vehicle, again saying something unintelligible as I pass. He continues to do this for the remainder of the day, so that by the time I arrive at the state campground and find it totally deserted and remotely-`

positioned, there is no way that I am going to risk staying there, freaked out by the antics of this man.

As there is nowhere away from the road where I would feel safe, I ask at a house if I might put my tent up in their grounds. The two women on the balcony mention lodges about five miles up the road where I should be allowed to camp. They sort of offer a pitch in their grounds, but reluctantly, so I carry on to the suggested destination, a motel and restaurant. The predatory pick-up is parked outside.

I cannot cycle any further. I have already done more than intended and now my day's cyclometer reads seventy-four miles. At least there are people here. I go in and ask to put my tent up in the grounds. The woman replies, with an emphatic, 'No.' She has not allowed tents to pitch for many years. I explain I can go no further and that I am concerned for my safety from a stalker, who happens to be here, but still she does not relent.

'Oh, him, he's harmless', she dismisses, 'However, there is a lane just past the motel. It's not necessarily owned by anyone. You might find somewhere there to camp. Although there is a group of workers who are having a bit of a noisy party.'

Gladly, I head towards the lane, hoping to pass the party surreptitiously, under the cover of darkness, but, no chance.

'Where are you going?'

'Up the lane to put up my tent.'

'Come and have a drink.'

'What's with the bike?'

'Stalker, eh? Don't worry, sleep here in the trailer.'

There are nine people, one working for the FAA (Federal Aviation Administration) setting up solar and wind turbine towers on top of the mountain to help improve communications for air traffic. The panels are transported by two-man helicopters. The group are sleeping in the motel rooms, hence the vacant trailer; an office during the day, recreation room and drinks bar in the evening. They are a fantastic bunch of guys and I have a safe haven. They invite me to join them in the motel for a meal and I am able to take a shower in one of the motel rooms. I am very thankful things have turned out so well.

The stalker hails from Tok Junction, my next destination. I am wary the whole of the following day, the woman's dismissal that he is harmless holding no sway with me. This time when I stop at a state campground short of the Junction, it is well-populated. They are all a fixed price of $15, which seems a great deal for not very much, not even drinking water. Here there is no river nearby, the only water being from a pump at a well, with advice to boil before drinking. Toilets comprise a loo seat over a large metal tank filled with chemicals, a notice strategically positioned requesting the lid be put down before leaving. This seems frequently ignored, instantly giving away the gender of the previous occupant. The other facility on these campsites generally includes bear bins: a large, bear-proof box to store your smellies at night away from your tent. Re-assessing my churlish thoughts about the cost of these campgrounds; we are, after all, in a fairly remote part of the world for convenient mains water and flushing loos.

The next morning, a neighbouring family invites me for pancakes and bacon, plus a water bottle fill-up before I leave. An adequate drinking water supply is the single biggest challenge for me at the moment. The bizarre thing is that it is easier to find alcohol than water, having passed liqueur stores set up in preference to a general store.

Tok Junction stands at the crossroads of the Alaska Highway (which stretches from Delta Junction in Alaska, down to Dawson Creek, British Columbia in Canada) and the cut-off to the Glenn Highway (Anchorage to Tok Junction). It is comparatively well provided with stores, visitor centre, post office, eating places and campsites.

Road works on a bridge over a wide river mean that I have to wait for the queue of traffic to be escorted over the bridge by an official car before my own personal escort repeats the same procedure with me. I chat to the driver as I ride alongside him, mentioning the shortage of drinking water. He assures me that there will be clean water in a culvert about ten miles along, although I fail to find it.

The road stretches out into the distance, for most of the time devoid of traffic. This is interrupted momentarily by a couple of Harley bikers on their way back to Salt Lake City, one riding alongside for a while asking about my trip. He is friendly and rather good looking.

A dearth of habitation leads me to request water refills when I come to a solitary property. Leaving my bicycle at the gate, I walk tentatively up the drive, nervous from the warning of the presence of a security dog, all the time calling, 'Hello, anybody there?'

I hear a low growl, and instantly freeze when a huge dog advances towards me, changing his pitch to a loud barking. Oh help. Still no one appears and still the beast does his security dog act. In the end, I judiciously turn around in retreat, heading slowly back to the gate. The dog follows me barking loudly. I stop, turn around to him; he stops advancing and barking; I repeat my action; he repeats his. In the end I walk backwards, at which point he stays where he is. Reaching the safety of the gate and my escape route, I call out loudly, 'I only wanted some water!'

At this point, a man comes running down the drive, apologising profusely for his dog's behaviour, urging me back to the house for water. As he turns, I see a handgun tucked into the back of his trousers. In his cabin, are rifles galore (well, at least three) hanging on the wall by his chair. As he says, 'A great deal of wildlife uses my land as a crossing point. I have to be prepared.'

Rick is a widower, a retired state trooper who used to live down south but, after the death of his wife, decided to move with his four young children up here to Alaska, building the small log cabin in which he brought up the children on his own. There is no running water or electricity; cooking and lighting is provided by gas cylinders; water for cooking and washing from a well, drinking water bought in bulk in bottles. His children are grown up and living away, but have recently built the new log house at the top of the drive. It seems weird that it is set up with mod cons (such as satellite internet) but has no running water. I sleep there on the settee in the living room; Rick prefers to live in the cosy original cabin. A visit to the outhouse is quite a joy, the door short in height, treats the occupant to an idyllic view whilst in quiet contemplation.

Recently, a daughter-in-law stayed in the new house. When awoken during the night by the dog barking, concerned for his safety she went outside, noticing something in the bushes. For some reason, she went towards that spot, only to be accosted by a bear suddenly emerging.

Now there are two things constantly emphasised that you must *not* do on encountering a bear, neither to shriek in a shrill voice nor to run. Instead, you should stand your ground, make yourself look as big as possible, talk in a calm, lowish voice so that the bear in question can identify you as a harmless human and not worth any hassle.

The daughter-in-law, not being calm and self-controlled at that precise moment, opts for the intuitive reactions. She screams in a high-pitch fashion and she runs. As she is running back towards the house, the bear runs alongside but makes no attempt to attack her. Rick explains this as the bear not being hungry, merely curious. The mental picture of the bear and the woman running along together, with the bear looking sideways at the woman, thinking, 'What a noisy, funny little thing you are,' is strangely amusing. So glad it wasn't me in her shoes.

Alaskans believe in co-existing with the local wildlife, rather than eradicating the dangerous ones. It is illegal to kill animals, except in obvious self defence, the expectation is to protect themselves as much as possible by avoidance of risky encounters.

Bears are becoming increasingly used to humans, even venturing into towns. Many photos have been taken of them opening bins outside houses to forage for food, even, as happened in Tok, venturing inside houses. One woman returned home one day to find a grizzly rummaging around in her kitchen. I do my best to dispel the instant assumption that it is wearing a floral pinny and yellow washing-up gloves.

The following morning, Rick tells me of the pack of wolves that crossed his land last night at two in the morning. I set off after breakfast, full of his bear and wolves stories from the evening before, constantly interjected with, 'But you'll have a great adventure.'

Northway Junction is a one café, one grocer place, where I stop for a hot chocolate and top up supplies of food and water. Continuing to Deadman Lake campground, only one other pitch is currently taken: a couple from the Netherlands in a rented RV. I choose a secluded pitch with picnic table and bench, swim in the lake, taking care to avoid any deceased bodies, and wash clothes, hanging them to dry on my bungee washing line.

Another couple turns up, Kip and Marya, on their way home to Washington State after a year in Seward, where Marya has been teaching gifted children. Neither of them has a job to which to return, but they do not seem fazed by this. They live along the route I shall be taking and invite me to stay with them. This means I can have an oil change kit sent to their address from UK; and Kit will try and locate a cycle shop, so that Raven can undergo a service. Their camp kitchen is a well-organised affair, pans simmering away on the fire cooking tuna pasta, undaunted by the rain. I eat with them, sharing my remaining home-smoked salmon; and they give me a useful container filled with cocoa almonds.

The trees have no sturdy lateral branches over which to sling my rope and hoist my bag above the ground. Unusually, neither are there any bear bins. In response to my concern, I am blithely assured by a group of campsite-workers, 'Oh, just leave your panniers away from your tent. You shouldn't have any problems.'

'You have to be joking, surely?'

Apparently not. I sleep little in the night, starting at the slightest sound.

I leave before Kip and Marya the following morning, and a short while later they pass by, taking photos and video of me cycling along.

I exit America at the United States Border Inspection Station; they are not huge on friendliness. Twenty miles later, I arrive at Canadian Customs. On the contrary/au contraire, they are friendly, with an uncomplicated approach to life – except that everything is bilingual. But they try incredibly hard to be as helpful and clear as they can at all times, fabulously demonstrated by the series of signs I now pass over the next mile or so.

First up, a large white board, informing me of a 125-year anniversary in 1998 and announcing that I am in Yukon, pictorially indicating I am in Canada by the addition of a large cutout Mountie.

Further along, a sign with map outlines of Alaska and Yukon, a clock in each country, showing 12 and 1 respectively; below, the words, 'You are entering a different Time Zone.'

Continuing on, we have an aesthetic, no doubt eco-sustainable, wooden sign proclaiming 'YUKON', adjacent to a couple of colourful flags on 20-foot poles, red for Canada, blue for . . . Yukon?

Last but by no means least:

Entering CANADA.
Canadian Highway signs are now in Kilometres
Maximum 55 (one assumes, miles per hour) Maximum 90 km/h

Having firmly established where I am, and what time of day it is (I have lost an hour), I arrive at Beaver Creek. I try to stock up on fresh food, but there is no fruit and the bread has seen better days. I eat in Buckshot Betty's; check emails, responding to one from Elliott, who has now bought a vehicle and made the Arctic Ocean in time for his birthday. There is always a chance we might meet up again. I send an email to Joe, as I am considering returning to Prince Rupert with a view to taking the ferry to Vancouver Island. Then I receive one from cousin Jonathan, who lives on the overland route to Vancouver, which negates the ferry option. Having arrived in Alaska a couple of weeks later than

301

intended, I am concerned at being caught napping in the snow and so decide to slightly shorten my time here, my best alternative options now under consideration.

The campground people give me a free pitch, plus use of showers, internet and endless coffee. A cyclist, Thien from Toronto, is returning from Prudhoe Bay; he sleeps in a bivvy bag, extolling its virtues of simplicity and fun. I am not sure. He does not have much money left, surviving on a porridge of peanut butter, oats and raisins, mixed with hot water. We discuss my route options, he suggesting ferry from Haines to Prince Rupert, cycle to Prince George, thence to Vancouver. It seems an attractive possibility. I breakfast in Buckshot Betty's, meeting a cyclist, Scott, on his way to the chilly north; another nice nutter who revels in extreme challenges.

On a lonely stretch of road my complete lack of wildlife spottings is momentarily interrupted when a lone wolf ambles across the road ahead. As I pass, he watches me from the scrub. I am thrilled, wanting to stop and photograph him, but think that might not be too sensible; perhaps lone wolves are dangerous, miffed that they are no longer part of a group. I adore this isolated landscape of long, empty roads stretching out into the dim distance, a vast unpopulated wilderness housing a host of indigenous creatures. Unfortunately though the air is currently thickened with smoke from multiple forest fires, spontaneously igniting from a thunderstorm a couple of days ago.

My mood is positive, happy with life generally. I feel emotionally buoyant, not worrying so much about things over which I have no control, letting go of thoughts of the future, living more in the moment. It is a good feeling.

After a particularly long empty stretch, I arrive at a cluttered, quirky place, The Old Buzzard: café, grocery, bric-a-brac, fuel, camping stop all rolled into one. A couple no longer in their first flush of youth run the place in a charming way, at the moment visited by an old friend from the lower states. He is more than eager to show off to me his right to bear arms, suddenly pointing his leg, impressively high, in the air and rolling up his trouser leg to display a neat little pistol in its leg holster. And, as he proudly tells me, 'Believe me, I won't be afraid to use it.'

At Lake Creek campground, Gako, a Japanese cyclist, is on the top-to-toe trip, from the Arctic Circle to the tip of South America, anticipating it will take about two years.

I feel chilled during the night, cold and moisture seeping up through the groundsheet. In the morning, ice glistens on the panniers. I have set a destination today for Destruction Bay, seventy miles away, but I am finding the going rough, gravelly, tedious.

'If someone comes along and offers me a lift, I could well be tempted to accept.'

At the next layby (pullouts in America), a man asks me about my cycling, hands me some fudge, tells me he and his wife are from San Diego, then, 'Would you like some lunch?'

We sit in their cosy RV to eat and they are happy to replenish my water bottles. As I am about to take my farewells, they hesitate.

'We appreciate you are on a cycling trip, but would you like a lift?'

Three hours later we come to Haines Junction; on my own I would have arrived three days later. Ron and Mary-Kay are kindness personified and Christians, always saying a prayer immediately before driving off at the start of the day.

For all its ease and comfort, being cocooned in the controlled atmosphere of a vehicle rightly emphasises, to me at any rate, the pleasure of cycling. As we drive and chat, oblivious to the beautiful scenery outside, I have feelings of frustration to think that I would have stopped there . . . and there . . . oh, must take a photo there. But, of course, I do them an injustice; after all, I met them when they had taken time out to appreciate the view at the beauty spot.

At Haines Junction, we meet a cyclist with a puncture. He is thinking of busing up to Tok. We encourage him to do so, the road not really having improved for the remainder of the way.

We continue to Kathleen Lake Lodge to camp. I pass another chilly night in the tent (the RV is not very big), wearing thermals, jumper and fleece, invited into the cosy RV the next morning for a hearty cooked breakfast. I buy a couple of jars of Fireweed Jelly for sale in the lodge, giving one to Mary-Kay.

We continue along the bumpy road, noticeable even in the vehicle. Smoke still pervades the air, veiling what must be spectacular scenery: lofty, majestic, snowy mountains, deep canyons with fast-flowing rivers, wide open plains alive with pink Fireweed (American pseudonym for Rosebay Willowherb). We arrive at the border post to re-enter Alaska. Here is my first encounter with a relaxed and amicable American immigration official. Welcome.

Shortly after the border, (where we gain an hour as the clocks go back again), we pull into a pullout for lunch, afterwards parting company; although only temporarily as we are likely to meet again on the ferry in a couple of days. The thirty-eight miles to Haines, now a good surface, is totally enjoyable. I meet an elderly couple in a multi-person vehicle, its back seats removed, curtains at the windows. They are having a whale of time, having dispensed with the obvious comfort of their RV in preference for this more basic setup. They send me off with an apple and good wishes. I fill my water bottle from a rockface waterfall, stop several times for the view, photos and delicious thimbleberries. Joe put me on to this scrumptious fruit, which I had never heard of before let alone seen, but recognising them instantly from his description and their name. They are growing in abundance by the roadside and I gorge juicily.

Haines is surrounded by mountains, situated on the Lynn Canal of the Inside Passage and a visiting port for cruise ships. Sitting on a sunny bench near the visitor centre chatting to some of the passengers currently in port, all of us indulging in an ice cream, I receive open invitations to Fort Worth in Texas and Pensacola in Florida. A couple of miles along the waterside is a campground for walkers and cyclists only. It is grassy, with picnic tables and firepits, even potable water; plus a tall frame, ropes suspended from the top bar, complete with carabinas for hanging bags. The view is gorgeous, but only if you like snow-topped mountains and mirror-calm lakes.

Three other tents turn out to contain a lone man, who seems to go off in the morning and return at night, a pair of cyclists, and a bilingual mum and two young children who live in Haines Junction. I go beachcombing with them at the head of the sound, excited to come across bear-prints in the sand. On our return, we stop off with a host of other people by the side of a wide river, watching as a grizzly bear ambles down to the swiftly-flowing water, fishing with its paws until it catches a salmon, then ambling back into the woods. It is a thrilling moment.

Emails from Joe includes an invitation to camp in his back yard.

'Better still, stay in my motorhome. It comes with shower, loo and wifi. And, when you arrive next, I'll take you for a Canadian special breakfast.'

A group of river raft guiders run past the campground, stop for a chat and invite me to their BBQ that evening. They are a sociable bunch and I enjoy the evening. They even offer to take me rafting if I was to stay longer.

When I find myself on the campsite with only the lone tenter, it is about time to find out if he really is as weird as my imagination has dubbed him. Invariably, as is the way, he is not; it turns out he has been on the campground for about a month, working in Haines in order to continue trekking around the Americas.

At the ferry terminal, I buy a ticket just for my bicycle and me, a cabin being far too expensive (no roomettes on this boat) and anyway, I have decided on The Solarium Experience: sleeping on a sunbed on the sundeck, a popular accommodation, even encouraged by the ferry authorities. Raven, as usual, is down below on the car deck. I take with me mattress, sleeping bag and small panniers containing the basics for the next couple of days, then bag my bed in the covered area of the deck, in the company of many other like-minded souls.

Ron and Mary-Kay are on board; also, the elderlies in the converted MPV; the whole atmosphere one of familiar camaraderie. Later, I chance upon Lyn, the woman with the little dog, Plato, only to be told that he had died suddenly four days ago. He had retched up blood in the morning, dead by the following day. Poor Plato; and poor woman, she is deeply distressed at the loss of such a wonderful companion.

My immediate neighbour on the sundeck is Karen, a 59-year old woman who works for the Canadian Development Agency. She has recently returned from a year in Afghanistan project-managering various civilian projects, including rebuilding fifty schools. She has worked abroad for much of her life: Ethiopia, Australia, Yougoslavia, Macedonia, Afghanistan.

The main stop on this ferry's itinerary is Ketchikan, six hours shore leave providing plenty of time for visiting Creek Street: rows of restored wooden buildings hanging over the water, supported on a network of stilts. We follow the sign, 'Where fish and fishermen go up the creek to spawn,' and watch the salmon repeatedly trying to jump up the waterfall, willing them with all our might for them to succeed, but so often knocked back into the frothing, swirling waters at the foot of the fall. They rarely notice the ladder at the side, placed there to make it so much easier for them, so why don't they use it? Can't they read the signs?

Sleeping on the sundeck is glorious; benefits over a cabin include a much nicer view, more room, greater sociability, fresh air. We are protected from the rain by an overhang that covers half of the deck; lights switch on in the evening, those at the rear staying on all night; ceiling heaters turn on at two in the morning. These actually become too hot, causing us to move further forward, but not too far to be out of cover against the rain beating down. It is a perfect way to travel the Inside Passage of the Alaska Marine Highway System.

*   *   *

Canada

8 August – 13 September 2009

*Prince Rupert, ferry to Queen Charlotte Island, Pure Lake,
Sidegate, Prince Rupert, Prince George, Hixon, Cinema,
Marguerite, Williams Lake, 100 Mile House, Bridge Lake,
Heffley Creek, Monte Lake, Okanagan Centre, Peachland,
beyond Oliver, Keremeos, Princeton, Manning Park,
Hope, Chemainus, Sidney, Victoria*

We dock in Prince Rupert at 5.15 am, back in Canada, losing an hour. On paper, this oscillating hour is easy to assimilate; in the field, on the other hand, over the past two weeks, the constant time zone shift has had me reeling, having no idea what time of day it is, nor even in what country I am. Hopefully, at last, there will be a respite.

Even at this unearthly hour, Joe is waiting in the terminal car park to greet me in person, before zooming back home, whilst I follow on at my more leisurely pace. Having then installed me in his mobile home, we drive to an out-of-town diner for the promised Canadian special breakfast, a huge fry up, maple syrup included somewhere. Replete, we head into the surrounding countryside of waterfalling creeks and nerve-wracking forest trails. Regaled with stories of Joe's encounters with bears, I follow his example, stalwartly arming myself with a couple of stones in each hand against bear attacks. Ha ha.

In the evening, I cook us a meal in the RV, after which Joe produces a joint, which I refuse, on the basis that it would be wasted on me as I am immune to its effect. He persuades me to give it a go, and I subsequently become euphorically stoned and high as a kite. I feel as though I have undergone some kind of rite of passage; maybe a delayed adolescence.

Queen Charlotte Island is a night-ferry away from Prince Rupert, a mattress on the lounge floor affair, arriving by six in the morning at the southern end of the island. It is not hugely big, camping on the north beach this night a doable option.

As my wheels roll along the forested road, I take time out to enjoy the tantalising side glimpses of the sea through the trees on my right-hand side. At Port Clement, the heavenly smell of an in-house bakery lures me inside to buy lunch and to sit overlooking the bay to eat it.

The road now becomes tedious and unattractive and I decide to dispense with the remaining twelve miles to North Beach, veering off instead along a forest trail down to a secluded picnic site on the shores of Pure Lake. I make sure to ring my bell and sing all the way, in friendly warning to any lurking bears. There are one or two other visitors about and I wait until they have left before risk putting up the tent, unsure how much the 'No camping' notice should be obeyed.

I have a wonderful night: no animal noises, no ringing of the warning bell attached to my 'smelly' bag twenty yards away from me, no people down for a moonlight stroll. The place is all mine. In the morning, I strip off and swim in the clean, clear water in this rural idyll, the unadulterated freedom intoxicating.

I meet other touring cyclists, unusually, all women: Tamara is on a touring taster trip and seems to have caught the bug; Melanie and Jan are combining their island cycling trip with attending the Edge of the World Music Festival.

The weather has been kind of late, but today I am forced to take cover in bus shelters when Heaven turns on the garden hose. I arrive too late to catch the Haida museum before it closes for the day, so am in plenty of time to board the overnight return ferry to the mainland and Joe's RV. Bless him, he has switched on the heater to warm it up for me.

He and his son and a friend are driving to Prince George the following day and Joe offers me a lift. His main reason is to stop me cycling an infamous stretch of road dubbed, 'The Highway of Tears,' along which about forty women have disappeared or been murdered over the previous forty years. No one has ever been brought to account and, although they are mostly native American women, local people are generally concerned for the safety of all women.

Before we set off, Joe presents me with a leaving gift, previously given to him by a local Haida Indian: a piece of silver jewellery, a unique first pressing from the original mould of a traditional Haida design central to their culture, coincidentally a raven. I feel honoured to receive it.

Driving out of Prince Rupert along the picturesque Skeena river, I partly regret not cycling, compensation coming in the stops we make en route. The first, a bare rock face on which, faintly painted in red, is the face of a Skeena chief, a warning that this is his tribe's land. Next is a salmon-jumping spot, the local Indians standing at strategic places on the slippery rocks by the water's side, large, long-handled nets in hand, selectively choosing their haul. They meticulously release any females (to continue up the river to spawn) and undersized males. The salmon are sold to passing tourists, who may well later be stopped by the police and have their fish confiscated because they should not have bought from the Indians. The Indians themselves are not supposed to be selling the salmon they catch; they are only allowed to use them for their own consumption (as for all Alaskans).

A collection of original wooden totem poles are on our impromptu itinerary. Some of them indicate alliances between clans and tribes, the representative animal or bird carvings placed in order of superiority of the alliance: eagle and bear, beaver and bear, frog and eagle. Other totems are burial poles, depicting a lineal history of the deceased in the vertical epitaph.

When we reach the main part of the infamous stretch, I have no qualms at having accepted the lift. The road now stretching before us is long, lonely, darkly flanked by dense pine forests, scant phone signal, no store stops. Shivers run down my spine as I imagine cycling along, constantly aware of the road's deadly reputation, nerves jumping and heart pounding at the sight of approaching vehicles, or the sound of cracking branches in the menacing undergrowth on either side. At the same time, logic tells me that, subconsciously, this heightened trepidation is in part due to my knowledge aforehand, as well as to the prominent warning signs at intervals along the road:

CAUTION.
Girls don't hitchhike on
THE HIGHWAY OF TEARS.
Killer on the Loose

Pictures and names of three of the victims look out from the poster.

A second sign:

Hitchhiking
Is it worth the risk?

incorporates a picture of a young woman hitchhiking, ethereal spirits of death floating around her, car lights approaching. An extra comment below:

Ain't worth the risk, sister

We drive this stretch in one day. On my bicycle, it would have taken me ten days.

I say goodbye to Joe and the boys in Prince George, cycling out along Highway 97 in the company of logging trucks speeding south; time is money. Even so, they are thoughtful enough to sweep as wide a berth as they can, which is more than can be said for many of the, generally elderly, RV drivers. Maybe they are so busy concentrating on driving these whales that they are oblivious to sprats like me. It is nerve-wracking to be passed at close quarters, feel the sucking whoosh of their draft threatening to topple me.

Normally when I mention I am cycling round the world, I receive a fairly positive reaction from people, so I am rather taken aback with the owner's dismissive comment at tonight's campsite.

'Oh that's nothing. I had a couple here recently who have already been round the world and are now cycling the length of the Americas.'

I reply that this is the first time anyone has referred to my trip as 'nothing', which of course is not how he had meant it to sound, offering me free wifi and a beer in appeasement.

It seems hit and miss whether I am able to connect to the internet: at this campsite I cannot, a mile down the road at another campsite, I can.

I am following the Fraser river and at Quesnel, have the choice of swapping to the other side for a change. Assured by the tourist centre staff that the road in question is fully paved with flat terrain, I cross over the river on the wood-planked pedestrian bridge. And it is as promised – at least for the first twenty miles. But now a long steep gravel hill, up which I heave and push, skidding and slipping on the loose stones beneath my sturdy sandals, gaining just a few feet at a time in a feeble bid for the summit. It takes for ever. Finally, at the top, shattered, I stagger shakily into the shade, well away from the sadistic sun, content to collapse on the parched grass for a couple of hours afternoon siesta.

On the move again, I am on the lookout for possible places to camp. But numerous signs are acting as a deterrent.

'Private.'

'Keep Out.'

'No Trespassing.'

This surprises me, as I thought this part of my trip would produce the easiest opportunities for wild camping. I am nervous of taking the risk of ignoring them because of the aggressive attitudes I have encountered in respect of people's right to protect their lands, many carrying guns, proudly proclaiming that they will have no hesitation in discharging them on any wilful perpetrator.

A solitary woman walking along the deserted road is the first person I have seen in a few miles. I ask her where I might camp; she of course invites me to stay in her home, at the end of a rough and bumpy track. She has home-schooled her three children, seemingly a widespread choice in these parts; I have already met one or two others who have done the same. Sometimes it is due to remote locations or a mobile lifestyle, most frequently to give a better quality of education to children, considered by some to be lacking in the local schools.

Another common activity in Alaska and Canada, is that of providing for oneself as much as possible. Many people grow, catch, hunt their own food. This family is no exception. One of the children will be married the following year, the food for the two hundred and twenty guests being produced entirely from their land: fruit, vegetables, beef. With the exception that they will buy in the pig.

On to Williams Lake, but no campsite. I eat in a curry buffet restaurant, afterwards allowed to pitch my tent on the titsy patch of grass behind, but only after the last customer has gone. The following morning on the outskirts of town is a colourful board, incorporating a picture of a man in a wheelchair, declaring, 'Williams Lake, Home of Rick Hansen, Man in Motion World Tour 1985-1987.'

At age fifteen, Rick Hansen suffered spinal chord injuries in an accident, leading to paraplegia. He became an athlete in the Paralympic games, winning gold medals. Inspired by Terry Fox, who had lost a leg to cancer and set out to run across Canada to raise awareness for cancer research, Rick Hansen embarked on his own venture, the mammoth *Man in Motion World Tour*. He wheeled himself around the world, a 26-month endurance of 25,000 miles and 34 countries, raising $26 million for spinal chord research and Quality of Life initiatives. What can I say? The world is made up of extraordinary people.

Through Lac La Hache, the Longest Town in the Cariboo according to the sign, and on to 100-Mile House, so called from the original roadhouse that accommodated prospectors on their way north to the gold rush towns of Alexandria and Barkerville. From Lilloet in the south, the starting point of the Old Cariboo Road, there sprang up roadhouses every ten or fifteen miles along its length, helpfully named according to the mile-mark from Lilloet. Some of these stops, 100-Mile House, 70-Mile House, 108-Mile House, expanded into sizable settlements.

The sky has a most peculiar hue: a vast expanse of murky purple and a low horizon of pinky-orange with a glaring white light. Forest fires are burning almost out of control forty miles away. Even at this distance the air hangs heavy with the smell of smoke. Weather and fire reports are referred to constantly by the local inhabitants, rightly anxious that they might be in the path of peril.

The 100-Mile House campground is run by a genial host, Vern, who lives on site in a tent from May to October. He took on the role the previous year in order to provide a safe and pleasant haven for campers, as opposed to the unruly, aggressive people who had been frequenting it before the advent of a live-in host. Vern sits in front of his tent, sewing moccasins from an assortment of furs. People regularly come by to see him, often to talk – he is a good listener. His philosophy is to do what you enjoy doing and then everything else turns out well. For instance, he made a pair of moccasins for each of his children one Christmas, in response to complying with his own instruction to them to give him a present that cost no more than $10. His daughter wore her moccasins to school and friends loved them, subsequently placing orders for their own. Visitors to the campground do likewise: order and pay, then patiently wait for the indeterminate date when they will receive the footwear in the post, for, as Vern stipulates, 'This is a hobby, not a business.'

I stay three nights at this convivial woodland campsite, even braving dips in the invigorating pool below the nearby waterfall, finally tearing myself away to get back on the road. I now leave the 97, to cut across towards Kamloops. At Bridge Lake campground, I receive a visitor at my breakfast picnic table: a coyote strides confidently towards me requesting breakfast. I decline, but he persists, sidling up to the table when he thinks I am not looking, swiftly ducking away when I shoo him, eventually moving on, thinking, 'Huh, what's with her? Most people give me something.'

I arrive at the top of the steep hill, of which everyone has been forewarning me. It is a downhill of eight percent, which does not sound too steep, but actually requires excessively hard work in the braking department, nearly but not quite all the way down. Since coming off my bicycle on the way to the Dead Sea, I approach such descents with trepidation, whereas previously I would fly down them nonchalantly. Here, however, some of that adrenalin-pushing fearlessness returns and I shoot down, heart attempting to escape through my mouth. I glance excitedly at the speedometer, grinning broadly, with mouth firmly closed (to save my teeth, if I come a cropper?!) – and hit 41 mph. This could possibly be the top speed for the trip. Checking in my little black book at the end of the day, I see it is a reasonable second to the day I arrived in Petra, at 42.9 mph.

From Kamloops, having stayed with a couple whom I had met at the previous evening's campground, I brave the TransCanada Highway for fifteen miles, more than happy to turn off onto the much calmer road to Monte Lake. As there is no campground in the immediate vicinity and the layby already has three campers, I venture up a lane around the lake, stealing surreptitiously through a gate onto private property and speeding for the cover of trees by the lakeside before anybody spots me. To be honest, I have only been confident enough to do this because a woman in the local shop had mentioned it. Shortly after, Lee, a guy on a motorbike I had met in the lane, also comes to camp. I have a refreshing swim in the lake, whilst Lee filters lake water for a brew of fresh coffee to share.

The next morning, somewhere near Falkland, a man in a car pulls alongside, inviting me for lunch in a diner up the road. His ulterior motive is to ply me for advice to pass on to his 18-year old son, who plans to cycle the Oregon coast.

Towards Okanagan, I develop a wobble in my back wheel and stop to check it. A passing cyclist asks if I am OK and then suggests an alternative route to take me away from this busy road, incidentally directly passing his house.

'I am happy to give you a lift to your cousin in Okanagan.'

I thank him and he goes off; the wobble turns out to be a slow puncture. Marvelling at the timing of my encounter, I make my way to the cyclist's house a couple of miles away, from where, true to his word, he brings me to my cousin, June's, house some fifteen miles away.

My cousin and I last met when I was four – ah yes, I remember it well. She has a brother in Hope and their mother lives on Vancouver Island, all conveniently placed for me to visit. I spend a fabulous five days with June and family, luxuriating in their lake view, nipping across the road to the water's edge to go canoeing and swimming, or zoom through the water in the speedboat, the daughter skillfully wakeboarding behind. A visit to June's hairdresser is on the house and one of the best cuts I have ever had. And for one of the nights I am here we haul mattresses outside on the balcony and sleep under the stars.

I mend the slow puncture, cracking a rib in the process. Whilst pumping up the tyre with a stirrup pump, the nozzle insists on slipping off the valve and so I hold it on with one hand. Not enough strength to pump one-handedly, I add more force by pressing down with my chest – only to feel something crack. I do not think too much of it at the time but, over the ensuing days, breathing is painful.

Buoyed by my family reunion, I resume cycling through the fertile, fruity sunshine valley of Okanagan, irresistibly taking a break in a place called Peachland. A chat with a woman in the visitor centre is followed by an invitation to stay the night. I even get to see the inside of a yurt, when we visit her son and family, who live in a large self-built, one-roomed affair, divided by screens into the different living areas.

Onwards through Oliver, Wine Capital of Canada, to follow a track beside a river, eventually to make camp. I adhere to the signs indicating no tents by merely hanging my mosquito net from a tree and over my mattress. The mozzies are out in droves and drive me prematurely into my net, not without a substantial number following me, so that I spend the night swatting and swiping them. During the night I consider the possibility of bears in the area, especially when I hear a loud splash nearby in the river, but in the end I do not move my food panniers away from me as they are shaping my net as a tent. But as a result, I hardly sleep.

Next day I cycle through desert, arid hills and endless road, the US border a few miles away on the left. Smitty's diner stands at the foot of Richter Pass, where I duly stop for eggs benedict on an English muffin. The local paper reports a recent Iron Man competition held in Penticton, in which a 79-year old nun became the oldest woman to complete the competition, in a time of seventeen hours. Wow. The separate components of this competition are daunting in their own right: a swim of 2.4 miles, cycle ride of 112 miles, marathon of 26.2 miles. Back-to-back is just insane.

In Keremeos, severe weather warnings cause me to scuttle for shelter to Eagle RV Park. In the grounds stands a large picnic marquee with a boarded wooden floor, specifically for tenters in the event of inclement weather. This is a thoughtful facility I have not yet come across and the timing is perfect; the storm that follows is almost terrifying.

There is not that much rain, or thunder and lightning; the worst thing is the wind, sounding and feeling like it is going to rip up everything in its path. If I had been in my tent, I would have been halfway home by now, but not in the fashion I would have chosen. If I had been in my tent, my bicycle would have been parked outside, except that it would not have been there now. If I had been in my tent – I would have wished I hadn't been.

The owner's generous attitude extends to charging me nothing for my stay; just as in Hedley Tea Rooms the next day, when my lunch bill is waived by the owner, a German Canadian, who has cycled trans-North America from Hedley to Halifax. On retirement next year, he plans to cycle up to Prudhoe Bay.

The private campground in Princeton turns out to be much cheaper than the municipal site and an attractive pitch near the noisy river, inviting me to take a dip in the shallow rapids. Afterwards I go to sit on a chair, squeaking in startled shock when, unfolding it, a slumbering snake slithers out. The next morning, the option of cycling in torrential rain, thunder and lightning loses out to the comfort of a local diner for a breakfast fry-up, in the company of two couples from the campsite. They are retired, currently mountain biking across Canada, each day setting up a relay system with their vehicles in order to cycle the sections in between.

Newfoundland jokes are included on the menu, in line with the theme of the diner décor. Did you know that Newfoundland binoculars consist of two beer bottles? Or that a square rolling pin is used for making four square meals a day? They have a definite ring to their Irish and Norwegian counterparts.

The rain eases, thankfully preventing me from lazily taking up cousin Jonathan's thoughtful offer to drive out and pick me up. I end the day in

Coldspring Provincial Park, a beautiful woodland setting with softly flowing river; but an uncomfortable hard, gravel tent pitch, emphasising the discomfort of my increasingly painful rib. The night is sleep-deprivingly cold, despite donning my thermals, not helped by tent and sleeping bag still being damp from the previous night's downpour. In the morning, although it is a sunny sky, I pile on five top layers in an effort to warm up. The cold is understandable, Sunday and Allison passes both summit at 4,400 feet. From the second pass the road plummets down for thirty-five miles to a mere 157 feet above sea level, where here is Hope.

I take the first of four exits from the freeway towards the centre. On the edge of town the driver of a car in front waves to me in his rear-view mirror; I wave in return. He continues to wave, so then I feel silly, he is obviously waving to someone else, someone he knows. He turns off into a car park and I pass by. But then the driver jumps out calling my name, jumping up and down, waving frantically. It is Elliot! We greet each other with ecstatic hugs, then catch up with each other over lunch. He proudly introduces his mini camper to me, converted from an MPV, complete with dinky curtains.

He then goes off to Vancouver, I go to meet my cousin and his wife for another lovely family reunion.

Hope holds an annual chainsaw wood-carving competition, past entries displayed at various points around town. Unfortunately, I shall miss this year's competition by a week. I should love to have watched the carvers in action, just to see how it is possible to sculpt so delicately using such hunking great machines.

When it comes to leave, the rain this time beats me and I accept a lift to Vancouver from Jonathan and Carolyn. We arrive in time for the mid afternoon ferry to Vancouver Island. After grateful thanks and promises to keep in touch, I board the vessel for the 2-hour sailing.

The island welcomes the ferry with low cloud and dull sky. I manage twenty-six miles as far as Chemainus, head for a church, which is closed, but ask at the house next door if I can set up my tent in the grounds behind. The woman is renting from the church, but readily agrees.

Snug inside my tent and settling into sleep mode by 11.30 pm, I am rudely disturbed by a torch glaring at my front door, a dog barking and a man's aggrieved voice.

'Hello, do you know someone in the house here? What's their name?

Do you have permission to be here? You are in my back yard. How long are you intending to stay?'

His wife had been startled to see my tent when she looked out of a window on her way to bed.

'Yes, I have permission, from the woman in the house opposite. It didn't look as though I was in your back yard; I'm on the other side of your fence. Are you expecting me to pack and find somewhere else tonight?'

'Well, no I suppose it will be alright. But you must leave in the morning.'

'Oh, alright then, if you insist,' I murmur to myself.

Chemainus is well-known for its many lively colourful murals on the buildings around town depicting its history. They were created in 1981 as part of a programme to revitalise the community and have since become a healthy tourist attraction, famous worldwide as, 'The Little Town That Did.' From here I make my way to Mill Bay, catching the ferry for the 25-minute trip to Brentwood, then over the hill and down to the far side of the island, arriving to enveloping hugs from cousin Ruth and her delightful home on the seashore.

From here I spend a day in Vancouver, taking the ferry from Sidney. My older brother had spent a summer here thirty years previously teaching sailing. On return to UK, he eulogised over the wonders of the place in a vain attempt to persuade my family to emigrate, so that he would be able to visit. (Wouldn't it have been easier for him just to have emigrated himself?!) He talked about snow skiing in the morning, waterskiing in the afternoon and sailing amongst the archipelago of islands. Seeing it now for myself causes me to agree with his efforts. The vivid blue water, seaplanes skimming the surface and parking at the pontoon taxi ranks, sailing boats idling at their moorings, a pleasure paddle-steamer passing by; all to a background of forests and mountains.

In Sidney, my squashed handpump, distorted in India (so long ago) when caught between the chainwheel and the frame, is replaced with a super-efficient mini pump, which includes a valve adaptor for US car pumps. I take my party shoes for re-re-heeling and repatch the patches on my extremely-patched trousers, losing any hope that I can keep them alive until I return home.

Ruth and I visit the fabulous Buchart Gardens, spend a day in Victoria and get together with friends, social invitations to Ruth also extending to me. I try, although not too hard, to keep my head from swelling uncontrollably with the acclamation and complimentary comments from one person after another, be they the guys in the cycle shop, Ruth's friends or people at church. Time to hit the road again.

The cycle route to Victoria saunters through forest trails and along pleasant lanes, past fields strewn with low-lying orange pumpkins; mid-Autumn leaves begin to scatter the ground. I stay the night in Victoria with an octogenarian cyclist, friend of the British cyclist from New Zealand whom I met at the ferry terminal in Tomakomai, Japan. The next morning he waves me off at the ferry.

Goodbye Canada. I shall miss you.

*   *   *

USA: West

14 September – 3 November 2009

Washington	*Sequim Bay, Port Ludlow, Shelton, Lake Sylvia State Park, Bay Centre*
Oregon	*Fort Stephens, Cannon Beach, Nehalem Bay, Cape Lookout, Lincoln City, South Beach, Florence, Lakeside, Sunset Bay, Humbug Mountain, Brookings.*
California	*Redwood, Patrick's Point, Ferndale, Richardson Grove, Westport, Manchester, Ocean Cove, Tomales, Fort Barry, Benecia, Santa Clara, Big Sur, San Simeon, Arroyo Grande, El Kapitain, McGrath, Santa Monica, Los Angeles, Santa Monica, San Divias, Crestline, Victorville, Yermo, Baker.*

Boarding the ferry in Victoria is not without its challenges. US Customs frustratingly fob me off for the third time about my white card extension, telling me they cannot issue them or even confirm I shall be able to obtain one and that I need to go to a CIS office (whatever that is) once I am actually in the States.

Once on board, I forget the truculent officiousness, simply enjoy the 90-minute crossing to Port Angeles, Washington State, USA. The sea is at first calm, becomes turbulent, a sudden drop in temperature prompting a swift change from shorts to trousers. Another tourer on board, a similar age to me, is at the start of cycling the west coast for a few weeks, the longest trip he will have done. He goes off as soon as we land, whereas I am off to see a man in Customs, this time a very amenable supervisor who could not be more helpful and affable, even allowing me to determine the duration of the extension period, and waiving the extra fee. And welcomes me to the United States. What a lovely man.

Initially I follow a dedicated cycle route by the sea, through forests, along elevated boardwalks, eventually continuing along quiet lanes. I meet a middle-aged couple touring on 3-wheeled recumbents, their daughter on a bicycle. They are circumnavigating the Olympic Peninsula along cycle routes and quiet roads. I have never seen the attraction of recumbents, mainly because eye-level view is knee-high to a grasshopper but, for those with dicky backs, it is a godsend, I am informed. I am invited to have a quick go. Still not convinced. The couple issue me with a firm invitation to a night's accommodation in their home, somewhere between San Francisco and Los Angeles.

I now discover hiker-biker camping. State campsites in America generally provide a specific area solely for people cycling or walking. Essentially, they are a great deal cheaper than the main campground, usually set away from the amenities. Sequim Bay campground gives me my first delightful experience of this. It includes meeting a different kind of traveller to those in the home-from-home RVs.

My evening companions include the west coast cyclist I met on the ferry, a young Aussie woman cycling for an indeterminate time, as well as a family of five who impress the living daylights out of me. They come cycling up the hill in the late evening: the French father pulling a trailer, the American mother also towing a trailer, their 6-year old daughter on her own bicycle. In one of the trailers is a few-months old baby; in the second, a 3-year old severely-handicapped son, as floppy as a new-born. They have been living on a boat in the Caribbean until recently when, deciding they have now outgrown it with their expanded family, are cycling for a few months until they decide what to do next. The daughter is being home-schooled as they travel. I might well be impressed with them, but there is one thing I have that the French guy admires – my bicycle stand. He has gone through four of them – in a week.

I have heard that Port Townsend is worth visiting and duly head there the following day. On the way, a stream of vintage cars toot past me, several occupants in period costume, presumably heading to a rally, possibly in connection with 'The finest example of a Victorian seaport in the United States.'

Just south is Port Hadlock where I meet up with Meredith, a friend of one of the Americans I met twelve months ago in the Christian guesthouse in Cairo. She and her husband designed and built their beautiful log house in the middle of a forest, living in a mobile home during the three years of its construction.

The next day's destination is a real bonus, staying with Kip and Marya, whom I met at Deadman Lake in Alaska. My oil change kit is waiting for me, as well as a package from cycling Rachel from work, enclosing her original copies of the west coast route from the supported ride she did last year. Kip has watched the demo video for the oil change and now reads out the instructions, whilst I perform the operation. What a team and what a painless exercise. We visit Seattle, including a visit to a large outdoor store where I am able to replace my cycling trousers, albeit reluctantly; but it has to be done, the seat of my trousers so tissue thin I could suddenly embarrass myself any time now.

Pike Street is on the itinerary, Pike's Place Fish Market drawing in the punters with demonstrations of their fish-throwing skills.

After my 6-day sojourn in Shelton, I continue south, meeting again the recumbents, just finishing their Olympic tour, who eagerly confirm their invitation to me. A plethora of cyclists now keep popping up on their way down the west coast: Wes, a newly-graduated student, Mark, a rumbustious Scot recruiting TEFL teachers for China, Paul from Pennsylvania.

Astoria, Oregon, is the start of the Pacific Coast cycle route, mostly running along Route 101, ending in San Diego, California; next stop Mexico.

I decide to forego a dirty, expensive hotel in the town itself, continuing a further twelve miles to the State Park campground. On the way, I happen to go into a cycle shop, the owners remembering Tom, the Hungry Cyclist, whom I met in Jerusalem, when he stopped here four years previously.

Fort Stephens State Park is undoubtedly to be recommended as an excellent start (or finish) to the west coast trail. I arrive at a large, well-run park; charmingly welcomed in the smart reception centre. But, as the receptionist goes through the list of all the amenities in the park, my heart sinks, wondering what the asking price is going to be for so much luxury, especially when the previous State Camp with only a pit toilet was $10 (I had stayed in a private one nearby with shower and shop for $14). Eventually she comes to the end of the list.

'That will be $4, please.'

'Pardon?'

'Four dollars, please. You're in the hiker-biker area,' says she, grinning broadly. And the topmost excellent thing about this wonderful State Park is that the shower block has *under-floor heating*. Maybe I could sleep in here.

During the night I have first a squirrel attempting to pick his way into one of my panniers, then a raccoon, who succeeds, until I shoo it off, whisking the pannier into my tent. Later, I make a trip to the loo, surprising four raccoons, who self-consciously troop out from the toilet block in single file.

The west coast of America is understandably popular, the scenery is breathtakingly stunning. At almost each turn of the road, I stop and gasp at the view thinking, 'It can't get better than this.' And I think, how can there *not* be a Creator?

I stay in Cannon Beach for a couple of nights in the home of the parents of a student of one of the guesthouse visitors in Cairo (hospitality connections can be quite convoluted). Even though the owners go away on my second night on a church weekend, they gaily entrust their place to me, a stranger. I leave them a bottle of red wine, carefully chosen, not for its bouquet or body, merely for its label, Red Bicyclette.

Route 101 is surprisingly horrible. The hard shoulder is one of the worst I have encountered: very narrow, broken surface, scattered with detritus from shredded tyres and slippery gravel, overgrown with vicious briars. I am amazed there has been no investment in improving the condition of this most famous of cycle routes, if only for the obvious increased level of safety for cyclists and motorists alike. When the hard shoulder is particularly impassable, the cyclist is forced into the main lane, thus encouraging a higher risk of encounters with motorists, not the most cycle-friendly people in this part of the world. Personally, I think road engineers should be obliged to cycle their roads of responsibility. They could then assess and improve the cyclists' needs, by default this would best serve the motorist and lower traffic incident statistics.

Meanwhile, I endure a puncture from a metal staple.

One of the many cyclists I meet is Patrick from French Quebec. He is cycling down the west coast this year, having gone up the east side the previous. He cycles alone, his girlfriend not much of a cyclist. But in five years' time they plan to travel together for a year, made possible by a work scheme his girlfriend has joined whereby she works four years at eighty percent salary, living the fifth year on the accumulated eighty percent. What an attractive scheme.

Cycling Rachel's unstinting recommendation, to stop to sample the glories of the Tillamook Cheese Factory, may be slightly surprising. Except that it is not cheese that is on offer, but ice cream. And little wonder the queue is endless and slow, not only is there a vast array of ice creams to choose from, but also wafers, toppings and quantities. At last, much umming and aahing results in a final choice of an obscenely-sized 3-scoop mountain: chocolate peanut butter (yuk), mountain huckleberry (acceptable), vanilla bean (mmm) piled high in a wafer bowl.

On then to Cape Lookout hiker-biker, and access to the beach for the Pacific, USA wheel-dip photo. As I leave in the morning, someone has thoughtfully left a book on my picnic table. It looks a potentially interesting read, *Odysseus' Last Stand*, recounting a cyclist's seven-year tour.

Of other cyclists I meet, one in particular is pretty impressive: Vicky from England. Whilst working in North America, seemingly on a whim she thought she would like to cycle the west coast. So, off she trots to Walmart supermarket; five hundred dollars later coming away with bicycle, panniers, tent and sleeping bag. West coast, here I come. That, coupled with the fact that she is not particularly, well, svelt, has never done any cycling before and who maintains a smile on her face in the drenchiest of rain and the gruellingest of hills, are the reasons why I award her the most-unlikely-to-but-impressive-she-did accolade.

Vicky and I stop in Newport at Bike, a one-stop cycle shop equipped for all your touring needs. If you go upstairs, you will also find showers, laundry and comfy settee. Our cycling day is rounded off by a tour of Rogue's Beer brewery, followed by a tasting session of the local tipple, comprising small-ish samples of four beers, a complimentary one thrown in for good measure.

Scottish Mark is at the campsite tonight, along with Irish girlfriend; both sleep in hammocks under tarpaulins. They are adamantly enthusiastic about their accommodation and it certainly does seem to be a compact and effective night shelter – as long as there are trees around.

My stay on the five-acre homestead in Alaska now reaps dividends, not only by being able to stay in Florence with Doug's sister and husband, but also because there is something of a mass reunion, my stay coinciding with Doug and his family visiting as well as his wife's parents. During my short stay an interview is arranged with the local rag, the *Siuslaw News*. I also find replacement shorts for my threadbare ones in a local charity shop, coincidentally St Vincent de Paul, a reminder of the Santiago pilgrimage. We take afternoon tea in Lovejoy's, an English-run, English tea room.

The sunsets each night are mesmerising. Standing barefoot on a sandy beach to the sound of the shallow surf and the sight of the setting sun glowing in glorious technicolour, sets my heart and spine tingling with emotion.

Vicky and I arrive in Brookings, the end of Oregon, the state with the most beautiful and memorable coastline I have ever seen.

Seven miles on, California produces a wavey welcome and cheery smile from the border control. Warnings of confiscation of forbidden fruit come to nothing. Californians are careful about bugs entering their state, serious danger of disease possibly resulting in fiscal failure of their famed Napa valley products.

We break from our usual canvas cover and stay in Redwood Hostel, a stone's throw from the sandy beach and sea. I sit my camera on the sea wall and set up the timer, then charge down to the water's edge in the nick of time to prance a pose. After performing these peculiar antics half a dozen times in attempts to frame the perfect frolicking photo, a carload of observers can stand it no longer, one of them leaping out insisting that he would love to alleviate my and their pain by helping me out. As for the hostel, the luxury of a bed goes down a treat.

Next day sees us upping a few hills, the brow of one inviting an ever expanding group of motley cyclists to stop, each newcomer hailed by outstretched hands proffering a beer. A photo call is organised in recognition that all six of us are wearing normal, blend-into-the-background clothes for touring, not a set of luminous, padded lycra in sight. This also applies to Star, who travels sedately on a trailer standing on all fours and surrounded by her master's baggage, but condescends to alight at the start of each hill, dashing madly to the brow, whereupon she returns to her chariot throne.

The nights and first thing in the morning are becoming cold and foggy, insidiously chilling bones and emotions. I leave Patrick Point campsite before the others, paying on exit as there was no one around the previous evening. A couple of miles up the road, two of the three young guys from the same campsite scoot by on their bicycles with nary a wave. In a few minutes I see why: one has been stopped by a park ranger – for dashing away from the campground in an effort not to pay the measly five dollars. How stupid can you be?! I don't know what their penalty will be, but it would not surprise me if they would then be blacklisted from other state parks.

Some towns have fairgrounds that double as campgrounds when there is no fair in town. In Ferndale, the receptionist and her passing friend insist on paying the $10 for my pitch. Another cyclist arrives later in the evening, tall, gangly Romain from French Montreal, cycling for five months. We keep in company for the next couple of days, marveling at the magnificent thirty-two miles of grandiose Redwoods through the Avenue of Giants. I succumb to the impressive but naff tourist attraction of cycling through the archway of one poor giant, conferred with the dubious honour of being old enough to have grown to such a size as to be a drive-through money-spinner.

Some drivers are very unpleasant. One redneck in particular drives up close behind me, sitting on my tail, hooting his hostile horn as I struggle against a hefty headwind on a not-insubstantial hill. He then pulls out and overtakes so closely he barely misses me, cutting sharply in front so that I fall off my bicycle. Similar incidents continue but not as aggressive as this one.

The winds and the rains now make their presence undeniably felt. After a couple of drowned-rat days, Romain eventually continues on his own, I taking the soft option of keeping company with the wifi for the rest of the morning in a steamy coffee shop, in a pointless attempt to drip myself dry.

Contending each day with a constantly wet tent inside and out stretches my camping *joie de vivre*. Coupled with my stove not working, so not even comfort food available at the end of the day, I head for the doldrums. After one such day and night, and feeling decidedly weak at the knees, I pull in to the upmarket Timber Cove Inn. Undeterred by my unwashed, unkempt attire, I treat myself to a luxury breakfast: bacon and eggs, scone (American: biscuit) heaped with jam and cream, fruit, coffee, clifftop coastal view. Ah, so much better for tackling the up, down, round a hairpin inlet, up, down, round . . . of the coastal road.

From Sausalito, a long trawl up brings me to a large car park overlooking the bay below and the teensy island of Alcatraz. In the dim distance, numerous bridges span extensive expanses of water. Directly ahead looms the Golden Gate Bridge. I have cycled three quarters of the way round the world for this sight. It is a moment to be savoured – and shared. Pity there is no one to hand.

I cycle over the bridge slowly; no choice, packed as it is with pedestrians, bicycles and inexpertly ridden hired tandems. On the opposite side, I look back at the bridge; the red-runged vertical supports gleam in the sunshine, the only part of the bridge now visible above a bank of low-lying cloud.

I take a ferry to Valléjo to stay with Suzy and Mark, friends of freighter-companion Krista. I receive a warm welcome from them and generous hospitality during an enjoyable weekend, which includes a drive out to Napa valley for wine tasting at one of the numerous domains.

Returning to San Francisco, I cycle around the recognisable car-chasing hill roads before exiting along El Camino Real (The Royal Road). This route was established by Spanish missionaries, mostly during the seventeenth century, outposts set up at intervals of a day's ride on horseback (about thirty miles) to facilitate travel between missionary stations, along the length of what is now California.

In Santa Clara, I stay with Alaska Doug's other sister and husband, Diane and Mike. The following day Mike drives me to Big Sur, on the way passing through Monterey and pausing in Carmel for a quick peek at the Hog's Breath Inn owned by the mayor, a certain Clint Eastwood; before depositing me in a layby to continue cycling.

As evening approaches and no campsites appear, I find a discreet spot between the bank of earth acting as a road barrier and the wire fence of a forested property through which I can make out the house, hoping that their daily habit is not to walk the boundaries at night. At the same time, I am surprising myself at the certain amount of pleasure derived from wild camping in the most unlikeliest of places.

The recumbent Olympians, Joy and Gary, live in Arroyo Grande, my next night's destination. Prior to my arrival I had mentioned the need for a hair trim and leg waxing, an appointment efficiently organised by Joy. In the evening, invited friends appear after the main course, for the dual pleasure of apple cake dessert and to meet me, so I am told.

The following day, I accept a lift to Guadeloupe and the sand dunes where *The Ten Commandments* was filmed, in which the scenery is now buried. I half expect Charleton Heston to come striding over the dunes.

As I approach Los Angeles, I am warned increasingly of homeless people on campsites. At one particular site a thick fog floats silently, outlines of one or two distant mobile homes just visible a hundred yards away. The only other camper, ten yards closer than I should like, has an unnerving line in conversation.

'God has told me I am not from Earth but from Atlantis, a place with two suns, one moon, a sea and palm trees and many women; although I can choose only one for eternity. I have been sent here to Earth for a purpose: to expose the world domination of Jews in league with Satan, Bush and Obama.'

At this point, I decide I am out of my comfort zone and make a tactical retreat to my tent as soon as possible.

I reach Santa Monica, leaving the road to follow the ultra-wide concrete cycle path along quirky Venice Beach to Los Angeles, find the appointed hotel, where I leave my bicycle and catch the courtesy bus to the airport to meet GR from his flight. We have been in sporadic contact these last few months, he now coming to cycle with me for an unspecified length of time.

After the inevitable sightseeing trip to Hollywood, we set out from Los Angeles, more sprawling than one might think; it takes a day to cycle clear of its environs. Much of the area we pass through is Spanish-speaking, then Chinese.

From LA we continue to Victorville, stocking up with enough 'vittals' for a couple of days, as we do not know what the Mojave desert will offer in the way of provisions. Although advised by the locals not to cycle along the old Route 66 because it is busy, fast and no hard shoulder, we opt to do so anyway, if only for its sheer historic value. In going against their suggestion, we are smugly satisfied, although still slightly surprised at the inaccuracy of local knowledge, in that it is neither too busy, nor too fast and does have some hard shoulder.

We camp in a public park in the small outpost town of Baker, the park staff even switching off the automatic water sprinklers to save us from a soaking. From town it is a long, tedious trawl to the first of two summits, the second reaching to a lofty 4,500 feet before plunging down almost to sea level, as we leave California and enter Nevada.

*   *   *

USA: Central

4 November 2009 – 7 January 2010

Nevada	*Primm, Las Vegas, Bryce Canyon, Page, Keyanta, Grand Canyon, Las Vegas, Henderson*
Arizona	*Searchlight, Bullhead City, Golden Shores, Parker Dam, Bouse, Wenden, Wickenberg, Phoenix, Queen Valley, Globe, Bylas, Safford, Duncan*
New Mexico	*Lordsberg, Deming, Las Cruces*
Texas	*El Paso, Fort Hancock, Van Horn, Marfa, Alpine, Study Butte, Chisos Basin, Rio Grande Village, Marathon, Sanderson, Langtry, Del Rio, Uvalde, San Antonio, Austin, Carmine, Independence, Navasota, New Waverley, Rye, Silsbee, Kirbyville*

In the middle of the Mojave desert is a strange town, Primm, all casinos and billboards. The latter advertise outlet shops, amongst them The Gun Store, complete with a picture of an automatic machine gun loaded with a belt of bullets seductively draped over the barrel, inviting you to, 'Try One of the Real Full Autos.'

The request for directions to a campsite, park, police station, fire station, church, community services centre elicit negative replies.

'Oh no, none of those here.'

How weird. What town has nothing of such standard amenities? In the end, and by now it is dark, we can only find a quiet street to put the tent up on a patch of grass by the roadside opposite a hotel. Relaxing as much as we can in our conspicuous location, we sit outside the tent, eating the food bought at the filling station. A car drives slowly past, turns at the end of the road, drives slowly back, stops, positioning itself at an angle that directs its glaring full beam onto us. A security man emerges from the car.

'You can't camp here. This is private property.'

'No, it isn't.'

'Yes, it is. This is a private town.'

And so it turns out to be, complete with its own 'police' force to protect the local inhabitants, almost all of whom are employees of the three casinos in town. We explain why we resorted to pitching our tents here and will be glad if he will direct us to somewhere more suitable.

'How about the next town?' the security officer suggests.

When this does not go down particularly well with us, he says he must now call the vice-president of the town for further action. The solution is that we are given free board and lodging in the hotel opposite. Anything to keep us from littering the streets.

Next stop Las Vegas, staying at the far end of the Strip along Las Vegas Boulevard at the Sahara Hotel. We enter the reception and I like the place instantly; on the wall hangs a photo of Elvis.

Tinsel Town is just as the name implies, but an experience to be had, nonetheless. Every hotel has a casino and hundreds of slot machines, at which the same people sit throughout the day (and night?), plying them with tokens, occasionally receiving a payout. We play the roulette table, GR loses his $20 in ten minutes, I come away smugly excited, up $40. Granted, not exactly mega-bucks.

We hire a car for four days, cross briefly into Utah to be amazed by Bryce Canyon, pink sandstone rock pillars intricately carved over centuries into weird and wonderful shapes by the mighty Colorado River. A couple of cycle tourers turn up and, unable to contain my curiosity, I ask about their trip, the length of the Americas. I mention my trip. Instantly the man comes out with, 'Is your name Astrid?'

It transpires they are Philip and Manu, two cyclists who had stayed with Kip and Marya a couple of weeks before I arrived. How extraordinary.

Crossing into Arizona, we visit the wilderness of Navajo country and Lower Antelope Canyon. The entrance necessitates squeezing into an underground gully to access the canyon; then to marvel at the softly-striated, smooth spirals of its pastel pink-grey interior. Our route then zig-zags back into Utah and mammoth Monument Valley, a flat, red landscape studded with eruptions of colossal rocks given self-defining names: Elephant Butte, Camel Butte, Three Sisters, Totems.

Back once more into Arizona, we head for the Grand Canyon to peer into its vertiginous depths, tentatively sidling to the edge of the rim to capture a pose for digital posterity. We stop at the Hoover Dam, walk from one side to the other, in the middle crossing from Arizona into Nevada and back into Arizona, a change of time each way. We continue back to Las Vegas, and our seventh time change in four days. You begin to ask yourself, 'What is time?'

We cycle for ten days to Phoenix, Arizona, much of it through open desert, incurring almost as many punctures during this time as for the whole of my trip so far. The main culprits are fine metal filaments from shredded lorry tyres, vicious cactus thorns competing for a close second. Nights now being excruciatingly cold, we plump for motel rooms more often than camping, their affordability being one of the advantages of travelling in company.

GR and I have been cycling together for three weeks and there seems to be an unresolved tension between us. He now talks about his own ongoing plans, not wanting to cycle all the way to the east coast.

We cycle past swathes of cotton fields, pockmarked with huge rectangular blocks of harvested crop awaiting transportation for processing into textiles. We pass acres of red hot chilli peppers, orchards of vines and pecan nuts.

At my 15,000-mile mark we arrive in Duncan, a place dumped in the middle of the desert adjacent to a railway line, a train passing once a day, if lucky. It has a certain charm to it, reminders of the old Wild West retained in the decrepit wooden buildings of the Duncan Hotel and the Court House, and a hand-painted wooden Public Notice unreasonably declaring:

Gunpowder and dynamite
will NOT be sold to questionable,
disreputable or unsavory characters

It is my birthday. GR shakes my hand (maybe it is a Dutch thing), wishes me, 'Happy Birthday. You are a lovely woman,' then removes a silver chain with small cross from around his neck and fastens it around mine. He bought it when walking the Santiago Camino a couple of months ago.

There is now a sudden change in weather, from happy sunshine and cloudless skies, to dark, thick clouds emitting dismal rain in the afternoon, a rumbling storm on the advancing horizon.

I read birthday emails and manage a Skype call with Cogs, my younger brother. Whilst we are online, he googles the B&B in which we are staying, going on to describe in detail the front and side of the building, the restaurant opposite and the corner of the street. And when he pinpoints the bedroom window, I have to resist the urge to rush to the window and wave to him. It is a spooky sensation, to feel he is across the road rather than on the other side of the Atlantic.

On the morning of departure we breakfast at Ol' Joe's Café, then I layer up in snood and woolly hat, rain jacket and trousers, two pairs of socks and plastic bags and full gloves to contend with the freezing wind and rain. My feet soon become ice blocks. GR complains I am cycling too fast. I just do not feel the desire to loiter.

A momentary compensation for such lousy weather conditions arrives in the form of a most impressive rainbow. Each band of the spectrum is vividly delineated in the 180 degree arc, a shadowy double in the dark sky above, an ethereal pale purple aura below. The fabulous sight lingers for twenty minutes.

With a forecast of snow we hole up in Lordsburg for two nights, then back out into the cold. We summit the Continental Divide at 4,585 feet, the rivers now flowing down to the Atlantic, rather than to the Pacific. Ranges of snow-covered mountains paint the backdrop to the yuccas in the arid desert foreground, a strange canvas.

The Welcome to Texas state sign is swiftly followed with a stars and stripes 'God Bless Our Nation' on the front plate of a car. On the approach to El Paso, GR suffers a record three punctures in one sitting, a total of five by the time we reach the hotel. The road in town is ankle-breakingly slippery from the freezing, icy conditions; crossing the road to the hotel an exercise in dancing on ice. The Gardner Hotel is the longest continuously-open hotel in the city running since 1922, complete with original furniture and décor in the rooms – a dubious boast.

We walk over the busy border crossing into Mexico, joining the 70,000 people who cross each way, each day. In Mexican El Paso city centre, dull-grey army pick-ups disgorge soldiers, automatics slung nonchalantly across their bodies, whilst they mingle with the stallholders, shoe-polishers and seasonal Father Christmases, warily eyeing me as I surreptitiously snap a photo. The cathedral draws us in with external loudspeakers broadcasting the celebration of special masses for a pilgrim festival.

Back in El Paso, USA, we join the evening throngs for the switching on of Christmas lights in the town square, a full-sized nativity amongst displays of other topical scenes. A gala procession of illuminated festive floats leaves from the square to meander around the streets.

GR is booked on Amtrak, leaving after the weekend. His decision is to continue his 'free life' on his own, at least for the time being, his agenda including no particular commitment of any future contact with me. This comes as a bitter blow; I didn't think it would end like this.

We part on the platform at El Paso station after six weeks cycling together. I return to the hotel, attempt to eat breakfast, unsuccessfully choking back the tears. On the way out of El Paso, I remember to post my Christmas presents to my children.

I have a particularly amazing day with winds of 40 mph, gusting sixty, exhilarating when directly behind and blasting me up a hill at 13 mph, but putting me through my paces in attempts to keep cycling when attacked from the side. Only on stopping does the full force of the wind hit me, literally, as I struggle to stay upright, accentuated even more when, on arriving in town and in search of a hotel, I am obliged to turn full into the gale, battling inch by inch to reach the lee of the building entrance. Those inside express admiration at my venturing forth in such conditions. My average speed for the day is a notable 14.7 mph, fifty percent higher than my normal target.

On then to Marfa, a small town that boasts one or two claims to fame. A few miles short of the town is a Prada shop, plonked by the roadside in the middle of an empty stretch of desert road, a minimalist display of luxury handbags and shoes in the window. I see no signs of life, but who on earth would be going into it, anyway? It is a bizarre sight considering I have just cycled seventy miles of the same desolate road, barren of any food or water whatsoever. Turns out it is a piece of conceptual art taking the mickey, commissioned (or, maybe, just sponsored) by Prada itself.

Two other claims to fame for the town are its nationally-reported anti-nuclear activism and its unexplained strange lights phenomena. There is even a viewing station in the area of such sightings to make the observation experience as comfortable as possible.

I stay with Gary, a political cartoonist, who offers me a bed for the night after he was dragged to the Dairy Queen restaurant to meet me by one of a group of local elderlies, because they know he offers his little back garden hut to passing cyclists. Through him I sign up for Warm Showers, a hospitality organisation solely for cyclists of which I have vaguely heard mention during my travels. I contact my first host, Liz, for my next night's accommodation in Alpine.

Between the two towns is picturesque Paisano Pass, from where I watch the silently advancing snake of two hundred carriages slithering through the wilderness along the solitary rail tracks. I feel very lonely at the moment, then laugh at a huge sign that suddenly appears in the middle of nowhere in front of a prominent knoll.

'I will lift my eyes to the hills, from whence comes my help.'

Such signs are not the first ones I have seen in this country.

I am full of cold and, despite going away for the weekend, Liz is more than happy for me to stay in the house. She even contacts a friend, who invites me to dinner, which I graciously decline not wishing to spread my germs. Much improved by the next evening though, I accompany her to a Christmas drinks party, followed by a ladies' lunch the following day. One of the men at the drinks party is a cyclist, who presents me with a marvellous little gadget: a small mirror that fits to my spectacles, thereby obviating the potentially hazardous act of physically turning round when checking traffic approaching from the rear. Since that day, I have never looked back.

I am persuaded to detour through Big Bend National Park, a hidden treasure of the United States. Pitching my tent behind a motel prior to arriving in the park, a greybeard rumbles up on his BMW. Ara has been on the road for three years, spending his time travelling on his bike between various favourite 'base camps' after selling his house. He rides this huge contraption, its width doubled by the attached sidecar, in which sits his demure four-legged companion, Spirit, her brown muzzle sporting a fetching pair of red-framed goggles.

From the campsite in Chisos Basin, I walk along the signposted trail to The Window, a wide gap between two rocks on the edge of a slippery precipice, offering a fabulous view of a rocky moonscape beyond. On the way, I take heed of the warning notice that bears are active in the area.

'If a bear approaches, scare it away.'

'Boo!'

Camping elsewhere in the park is not as easy as one might think. Unsuccessful in obtaining a permit for one of the primitive campsites, they are already full, I am faced with the prospect of a long haul to the nearest campground. Happily though I am offered a lift by a couple and their dog in their RV to the campsite in Rio Grande village, incorporating a detour to bathe in a hot springs pool on the banks of the Rio Grande, Mexico a hop and a skip away on the other side of the narrow river. I also meet a couple of women cyclists, who instantly ask me, 'Are you Astrid?'

They have been speaking to Liz. The three of us may well be staying the same night in Liz's other property in Sanderson, also open to Warm Showers over-nighters. In fact, I meet them the next night in Marathon at another Warm Showers. This is very much an alternative lifestyle type of place, all sorts of wonderfully weird people, including amiable Eric, forehead and neck bedecked with crazy tattoos. The following day I cycle to Sanderson with the two women, Nicole and Judy. Their bicycles have narrower tyres than mine and lighter loads and it is hard going for me to keep up with them. I am therefore quite happy that they are staying two nights. In the evening I manage to hook up in a local restaurant for a Skype birthday call to my daughter.

The tourist town of Langtry offers camping behind the community centre, but no facilities. A museum historying the life and times of Judge Roy Bean includes the original saloon-cum-courthouse and his Opera House home. He named the saloon 'Jersey Lilly' after his idol, the Jersey-born British actress, Lillie Langtry, the judge infatuated with her although they never actually met. He kept a strict saloon, the house rules displayed clearly on a wooden sign.

'No shooting, cutting, fighting or loud cussing allowed, and absolutely no spitting on the floor.'

Spoilsport.

The road continues to cut through a desert landscape, the lonely strip of tarmac stretches endlessly before me for the majority of the day. Stops are rare but welcome, especially when a sign invites customers to free chilli and snacks during the football on Sundays. Providentially, my timing is spot on.

It is four days before Christmas when I arrive in Del Rio to Jon, another WS host. He is not at home when I arrive, but has said for me to park my bicycle in the garage and let myself into the house. He comes by after a couple of hours with a group of friends and neighbours, all riding bicycles. They are going around the neighbourhood admiring the many Christmas light displays in gardens and on houses.

I join them for a magical and fun evening, particularly at one elaborately decorated house, the garden directly opposite surrendering any notion of competing against such ornateness. Instead it resorts to a simple display of white lights in the middle of the lawn, one display forming an arrow pointing to the Santa's Grotto opposite, the other, the word, 'DITTO.'

Jon and two of the other cyclists, one a woman, work at the US Air Force base nearby, all three trainers of F1-11 fighter pilots.

Three days before Christmas I am cycling along a quiet country road away from the busy highway. A woman standing at the roadside by her car flags me down as I draw level. She had overtaken me further back, saw my loaded bicycle, and was now waiting to ask me where I would be spending Christmas.

'I thought you must be travelling and so, if you have nowhere to stay for Christmas, I should like to invite you to stay with me.'

I am almost in tears at this astonishing invitation but, as I already have plans, I reluctantly decline. My Christmas Angel then sends me off with a big hug. In high spirits, I continue to the youth hostel in Austin, the final three miles with a nail embedded in my front tyre, but which remains inflated.

I arrive on the eve of my son's twenty-first birthday. One-thirty in the morning finds me at my computer in the lounge of the hostel, tuning in for a prearranged Skype call with my daughter at 7.30 am their time. Besides Jessica, three friends have dragged themselves dressed to be part of this family tradition.

We gather in the hallway, whisper confirmation that everybody is ready, light a candle, tip-toe to the closed door, open it quietly, then all burst into a rollicking rendition of, 'Happy Birthday to you,' and ply Daniel with his presents. I am placed on a chair in full view of all that is going on, thrilled to be in the midst of the proceedings.

I cycle into the centre of Austin on a bitter-cold Christmas Eve. Stopping by Lance Armstrong's 'Mellow Johnny's' cycle shop, I inadvertently, but sensibly, come away with a new set of brake pads, 6,000 miles after the last change in Japan.

Lance Armstrong has won the Tour de France a record-breaking seven consecutive times, even more astoundingly achieving this after successively combatting cancer.

I park my bicycle in the foyer of St David's Episcopalian Church, slipping into a cosy warm pew, a Children's Pageant Service just beginning. The pageant takes my thoughts to the candlelit Christingle Service currently in full swing back home.

The hostel is friendly, relaxed and comfortable and I spend quite a social week here. On Christmas Day, one of the staff cooks a turkey meal for the itinerant guests, greatly appreciated by all sixteen recipients. After Christmas, I go in company with another traveller from the hostel, Debbie, to the old Paramount Theatre in Austin to watch Woody Allen and his New Orleans Jazz Band in concert.

I manage to find a cycle route map for Louisianna and buy road maps for Florida, Mississippi, Spain and Portugal. I cannot help but feel excitement at the European maps.

A lovely couple, Holly and Gary, are also staying in the hostel and I spend some time with them. When I leave, Holly presents me with a leaving present of her favourite book, *The Hiding Place*, by a Dutch woman, Corrie Ten Boom. I read it as a teenager and loved it. The book recounts the story of Corrie's family during the Second World War, during which they helped and hid Jews, eventually being sent to death camps themselves. Corrie was the only surviving member of her family. One might wonder why or how it could be termed a favourite read.

At the heart of this book is the family's solid, unwaivering relationship with God and how this reflects and determines their whole attitude, not only towards themselves but towards all people without exception, including their cruel perpetrators. Above all it is a book of hope, trust and love.

After a rejuvenating 9-day break in Austin and seeing in the New Year, I depart on New Year's Day. The weather is cold, very disappointing, as all the way down the country I was being 'reliably' informed otherwise.

'Once you are south as far as you can go, it will be fine and warm in the winter, shorts and T-shirts weather.'

I meet up with Nicole, one of the two 'thin-wheelers', a hundred and eighty miles east of Austin. She had emailed me offering herself as a companion after her friend had departed back to Santa Fé and she didn't fancy cycling on her own.

Nicole is on a taster trip. She has sold up most of her possessions and owns no property, cycling now to her parents in Florida, at the same time keeping her options open as to whether or not she will then continue a nomadic life. She mentions an organisation called Bicycling Superheroes who, for a month each year, cycle from town to town setting up camp and finding out in what ways they can best help the local community for the time they are there. Each volunteer is costumed in a character of their own creation, such as Great Gitchigumi, Queen Bee, Believe-Oh, Super OK with Himself Guy, Wander Woman, Infinity Kid, Atomic Calm, Zing. Nicole was Metta Mime: face painted white, white gloves, no talking – for a whole month!

A few days after meeting up with Nicole, the vast state of Texas is crossed, four and a half weeks after entering from New Mexico.

*   *   *

USA: East

8 January – 5 March 2010

Louisianna	*Deridder, Oberlin, Opelousas, Baton Rouge, Convent, New Orleans, Memphis (Tennesee)*
Mississippi	*Bay St Louis, Ocean Springs*
Alabama	*Dauphin Island*
Florida	*Pensacola, Fort Walton, Seagrove, Mexico Beach, St George Island, Sopchoppy, Monticello, Suwanee River, High Springs, Micanopy, Palatka, St Augustine, Port Orange, Cocoa, Vero Beach, Jupiter, Fort Lauderdale, Miami, Key Largo, Florida City, (Nova Scotia), Miami, (Santo Domingo), Florida City, Miami*

It is too cold to camp – it really is glacial – but the search for affordable accommodation brings its own rewards. Nicole and I are invited to stay in someone's trailer in a field, after a chance encounter in a local store. The owner drives on ahead of us to switch on the heater and water and to leave a pizza for us. In subsequent searches, we are turned away from a couple churches in one town when we ask if we can sleep inside, but the following couple of nights we are put up in motel rooms paid by local churches, their policy after negative experiences with travellers staying in their churches. After the second night, we admit to some reluctance in continuing to accept such humbling charity, fantastic though it is not to be sleeping outdoors.

Fire departments also come up trumps, providing cosy warm rooms, hot showers, kitchen facilities, and grapevine to the next fire station. Another grapevine, a fellow guest in the hostel in Austin, provides us with a homestay contact in Baton Rouge, plus an evening meal in a restaurant. A bar encounter ends with another homestay on a sugar plantation in Convent.

Encounters with not so friendly locals provide a bit of light relief. Pedalling against a sub-zero headwind, layered up to the eyes and beyond, hands and feet in need of thawing, we spot a dilapidated barn a hundred yards past a ranchhouse. Relieved at the prospect of temporary respite from the wind, we push our bicycles into the shelter of the barn, sandwiches out at the ready to make good use of this break.

We hear dogs barking from the house, a man emerges, wearing what looks like pyjama bottoms and check flannel shirt, hillbillies springing to mind. The man walks purposely and menacingly towards us, brandishing a revolver and cocking a rifle. Nicole and I exchange rather nervous looks. Then, fixing her face with a huge, maniac grin, she steps forward and explains our trespass. Thankfully, he is assuaged when he realises we are not after all about to hitch his boat to our bicycles and run off with it, and returns to his home. We should dearly love to take his photo, but think it might be pushing our luck.

Wildlife is visible in abundance: bluebirds and vivid red cardinals, turkey buzzards gorging on road kill, white herons, small stripey birds with a song like a laugh. Road kill includes dogs, owls, skunk, possum. Poor innocents. We pass waterlogged fields in which rice is grown as food for crawfish, piles of net pots waiting to harvest the farmed creatures.

And so we arrive in New Orleans, from where I take a side-jaunt by train to Memphis, Tennesee to visit Graceland. I stay in a motel on Elvis Presley Boulevard for a couple of nights, to spend a whole day looking around his home and the museum. The house is smaller than I had imagined and has a certain charm about it, despite some of the garish décor.

Back in New Orleans and I remember the dire warnings of well-meaning advisors.

'Far too dangerous to go there.'

'Steer well clear.'

In reality, New Orleans is a vibrant, friendly, fun place, albeit coupled with poverty and still dealing with the aftermath of Hurricane Katrina, four and a half years down the line. I stop to watch street musicians, Shoeshine Fine, a lively couple jazz dancing to their songs. Further on, a puppeteer performs with his string-held puppets. Mardi Gras is in the air, the colours purple (justice), green (faith) and yellow (power) are visible everywhere adorning balconies and special cakes. A Mississippi steamboat paddles up the wide river concourse.

But all along the coast the flattened devastation from Katrina is dauntingly, depressingly extensive, swathes of houses yet to be reinstated. Nicole and I find ourselves staying in Bay St Louis with a volunteer group, the Lutheran Episcopal Services in Mississippi. This is a truly amazing organisation, set up immediately after Katrina struck, with the sole purpose of helping people to rebuild their destroyed homes. It is run by one paid staff, a committee of volunteers and the labour of love from 40,000 other volunteers in the last four years. Even after so long, its services are crucial; hundreds of people are still without homes or with no basic services, such as electricity.

Volunteers stay for anything from one day to many months, the spectrum of their ages spanning youth groups to retirees. Displays of handmade posters decorate the walls of the warehouse base camp, creating a chequered map of the widespread concern for fellow human beings from all corners of America. The posters each include the distance from New Orleans to the hometown of the volunteers: 319 miles, 611.24 miles, 1,123 miles, and, attracted by the Union Jack, I notice a whopping 4,702.3 miles, from York St John University, England. A group of 18-year olds are here for two months with a youth organisation, Americorps. This is one of five projects that takes the group through a 10-month term.

Into this Nicole and I are effortlessly incorporated: homecooked communal meals, warm bunkhouse, hot shower, easygoing, dedicated, philanthropic people. We are so impressed and touched by their work that we stay the following day, offering our services for a painting job of the kitchen doors.

We continue along the coast, staying next at the sister organisation, Camp Victor in Ocean Springs. An English guy with a degree in Disaster Management has recently arrived for a couple of months, considering whether at a later date he might be able to help with the longterm aftermath of the recent earthquake in Haiti.

These under-cover stays are timely, as fierce storms invade most nights: bucketing rain, clapping thunder, sheet lightning. The intensity of the weather accentuates the many reminders of Katrina: the Bay St Louis place sign proudly declares, 'Discovered 1699, survived Katrina 2005.' The Friendship Oak boasts, 'I am 500 years old and I survived Hurricane Katrina.' In a hotel lobby, a high water mark is painted onto the wall almost at ceiling height.

'Hurricane Katrina, 8.29.05, 28'10" above sea level.'

Cycling has been along completely flat terrain for the last couple of weeks, promising to continue so for the remainder of my time in the States. On the whole the effortless exercise is appreciated, and the landscape is varied enough to be enjoyed, even though it rarely rises above sea level. Along this stretch through Louisianna, Mississippi and now briefly Alabama, swamp tours are plentifully advertised, enticingly promoting the local 'gators and crocs.

Our only night in small-state Alabama is memorable for being able to change into shorts after so long wrapped up against the arctic temperatures.

This winter has seen extreme conditions throughout the States (and, I understand, northern Europe), the weather channels having a field day with round-the-clock updates, reporters animatedly shouting into their microphones against the noise of swirling snowstorms, knee deep in snowdrifts. Even Florida has seen snow in the north of the state, shocking its inhabitants; many properties are not installed with heating of any kind because in fifty years they have never been in need of any.

We take the ferry to Dauphin Island, to camp in the comfort of a warm evening sun. The next day, six months after arriving in the northernmost state of America, I arrive in the southernmost, Florida, the Sunshine State. And for the first day it lives up to its name, as we frolic in delight on a dazzling, clean, empty beach and prance in the surf, Nicole performing circus handstands across the sands. Our first night in Florida sees us put up by Pensacola Fire Department, the firemen even paying for our meal at the pizza place opposite.

The following day is one of impossible headwinds, sand propelling across the road stinging legs and faces. The swirling sand looks just like snow, a surreal scene, fascinating to see despite the arduous cycling.

The local news issues an announcement of a Tornado Watch. Before committing ourselves to setting off for the day, we phone the Warm Showers host for the coming night, who thinks the warning will probably come to nothing. We set off mid morning, stopping in a state park for lunch and puncture repair for Nicole, grabbing the opportunity to ask a pair of park rangers for an update of the tornado, the warning still in force. In the end, I'm glad to say, it does indeed come to nothing.

Our WS host, Jeff, is an enthusiastic competitor of triathlons, Iron Mans and marathons. His wife is currently on a yoga retreat. In the morning he prepares a healthy, energy-packed breakfast for us: triathlon smoothie (banana, peanut butter, orange juice and other stuff), poached egg on pitta toast, orange juice, coffee, fruit, porridge with raisins, cranberries and nuts. He stocks us up with gaterade and other energy salts in our drinks' bottles, plus extra sachets of powder and gel in reserve for when we need a bit of oomph.

Florida motorists are notorious for being amongst the least friendly road sharers. This is not helped by a dearth of hard shoulders giving rise to numerous disgruntled horns. But, towards the end of the day, we can forget all that as we cycle over a long, low, elegant bridge to St George Island. As we come off the bridge, we meet up again with Jeff, this time with his wife. They have a second property here on the island to which we have been invited. At the same time, a cyclist at the side of the road asks if we have somewhere to stay the night. He had seen us on the bridge when he went by in his car, then rushed home in order to sprint back on his bicycle, all the time afraid that he would miss us. Maybe he thought being on a bicycle was a more appropriate way by which to issue his invitation. He happens to be a neighbour of Jeff and we all end up together for the evening at a restaurant, where I choose a local speciality.

'Alligator burger, please – and make it snappy.'

Travelling with Nicole is a healthy and eye-opening experience. She passes over all foods with high fructose corn syrup (HFCS), thus dramatically limiting her choice of foods, the vast majority of packaged food in America being full of the stuff. I am completely oblivious to the issues surrounding the manufacture and use of HFCS in processed foods, which is widespread in the States but, as far as I know does not feature to the same extent in Europe. Whilst staying in a particular Warm Showers' home, we watch a film, *King Corn*, about the production of HFCS and the side effects. It is in nearly all foods and leads to high level obesity and an increase in diabetes.

The obesity factor involves vital hormones that help to regulate hunger. Insulin and leptin tell you that you are full, whereas ghrelin tells you that you are hungry. By ingesting high fructose corn syrup, insulin and leptin are inhibited, so that you do not feel full, ghrelin is overproduced so that you still feel hungry. The ensuing double whammy contributes vastly to the enormous obesity in an increasing proportion of the American population.

The colossal levels of production of corn in an area leads to monopolies obliterating small, independent farmers, giving them no option but to work for their ruthless conglomerates.

I didn't realise how instructive my trip would turn out to be.

We continue to receive hospitality from churches, even arriving with impeccable timing for a midweek communal supper in a church hall, at which we are fought over as to who will take us home to put us up for the night.

Nicole and I now arrive in St Augustine and the east coast of America. Her parents are already installed in their spacious RV on a campsite on the outskirts of town. Nicole is greeted by her father with a sustained heartfelt hug of relief and happiness, after which he embraces me with a grateful, 'Thank you,' for ensuring his daughter's safe and sound arrival. All I did was accept her offer to be my travelling companion. As reward, I experience the luxury of a stay in one of these home-from-home extravaganzas.

St Augustine is the longest, continuously-inhabited-by-Europeans city in the U.S of A, dating back to 1565. The fort and remaining original buildings were built from a natural local seashell rock, coquina, which replaced the initial wooden structures and was more effective for the resident Spanish to withstand the annoying marauding activities of the likes of Francis Drake.

Nicole and I make our way to the beach for the traditional coast–to-coast wheel-dipping in the Atlantic. Having wider tyres, I can strike an elegant pose cycling across the wet sand and through the shallow surf. We then spend a damp last night in the State Park campsite by the coast in the drab rain, speculating on the peculiar notion of swapping the cosy comforts of an RV for the dubious delights of noisy neighbours disregarding the campground curfew.

After five weeks cycling together, it is time for Nicole and me to split. She will stay in Florida for the summer planning her next stage, the concept of living permanently on the road not yet a fait accompli.

Having been warned that the east coast of Florida is exorbitantly pricey, even the campsites, I have booked Warm Showers wherever I can. In between, I wild camp, on one occasion unobtrusively in the grounds of First Baptist Church. The following morning, I am up and away before being discovered, stopping at nearby Grace Episcopalian church in time for the early service. On the way out, a sidesman presents me with a small home-baked loaf wrapped in foil, tied with a pink ribbon and containing a Bible verse.

'I am the Bread of Life; whoever comes to me will never be hungry.'

At which, we eagerly transfer to the church hall for the regular monthly, full-cooked breakfast.

In Cocoa, a friend of the Warm Showers host works a few miles away at Cape Canaveral. He obligingly rings her at 4 am, she in turn wakes me, we then stumble sleepily in our pyjamas to stand outside her house, gleefully awaiting an historic event. It should have taken place the previous night, but was delayed due to adverse weather conditions.

We stare into the darkness, ears and eyes bristling. Eventually, a yellow light appears on the horizon, soundlessly spreading in a radiating band, silhouetting trees. After a minute a white light like a brilliant star, rises upwards into the pitch black. Gradually, we become aware of the noise of the engines, short lived. The star appears to pause, suspended in mid black, our unblinking eyes transfixed, until . . . poof! The Shuttle disappears through the atmosphere and into space. This is the last night launch of the Space Shuttle *Endeavour*, in the early hours of Monday 8 February 2010. Momentous event over, we return to our beds.

This trip is nothing if not varied. My Warm Showers host is not feeling well and arranges for me to stand in for her with her dancing partner for their weekly tango class, then on for a curry. I enjoy this unexpected evening, having over the years attempted and survived salsa and jazz classes.

The disarming trust and generosity of Warm Showers' hosts is patently portrayed by one in particular who, currently away in Asia, is nonetheless happy for me to stay. He even attaches photos of useful landmarks to help me locate his beachside home, exhorts me to make myself at home, and apologises for not being there himself.

The weather is now almost continuously glorious as I make my way to Fort Lauderdale, the place a reminder of watery Venice with its intricate network of canals and bridges. Hardly have I set foot in the home of Warm Showers Ray and Denise, than I am donning a bikini and stepping out onto the patio and into the steaming bubbling hot tub; swimming pool on one side, canal on the other, a bevy of boats behind. Glass of red wine in hand, I raise a 'Skol' in toast of mine hosts.

Ray has worked out a sightseeing cycle route of the city, along which I follow him the next day. We take a breather at the highest elevation point, all of eighteen feet above sea level. We spot ibis, mallard ducks and small turtles, the latter treated with great fondness by Florideans, seaside street signs stating, 'Turtle Nesting Beach. Street lights turned off March through October, next 5 miles.'

We pass the wonderful sounding gumbo-limbo tree, with so many properties to its credit you wonder why it is not suffering from an inflated ego. It is salt tolerant, hurricane resistant; its turpentine-scented resin is used for making glue and varnish and coating canoes; its sap used to treat gout; leaves brewed into medicinal teas. Fence posts built from its wood are known to have taken root and grow. Its red berries provide sustenance for mockingbirds and others during the year.

From Fort Lauderdale I cycle along the picturesque Atlantic Intracoastal Waterway to arrive in Miami. The first area I pass through is the Jewish quarter, many people heading towards the synagogue for Sabbath prayers. I cross the Venetian Causeway, in full view of the Miami skyline.

My Warm Showers place tonight is an Intentional Community, an interesting experience for me, having led a rather sheltered life. Art owns the place, lives here with his partner, Luigi. Nick is straight, even though he met Art and Luigi at the 'Radical Fairy Gathering, and rents a room here. Two other guests are cross dressers, performing in their own show in a club in town for a couple of nights. One of them wears a skirt topped with a low sweetheart-neck blouse sitting incongruously on his mildly hairy chest; he is soon to be a father. I receive a lovely hug from him when he leaves, possibly feeling a kinship with me, having himself cycled across Florida last year. In fact, everybody is very friendly, attempting to set the oddball amongst them at her ease.

On my way out of town, my gears start behaving like a truculent teenager, not giving much away before obstinately digging its heels in against a required activity. My gearshift is totally stuck in ninth gear and I am going nowhere. This cannot be happening. How on earth am I going to complete my trip with my bicycle incapacitated? Whoa. Hang in there, deep breaths, calm down. Remember, *everything* has turned out well in the past. At least it is stuck in a mid gear. I ask a handy police car for directions to a cycle shop and set off as instructed. Half a mile down the road, a loud voice from a PA system scolds me.

'You've gone the wrong way. I told you to stay on the 136!'

It is a Sunday, but thankfully the cycle shop is open; what is more, the owner, Manni, is the perfect guy for this job, completely on the ball. Although unfamiliar with my bicycle, he looks at it, tries a few things, goes to his workbench, returns with a can of lubricant. He proceeds to spray the inside of my gearshift, twisting it backwards and forwards until gradually the twists become bigger and smoother, the gears shifting once more. The teenager has been brought to bear.

The famed hostility of Florida motorists to cyclists, especially along the thin protrusion of the Florida Keys, precedes my arrival, extending even to the occasional fatality arising from bouts of extreme aggression. It is maybe fortunate therefore, that I have only a few days to spare, my short incursion extending only to Key Largo, a good choice as it happens. Campground fees are highly inflated, but the sites are also fully booked, with no margin of favour for a weary cyclist. Instead, I knock on the door of a local Church of Christ, the pastor directs me next door to an outward bound centre for underprivileged children, where I am allowed to pitch my tent amongst canoes and motorboats.

In the morning, a group of half-a-dozen teenage girls and their leaders return from a 21-day canoeing trip to the Gulf of Mexico, during which they slept at sea on boards on their canoes at night. The girls have had an awesomely wicked time, quite rightly on a jubilant high from their achievements. We instantly form a Mutual Admiration Society.

Breakfast at the Paradise Bar up the road results in accepting the offer of a night's accommodation from one of two old codgers at the next table. When he phones and tells his lady friend, she throws her hands up in fearful horror that I might be coming to murder him in his sleep. Orestes is a sweet, 83-year old gentleman, who keeps himself spritely with a 5 am daily workout at the local YMCA, in the company of four other elderlies.

I cannot visit the Keys without eating a slice of Key Lime Pie. I have already sampled a few, therefore am sagely sceptical at the current sign proclaiming, 'Best Key Lime in the World.' The pie is pleasantly mediocre at best; but I have eaten a Key Lime pie on the Keys.

Back in Miami and the home of another Warm Showers, Ellen and teenage daughter, Beth. They live in the midst of a Cuban area, neighbours and shopkeepers Spanish-speaking *only,* feeling no need to integrate into the wider American community; in fact, reverse integration is the case here.

Warm Showers exists to provide accommodataion for travelling

346

cyclists as a one night stand. If, by mutual agreement it extends to two, a contribution by the guest (commonly cooking a meal) is appreciated. Ellen and Beth are inordinately kind and generous, with a fortitude and tolerance level that should have put them in line for a Nobel Prize. Around New Year, they accepted the request from a Polish couple to stay. But the couple kept asking to extend their stay to sort out ongoing arrangements, finally leaving after seventeen days. When asked why she put up with them it was because she did not want to give a bad impression to foreigners of Americans. It is just a shame that her visitors did not feel the same compunction towards the reputation of their country.

I must have done or said something right to offset their unfortunate experience, as I am able to leave my bicycle and baggage with them when I fly off to Nova Scotia in Canada, to meet up with a friend for a long (and snowy) weekend. Afterwards, back for a couple of days with my saintly hosts, I then fly to Santo Domingo in the Dominican Republic.

My Norwegian great-grandfather was a sea captain of merchant tallships, sailing around the world. Occasionally, his wife would accompany him on his voyages, one time arriving in Santo Domingo. She was pregnant and her time to give birth occurred when they were there. The governor of the island became godfather and, in honour of the baby being the first Norwegian to be born there, bestowed on him the name Domingo. He therefore was my morfar (mother-father. Likewise, his wife was my mormor. The Norwegians are a sensible lot). I am hoping to find the record of his birth here in the city register.

The tourist office makes a few phone calls, tracks down the Departimenti de Restoraccion. Here I end up in the old records area, but they do not extend as far back as 1892. I am re-directed to Archivo de la Nacion, where I am shown into the hushed atmosphere of an archival library. A solemnly-bound index book is brought to a viewing desk. It is entitled

Registro de Nacimientos
SANTO DOMINGO
AÑOS
1891–1896
REF: ANTERIOR

I feel an excitement and a hopeful anticipation. This is one of the specific goals I made sure to include on my trip. I turn to 1892 and scan through the Ds, looking for Domingo Olsen, then the Os. His birth date is 1 May. I repeat the exercise, searching more carefully. But no, his name is not there. I had taken it as a given that it would be and I am now quite deflated. A final wild card attempt guides me to the huge Mormon Church, but they can only give me internet access to names and dates, not to locating actual records. It is a shame I did not find what I was looking for, but am very glad I came here and tried.

In the port area, a tallship happens to be berthed, but on the other side of a security fence. Would it not be appropriate to have a photo taken in front of her? I enter the building of the port offices to ask how to gain access to the quai. But they are not in an obliging mood and all I come away with is a picture of me in front of the wire fence, sailing ship in the background.

I return to Miami for a further couple of nights with the mum and daughter duo, thence to the Everglades Hostel, signing up for a day trip into the swamps. There are six of us in the group and one guide. It is a fabulous day. We tread the boardwalks elevated above the swamps inhabited by alligators, where we spot great blue heron, ibis, pelicans, woodstorks, turkey buzzards, red-shouldered hawk and little green heron. We lunch on the river bank within ten feet of a crocodile – scary. Our guide, Graham, warns us repeatedly that the Glades contain wild wildlife, not to be taken lightly or blithely, and to respect that this is their habitat.

We pair off into canoes, forming a convoy through the mangrove forest, the low slung vegetation creating tunnels through which we do our inexpert best to negotiate the narrow channels. We are invited to get out and swim.

'But mind out for water snakes and alligators.'

Feeling very intrepid, I lower myself into the thigh deep water, but within minutes I am safely back in the canoe.

The biggest challenge though is the walk through the mango forest, in which there could be snakes sliding down from the branches or skimming the surface of the water, or there could be alligators or crocodiles buried in the mud to step on and become the daily special on today's menu. I question my sanity as to what possessed me to participate in this nerve-wracking foray into the mangrove forest.

A redeeming feature, and one that helps to take the mind off the clear and present danger, is the bromeliads, bright orange spiky flowers hanging onto the grey and white blotchy trunks of the mangrove trees. And now ahead of us is an alligator, bulbous eyes, long snout, top of his back just visible. He eyes us silently as we keep our distance and try hard not to make any sudden movements, valiantly quashing the urge to beat a hasty retreat. But we are all friends, not wishing any harm to the other.

The Everglades Hostel has gorgeous grounds and an alluring atmosphere, enticing the guest to stay longer than their original intention. I drag myself away with difficulty, staying with yet more Warm Showers' hosts, Jealanne and Ken, in Miami Beach. Ken cycles, but has had so many nasty scrapes with aggressive motorists that he has a camera on the handlebars of his bicycle to record future incidents.

I sightsee around Miami harbour and waterfront. A towering black statue on a 10-foot high white pillar draws my attention. The figure is looking upwards in a pose of serene supplication. I am introduced to Christopher Columbus by the inscription on the brass plaque beneath.

> Christopher Columbus
> He dreamed greatly
> He dared courageously
> He achieved mightily
> Guided by the hand of God

I tingle on reading those words. Okay, I have not discovered America, but I have discovered a great deal about myself and about the world. I have discovered that you can do more than you think you can; that the world is a safer, friendlier place than you might think; that God is a great travelling companion; and that you don't need padded lycra to stay free from saddlesores.

I allow the words on the plaque to resonate with me. I *do* feel I have dreamed, dared, achieved, 'Guided by the hand of God.'

I receive a surprising invitation from Ellen to stay with her and Beth for my last night, not only in Miami, but on the North American continent. In the evening, the two of them cover Raven with fabric stickers of white doves and pink flamingoes, a uniquely distinctive reminder of my stay with them. In the morning, after affectionate adieus, I depart for the rendezvous that will mark the beginning of the end of my trip.

Port of Miami. The green overhead sign gives my heart a jolt. My excitement is palpable. I shall be back in Europe in just thirteen days. I can hardly believe it.

* * *

Atlantic

6 – 18 March 2010

CMA-CGM Amber

The 30,000 tonne freighter ship has a capacity to carry 4,500 containers. On this trip she is sixty percent full, a hundred and fifty of the containers are refrigerated so bring in a higher revenue. The Amber is just over a year old, Korean built, French owned, sails out of London. Her running speed is 14-15 knots, although on alternate days for a couple of hours this is increased to 24-25 knots to give the engines a workout. Peering tentatively over the bow, the eery sight of the the the bulbous bow underwater strongly suggests a menacing missile. This feeling is tempered slightly by being told dolphins are sometimes seen playing around it.

On this voyage I am not in the splendour of the owner's suite, merely a humble single cabin. Emboldened by the premise, nothing ventured, nothing gained, and being *the only* passenger, I suggest they might like to upgrade me.

'Yes, if you wish to pay the supplement.'

I have not yet developed Tomasz's smooth-talking charm.

I spend a fair amount of time in my cabin: resting (to catch up on the lost hour on alternate days), reading (*Tuesdays with Morrie*, *The Will of God*, *Reading Lolita in Tehran*, *A Walk in the Woods*), writing (my book), reorganising (my profusion of photos).

My room is cleaned each morning at ten by Anacita the Filipino steward, when I embark on my daily constitution. I phone Bridge to inform the duty officer that I am about to go out on deck. In the Ship's Office, I don the compulsory fluorescent jacket and hard hat before stepping out onto the Upper Deck, the only one on which to circumnavigate the entire ship from stem to stern. The sea is calm, sun hot, the lee area at the bow still and silent, a sheltered, windless suntrap. Here I sit at length with Bill Bryson, guffawing with laughter. On my safe return inside, I phone Bridge to let them know I have not fallen overboard.

The Filipino crew spends each day cleaning decks, servicing the ship's engine, re-painting the fire faucets red. The Croatian captain and officers take in turns to man the bridge, plot the course, make coffee, gaze out to sea. The odd fire drill and evacuation is organised; alarm bells sound, we gather at the muster station complete with fluorescent orange bag containing self-preservation immersion suit. A half-hearted demonstration of how to get into it is performed by the young Ukrainian cadet, a learning curve for him as well as his assistants as nobody seems to have the vaguest notion as to what fasteners go where and how. Let's hope we don't have to apply our ignorance in a real emergency situation.

Halfway through the voyage, with no more than the horizon for company for the previous six days, the phone in my cabin breaks the solitude. The Chief Officer is letting me know that dolphins have appeared off the port side. I rush out on deck, on the way grabbing hat and vest. As I speed towards the bow, I see the smooth arc of a dolphin glide cleanly out of the sea. Such a beautiful sight. I arrive at the bow and lean over eagerly. One, two, three . . . half a dozen dolphins in formation take turns to play in front of the bulb. I squeal in delight, especially when three more veer in from the starboard side eager to join the party, leaping smoothly and effortlessly, interplaying with each other. It is an enthralling spectacle and I am not the only one who is enjoying it. A dozen or so seagulls now come skimming across the surface to watch the show. Odd, isn't it? We are the furthest from land that we shall be on this voyage and suddenly the world and his wife are here.

Meal times are a self-conciously lonely affair when one is a solitary passenger. The chatty officers' table (including the captain's wife on this Atlantic leg) always speaks Croatian, sadly therefore excluding the Filipino master-in-waiting, who will take over when the captain disembarks in Spain. The extent of my lingual input is a daily good morning ritual of '*dobro utro*' and '*magandangoomaga*', Croatian and Filipino respectively.

I love the voyage. I love the sea. I love the ease of travelling by ship. The contrast to flying could not be greater. On the one hand: reduce bicycle to pieces, pack it up, somehow reassemble at the other end, hoping no damage has been sustained in transit; fear of crippling cost of paltry, penalty-bearing weight allowances; encounters with pompous airport personnel.

On the other hand, comparatively stress-free boarding and disembarkation; wheel whole bicycle onto ship or have a jolly sailor bear her up the gangway on brawny shoulders. Cycles and ships make serene, harmonious couples.

However much I enjoy sea travel, I realise that I am showing signs of going stir crazy when, after twelve days in my own company, I find myself in the passenger's recreation room avidly reading a celebrity gossip magazine from cover to glossy cover. Definitely time to jump ship. Fortunately, we arrive in Algeciras just in time.

*   *   *

Spain/Morocco/Spain

19 – 31 March 2010

Gibraltar, Ceuta, Tangiers, Torredd Pena, Zahara, Chichane, Costa Ballena, Dos Hermanos, Seville, Matalscañas, Isla Cristina

After breakfast I wait in my cabin until the (new) captain phones down to say I can leave whenever I wish. It is as a simple as that. No airport customs, no security hassle. Passport control is the captain handing my passport back to me.

My panniers are carried down to the quai, Raven is extracted from the bo'suns store, and we wait for the bus to take us to the port perimeter. I finally catch a bus after I realise I am standing in the wrong place, duly deposited at the exit. I load up and approach the man in the kiosk, who has to confirm my legitimacy with a phone call before allowing me to cycle through the gates. All very painless.

Gibraltar is not far away just around the bay. A courtesy call is the least I can offer. On the way, the only ongoing road seems to be along a motorway, memories of previous awkward occasions come to the fore.

'You are OK.' say a couple of policemen, waving me onwards, 'It is permitted.' Nevertheless, I remain daunted by the blue *Autovía* sign urging, 'Precaucion.'

The Rock is shrouded in cloud as I approach, but clears in time to display its dominance of the skyline. As I enter the main square in the centre of Gibraltar it seems almost surreal to be in England – but not. To be so close to home – yet still far, far away. A pair of smiling British bobbies direct me to Tourist Information, the familiar domed helmet perched on their heads, hands clasped behind backs, ready to issue, 'Evenin' All, let's be 'aving yer, then.' I buy sterling to pay for purchases; Union Jacks, British pubs, English tea rooms abound.

My uncle was a naval chaplain posted here for a time at one of the churches. The Anglican Cathedral of the Holy Trinity is worth a go and so it proves. The organist is having a quick blast on the pipes as I enter. I mention the name of my uncle.

'Oh, yes,' he rejoins, 'he married me fifty years ago.'

He qualifies his response by adding that he and his wife are currently celebrating their fiftieth wedding anniversary and that they knew my uncle very well.

At the bobbies suggestion, I head for the Gibraltar Chronicle, who carry out an interview with me, even sending a photographer to where I am staying to take pictures of my bicycle with The Rock in the background. I am told it will most likely be published within the following couple of weeks. The additional local slant of my uncle marrying the organist and his wife might help the story to run. (But as with the Dubai newspaper nothing comes of it after all.) The cable car to the top of the Rock provides plenty of opportunity to absorb the panorama and enjoy a brief encounter with the resident Barbary Apes.

After one night, I return to Algeciras by ferry across the bay, thence by another for a quick pop over the Strait of Gibraltar to North Africa. The ferry brings me into Ceuta, a Spanish Gibraltar, on a tip of land to the right of Morocco. When I arrive it is raining cats and dogs, so possibly I do not see it at its touristy best. I cross over into Morocco, choosing the scenic but mountainous route to Tangiers. However, any beautiful views remain hidden the higher I climb, a judiciously-placed road sign in bilingual Arabic-French is slowly making an appearance through the grey precipitation.

'بابَض Brouillard.'

'Fog? Yes, I can see that (or not) for myself, thank you.'

Descending to sea level, the skies clear once more and the temperature increases exponentially.

Somehow or other I find myself on a motorway.

'But there is no alternative road,' I reply to the man in the yellow van, 'Assistance' written on the side, when he pulls over to say I should not be on this road. He drives off without further dispute.

It is a beautiful motorway: virtually empty of traffic, wide clean shoulder. My validity to cycle on the motorway seems justified when I see a van parked on the hard shoulder, a bunch of men seated next to it lazily watching the traffic go by as their Sunday pastime. Later on, I pass someone walking along the hard shoulder. Another van then overtakes me very closely, pulls in sharply just ahead, two men spring out.

'Uh oh,' I react, alarmed. It is a lonely, empty road, after all.

But they make every effort to reassure me that they mean no harm. They are motorway security staff responding to a phone call from a certain yellow van. They insist it is too dangerous for me to be on this road, further insisting they drive me to an appropriate exit and a non-motorway road. The totally bizarre thing now is that the 'safe', non-motorway road is bristling with speeding vehicles unconcerned with my vulnerability or right to be on the road. Self-preservation tactics come into force, as I deliberately cycle in the middle of the inside lane in order to force cars into the next one to overtake me. This is to prevent them forcing me off the road when overtaking in the same lane. It is a tactic I learnt from Nicole in America, but I feel more confident carrying it out here than there, sensing that these locals would respond more readily to such an action.

I find a cheapish hotel in Tangiers, spend the afternoon sightseeing and checking out the port for ferry information back to Spain. I am in need of a good meal as the lack of sufficient nourishment these last couple of days has made cycling hard work. Les Celliers de Meknes serves up a tasty beef in creamy Balkanais sauce. Orange and whisky crêpes suzettes are on the house. No tip accepted.

The following day, instead of returning to Algeciras, I plump for the pretty little town of Tarifa. For such a small place, it boasts some significant markers: the southernmost point of Europe; the point where the Atlantic and the Mediterranean come together; the meeting place for two continents, Europe and Africa.

I spend the afternoon relaxing on squashy cushions at low tables in the colourful, bohemian Bamboo Café, internetting and sending pics and text to The Leprosy Mission for inclusion in their Annual Report, also to a reporter for *The Church of England Newspaper*. And I send an email to my family.

'Hey, I'm back in Europe – not long before I see you.'

I linger along the coast as I make my way to Seville, meeting retired British merchant seaman, Jan, and his sweet companion, Dotty Jack Russell. I absorb history in the Roman ruins at Baelo Claudio; become mesmerised by the graceful, slow motion somersaults of countless windmills on the far hillsides, a piece of conceptual art in functional disguise.

A lighthouse marks Cape Trafalgar in a surprising and gracious reminder of the renowned battle, in 1805, where the English navy defeated the combined Spanish and French navy. On then to Cadiz, bumping along its ancient cobbles and a chance meeting with a local cyclist, who mentions the ferry across the bay to Puerta Sainte Maria, undoubtedly more pleasant than the dangerous road would have been.

I achieve only the second 100-mile day of my trip, quite inadvertently and only because I try a scenic cycle route through a forest, but end up returning to exactly the same spot four hours and thirty-five miles later. I set off for a second attempt to cover sixty-five miles to a campsite just short of Seville, arriving exhausted and in the dark. The next day, I pick up a green cycle route on the outskirts of the city for an easy pleasant ride through the suburbs and into the centre. A plethora of ornately-tiled buildings hinders my progress as I pause to admire their attractive shapes and styles.

I happen to arrive on the weekend before Easter at the beginning of the Semana Santas, a week of countless street processions in towns and cities throughout Spain, of which Seville is the biggest celebrant. Each procession has its own local starting point, then follows a prescribed route through the city at a specified time, returning to its starting point after twelve sweltering, exhausting hours.

The basic components of each procession comprise full-sized icons of Jesus or Mary mounted on a dais and carried on the shoulders of sturdy teams of strongmen, themselves hidden by fabric screens hanging down from the dais, just their feet on show. Sombre strains of emotive music come from groups of musicians, a sedate drumbeat emphasizing the solemnity of the occasion. The procession includes hundreds of participants in long white tunics and flowing capes endlessly filing by. Some are barefoot. But it is what is on their heads that is the most interesting thing about their dress. Each wears a very tall pointed hat in dazzling white or marine velvet that extends down over the face to the shoulders, ending in a point over the torso and back. The face is completely covered except for eye holes to break it up. In other words, exactly the same garb as the Ku-Klux-Klan.

But of course this is not that. This ceremony is a symbol of cleansing – in the spiritual sense. I can only surmise this is the reason behind the KKK adopting it as their emblem for their inhuman brand of cleansing; anonymity an additional advantage.

I follow a procession for a few hours through the streets of Seville, one of the floats a statue of the Virgin Mary dressed in a long white gown and mantle, an elaborately-decorated crown and halo on her head, in a posture of grieving for the death of her son Jesus.

These processions mark the event when Jesus processed into Jerusalem on a donkey, leading on to his arrest, trial and execution. A float of Jesus in prayer, head raised in supplication, is adorned in richly-embellished gold decoration. The processors each bear a black cross over one shoulder, their pointed hats folded down on the backs of their heads. Behind, the slow beat of the band adds great poignancy to the scene.

Amongst the spectators, a distinctive man in a three-quarter length black coat and flat-brimmed Andalucian sombrero catches my eye. As does a group of four young men jaunting along in Sunday black suits, reminding me of Vettriano's, 'The Billy Boys'.

I stay one night in a backpackers' hostel near the centre, the other two nights on the other side of the river. The second, Hostel Triana, happens to be a popular one for Santiago pilgrims, Seville being the start of the *Ruta de la Plata,* Silver Route. Dotted around the city are the now-familiar blue and yellow scallop shells, reinforcing my excitement that I am in the final throes of my trip. I shall not be following the Silver Route, which goes due north through Spain to Astorga, then turning left to join the French Camino for the remainder of the way. Insead I shall be travelling up the coast through Portugal, picking up the *Camino Portugués* in Lisbon.

I need a new tyre but Seville is unable to produce anything remotely akin to a puncture-resistant Kevlar, Hobson's choice presenting me with a £5 cheapie. I replace batteries in my rear light, clean and oil Raven and purchase maps of Portugal and northern Spain.

Armed with a stamp in my pilgrim passport, I embark northwards, back on the pilgrim trail. It is now nearly four months since GR and I parted in El Paso and it has been a tough time. Still is. My big question to God is *why* did GR and I meet and go through all the ups and downs for it to come to this pithy end? My confusion causes me to become frustrated, almost angry with him, or is it with myself at my lack of discernment? I cycle along berating both God and myself.

Fortunately, this internal raging does not blind me to the splendour of the wayside and fields, an artist's palette of natural beauty. I decide to allocate different colours of flowers to specific people, so that every time I pass them, I pray blessings on the designated person. I assign yellow flowers to my children (a reminder of the sunflower letters). As these appear in profusion, they have blessings coming out of their ears. Blue flowers are for my father (because sometimes he is), green cacti my brothers (but not because I consider them a prickly pair, I hasten to add), white flowers for some friends, orange for others, pink for my charities, even red 'glomp roses' for GR. And when I pass pine forests and olive groves I give thanks for all the blessings I have received.

At the end of the day, wrapped up against the cool air, I write my journal sitting ouside my tent, next to pretty yellow flowers on slender stems that frivolously frolic in the breezy sun, the heady breath of the salt sea air combining with the mellow smell of fresh cow pats. Ah.

The time of year dictates that mornings are cold and dark, but small mercies come in the shape of Juan, my campervan neighbour, bringing me a steaming mug of sweet tea and a chunky slice of buttered toast. So too, the green cycle route temporarily removing me from busy roads to ride along the coast on raised boardwalks.

I manage a final wheel-dipping, Atlantic, Europe-side, thus completing the quartet.

* * *

Portugal

1 – 14 April 2010

Vila Real da San Antonio, Faro, Alvor, Aljezur, Porto Covo,
Vila Nogueira, Lisbon, Azambuja, Fatima, Coimbre,
Porto, Viana da Castelo

At Ayamonte, the 20-minute ferry crosses the River Guadiana to Vila Real de Santo Antonio, Portugal and the beginning of the Algarve. Onboard is a group of lively young cyclists, singles on a cycling holiday. I cycle through the town to a large lush campsite, taking the lead from the northern European winter-sun seekers in spending a lazy, do nothing afternoon. I am invited by a Dutch couple in a campervan for a yard-arm beer in the sunny lee of their winter holiday home. Another offers a touch of civilised comfort in the form of a table and chair he brings over to my tent.

I arrive in Faro, at the youth hostel near the ancient walled city, staying for two nights. At the cathedral, I gain free entry as a pilgrim and request a stamp. The pleasant young man hunts around for a while, eventually finding two pretty ones in a store room. He asks which I would like and is about to press it into my passport when his boss comes along. Presumably unimpressed by the way his junior is using his initiative, he stops the proceedings and leads me to an office, whereupon he produces an extremely plain stamp to deposit in my *credenciel*.

Claustrophobic stairs spiral stonily upwards emerging eventually into the open-aired bell tower, magnificent views extending over the pink-tiled roofs of Faro to the grey smudge of distant hills. A Ryanair plane flies overhead. A moment of déjà-vu from nearly two years ago.

I leave Faro on Easter Sunday. I cycle along, my thoughts still trying to analyse what went wrong with GR and me. I like answers to things,

359

reasons why they happen. In this vein then, I cycle along, successfully working myself up into a pretty heated frustration.

And then I have an ahha moment. A light switch flicks on as a simple uncluttered thought enters my mind.

'Stop demanding answers and trying to control every aspect of your life. Start believing in yourself and living in the present. The past will eventually become clearer and the future will look after itself.'

And that is all there is to it: live each moment as it is. My own little Easter epiphany.

The landscape now displays a cheerful countenance of white-housed villages with terracotta sunhats. As I cycle along, past acres of nature's beauty, words play in my mind, gradually ordering themselves into a single sentence: frivolous frolics of fluttering flowers festooning fragrant fields. Such is the creative loneliness of the long-distance cyclist.

The ferry at Setubal carries its passengers across the River Tagus to Lisbon, affording us a generous view of the popular capital of Portugal. It is the oldest city in Europe, pre-existing London, Rome and Madrid by hundreds of years. The waterfront is dominated by a long yellow and grey building, forming three sides of a square, in the middle a monument on which poses a majestic monarch mounted on a spritely steed. The city is built on seven hills, its transport infrastructure including three funicular railways, introduced no doubt to extend the lives of those living here by minimising the sheer exhaustion from the SAS workout otherwise required, in order to buy one's daily bread from the bakery up the hill.

Tourist Information gives me directions for the youth hostel eight miles out of town, but when I happen upon Yes! Backpackers Hostel in the middle of the city, at a cheaper rate than the antisocially sited alternative, I grab the offer eagerly. I climb to the cathedral and castle, ensuring I am not mown down by the funiculi-funicular as I bump along with the bustling tourists through the narrow streets.

On my exit from Lisbon a cyclist urges me to follow him along the waterfront cycle route past a statue of Catherine of Braganza, Queen Consort of England, wife to Charles ll. When I later find myself on the unpleasant N10, I decide to veer away into the hills. Everything is lovely: pretty hills, villages, views, flowers, no traffic. Bliss.

But then, disaster.

The handlebar gearshift turns freely but there is no power, no take. It is as though I am ten gears below bottom gear, pedalling furiously but going nowhere. I am just three weeks from home with a defunct bicycle. I do a McEnroe, 'You can*not* be serious!'

Okay, so let's calm down. Do *not* cry. You are done with that. All will be well. Take a deep breath. Or two. All will be well. Stop crying. All will be well.

I flag down three cars, but they are not going in my direction (?!). All will be well. I have stopped outside a garage but it is closed. Maybe somebody will come along after siesta and open for business. After forty-five minutes, nothing, nobody.

I look at my gears. There seems to be an unusual amount of slack wire protruding from the direction of the rear hub. I try fiddling with them because it does not look right. I attempt to visualise myself into becoming an instant cycle guru, miraculously diagnosing and mending this minor glitch. It does not work. All will be well.

And of course it is. A vehicle eventually comes along who stops to help. A charming couple, the woman speaking English, gives me a lift to where I am headed, depositing me at the *Bombeiros* in Azambuja. There is no cycle shop in town but, after locating an elusive phone box, stuffing it maniacally with money in an emergency call to Robin, a real cycle guru, I receive the calm and confident reassurance I need.

'It can be fixed.'

He suggests what might be the fault, I perform the diagnostics which confirm his assumption – pause for breath of relief – fish around in the depths of my panniers, gleefully extracting the thingummy from the spare parts' bag that needs to replace its counterpart. Firemen being what they are, lo and behold and hey presto, they whip off the old part and slip on the new one. And off I go the next morning as if nothing had gone amiss. Oh joy. Oh thanks.

As well as the yellow arrows indicating the Santiago Camino, similar blue markings lead me to Fatima, virtually on my route anyway. A huge plaza spreads out in front of the Shrine of Our Lady of Fatima, erected following a series of visions of the Virgin Mary by three young children in 1917. Hundreds of people mill around, but in a quiet fashion that gives the place a special air.

I wonder around the square, trying to spot likely people to ask for accommodation. Ah, a group of frocked clergy. They will help me, a tired pilgrim. As I approach, one of them looks at my bicycle in shock, shakes his head and is about to say, 'You can't bring that in here,' when

I interject in my best Anglo-Spanguese.

'*Donde is refugio de peregrinos, por favor?*'

This priest obviously does not consider me a worthy recipient of his time as he impatiently dismisses me with, 'No English, no English.'

But another of the group quietly detaches himself, comes up to me, and speaking gently in English, gives me directions to the *Sanctuario*, even writing the name of it on a piece of paper. He is so lovely, more than making up for the rude rebuttal of the first priest.

I wonder if it is the latter's cousin who works at the pilgrim refuge to which I now arrive, judging by the brusque greeting, the curt demand to see my pilgrim credential. What happened to 'Hello and welcome?'

In the large dormitory are three gregarious adolescents, massaging each other's suffering feet after two days of hard walking, covering an incredible sixty miles.

The roads in Portugal contrast markedly with those in Spain. The maintenance level is much lower, resulting in a high proportion of poor surfaces impeding pleasant cycling conditions. There is often no hard shoulder which, considering the habit of Portuguese drivers to drive in as direct a line as possible, poses potential hazards for the invisible cyclist.

Along the Coimbre road waiting for traffic lights to change, a multi-coloured mêlée of mucho macho suddenly swoops down to the junction from the little side road on the left. Whipping out my camera before the lights require me to continue, the entire horde cheers, laughs and waves, as I snap their infectious jubilation. My own Cheshire grin extends for many miles along the road.

Preparing for departure from the youth hostel in hilly Coimbre, I notice a missing screw on one of the pannier retaining clips. However, a smug smile slips into view, because I have a bag of nuts and bolts that Dan, the impolite cycle man back home reluctantly bestowed on me when collecting my brand new bicycle two years ago. I now spend ages screwing in the bolt with my Leatherman pliers, pop on the washer, then the nut, which goes on just as easily – because it is too big! I try another and another . . . Aaargh! They are *all* a mismatch. Thanks, Dan. Instead I have to resort to securing the pannier with a bungee strap until I find a garage which furnishes me with a fitting partner.

Portugal has some interesting aspects to it. I can't fail to notice the blatant billboards advertising sex shops and, along this current section of road on the way to Porto, it appears I am cycling through Call Girl

Corridor. In the middle of nowhere a woman stands nonchalantly at the roadside, to whom I give my customary hail as I pass by. Ten kilometres on there stands a second woman with similar stance, thus setting the pattern as periodically, lone women line the lonely stretches of road. And they are definitely not dressed to walk the Camino.

A driver standing by his car, obviously having waited for me to catch up with him, asks if I am travelling to Santiago, then suggests I leave this busy N2 and head down to the coast. Result: a flat road and quiet route all the way to Porto.

I like Porto. Spreadeagled either side of the Douro estuary, curving terraces of terracotta-roofed townhouses press close to the river's edge. On approach, a sleek modern bridge frames a view of the ornate old bridge that links the two halves of this pretty city across the watery divide.

I like the towering pastel buildings, front entrances elevated by bricked steps; the 100-year old blue and white tiled roof of Porto railway station is worth a visit. Quirky statues have been placed in a random fashion around the city: a bronze man in flat cap stands alongside a red English pillarbox, arms outstretched, a postbag dangling from his left shoulder, large board in his right hand. A shaggy-haired pilgrim in an orange hair shirt stands to quiet attention holding a thin metal cross. He looks down from his lofty perch in an alcove halfway up a monument, behind the Fonte da Praça da Ribeira and turns out to be John the Baptist.

I like the tourist chap in his little kiosk, who is not disgruntled when I roll up ten minutes before closing requesting help in locating accommodation. He also remembers me when I return the following day asking for information on the Camino route, directing me to the cathedral for a *calibra* (stamp) and helpful literature, under the impression that they have taken on the task of helping pilgrims along the way. Not so. I just about manage a stamp. But no other information is available, nor advice on where to obtain any, despite this being a major starting point for both Fatima and Santiago. Most odd. Well, at least I can sit in a pew for a bit of personal meditation. Not so. One minute after settling myself in a suitable seat I am asked to leave; the cathedral closes for lunch.

I like the jolliness of the stallholders and the gaudy-coloured displays of oranges and lemons, apples and pears, plums and peppers in the glass-ceilinged market place. I enjoy discovering the narrow lanes leading down to the laidback leisure-trip lads touting for trippers for a sightseeing tour up the river. I should like to have had more than a day in Porto.

My last day in Portugal includes a pleasant encounter with a day cyclist, a retired Professor of Cardiology who invites me to his members-only sailing club for coffee and to mark my map with the towns on my route. I then follow him along a diversion (helpful because they are notoriously badly signposted), before we part company. However, his prescribed route takes me along miles upon miles of cobblestones! Very hard work, very tiring, horribly bumpy and downright tedious. I can see no escape; whichever direction I turn there is more of the same. I travel along at 7-8mph, even an excruciating 5mph. I must have taken a wrong turning.

My last night in Portugal is at another *Bombeiros*. Hot shower, comfy mattress in sport hall; no donativo accepted.

*   *   *

Spain

15 – 29 April 2010

Pontevedra, Noia, Finisterre, SANTIAGO, Arzua, Vilalba, Ribadeo, Cadavedo, Oviedo, Poo, Cobreces, Santander

My intention had been to follow the river inland to Tui. On the 10-minute ferry crossing to Spain I chang my mind and turn left, preferring to stick to the coast to Baiona. An excellent decision as all the boxes tick positively: road surface, hard shoulder, traffic (Spaniards drive more thoughtfully than Portuguese), scenery, sea, flat terrain. I even spot a sign for Santa Tecla, a surprising reminder of St Tekla convent in Syria.

In Baiona, the heavens produce a honker of a hailstorm, well and truly drenching me before I can take refuge in a café. This continues for the remainder of the day all the way to Pontavedra where I stay in an *albergio*, meeting pilgrims again for the first time since returning to Europe. I like the familiarity.

I stop at the pilgrim refuge in Padron for a stamp, before negotiating a number of hills to arrive in Noia. I have no joy with accommodation at two churches, spend a couple of hours in the warmth and dry of the library until it closes, then transfer to a friendly local café-bar. They serve up a mean homecooked meal of rabbit stew, homemade crème caramel, coffee, beer, wine. I prolong the point of departure into the fog-chilling darkness as long as possible. But at ten o'clock they shut up shop and I cycle unenthusiastically to the Cruz Roja (Red Cross) to pitch my tent.

I am not the only one camping here. Two gaily-painted traditional gypsy caravans are stationed on the grass, three horses graze studiously nearby. A Dutch family, André and Eunice and their two teenage daughters, have been on the road for the last ten years. Just two months ago they built the second caravan, the two girls needing their own space.

They rarely stay more than a night in any one place; live by making jewellery, face painting at fairs and festivals, odd jobs. They love their simple, uncluttered lifestyle.

Sixty miles along the coast I approach my destination. I feel myself welling up. On the final stretch up a long, gentle uphill, I pass a statue of a pilgrim, her eyes fixed on the end, now within sight. And half a mile further on I arrive at that end, Cap Finisterre, Land's End. The traditional end for many Santiago pilgrims.

My first reaction, though, is not the spiritual import, but the human accomplishment, the dawning realisation that I have cycled round the world. I have done it. On my human own. For two years I have been on the road, away from my children, family and friends; meeting and cycling with people, and departing from them; receiving kindness and hospitality from strangers; being blown away by the beauty of God's earth and Man's creations.

I have cycled round the world.

I stand in solitary celebration, unchecked tears streaming down my face. I need to share the moment with someone, anyone. I turn to the nearest person a few yards away, a lovely German woman who comes up trumps, bless her. She gives me a huge and generous hug, then calls over her companions to share my news. It's exactly what I need. Thank you, wonderful woman.

I watch the setting sun. Tradition also states that the path of light from the setting sun on the surface of the sea symbolises a person's eternal pilgrimage towards the light of God, to new life. My journey has taken me each day in the direction of the rising sun, a new beginning, a fresh start. I have tried to be open to God. I have learnt to live in the present because I have learnt to trust. I recall the words of an Elvis song.

> 'I don't know what the future holds,
> but I know who holds the future.'

And my spirit soars, free as the seagulls overhead.

I return to the town of Finisterre and the hostel at which only bona fide walkers and cyclists are allowed to stay (many people travel this additional leg by bus). The holiday atmosphere sends a motley bunch of us out for a celebratory meal in a restaurant overlooking the attractive harbour. We drink and toast and drink a great deal. Just as well I am not cycling the next day.

It is only now that many of us become aware of the Icelandic ash cloud that appears to have brought the world to a standstill over the past week or so. A couple of New Zealand women merely shrug their shoulders when they hear their flights have been cancelled, planning to carry on walking until aeroplanes resume flying; better than sitting at an airport. I try to book my ferry from Santander to Plymouth online, in case this alternative viable mode of transport suddenly becomes popular. I have a specific date to be home if I wish to attend the welcome home party my daughter is organising.

'No pressure, Mum.'

But first it is difficult to get through to any ferry booking sites and, when I finally succeed, my card is not accepted.

After a couple of days, I prise myself away from the soporific air of Finisterre and proceed to Santiago, arriving for the second time. I came here at the beginning of my trip and now having cycled full circle, I return. Just as before, I attend the daily midday pilgrim service in the iconic cathedral, enthralled and thrilled by the pervading solemnity and celebration, although disappointed the giant swinging incense burner is not in action. I even join the queue to embrace the statue of the apostle, James, the brother of Jesus, who is unintentionally responsible for the establishment of this most popular of pilgrimage destinations.

And now I want to go home.

This is the single thought that dominates my mind. I want to see Jessica and Daniel again. The timing is perfect. Mentally and emotionally, I am ready to return home. My trip has been exactly the right length of time, neither too long nor too short. I remember the words that Jessica wrote in her secreted letter to me.

'I love you so much, I can't wait to see you again, but not for two years! You can't come back until you're ready, and when you do we will still be here.'

I try again to book the ferry, on the internet, by phone at the travel agent, using their card as well as mine, but still the transaction is not successful. At the start of my trip I had about six different cards and various cash currencies. I am down to one that only half works (at least I can withdraw money from a machine).

I take the high road to Santander, the northern coastal Camino route. It is far less popular than the Camino Francès with fewer pilgrims, although still a generous sprinkling, especially for the early season.

They are all going in the opposite direction to me and I allow myself a hint of smugness – but only because whenever I had met returning pilgrims I thought, 'I could *never* do that, go *all the way home* the same way I had come. Far too tedious.'

Even though I am desperate to be home, I still appreciate my scenic route and the friendly pilgrims and refuges, the weather kind much of the time. I turn left in Arzua, up to Vilalba; pay my respects to the English Madonna in Mondonedo, arrive on the coast at Ribadeo. At Cadavedo I decide to turn inland into the hill country to Oviedo.

In the past, Oviedo was a significant pilgrim destination as a warm-up to Santiago. I stay in a refuge opposite familially-named Santo Domingo church and college. From here an easy downhill river road returns me to the coast and a private albergue in pretty little Poo. As I draw nearer to my port of exit, I mark the diminishing distance by taking photos of roadsigns every ten kilometres. And finally I arrive in Santander.

In three days I shall be back in England.

But first I need to buy my ferry ticket. Of late I have been imagining this final voyage to be spent in the unexpected luxury of a deluxe cabin, after a friend had emailed me a few weeks ago kindly offering to pay for something that I might otherwise consider frivolous or an indulgence. After a fleeting thought of selfless altruism had been dismissed, I went for an upgrade from sleeping on the floor of the ferry lounge to a deluxe cabin. However, because of difficulties with the card, this lovely scenario does not actually now come to fruition (although with current means I can just manage one level up from the floor to a pokey little cabin).

On the morning of departure, a couple of young, free-spirited Czech pilgrims leave the refugio the same morning as me and together we wander down to a café near the ferry port to sit in the sun. Patric brings out his guitar, finally plucking up courage to strum softly, singing a wistful Czech folk ballad. He and Leike have no tents, often sleeping rough in their waterproof sleeping bags on mattresses. They are totally laid back about when they set off to walk for the day, lingering until it is time for me to embark at 2 pm. They walk with me to the ferry and wave me off.

*   *   *

England

30 April – 2 May 2010

Dawlish Warren, North Petherton, ALMONDSBURY

And so I watch, as the land recedes and Spain eventually disappears over the horizon.

First things first. Although I have had to forego the much-anticipated pleasure of a luxury cabin, I still book a table in the posh restaurant on board after remembering my emergency cache of a fifty-pound note in its hidey-hole.

Dressed as smartly as my limited wardrobe allows, the charming waiter seats me at my solitary table, surrounded by the usual 2-plus diners. For once, I do not mind in the slightest. I am on a high. Especially when my silver service nouvelle cuisine celebratory meal is served: a gourmet feast of Noux St Jacques (scallops), creamy artichoke risotto, deluxe cheeseboard; the finale, café gourmand of pungent, rich coffee accompanied by dainty dishes of chocolate mousse, crème brûlée, ice cream in chocolate box, choc and nut wafer, sugar-cluster swirly coffee stick. The bubbly contents of a sparkling bottle of champagne complete the menu.

The waiter becomes party to the cause of my celebration, to which he responds in a friendly, dutifully-impressed manner. The couple on the neighbouring table are the next to be given the opportunity to join in my unsuppressed joy. In my mind, I want to stand up and give a stirring and emotional speech to everyone in the restaurant, inviting them to lift their glasses in a toast, 'To the desires and dreams of derring-do and undaunted determination.' Being English, I remain seated, but continue to bask in my euphoria.

The shores of England are in sight, drawing ever closer. We approach the mouth of the bay, Fort Bovisand over to the right, ahead a distinctive sign looming ever larger: PLYMOUTH FERRY PORT.

There is a scant glimmer of a hope that Jessica and Daniel will be waiting for me, but it is a silly notion: to drive all the way down here for a few minutes and then return home? The thought occurrs to me only because my daughter had asked for specific time and port of arrival, so I just wondered . . .

I disembark at 9 am, along with another cyclist, a young German, Achim. We cycle into Plymouth's attractive city centre. On the way, I chance upon a large golden scallop shell on a wall, a plaque beneath describing the Way of St James. It is delightfully unexpected. After sorting out maps, money and a mug of coffee, Achim sets off westwards to Land's End, I head northeast and homewards, a mere hundred and fifty miles away.

What hits me most forcefully is the verdant English countryside, lush and green like no other country. Hedgerows bloom with colour; fields are awash with yellow rape. Two years away seems to have offered a new appreciation of my home country.

After camping at Dawlish Warren, I follow the towpath alongside the River Exe, then the canal up to Exeter. At the beginning of the path I come across a locked gate, kissing-gate access only at the side. Is this really the cycle route? It would mean unpacking and re-packing my bicycle to squeeze through. Whilst I am wondering what to do, a car arrives, a man emerges, produces a key for the gate and proceeds to unlock it for me. Thank you, kind sir.

By the time I reach Exeter, torrential rain is chucking down. Cyclists give me directions towards Taunton; one on a Thorn bicycle shares with me his intentions to cycle the Americas in a year's time.

I stop for the night in a homely, comfortable, very English B&B, cycle in very English rain to a very English pub for a very English homecooked steak and kidney pie and sticky toffee pud heaped with clotted cream. It is the eve of my prodigal return. Fifty miles remain to arrive in time for the party at 3 pm tomorrow afternoon.

My final morning and, full to bursting with a full English breakfast inside me, I set off into a cold, wet headwind, a fully layered Michelin woman of jumper, wind jacket, rain jacket, rain cape, socks, plastic bags, sandals, full gloves, head buff and hat. I make the mistake of keeping to the A38 when I should have done better to taken the A370. Next time.

The demanding hill to Bristol Airport slows down my finely-timed progress and I begin to feel the pressure of my deadline.

After what seems hours, I eventually find myself cycling along the Portway under Brunel's familiar Clifton Suspension Bridge, turn right then left, past Blaise Castle, down the hill to Hallen, along the country lane to Easter Compton, a route I have always enjoyed cycling, often on the return ride from work.

I am in constant phone contact with Jessica, progress reports relayed to whoever is now gathered, awaiting my 30-minute delayed arrival. By the time I am three miles from home, I have gradually delayered to camisole and unfettered sandalled feet. As I come over the brow of a hill a mile from home, I see first my nephew, then my younger brother, finally my son, Daniel. I have been looking forward to this moment for soooo long. And what do I do? I hug my nephew first. Why? In terms of who I saw first? Bizarre. But then a tight, lingering, loving embrace with Daniel. At the same moment, friends from church pass by, delighted that they happened along at the very point of my return.

Flanked by my family escort, a delighted grin on my face, I carry on to the main road, recapturing the point of departure two years minus two days ago when I cycled past this same view of the two Severn bridges. This time though, 20,000 miles later, I am looking at them over my left shoulder.

I continue the last half mile, turn right and a final right into my road. I cycle towards the far end, to be greeted by clicking cameras as I round the corner, my right arm thrust upwards in jubilant victory. And – oh my, what a reception: cheering and clapping, hooters, balloons, a banner on the roof of my house proclaiming 'Welcome Home.' I see smiling familiar faces, amongst them that of my daughter. She steps forward as my son and I cycle into the driveway and dismount. We hug, long and hard.

Did you miss me, children?

*   *   *   *   *

371

I have learned, in whatsoever state I am,
therewith to be content.

Philippians 4

Acknowledgements

I should like to extend heartfelt thanks to everyone I encountered on my trip, whether it was as brief as a passing smile or the hospitality of an extended stay; whether a spontaneous gift of a packet of tissues or a meal with cinema thrown in; whether cycling with me for half a day or for a month and a half.

And in an attempt to show my appreciation to all these people who touched my life in such a profound way, I mention those with whom there has been ongoing contact since my return, but including in spirit the countless others, in an all-inclusive package of thanks: Krista, Joe, Marya, Kip, Nicole, Suzy, Mark, Liliane, Jean, Monique, Patric, June, Jonathan, Ruth, Tim, Antoon, Jan, Salim, Elliott, Hande, Karfori, Romain, Debbie.

It is highly unlikely that I shall ever know anything of the ongoing lives of my unsung angels, but they are frequently in my thoughts which, inescapably as I write (May 2012), tend towards Syria. I think particularly of a young Christian family, Dara, Amer and their young daughter, Elisa, living in Homs. They showed me spontaneous hospitality when they invited me into their home. They shared with me aspects of their lives, mentioning some of the challenges of living as a minority faith. They were understated shining examples of the spirit of love.

* * *

My sincere thanks go to all back home, especially those who kept an eye on my children during the two years. And of course gratitude to all those who sent fabulous emails with news from home and about themselves, worth their weight in gold when far away.

* * *

In order to produce this account of my journey, critique, comments and encouragement have been donated in the shape of Rick, Marya, Steph, Clare, Joe. But particularly I am indebted to Trish at Quicksilver Publications. She wore herself out with her vast contribution of time, effort and guidance, that my thanks are totally inadequate. But thank you hugely anyway; particularly, thanks for your honesty in your many useful comments.

* * *

My undying love goes to my family: my father and my two brothers, Rick & Cogs and family, Kirsty, Poppy and Rory. But most of all my love goes to my two gorgeous children, Jessica and Daniel, who presented me with my biggest challenge by deserting them for two years, but from whom I drew a huge amount of strength, especially from their letters (which were well worn by the end of the trip), and by the knowledge that they would be around when their prodigal mum returned. I'm sure they agree that, for their part, the whole experience was good, character-building stuff!

* * *

Lastly, I give praise and thanks to my stalwart and constant companion; who never deserted me, always protected me (as much from myself); and who persisted in his attempts to guide me in the right direction as best he could with such a wilful disciple. I shall be eternally grateful for the opportunity that presented itself so readily for me to take this journey of faith and discovery.

* * *

Equipment

Bicycle

Bicycle, Thorn Raven Tour
saddle, Brooks B17L
saddle cover, Brooks
wicker basket
panniers x4, Ortlieb
waterproof rolltop bag, Ortlieb
bicycle pump
cycle computer, Cateye
multitool
drinks bottles x 3
bicyle stand
fluorescent strips
helmet
rear light, Cateye
cable lock
stop block
map holder
dubbin + cloth
bungee straps x 3

Spares

inner tubes x 2
tyre
spokes x 6
gear cable
brake cable
Rohloff axle ring assembly
brake pads set
puncture repair kit+levers x 2
puncture repair – no glue

Camping

tent, Hilleberg Nallo 2
sleeping bag, Blue Kazoo down
mattress, Thermarest
stove, Primus omnifuel
cooking pans, titanium
storm matches
storm lighter
spork (fork/spoon combined)
mosquito net
emergency blanket
inflatable pillow
vacuum-packed meatballs

Clothing

underwear x 3
sleeveless camisole x 3
vest
sh/sleeve top, merino wool
sh/sleeve cotton x 2
long sleeve top, merino wool
shirts x 2
light fleece top
trousers x 3
shorts
thermals, top and bottom
fleece outer jacket
down jacket
socks, long x 1 warm
socks, short x 1 cotton
socks, sports x 2 cotton

sandals, Teva Terra fi 2
shoes, Ecco
waterproofs, jacket + bottoms
cycling cape
warm hat
buff
sun visor
fingerless cycle gloves
ski mitts
shawl, silk+cotton
neckscarf, cotton
pyjamas, cotton
bikini
silk skirt
silk camisole
silk sh/sleeve blouse
black heeled sandals
small black handbag
pashmina
earrings + necklace

Other
Bible
reading books x 2
journals x 3
small notebooks x 3
pens
French dictionary
Spanish phrasebook
Sudoku puzzles
Puritabs

malarial tablets
insect bite cream
insect repellent spray
antibiotics
lip protection SPF30
first-aid kit (sterile)
memory cards + sticks
camera – Canon Ixus 65
spare camera battery
mobile phone
ipod nano
ASUS netbook
battery chargers
solar panels
bank cards x 4
preloaded money cards x 2
cash and travellers cheques
waterproof money belt
waterproof day backpack
stuff bags
bendy tripod
travel alarm clock
karabina x 2
small zip bags
universal plug
sewing repair kit
gaffa tape
travel toothbrush
wash bag
rubber door wedge
Christmas tree earrings